P9-DVC-071

LATE INNINGS

A BASEBALL COMPANION

ROGER ANGELL

BALLANTINE BOOKS • NEW YORK

Copyright © 1982 by Roger Angell

All rights reserved including the right of reproduction in whole or in part in any form. Published in the United States by Ballantine Books, a division of Random House, Inc., New York, and simultaneously in Canada by Random House of Canada Limited, Toronto.

Except for Chapter 1, all the material in this book first appeared in The New Yorker, *some of it in different form. Some passages in Chapter 1 first appeared in* A Baseball Century *(Rutledge Books/ Macmillian), and are reprinted with permission.*

Library of Congress Catalog Card Number: 82-764

ISBN 0-345-30936-7

This edition published by arrangement with Simon and Schuster

Manufactured in the United States of America

First Ballantine Books Edition: April 1983
Third Printing: August 1984

ROGER ANGELL

"LATE INNINGS...reaffirms Angell's position as the most astute and graceful chronicler the sport has known...brilliant and inimitable...a splendid work...perceptive, opinionated, informed."
Washington Post Book World

"Blessed with an artist's eye and a writing style that could make a laundry list fun to read, Angell holds baseball at different angles and describes how the sunlight slants through it...a passionate historian...a heavy hitter who...focuses on real people...LATE INNINGS is graceful...elegant... tender and lyrical."
Chicago Sun-Times

"If all the tributes to Roger Angell's writing on baseball were tacked end to end, they would stretch farther than a Mike Schmidt home run. And every compliment is entirely deserved...no writer...is more skillful than Angell in conveying the essentials of personality in a professional ballplayer away from the diamond...keen and witty coverage...a memorable book."
St. Louis Post-Dispatch

"Extraordinarily perceptive...absolutely brilliant... This type of analysis is rarely found in conventional sportswriting or conventional journalism. A reader is able to relive the action with the joy of a child...Angell is in a league by himself."
Chicago Tribune Book World

"Roger Angell has...been writing about baseball for twenty years, and he's better than ever...Athletes have a throwaway line for star-quality performers that goes, 'Ted Williams can *hit*,' or 'Bob Gibson can *throw*.' Well, for my money, Roger Angell can *write*."
Jean Strouse
Newsweek

LATE INNINGS

Also by Roger Angell
Published by Ballantine Books:

THE SUMMER GAME

CONTENTS

Foreword

THIS BOOK IS ABOUT BASEBALL GAMES AND PLAYERS AND
seasons that I watched from the spring of 1977 to the late
summer of 1981, and also about the substrata of the sport—
money, celebrity, power, traditions, and social change—that
lie beneath its green and ordered fields. Most of the autumn
chapters include a summary of the campaigns just past, but
readers are advised not to take these as history. Many deserving
ball teams and outstanding players have been slighted in these
pages, because I did not see them play over an extended span
of games, and other clubs and stars reappear so frequently as
to suggest some bias at work. I admit to the charge. I am still
a baseball fan as well as a baseball writer, and old fans like to
retrace their steps; I like to be in Scottsdale and St. Petersburg
in March, in Fenway Park in July (September there hurts too
much), at Shea whenever the Mets appear to be breathing, and
in Yankee Stadium or Chavez Ravine or walking over the
bridge across the Allegheny to Three Rivers Stadium in October. I take sides during most games and through every summer, and although this disqualifies me as a Gibbon, it has
probably kept me cheerful. As Bill Veeck always says, it's
meant to be fun.

Some readers may hear a somber, almost funereal murmur
in this book's title. This is not intended, for although big-league
baseball is long past its innocent youth and well into what
appears to be a disordered and self-destructive sort of middle
age, it is a flushed and vigorous reprobate, with astounding
recuperative powers. I suggest two lighter alternative read-
ings—"Late" as in the late news: the baseball news of recent
years; or, perhaps better, the later, most absorbing innings of
a good game, when we in the stands begin to understand its
particular pace and patterns, and even to pick up some glimmering of its resolution. More than half of my own baseball-
watching is behind me, but I have no intention of leaving the
park.

It occurred to me more than once to dedicate this book to the fans of the game, but such a gesture would have a patronizing and self-serving look. One cannot send a personal message to forty millions. The wish is still with me, though. I have learned many things in the twenty years since I began to write about baseball, and one of the real surprises was to find that not all players are fans of the game. This didn't matter much, to be sure: a double off the wall is not less satisfying if the young man who hits it has never heard of Alexander Cartwright. More and more, though, I have come to appreciate anyone who appreciates this game—the fans most of all. Their abiding loyalty to the pastime is shown not only in their dogged, comical attachment to this hopeless team or that fading star but in their adherence to the sport in the face of the repeated injuries they have suffered at the hands of the careless men who have bought their way into baseball's seats of power. Such heroic resilience has raised my own spirits and renewed my hopes about the game at times when I have almost despaired of its future.

Fans, of course, are habitually ignored by the media and merely counted by the front office. Even the word "fan" has a contemptuous, nicknamey affability. None of us can quite identify with the noisy, heedless, cheerful or irritable mob at the park, which always includes so many children, front-runners, foulmouthed partisans, idlers, tourists, and drunks. In among them, though, are the *fans,* and I think we should remind ourselves from time to time that it is the attention and mass memory and grave, judgmental expertise of this attendant crowd that give each game its resonance and seriousness. I have tried to let the voices and opinions of some fans be heard in these pages, but there are countless thousands more of them out there who deserve the same, and more. I feel fortunate to have been a writer about baseball, but I am proud to be a fan. It's great company.

—R. A.

So Long At the Fair

SUMMER 1981

STATISTICS ARE THE FOOD OF LOVE. BASEBALL IS NOURISHED by numbers, and all of us who have followed the game with intensity have found ourselves transformed into walking memory banks, humming with games won, games lost, batting averages and earned-run averages, games started and games saved, "magic numbers," final standings, lifetime marks, Series, seasons, decades, epochs. With the right data at hand (such as Joseph L. Reichler's *The Great All-Time Baseball Record Book*) one can pass a rainy summer weekend in pursuit of such esoterica as Unassisted Double Plays, Outfielder; Most Complete Games, Rookie, A.L.; Stole 2nd., 3rd., and Home in One Game, N.L. (Pete Rose did it last, against the Reds in 1980), and so forth. Just the other day, while happily meandering among Mr. Reichler's figure-thickets (Dave Kingman is the Second-Easiest Batter to Strike Out in the history of the National League; Ty Cobb batted .357 in 1927, to lead all comers in the How They Performed at Age Forty category), I was suddenly taken by surprise—knocked flat, in fact—by a statistic that fell out of the sky, so to speak: I have been a fan for fifty years.

My first reaction, of course, was guilt. A half-century of

vicariousness? Fifty years (now that I think of it, it may be more like fifty-one or fifty-two) in pursuit of a *game*? For shame, sir! But age teaches us how to deal with guilt (I picked him off first base), and soon I permitted myself to smile a little about the multiple pleasures and discoveries that my foolish servitude has brought me. I have written perhaps too often (Most Years Overestimating Rookie Pitchers in Spring Training, Both Leagues) about the most immediate attractions of baseball, but now some longer, quieter rewards may be observed as well. The comforting inner glow that I feel while consulting *The Baseball Encyclopedia* or looking at Lawrence Ritter's and Donald Honig's wonderful baseball picture-album, *The Image of Their Greatness*, emanates in a strange way from the names those books contain. The many dozens or even hundreds of old ballplayers' names and faces that I can quickly recognize are accompanied in my mind—blurrily or else with a perfect, crazy clarity—by scraps of attendant statistics, mannerisms, nicknames, anecdotes, teammates, and immemorial feats and failures. All ballplayers are connected with each other through the record books, of course, but now they seem connected to me, as well, through this enveloping, delicate capillary network of memory and association. Baseball is in my blood. When I stop to think about the sport this way—to think about how much almost every fan comes to know, almost without effort—I am reminded of my earliest feelings about baseball, when I had just began to follow the fortunes of my first real heroes, Joe DiMaggio and Carl Hubbell, through the long summers of my teens. Even then, I must have sensed that more was involved in baseball than the accomplishments of a few athletes and teams, and that I was now attached in a rather mysterious way to a larger structure, to something deep and rooted, with its own history, customs, records, honored and dishonored warriors, founders, superstitions, and clouded lore. I belonged and I cared, and because I have been lucky enough to go on caring, I have belonged to baseball now for almost half of its history.

For me, going through the baseball record books and picture books is like opening a family album stuffed with old letters, wedding invitations, tattered newspaper clippings, graduation programs, and curled up, darkening snapshots. Here are people from my own branches of the family—the Giants, the Red

Sox, the first Mets—and, in among them, page after page, the names and looks of other departed, almost forgotten in-laws and cousins and visitors. Everyone is here. The White Elephants and Gashouse Gang and the Big Red Machine. Hank Aaron and Hank Greenberg. Clemente and Brooksie. Gabby and Pie and Sunny Jim. Doc Cramer. (Why do I always think of Doc Cramer the instant I think of Sunny Jim Bottomley? Because, each in his own league, they were the same kind of players—invaluable, indestructible, and somehow never quite famous. Because each of them got six hits in a single game— and did it *twice:* no one else has ever done that.) Harvey Kuenn. Willie and Duke and the Mick. Jackie Robinson. *Frank* Robinson. Country Slaughter. Catfish Hunter. Columbia Lou (Old Biscuit-Pants) and the Fordham Flash ("Oh, those bases on balls!"). Stan the Man. The Meal Ticket. Schoolboy Rowe. The Yankee Clipper. Ron Swoboda, sliding on his face. Bill Klem. (An umpire, yes. He spent five thousand afternoons on the field, far more than anyone else in baseball history, and invented the umpire's essential creed: "In my heart, I never called one wrong.") The Babe. The Dutchman. Christy Mathewson. Frank Chance, the Peerless Leader. The Big Train. Cap Anson . . . An Iliad of names.

Many of these players, of course, were before my time, but I have noticed that this makes very little difference to me now. I have read so much about the old-timers and heard older players and writers and fans (including my father) talk about them so often that they are almost as visible to me as the stars I have watched on the field. I did see Babe Ruth play ball—once or (I think) twice, I saw him and Lou Gehrig hit homers back to back—so he is in my mind's eye, all right, but the sight of him is less to me than some of the things I have read about him: things I know because I am a fan. Almost everyone remembers something large and unlikely about this unlikely man, but the deed I come back to most often—I can't get over it— is his final one. On the last Sunday of his career, only a week before his retirement—when he was fat and worn-out at forty-one and had gone off to play for the Boston Braves because no other team would have him—he came up to bat four times against the Pirates, in Forbes Field at Pittsburgh, and hit a single and three homers. The last home run—the last one of his career, No. 714—flew over the roof of the double-decked grandstands in right field. It was the first ball anyone had ever hit out of Forbes Field. Goodbye, baseball.

Baseball history has made some different prodigies visible to me as well—men who illuminated the game not with their play but with their imagination, their will, their passionate selves. Two such men leap to mind.

The first one was short and dumpy, only five feet seven, and the weight he carried in later years made him look even smaller. He played the game for sixteen years (his lifetime batting average was .334), but he was made to be a manager. He managed the same club for thirty years. In time he bought a piece of the team, but in another sense he had always owned it. For every day and every game of those thirty years he was unquestionably the most vivid figure on any field where his team was playing. He was a master tactician in a time when runs were scratched out singly, out of luck and speed and connivance. He was too impatient to qualify as a great developer of talent, but he was a marvelous coach and a cold and deadly trader. He kept a distance between himself and his players, and the only two for whom he permitted himself to hold a deep affection both died young and before he did. He had great success, but terrible things happened to his teams on the field—immortal bonehead plays, crucial bases left uncovered, pennant-losing collisions on the base paths, malevolent bounces off invisible pebbles in the dirt. The bitter, enraged expression that settled on his thick face in his last years was the look of a man who had fought a lifelong, bareknuckled fight against bad baseball luck. They called him Little Napoleon. His name was John McGraw. "The main idea," he said, "is to win."

The other man was a lawyer, a churchman, a teetotaler—a straight arrow who made an early promise to his mother never to play ball or watch it on Sundays, and who kept his promise. He had flowing hair and bushy eyebrows and bow ties that he wore like a flag. He was a rhetorician, a nineteenth-century orator, a front-office man who enlivened trade talks with torrents of polysyllables and quotations from Shakespeare and Pope. Ideas and cigar smoke streamed from him. He thought up baseball tryouts. He put numbers on uniforms. He invented Ladies Day. He had the most discerning eye for young baseball talent that the game has ever known, and it was appropriate that he should have been the man who thought up and perfected the farm system. By the time World War II came along, his club, the Cardinals, had a chain of thirty-two minor league teams that employed more than six hundred ballplayers. Each year, the best of his young phenoms came up to the parent club, crowding its famous roster and forcing so many trades that in time half the dugouts of the National League seemed to be populated with muscular, mountain-bred throwers and long-ball hitters whom he had first spotted in some cinder-strewn Appalachian ballyard.

Then he, too, moved along to other clubs, still spouting phrases and ideas. "Judas Priest!" he cried. There was something about him of the travelling medicine-show man, something of W. C. Fields. But his ultimate alteration of the game, the destruction of baseball's color bar, was an act of national significance—an essential remedy that had awaited a man of subtlety and stubborn moral courage to bring it about. He refused to accept awards or plaudits for the deed, since it had only reversed an ancient and odious injustice. It would shame a man, he said, to take credit for that. He was the Mahatma: Branch Rickey. "Baseball," he said, "has given me a life of joy."

Quite a pair of forefathers. Judas Priest! And here comes another one, walking east on 93rd Street, in New York, at eight-thirty on a spring morning in 1932—a square-shouldered, medium-sized gent with a double-breasted suit, a small bow tie, a small white mustache, pink cheeks, and twinkly, shoe-button eyes: Colonel Jacob Ruppert, the owner of the Yankees, on his way to work at his brewery, over on Third Avenue. Coming toward him is a boy in knickerbockers, carrying books and a baseball mitt—myself, at eleven, on the way to school. Just before we pass, I tuck the books under one arm and whack my fist two or three times into the pocket of the mitt. Colonel Jake stops me, there on the street, while he extracts a calling-card from the pocket of his vest and scribbles something on it with his fountain pen. "Young man," he says, handing me the card, "take this up to the Stadium tomorrow morning for a tryout. And good luck to you." Does he actually say this to me? Did this really happen? Well, maybe not on that particular morning, nor on several dozen others when our paths crossed, there on 93rd Street. But it almost happened, surely, and one of these days, in my dreams, the Colonel will relent.

Now travel north with me about sixty blocks and about two decades and try to pick up a bespectacled, prematurely bald editor-writer at the wheel of his beat-up Ford tudor, westbound on the McCombs Dam Bridge on an early-summer Saturday. Beneath him is the Harlem River; ahead of him, uphill and off to the right, lies the Polo Grounds. Seated beside him in the front seat is his first child—a daughter, age four. He leans forward to adjust the dial on the car radio, which is bringing in the sounds of a ballgame in progress, as described by Russ Hodges. Struck by something odd, I point to the ballpark up ahead and say, "Callie, the game we're listening to is being played right over there, right now. That's the game we're listening to, and this is the Polo Grounds, where the two teams are playing it, see? It's hard to explain, but—"

The girl nods, not much interested. Then she hears something in the broadcast and sits up suddenly and stares out at the great green barn beside her. When she turns, her eyes are wide. *"Giants* are playing in there?" she asks.

Among relatives, jokes mean more than triumphs or ancestors. In the press box, a cloud of gossip and one-liners and irritable, over-familiar bonhomie hovers over the absorbed, half-bored regulars, as it does at a family breakfast table. Baseball writers work hard, but there is always a sense of playful companionship around them, because they must spend so much time together over the endless season and because they share the knowledge that they have all escaped doing something drearier and more serious in their lives. Even the white-haired scribes have this gleam, this boyhood joy of their occupation about them. Baseball writing has some drawbacks, but it has its moments, too. Before the opening game of the 1970 World Series, an eminent baseball writer for one of the New York dailies was on the field at Riverfront Stadium during batting practice when he noticed that the flag-draped, front-row Commissioner's box, next to the home-team dugout, contained a telephone—an instrument installed for the occasion in order to keep Mr. Kuhn in touch with God knows what advisers in case of unforeseen emergencies: with God Himself, perhaps. The reporter idly jotted down the number of the phone, and after the game had started he informed his neighbors up in the press rows about his odd discovery. Then, between innings, he dialed the number.

Watched intently by the flower of the American sporting press, Mr. Kuhn heard the ring and reached down under his seat for the receiver. "Hello?" he said cautiously.

"Hello, Chicken Delight?" said the writer-genius briskly. "I got a big order here—it's a picnic. We want eight of the Jumbo Baskets of Southern-fried, nine barbecue specials, six—"

"No, no," said Mr. Kuhn. "I'm afraid you have the wrong number. This is the Commissioner of Baseball. I'm sorry."

"...Eleven orders of french-fries, eight cole slaw—no, make that *twelve* fries," the reporter went on, fully audible to us all. Weeping with pleasure, several dozen writers tried to keep their game binoculars steady on the Commish.

"No, you've made a mistake," Mr. Kuhn said, a trifle impatiently now. "I don't know how this could happen. This is the Commissioner of Baseball—I'm here at the *game.*"

"Hold the barbecue sauce on one of the specials," the writer said. "Lots of ketchup. Lots of pickles. Last time, you forgot the pickles."

"Goodbye," said Mr. Kuhn politely, his cheeks scarlet. He hung up.

The call was placed again in the fourth inning, of course—more urgently, because the big order hadn't turned up—and again in the sixth, to diminishing returns. By this time, Mr. Kuhn had figured it out—he was in on a joke—and, to his credit, he was laughing, too. Once, he replaced the receiver and directed a sudden long stare at the press box—where everyone was deeply absorbed in his scorecard and stat sheets or busily banging out his running story. Nobody here but us scribes, Bowie. . . .

Somewhere in my files, I still have my scorecard for the Series game, with "Chick. Del." scribbled on the margin, because I have no symbol for bliss. I keep all my scorecards, of course—hundreds and hundreds of them—but I don't consult them much, to tell the truth, once the season is over. Except one. This game-scheme, now matted and prettily preserved in a grass-green frame, hangs on my office wall, and every few days or weeks I take it down and play its innings over again, out by out, in my imagination. The card is filled out far more neatly than any other scorecard I have ever seen, the names and symbols and numbers executed with an almost Oriental calligraphic care. It is not a scorecard of my own making but one that came to me by mail, two or three years ago, with a modest covering letter from its creator, a Seattle artist named Alan Douglas Bradley. I do not know Mr. Bradley, but he seems to know me. He knows, for instance, that I am a Red Sox fan, of long and painful good standing. The game he has sent me is an invention—a fabulous all-star exhibition contest in which the greatest lineup in the history of baseball is pitted against a pathetic assemblage of nondescript Red Sox footsoldiers and benchwarmers, most of whom I did not recognize or know much about until I had consulted *The Baseball Encyclopedia*. They include Hobe Ferris, who compiled a batting average of .239 while playing third base for the Bosox between 1901 and 1907; right fielder Skinny Graham, who batted .246 in twenty-one games for the Sox in 1934 and '35; Mike Herrera, at second, with .275 in eighty-six games in the mid-twenties; and so forth. The pitcher for this hopeless nine is not to be found even in the all-encompassing agate of *The Baseball Encyclopedia*, for he is me. The opening lineup for the Immortals, by contrast, requires no elucidation: Cobb, Lajoie, Wagner, Ruth, Gehrig, J. DiMaggio, Traynor, and Berra. Cy Young is on the mound. They bat first (we are playing at Fenway Park), and in the top of the opening inning they load the bases, with one out—hits by Cobb and Wagner, a sensible intentional pass to Babe Ruth—but fail to score, because Gehrig unexpectedly raps into a 6–4–3 double play. This establishes a pattern; the All-Timers keep putting men on base—two walks in the third, a single and a double and a walk in the fifth, and so on—but somehow can't push across any runs. Babe Ruth strikes out with the bases loaded to end one threat—so weak with laughter at my curveball that he can't see straight, no doubt—and pinch-hitters Willie Mays and Hank Aaron fan, in the third and sixth, probably because the proximity of the Green Wall in left field has them overswinging at my 50-m.p.h. heater. With one away in the top of the eighth, Mickey Mantle triples, and an ugly little scene is barely averted when I am warned by the home-plate ump—it must be Bill Klem—for intentionally plunking the next batter, pinch-hitter Pete Rose. (I may be overmatched but I am all heart out there—a Don Drysdale glaring in at my enemies.) Then Johnny Bench flies out to center, and Mantle is doubled up at the plate, on a close play, to end the inning.

Meantime, my Sad Sox have been able to do almost nothing against the offerings of Cy Young and his mound successors: Dizzy Dean, Sandy Koufax, and Walter Johnson. In the home fourth, we do get a man as far as third base, with two out, but Old Diz fans me in the clutch. By the top of the ninth, the game is still somehow scoreless and the stands are going *crazy*. Tris Speaker leads off with a single, and another pinch-hitter, Stan Musial, also singles. I retire Eddie Collins on strikes but walk Honus Wagner, to load the bases. (I am bushed by now, almost done, but gamely refuse to quit the mound.) The next batter, Ruth again, hits a screamer up the middle, off the first pitch. I throw up my hands in self-defense (this part is not in the scorecard, to be sure, but a trained scorecard-reader learns how to sense such things) and the ball miraculously sticks in my glove; a flip over to third doubles off Speaker to end the inning, and the Gray Eagle, a step or two away from home, shakes his head in disbelief. In the bottom half, with one out, Pumpsie Green triples against Early Wynn (Pumpsie Green *triples?*), and then trots home with the game-ending counter, the only run of the game, which has been driven in on a sacrifice fly lofted to center by old Guess Who. What a game!

Alan Bradley's scorecard, it seems to me, is much more than a joke. It is also beyond art, for he has contrived to keep score during a game that only could have been played in my head. He can do this, of course, because we are both fans, he and I, and he knows that true fans still schedule these fanciful, unpardonably boyish entertainments to light up the miserable predawn darkness or the endless late-afternoon of middle age. He is thoughtful enough to remember, from some writings of mine, that I would want to pitch and that the scene of my triumph is always the Fens. He and I have never met, but we are friends now—friends in baseball. This way of connecting, this family feeling, means almost more to me, I find, than the boisterous excitements of the World Series or the aesthetic tingle of a neatly executed hit-and-run play. The game has kept my interest, over many years, for reasons I have tried to set down, but its most surprising attribute may be its effortless, disarming capacity to bring its adherents closer together. A great many strangers write me baseball letters throughout the year—men and women, teen-agers, junior-college players, retired minor-leaguers, a female concert violinist, a corporation lawyer, housewives, law students, a minimalist painter from Virginia, a college president, a soldier in Germany, an eighty-four-year-old widow in Maine, many others—to express their feelings about our pastime. Often they start by thanking me (or correcting me) for something I have written, but then there is a shift (and another page or two or three of the letter) as they begin to put down their own baseball recollections and attachments, and, very often, to express their anger and sadness over its recent alterations, and by the end of the letter I sense that I have been offered not just a view of the game but a view of life. I can never respond adequately to such a compliment—I am always weeks and weeks behind in my baseball correspondence—but now and then these disarming, funny, intensely private letters have led to a longer correspondence (with a Tiger-smitten oral surgeon in Detroit, say) and to the beginning of a lifelong friendship. The same thing—the same suddenly offered glimpse of self—happens sometimes when I am on the field or in some clubhouse or in the stands, in pursuit of a story. An old pitcher, now a scout, tells me about his farm-boy beginnings in North Carolina that were first altered one morning when a shiny black Cadillac rolled up the red-dirt road to his house and yielded a dapper, citified Cardinals' scout who had come to watch him throw. A great present-day pitcher unexpectedly begins to describe his work as art, as ballet, and, on another afternoon, a famous catcher points out the trifling, everyday patterns of the game—the arrangement of infielders in response to a foul ball—that he finds so moving and satisfying. A Hall-of-Fame fireballer and a never-was, one-season Class A southpaw talk about their craft with equal seriousness and passion, and suddenly and tragically failed Pirate hurler goes through an imaginary inning for me, pitch by pitch, against a great team—just as I do alone sometimes, in the dark, with Alan Bradley keeping score. We are all moved, or want to be, and the game invites us to that end. As E. M. Forster said (I can still see him, with one spiked foot up on the top step of the dugout and his keen, Ozark-blue eyes, under the peak of the pulled-down cap, fixed on some young batter just now stepping up to the plate), Only connect.

2

The Long Green

APRIL 1977

Last month, in scottsdale, arizona, i had a drink with a friend of mine named Jerome Holtzman, who is an eminent baseball writer with the Chicago *Sun-Times*, and after a very few minutes we found ourselves scribbling on bar napkins as we tried to draw up an all-star team for 1977. Everything in baseball is changing, and it is possible that our joint effort may be the first interleague all-star team ever to be seriously discussed some weeks before the beginning of the season. Here it is:

1B:	Steve Garvey (Dodgers)	283
2B:	Joe Morgan (Reds)	400
3B:	Mike Schmidt (Phillies)	450
SS:	Bobby Grich (Angels)	310
C:	Gene Tenace (Padres)	363
OF:	Joe Rudi (Angels)	418
OF:	Gary Matthews (Braves)	360
OF:	Reggie Jackson (Yankees)	580
DH or	Utility:	
	George Brett (Royals)	385
	Dave Cash (Expos)	300

	Sal Bando (Brewers)	300
	Don Baylor (Angels)	266
P:	Don Gullett (Yankees)	330
	Wayne Garland (Indians)	230
	Rollie Fingers (Padres)	320
	Bill Campbell (Red Sox)	250

The statistics accompanying this roster, it may be noticed, look impressive but peculiar, because of the missing decimal points. The stats become more understandable, and perhaps more awesome, when one perceives that the decimal points in this case do not belong on the left-hand side of the figures, as they normally do with batting averages, or one or two spaces to the right, as they do with earned-run averages, but *six* spaces to the right, after the addition of three zeros to each set of figures; what now must be added to the left-hand side of the numbers is a dollar sign. These—as well as Jerome Holtzman and I could work out—are the present annual salaries of some celebrated big-league ballplayers. A few of the names and a lot of the numbers are open to challenge (not many players' salaries have been actually announced this year, so careful guessing and a judicious computation of bonuses were some-times necessary), but never mind. This is the richest team in the history of baseball.

Selecting all-star squads is usually a harmless midseason or post-season pastime for writers and other baseball idlers, but this particular selection is more serious; in one form or another, these figures were the central subject of conversation, specu-lation, jokes, anger, and anxiety among the players, executives, writers, TV and radio people, fans, and hangers-on gathered at the preseason baseball camps that I visited in Florida and Arizona this spring, and there is no reason to believe that the daily headlines and box scores of the baseball season that has now begun in earnest will diminish their importance or (as most of the owners secretly pray) somehow make them disappear. Baseball is caught up in an immense redistribution of money and power and talent—one could call it a revolution, except for the fact that the same redistribution, in one form or another, has come to all the other professional sports—which has dark-ened the vernal gleams of the old game and presented us with disturbing new ironies and doubts. Fan friends of mine have confessed that the new salary scales and the sudden winter decamping of so many baseball stars to different cities and into strange uniforms have finally destroyed their attachment to the game and done away with the last shreds of their identification with some favorite old team. "It's just show business," they have said to me. Or "All the players care about now is money." Or "It's gotten cold-blooded and greedy. Even the minor-leaguers have those agents now. The game is dead." I sympathize with their feelings, for I have certainly shared them at times in the past year. Most of all, I think, the new salaries have vastly increased the distance between the players and the fans—increased it figuratively in much the same way that the machinelike, circular new ballparks have done the job literally and aesthetically on the field. Before last year and this year, baseball fans and baseball players—all but a few superstars, that is—seemed socially, and perhaps spiritually, united. Baseball was their game, owned in a complex partnership, and the man in the stands could be forgiven if he felt that only the inexplicable accident of skill kept him from the field itself. (The players always knew how wide *that* space really was.) There was a bond between fans and players in the wry shared knowledge that both groups were the victims of the businessman owner. In the nineteen-fifties and early sixties, when some old baseball franchises—the Dodgers, the Giants, the Athletics, the Senators, and the rest—were first ripped loose from their traditional cities and their fanatically loyal lifelong fans, and after that, when handfuls of new and vapid teams were invented, the fans saw, many of them for the first time, that the owners were in this game, first and always, for the money. The fans' pain on learning this hard, barely concealed old truth was exactly the same as the shock and outrage that any veteran player had suffered on being given the news that he had suddenly been traded away from his parent club. Now all this is gone. The players are businessmen, too—businessmen, with a vengeance, it seems—and the space between the fan and the player is the same light-years span that divides the television star or the famous rock singer from his patronized and wholly anonymous audience.

None of this is retrievable, but I must now add that my recent spring-training travels, during which I talked to a great many players and other baseball people about these issues, diminished my gloom, and I came home feeling pretty cheerful about baseball, and expectant, as always, about the long season ahead. I believe that while the players' new freedom to hire themselves out to the highest bidders and to employ young financial agents to arrange complex six-figure or seven-figure contracts for them has badly jolted some of the customs and continuity of the game, it will probably not destroy it, or even permanently twist it into some parody of its old and elegant self. The startling new salaries may represent both a contemporary reality and a historical inevitability, and are thus perhaps best approached with curiosity rather than horror.

One of the peculiarities of the great money shakeout is the difficulty that fans now have in getting hold of any accurate figures. In the old days, when a club signed one of its stars to a new contract the writers and photographers would be called in, cigars would be passed out, the florid owner and the beefy, bow-tied slugger would pose shaking hands over the fabulous document, and the price of the contract would instantly go out to the world. In their time, every fan in America knew about Connie Mack's Hundred-Thousand-Dollar Infield of Stuffy McInnis, Eddie Collins, Jack Barry, and Home Run Baker (the scale of things has so shifted that one usually hears this wrongly referred to as the Million-Dollar Infield), and about Babe Ruth's eighty thousand dollars in 1930 (a reporter asked Ruth how he felt about earning more money than the President of the United States; "I had a better year than he did," said the Babe), and about Sandy Koufax's and Don Drysdale's successful double holdout against the Dodgers in 1966, to gain admission to the élite hundred-thousand-dollar fraternity. The money became part of the star's reputation, part of his drawing power. Now the numbers are shrouded and somehow less splendid; the total is rarely announced, partly because the player's agent and the team's lawyers have usually worked out a document involving so many deferrals and life-insurance plans and mutually advantageous I.R.S-inspired subclauses that no single bottom-line figure can encompass them all. (Catfish Hunter, the first and most celebrated beneficiary of the money boom, has been omitted from my all-stars simply because his five-year, three-and-a-half-million-dollar contract with the Yankees, signed in 1974, calls for a deferred bonus of one and three-quarters million dollars, to be paid over a period of fifteen years starting

in 1979, which does not seem translatable into a 1977 "salary.")
Front-office people have also become evasive about announc-
ing gargantuan new contract figures because they are not anxious to deepen the unhappiness of their other (and now suddenly
underpaid) stars or to invite the rage of poorer or less ven-
turesome rival owners. When the Red Sox general manager,
Dick O'Connell, signed a little-known Minnesota relief pitcher
named Bill Campbell to a four-year, million-dollar contract last
November, another baseball executive said, "They ought to
shoot Dick O'Connell."

Most of the players on my roster (Bobby Grich, Joe Rudi,
Reggie Jackson, Gary Matthews, Gene Tenace, Don Gullett,
Wayne Garland, Rollie Fingers, Bill Campbell, Dave Cash,
Sal Bando, and Don Baylor) are new to their present clubs and
present salary levels, because they elected to become free agents
at the conclusion of the 1976 season. This was made possible
by a new basic agreement between the owners and the Players
Association, which was drawn up last July, after a winter and
spring of prolonged and bitter negotiations and maneuverings,
including a lockout that temporarily closed the 1976 training
camps. The document granted free-agency to all players a year
after the expiration of their existing contracts, including multi-
year contracts running through 1977 or later. Players signing
contracts after the agreement went into effect could achieve
free-agency upon the completion of six years' service in the
major leagues. As is perhaps well known by now, this baseball
earthquake came about as the result of a grievance procedure
won the previous winter by two major-leaguers, Andy Messersmith and Dave McNally, challenging the ancient "reserve
clause," under which players since the earliest days of baseball
had been forced to negotiate exclusively—and thus power-
lessly—with the clubs holding their current contracts. The
number of self-declared free agents last fall was much smaller
than many owners had predicted (there were twenty-five of
them, out of a total of six hundred major-leaguers), but the
size and nature of some of the new contracts they arranged for
themselves, it must be admitted, seemed to bear out the hor-
rified prognostications of those hardshell owners who had insisted all along that a few extremely wealthy clubs would attempt
to dominate their leagues by pouring great sums into the sudden
new player market. The Yankees and the California Angels

have evidently embarked on this course—the Yanks by spending a total of about five million dollars to pick up Jackson and Gullett, and the Angels (whose principal owner is Gene Autry) by investing five and a quarter million in Rudi, Grich, and Baylor. The pennant adventures of these two teams, and of the San Diego Padres, who also spent heavily at the free-agent counter, will be watched by the other owners with fervent ill will. There is no way to forecast how many players will decide to become free agents at the end of this season, either upon the expiration of their old multi-year contracts or because they will have qualified as six-year men, and it is still too early in the season to work out an average salary for a major-leaguer in 1977. A very recent count, however, shows that at least a hundred and twenty-five players will be paid a hundred thousand dollars or more this year.

Four starters on my Gold Sox team—Joe Morgan, Mike Schmidt, George Brett, and Steve Garvey—are holdovers who have signed lucrative contracts with their old clubs. They are irreplaceable stars. Morgan has won the National League's Most Valuable Player award for the past two years; Schmidt has led the majors in home runs for the past three years; Brett, at the age of twenty-three, is the American League batting champion; and Garvey is a lifetime .300 hitter and a former National League M.V.P. Their pay scale provides the owners with a disheartening measure of the price of club loyalty on the new open market. Wayne Garland and Bill Campbell, by contrast, represent high-risk fliers. Campbell, a reliever, achieved an impressive 17–5 record with the Twins last year, with twenty games saved—considerably better than his performance in 1975, when he was 4–6, with five saves. (His new two-hundred-and-fifty-thousand-dollar salary with the Red Sox is also an improvement; last year, with the Twins, he earned twenty-two thousand.) Wayne Garland, a twenty-six-year-old right-hander, finished up with a splendid record of 20–7 with the Orioles in 1976 and was paid twenty-three thousand five hundred dollars. He became a free agent and went to the Indians. Upon signing Garland to a ten-year contract worth two million three hundred thousand dollars, Phil Seghi, the Cleveland general manager, explained that the financially troubled Indians, who have not won in their league since 1954, could not afford *not* to sign him. This statement struck me as being insane but familiar, although it was some little time before I realized that Mr. Seghi sounded exactly like the Chairman of the Joint Chiefs of Staff testifying before the Senate Armed Services Committee about a new American missile system.*

In the middle of March, I determined to think less about money and more about baseball; I got out my summer shades and my suntan lotion and took off for the Florida camps—where everybody was thinking about money. At Al Lopez Field, in Tampa, I watched Tom Seaver work four innings against the champion Reds, in which he gave up two runs on five hits; it was a good, mid-March sort of performance, with a couple of steamy mid-July swinging strikeouts thrown in, but in the dugout before the game I had noticed that Seaver had a hooded, glowering expression. The Mets' left fielder in the game was Dave Kingman, who in the first inning played a little handle-hit by Ken Griffey into a stand-up double. It is no news that Kingman is a frightful fielder, just as it is no news that he sometimes hits tropospheric home runs, but his presence on the same team as Tom Seaver had become a distracting little economic morality play. Kingman, who was unsigned, was asking the Mets for an enormous new contract—a multi-year, million-and-a-half-dollar model, it was said, with a very large additional bonus for his having not elected to become a free agent—and he and the club were very far from coming to terms. Tom Seaver had

---

* Bill Campbell had one outstanding season with the Red Sox, in 1977, when he posted a 2.96 earned-run average and led his league with thirty-one saves. The next year, he began to suffer problems with the shoulder of his pitching arm (he is a right-hander), which became chronic and have limited his effectiveness and number of appearances in subsequent seasons. In 1981, he was 1–1, with an earned-run average of 3.19, and felt sufficiently encouraged to enter the free-agent market once again, where he was signed up by the Cubs. Wayne Garland had even less luck. He ran up a 13–19 record for the passive 1977 Indians, before *his* shoulder gave out. He missed a full year's work after undergoing surgery (the rotator-cuff operation, or Pitcher's Special) in May 1978, and has seen limited service since then. Last year, he won three games and lost seven, with an earned-run average of 5.79. Such professional ill-fortune is commonplace in baseball, and has almost nothing to do with free-agency or lofty salaries, but disappointed, pennant-hungry fans rarely notice that money is not an effective cure for pain.

announced that he wished Kingman nothing but the best in his salary dispute, but Seaver is also a proud and realistic young man, who knows that he is the premier pitcher of his era and that his own value to the Mets is immeasurably greater than Kingman's. Seaver is in the middle year of a complicated three-year contract that brings him a base pay of two hundred and twenty-five thousand dollars, with some special performance clauses that can further reward him for a good year on the mound; his contract struggles with the club last spring were marked by extreme bitterness. Dave Kingman hit thirty-seven homers last summer—only one less than the Phillies' Mike Schmidt, although Kingman played in thirty-seven fewer games than Schmidt, because of a damaged thumb. He also batted .238 and struck out a hundred and thirty-five times. The Mets, who have no hitting to speak of and who made no serious moves in the winter player market, clearly needed Kingman in the lineup, for his power and his gate appeal, but how could his value to the club be assessed against the contribution of a Tom Seaver? I wondered how any front-office executive could solve a problem like that, and how a ball team could be expected to hang together through the long summer's campaign if it *weren't* solved. Specifically, if the Mets were to sign Kingman to a contract that called for, say, three hundred thousand dollars, would they not then be under some obligation to come back to Tom Seaver and offer to remedy an apparent injustice? Was "injustice" an admissible word in these circumstances? What *was* justice? What was truth? Beauty? What ever happened to the ten-cent subway fare? Where was Casey Stengel, now that I needed him, and why did he always use to call Bob Miller "Nelson"? . . . I sighed and gazed moodily out at the young men at play on the warm green pasture before me; it was my very first game of the year, and already there was something glum about it.*

I did a little better after that. I began to put these new

---

* The Mets' front-office decision in the Seaver-Kingman salary dilemma was a final solution I had not envisioned even in my gloomiest spring musings. On June 15th, 1977, the club unloaded both stars, sending Seaver to the Cincinnati Reds and Kingman to the San Diego Padres, and in each case receiving a number of less skilled and much less well paid players in return.

questions and confusions to the players, thus freeing more of my attention for the old pleasures of the game. The next afternoon, I watched the Phillies paw gently at the Toronto Blue Jays, who are one of the American League's two newborn expansion clubs. The Toronto road uniforms are horizon blue and feature a large ventral blue jay's head superimposed on a baseball, with a scarlet maple leaf *supra*—everything, in short, except a view of Banff National Park. The earnest young men bearing this heraldry were almost entirely unknown to me (according to an American League roster, the six Toronto outfielders boasted a combined total of 1.389 years of major-league experience), but I was forced to take note of a large first baseman named Doug Ault, a draftee picked up from the Texas Rangers, when he smashed an enormous six-inning double off the center-field wall on a pitch by Wayne Twitchell. There was a good, hot sun, and by the middle innings a lot of writers were sprawled on the grass in short right field with their shirts off. I was glad to see that the Toronto scribes seemed to be in excellent trim, for they are going to have a longish summer of it up there in the provinces. I wandered out toward left field and began to watch a tall, extremely youthful Blue Jay pitcher named Butch Edge, who was warming up in the bullpen with a catcher named Ernie Whitt. Edge was working hard, and Whitt kept talking to him between pitches. "Keep it all together, Butch," he said, straightening up and flipping back the ball. "Don't hurry it. Keep that arm and shoulder all one."

The ball popped in the glove this time, and Whitt said, "That's it! Beautiful. Just keep it together, man."

A signal came from the Toronto dugout, and Edge picked up his jacket and walked in to face the Phillies in the bottom of the seventh. "Go get 'em, Butch!" the other young pitchers called to him from their folding chairs. "You can do it, baby!"

But he couldn't. He retired the first man on an infield out, and walked the next. He worked Garry Maddox to a two-and-two count, then threw a wild pitch, then walked him. He walked Tommy Hutton on four pitches. He bounced a pitch in the dirt, and the crowd began to get on him, clapping and groaning derisively. Butch Edge no longer had it together. The Toronto pitching coach came out to settle him down, but the boy was beyond reach, caught up in a bad dream. He gave up a run, and, with the bases again loaded, delivered three more balls to a Phillies rookie named Dane Iorg. He threw a called strike and then a swinging strike—a good pitch. Encouraged, he came in with a waist-high fastball, which Iorg smashed over the center-field wall for a grand-slam homer. Butch Edge walked one more man and was taken out, getting a nice, friendly round of applause as he came off the field: That's O.K., kid. This kind of small tragedy is a regular feature of the touring spring repertory companies, and each spring I find it more nearly unbearable to watch.

Tug McGraw cheered us up, strolling in to pitch the top of the eighth in a Phillies uniform with a shirt that had been dyed a gruesome green, in honor of his ancestors: it was Saint Patrick's Day. The umps would have none of it, of course, but they had a good laugh, too. Tug went back to the dugout to change, and I recalled a Camera Day at Shea Stadium several years ago, when McGraw rubbed shoeblacking on his face and arms and then slipped on Willie Mays' uniform shirt, with its famous No. 24, and ran out onto the field to oblige the Queens shutterbugs. The act received mixed notices.

Earlier in the day, before the game, I had asked a couple of the Phillies veterans what they thought about free-agency and the enormous new sums of money that some players have begun to earn. Tim McCarver, a catcher, with seventeen years' service in the majors, said, "I think the news about our money is written in sort of a derogatory way. I always used to feel that we were looked down on by the press and by other people for not being good businessmen, but now we're criticized even more if we *are*. Who determines this idea that athletes are overpaid? How much is 'overpaid,' anyway? If Elizabeth Taylor gets a million dollars for appearing in a picture, it adds to her attraction. Why isn't this true with ballplayers? I don't understand it. If the owners are offering this kind of money to players right now, it would be folly for anyone not to try to get it."

Jim Lonborg, the tall and extremely handsome veteran right-hander, who is thirty-four years old, said that he had been paid about sixty-five hundred dollars for his first year in the majors, in 1965; he had not yet signed with the Phillies for this season, but I had heard it said that he was expected to receive a two- or three-year contract worth about two hundred thousand per year. "It's fun to think about what the money might be if I were starting up right now," he said, smiling and shaking his head. "I feel fortunate to still be around when this boom came along. But what about the people who just missed it? How about somebody like Bob Gibson—what would a great competitor like that be worth today?"

Tom Seaver had been running in the outfield at Huggins-Stengel Field, which is the Mets' major-league training center in St. Petersburg. We were sitting on a bench in the shade just outside the clubhouse, and Seaver was wearing a pale-blue Mets warm-up jacket. The front of the jacket was streaked with sweat. He wiped his face with a towel and murmured, "All this damn running. I never *will* get used to it." He took a packet of Red Man chewing tobacco out of the side pocket of the jacket and helped himself to a good-sized wad, and began to talk baseball.

"Some of the owners seem able to understand the changes in the money levels that have come into the game as a result of the new agreement, but not all of them, not all," he said. "For years, you know, the owners were able to get away with almost everything in their dealings with the players, even if it ran up against—ran contrary to the teachings of a democratic society. They had it all their way, and they weren't willing to give that up. The Players Association kept suggesting that something could be worked out that would make for a fair distribution for both sides, but the owners said no, and they fought it all the way through the courts, and every other way. Now when we talk about money the owners say, 'What will the fans think?' but that's always a nebulous question. It depends which fans you hear from. I get letters that are pro-owner and letters that praise the players' position in all this, but most of the letters I get just say that the Mets fans want a winner. The owners hold up the spectre of increased ticket prices as a reason for not entering the free-agent market, but the fans I hear from don't have any interest in paying less money for the privilege of watching second-rate ball. I think a lot of fans understand that free-agency is going to help the game by cutting loose the good players that some clubs have kept sitting on the bench. That's the redistribution that matters.

"I think this industry just doesn't want to make progress. Maintaining the status quo has always been the first concern of the owners. There are so many examples. For instance, they've almost never worked at finding coaches who are really efficient in their teaching—people who have studied teaching and know how to get their ideas across. No other business would put up with such a thing. Or look how long the owners have been dragging their feet about interleague play. There's no question that the game needs it. You could build up natural rivalries—Cleveland and Cincinnati, New York and Boston and Philadelphia, and the rest—and the fans would eat it up. In any business, you have to think how to make things better, how to make the right alterations, how to use imagination and new ideas and forms. I'm not automatically in favor of change. I mean, I don't think much of the tricks and easy little gizmos that are beginning to alter the game on the field. The designated hitter takes away part of the beauty of the game. I think it damages the feelings we have about the age of the game of baseball and how it's always been played. You should be very careful about how you fool around with something like that."

I asked Seaver about his relationship with the Mets front-office people.

"There's no doubt that I'm being treated differently now, because of my part in the labor negotiations last year," he said. "The chairman of the board, M. Donald Grant, reprimanded me directly for that. I still can't believe it. I know what he thinks about player salaries, because last year he said to me, 'You're making too much at a young age. It isn't good for you.' My owner said that to me. And for me to say 'my owner' is the most ridiculous thing in the world. Does somebody own *you?* Does anybody *own* anybody else in this country?"

He stopped and stared out at the empty ball fields. In the distance, a couple of lawn sprinklers were sending up pale clouds of water that caught prisms of color from the sun.

"I don't think any of this has changed my feeling about how I play the game," Seaver went on. "I still love to pitch, and I love the game and the people I play with. I still bust my ass out there. The thing that depresses me, though, is that so many of the owners think of me and all the other players essentially as laborers. They have no appreciation of the artistic value of what I do. They think if I wasn't in baseball I'd be out digging ditches, or something. That really fries me. How can they be in baseball and not see what it's all about? Pitching is a beautiful thing. It's an art—it's a work of art when it's done right. It's like a ballet or the theatre. And, like any work of art, you have to have it in your head first—the idea of it, a vision of what it should be. And then you have to *perform*. You try to make your hand and body come up to that vision. When you do it, when you can sense sometimes that it's been done right, it's an extraordinary feeling. It's the most beautiful thing in sports."

The dialogue went on the next day, back in Tampa, where the Kansas City Royals were visiting the Reds. The Royals, who won their western divisional title last fall and came within a hair of beating out the Yankees for the American League pennant, experienced very few salary squabbles this year, mostly because their president, Ewing Kauffman, offered attractive multi-year contracts to the Royals' stars, and pointed out to them the long-term benefits of their staying together and sticking with a rising club.

"I wanted a five-year contract," the Kansas City shortstop, Freddie Patek, said to me, "but I settled for three. I thought they were always good to me here. Before free-agency, you weren't really bargaining at all. Now it's more realistic. But to tell the truth, I don't think anybody thought the escalation of salaries would ever go this high. I feel we're all overpaid. Every professional athlete is overpaid. I got a phenomenal contract—much more money than I ever thought I'd make. I wouldn't say I'm embarrassed by it, but deep down I know I'm not worth it. To my shame, though, I have to admit I asked for it."

Patek, who is thirty-two, is a ten-year man in the majors. He is five feet four inches tall, the smallest man in the big leagues, and he is so neat in appearance that he sometimes gives the impression that his uniform is a business suit, complete with vest and tie.

"I've heard the fans and writers complaining about money," he went on. "People are sort of upset about the kind of player who's getting fifty or sixty thousand now, even though he has hardly played as a regular in the big time. Sometimes he's even playing out his contract and getting ready to move on if he doesn't get what he asks for. Fans say, 'How can he do that?' but often it's a good investment for a club to give a young player that sort of a big jump, if he's proved his potential. But if they don't want to, then O.K., he can move along. Free-agency will stay. I've always felt that just because I was a major-leaguer I had no right to hold somebody else down in the minors. You have to think about things like that in this whole picture. Movement of players is a good thing. It's good for baseball. Being traded from the Pirates seven years ago was the best thing that ever happened to me. If I'd stayed with them, I'd still have the utility-man status, and probably I'd be out of baseball by now. The Players Association has made all the difference. I admire Marvin Miller a lot, but I think the players ought to be more content with things the way they are now. I hope it doesn't get out of hand."

I found Pete Rose over in the Cincinnati clubhouse. He had a sore elbow and was not in the Reds' lineup for the game against the Royals, but he had worked out that morning, and now he was getting into his street clothes. Pete Rose looks like nobody else in the world: round, hard, firmly packed, resilient, interesting—a bag of basketballs. He is thirty-six years old now, but is still one of the great hitters in the game; if he attains his customary level of two hundred base hits this summer, he will match Ty Cobb's all-time record of nine two-hundred-hit seasons.

There were a couple of large paper bags in Rose's cubicle, with dollar signs on their sides made out of adhesive tape; the bags were stuffed with crumpled newspapers, to make them look like sacks of money. These had just been sent over by two of the visiting Royals, George Brett and Hal McRae, and Brett had also sent along a signed personal check made out to Pete Rose in the amount of two million dollars. Down in one corner of the check, Brett had written "Your contract—no cut," and then he had thoughtfully added "VOID!"

"Too bad," Rose said, showing me the last entry. "I'd have cashed the son of a bitch."

It was all a joke, of course, but it was a message, too. Pete Rose's contract with the Reds still had a year to run, but it was known that he had demanded a new three-year contract worth a million two hundred thousand—the same four hundred thousand per year that the club had already agreed to pay his teammate Joe Morgan. Rose had announced that if he and the Reds could not come to terms, he was prepared to become a free agent at the end of the season. The Reds, of course, are the most successful team of this decade, and their manager, Sparky Anderson, has been a passionate advocate of short haircuts, absolute team loyalty, and other classic baseball virtues; the club president, Bob Howsam, has been a proconsul among the most conservative and intransigent club owners during the long labor wars. Rose, for his part, is a Cincinnati native who has been a home-town hero ever since he first came up to the Reds, at the age of twenty-two—a dedicated and hardworking team player who has perfectly embodied the Reds' "image." For the Reds and Pete Rose to wrangle openly about money was scandalous: it was the end of a famous marriage.

Rose finished dressing, slipped on his loafers, and put on a pair of dark glasses, and we walked out into the dazzling sunshine. I asked him if he thought it would be different for him playing for the Reds this summer.

He answered with a short word. "I've had trouble with them every year," he continued. "The only difference this year is I'm not forced to sign. It don't make any difference on the field if I'm signed or not signed—I'll still give a hundred and fifteen per cent out there, like I always do. If it comes down to playing out my contract this year, what good will it do me if I hit .220? My age has nothing to do with it. I'm asking off my record of last year. I led the league in runs, led the league in hits, led the league in doubles, I tied for the most games played—a hundred and sixty-two. That's all of them—the whole season. I ain't missed but one game in three and a half years, two in four years, four in six years, seven in seven. You can look all that up, but you don't have to, because it's the truth."

We were standing in the foul ground in short left field, and the game had just begun. We were joined by Pete Rose, Jr., who had been a part-time batboy with the Reds this spring. Young Pete, who is seven, was wearing a T-shirt with his father's number, 14, on it, along with a Reds cap and a pair of outfielders' snap-down dark glasses, and he was also carrying a glove. The Royals had a man on first, and now George Brett whaled a line drive that caromed off the center-field wall. Brett wound up on third, but the Reds had executed the relay perfectly, as is their custom, and the first base runner was cut down at the plate. Brett, with his toe on the bag, spotted Pete

Rose, and grinned cheerfully at him over his shoulder.

"Yah, yah!" Rose yelled at him. "Only, how come you din' bat his ass in?"

"Hey, Dad," Petey Rose said, "did that guy have more hits than you last year?"

"Naw," Rose said. "We had the same." (Pete Rose and George Brett each wound up with two hundred and fifteen hits in 1976.)

"Did you have more triples than him?" Petey asked.

"No, he had more triples. I had more doubles. But he plays in an easier league than I do."

Petey nodded, and then his father looked down at him and said in a quiet voice, "No, Petey. He's a real good hitter."

The game that afternoon was a rouser. George Brett, who is the kind of real good hitter I like to think about while I am in the dentist's chair or caught in a traffic jam, also cracked out a double and a single against the Reds' pitchers, and Clint Hurdle hit a home run, and there were two good-looking rookies on view—Joe Zdeb for the Royals, and Steve Henderson for the Reds. (Zdeb's name had a tonic but oddly familiar ring to it, but it took me a couple of innings before I could pick up the echo: "ZDEB" is the last draw in a Scrabble game.) Before long, swarms of second-stringers began to crowd into the lineup, quickly causing my scorecard to resemble a botched arithmetic test, so I cheerfully gave up following the game and ate some peanuts and listened to the jokes in the press box and watched the crowd and, lulled by baseball, perhaps fell asleep for a minute there in the sun.

On my way out, in the eighth inning, I saw a young groupie approach George Foster just outside the Cincinnati clubhouse. "Sign my pants!" she said to him. "Please, George, sign my pants!"

We both looked, and, sure enough, her bluejeans were heavily autographed.

"I don't sign clothing," Foster said.

The Yankees' dressing room in Fort Lauderdale Stadium is the most luxurious cabaña in spring training, but this year it seemed much too small. Some of this crowded feeling, I sensed, was caused simply by the names in black block letters up over the players' cubicles—HUNTER, GULLETT, HOLTZMAN, FIGUEROA . . . MUNSON, NETTLES, WHITE, CHAMBLISS, JACKSON, RIVERS, WYNN . . . and, over in the coaches' sector, BERRA, MANTLE, FORD, HOWARD. . . . The players, to be sure, were cheerful and relaxed, even raucous at times, but the place was claustrophobic. The Yankees are loaded with fame and money and expectations—oppressive with possibilities. Their high-priced, high-powered lineup is expected to spread-eagle the field in the American League East this year, and then, maybe, avenge their frightful beating in the World Series last fall, but there is always a chance that it will not. There is a possibility of failure— and any failure of this expensive, custom-built apparatus will be cosmic in its dimensions, and perhaps more entertaining and popular than the expected triumph. Flying molecules of news, trifling or epochal, zinged invisibly through the Florida air—Thurman Munson's moodiness, Dock Ellis' contract, Graig Nettles' silence, Mickey Rivers' lethargy, Reggie Jackson's money, Billy Martin's temper, George Steinbrenner's ambition—and the New York writers vibrated under a bombardment of intimations. All of us there, writers and fans and hangers-on, were no longer a baseball audience but attendants at a contemporary festival of personality and celebrity, and the event we were waiting for was not just a pennant race but something deeper and sneakier—perhaps (COMING SOON!) even the long-expected, much-predicted explosive row and bust-up between Billy Martin and his boss, George Steinbrenner. Even the ball-games in Fort Lauderdale had a different taste. During my visit, Mickey Rivers misplayed a single in center field in the seventh inning of a game against the Phillies and then trotted languidly after the ball as it rolled to the fence; on the next play he dropped an easy fly. None of this was exactly star-tling—Rivers' sputtering desire is a persistent mystery, probably even to himself—but after the game the writers subjected Billy Martin to a good twenty minutes of questions about his inevitable forthcoming psychosocial colloquy with his center fielder. Spring afternoons in Fort Lauderdale were *stuffed* with drama, exactly like "Marcus Welby, M.D."

Reggie Jackson, the new president of the Bronx, impressed everyone in camp with his cheerfulness and hard work. "You have to feel your way on a new club," he said to me. "Come early, stay late, be a diplomat."* Reggie in white pinstripes was dazzling; the change of costume from his Baltimore colors and his old green-and-gold Oakland frontier getup reminded me of Clark Gable no longer in the Klondike or on the China seas but entering a drawing room in a dinner jacket. Reggie talked about money, of course.

"I paid my dues," he said. "It took me seven years to get up to a hundred thousand, and I was in four divisional championships and two World Series before I made it. One thing I learned from Charlie Finley is how to be a tough bargainer. Sure, there's a lot of feeling against me. Some club owners have said they wouldn't let me in their clubhouse. The feeling is in the air—not so much an anti-big-money thing as an anti-Reggie Jackson thing. Some of it is because I'm black and I'm articulate. The owners don't like ballplayers who talk a lot. Some other people don't like black people who talk a lot. That's distasteful, but it doesn't surprise me. I think most of the flak about too much money has been aimed at the black players."

I asked Billy Martin whether the wealth and celebrity of his new stars would inspire deeper competitive hostility in the rival clubs in his league.

"You don't want 'em to *like* you," he said at once. "We always had the same thing on the Yankee clubs I was with. The amounts were different, but we were the ones making the big money back then, and everybody was laying for us. If you're any good, it'll only make you play harder."

That afternoon, in a game against some Dodger scrubs, Reggie Jackson singled his first two times at bat—singled noisily, with the pistol-like sound that his bat always somehow produces—and then struck out, swinging and staggering, in the same exuberant fashion. The crowd loved it all. Rivers, it could be noticed, ran everything out in the game. Martin had talked to him that morning, and so had Reggie Jackson.

* Like other diplomats, Reggie sometimes can't help starting a war. A few weeks after this, he was quoted in *Sport* magazine as claiming that he was "the straw that stirs the drink" on his new team—a line which Thurman Munson took as a personal insult and which contributed to the noisome and bitter atmosphere that infected the Yankee clubhouse all through the summer.

"Maybe Mickey Rivers needs to hear more about himself," Jackson said after the game. "All he hears around this place is Jackson, Munson, Hunter, Steinbrenner. He may need to be told how much he matters to this club. Sure, he ought to know it already, but some people have to be told that every day of their lives."

Jackson noticed some reporters writing this down, and he made an impatient, dismissing gesture. "Aw, come on," he said. "None of this counts. Hell, this is just spring training. But a couple of weeks from now..." He picked up an imaginary bat, knocked some imaginary dirt from his spikes, and took up a batting stance. He was smiling now. "Showtime!" he cried.

Out in Arizona, under a blinding desert sun, I watched the San Diego Padres and the Seattle Mariners inflict unspeakable indignities upon each other on a patch of barely reclaimed Tempe mesa. I had come mostly to look over the new San Diego assemblage—hitters Dave Winfield, George Hendrick, and Gene Tenace; pitchers Randy Jones, Rollie Fingers, and Butch Metzger—that had been given an outside chance to "back-door it" to the top of the National League West while the Dodgers and Reds wore each other out this summer. Here, in the very first minutes of play, the Padres whacked six consecutive base hits, good for four runs. The Mariners are the other expansion club in the American League, and I felt a brief, commiserating sadness as their overmatched, anonymous hopefuls trotted in for their licks in the bottom half of the first inning—brief because the boy Mariners instantly rapped out three doubles and five singles, good for *eight* runs. The unique Seattle style, I subsequently saw, is one of ferocity at the plate and unbridled generosity on the mound. Their pitchers now gave back those eight counters, in five- and three-run clusters, and after five innings the score stood at 12–10, in favor of the Padres. I looked up the Seattle Club statistics in my scorecard and discovered that after thirteen spring games the new club boasted a team batting average of .343 and an earned-run average of 8.20—with both indicators sharply on the rise.

Strolling the sunny casbah of Tempe Stadium, I ran into Mike Kekich, the former Yankee left-hander and marital celebrity, who had invited himself to the Mariners' camp this spring on the outside chance of winning a place on the Seattle pitching corps. Nothing has gone right for Mike Kekich in the last few years. He was traded away from the Yankees shortly after the famous press conference, four years ago, when he and fellow Yankee pitcher, Fritz Peterson, announced that they were switching wives and children. For Kekich, the new marriage didn't materialize. He moved around in the big leagues and played in the minors and in Japan. A year ago, on his way to spring training with the Rangers, he cracked up his motorcycle and damaged a shoulder, and last winter, playing in Venezuela, he suffered a ruptured spleen in a brawl on the field and nearly died. Here in Tempe, however, he looked fine. He was wearing bluejeans and sandals (he was sitting out the game because of a pulled muscle), and he was clapping and whistling for the Mariners' hitting. "Have you ever seen the likes of this!" he exclaimed. "These kids just don't know any better. They just hit the ball wherever it's thrown. Everybody knows it can't last, but there's always that crazy little glimmer—a little hope that we can keep some of this after the season starts. Don't look for us in August, but it's sure been fun in camp. There's a high level of excitement when everybody has a chance for a place on a club. Most of the players here are in their early twenties, which makes me an elder statesman or something. My motivation is that I need a job, but I don't think I've ever been so—so *stimulated*. I've never known a spring to go so fast."

Kekich was the only ballplayer I talked to this spring who never mentioned money.

I stuck with the game until the end of the seventh inning, by which time matters stood at 16–12, in favor of the Padres, and my scorecard looked like a volume report from the Chicago commodities market. As I stood up in the press box and prepared to take my leave, in search of less excitement, a Seattle writer murmured, "If you want to stick around, the pitching sometimes gets better near the end. I think it's because the batters are worn out." The final, I read later, was 17–15, San Diego, with a total of thirty-eight hits, including seven triples. The next day, the Mariners whipped the Cleveland Indians 16–13, on a field goal in the last two minutes.

* * *

Big scores in Cactus League games are partly attributable to the thin, high desert air and the commensurately spacious local outfields, but this spring there was a lot of speculation that the ball itself was livelier. Big-league baseballs are being manufactured this year in Haiti by the Rawlings Company, which has taken over the job from the Spalding people, and pitchers told me that the new ball did seem tighter and quicker. Pitchers, however, always think that the ball has been secretly doctored to their disadvantage. This is nonsense. Everybody knows that pitchers are crazy. What *was* happening this spring was that the baseballs were trying to tell me something. Me, personally, I mean. A message was being sent, or perhaps several messages, and the fact that I have not yet deciphered them doesn't change anything. During a batting practice in Clearwater, I was gossiping with a Philadelphia writer near the Phillies' clubhouse in foul territory, well up the right-field line, when we heard an urgent "Heads up!" As we all know, "Heads up!" on a ball field means "Heads *down!*" and I quickly cringed away and received a glancing blow on the back of my right shoulder—a line foul from the batting cage, hit by Ted Sizemore. My shoulder felt as if I had been grazed by a 37-mm. cannon shell, but I did not rub the spot (a man learns a few things about this game over the years), and that night in my motel room I was delighted to discover that the bruise looked large enough and purple enough to last, with any luck, until my return home, ten days later, when I could show it to my six-year-old son and thus qualify for the Croix de Guerre. Then, in Arizona, the following events took place: A foul ball descending into the stands in Tempe Stadium ricocheted past my chin and then catapulted a full container of beer out of the hand of a retiree two rows in front of me, distributing its contents impartially upon four or five blue-haired ladies immediately before him. The next afternoon, in Phoenix Municipal Stadium, a ball came down behind the foul screen, bounded about determinedly and curiously among several boxes, rows, and railings in the manner of a police-trained terrier sniffing out an illegal immigrant, and then, suddenly on the trail, scurried down three more rows, took a sharp left, and rolled gently up the aisle behind me and into my hand. It was the first foul to come my way in the stands since I was about fourteen years old. Next day, same park, and here came a *third* foul, almost in the same location. This one took a high, straight-up ricochet and then a quick sideways one; missing our rendezvous, it vanished somewhere close to a nice-looking woman in my section who was wearing a Giants cardboard sun visor. She looked frantically around and under her seat, and cried, "Where *is* it?" Don Drysdale, who is now a broadcaster for the California Angels, was walking by on a transverse aisle, and he stopped behind the woman and pointed. "There it is," he said. "In your pocketbook." Finally, over in Scottsdale, just after I had left another game in late innings, I was walking alone toward my car in the club parking lot when I heard the sound of quick, oddly spaced running footsteps behind me. I turned and saw a baseball— red-seamed, shiny-white, beautiful—bounding delightedly toward me up the alley between two rows of cars: a foul ball, out of the park. The ball saw me and inexplicably veered and went to earth beneath a mauve Camaro. I followed, getting right down on my belly under the back bumper, but, of course, that ball had vanished forever—done away with, no doubt, by the K.G.B.

Before a Giants-Angels game in Phoenix, I watched Bobby Grich take a long infield practice at shortstop for the Angels. It will be a new position for him this summer—he was a second baseman for his last four years with the Orioles—although he played short through most of his minor-league career. Last winter, after signing up with the Angels, he got in a lot of work at short with the Long Beach Rockets, a semi-pro club in his home town. Grich is six feet two and powerfully built, with high cheekbones, narrow eyes, and a dashing mustache— a Cossack shortstop. When I sat down in the dugout with him before the game, he seemed anxious to talk about his status as one of the new high-priced free-agent stars.

"It bothers me," he said. "I'm a .260 hitter, and I think a lot of the fans are going to expect me to be a .290 hitter because I got all that money. Well, it's not going to happen—" He stopped and laughed. "I mean, I don't *think* it's going to happen, unless I have some kind of great year. I hope in time the fans will understand what went on last winter. It was a bidding year, and I just happened to be there. It was almost the same situation that we had back in the early nineteen-sixties for kids getting out of high school, before the coming of baseball drafts. A lot of money was paid out for some eighteen-year-old ball-players then. I was in elementary school, and I remember reading about Bob Bailey signing for a hundred and seventy-five thousand dollars. He was in Woodrow Wilson High, in Long Beach—the same school I went to later on.

"The way I look at it is that professional athletes are among a very small group of Americans who are able to make a lot of money when they're young. People aren't used to the idea of that, and it worries them. It doesn't happen to many of us, but I can't see there's anything wrong with it. I feel lucky, but I don't feel guilty. I'm enjoying it. If this was twenty years ago, I'd take what was being paid then and I'd enjoy that. I love playing ball. It's competitive. It's a struggle. You're always pushing yourself, trying to be better. I think the ones that get to the majors and get to the top—get up to the big money—are the ones that work the hardest and challenge themselves the most. The self-fulfillment you get out of the work is worth a lot more than the money. It's the only thing that matters."

The game that afternoon was full of pleasures and interest. The Angels and the Giants both started lineups close to what they would put on the field on opening day. Grich and Joe Rudi and Don Baylor were there, in their new California colors, and the starting Angels pitcher was Frank Tanana, their terrific left-hander, who is considered on the verge of perhaps becoming the best pitcher in the game. The Giants' obligatory super-prospect—the Giants *always* have a fresh-hatched Willie Mays or Carl Hubbell in March—was Jack Clark, the left fielder, but Clark had already achieved special status as the *old* phenom, having been pushed out of the headlines by a non-roster ball-hawk named Randy Elliott, who was playing right field today; Elliott was batting .625.

Frank Tanana works from the outermost corner of the pitching mound on the first-base side, throwing with a swift knee-crick and a rapid motion. His money pitch is the curve, but his fastball is no insignificant article; for right-handed batters it seems to sweep in on their fists from somewhere out by the right-field boxes. American League batters often describe Tanana with the currently cool line "He's *unfair*." In the bottom of the second inning, I watched with condescending amusement as Randy Elliott led things off against Tanana—a typical spring mismatch, suddenly altered when Elliott smashed a drive to the left-field fence, good for a double. Randy Elliott led off again in the fourth: a first-pitch triple to the left-center-field wall, four hundred and twelve feet away. He is tall and heavy-boned, and runs in a sprawling, loose-footed manner, but he pulled into third base standing up, with an expression of careful unsurprise on his face: Nothing *to* this game, gang . . .

The Angels, for their part, kept working away at the Giants' Ed Halicki and his successors, twice tying up the game, and then going ahead by 3–2 in the seventh before Bill Madlock, the Giant third baseman, made a super, diving stop on his knees to cut off the California rally. Then the Giants retied the game, 3–3, in their half. The whole afternoon was like that. The desert sun hammered down on us, casting rocklike shadows on the infield and softer shapes on the thick green grass of the outfield, but there was a warm breeze blowing out toward center field and beyond, where a little windmill spun and glittered in the sunshine. In the stands, we yelled happily and almost impartially, admiring the ballplayers and the close, meaningless, money-free game, not wanting it to end. Then it did end, in the ninth, with a double by the Angels' Bruce Bochte and a useful, just-good-enough, wrong-field single, an inch or two above the first baseman's leap and stab, by Joe Rudi—by Joe Rudi, *of course*. In their half, the Giants put two runners aboard and got the tying run to third before a double play ended it all. You couldn't ask for a better game.

3

Goodbye, Tom

JUNE 1977

TOM SEAVER IS GONE—NO LONGER A MET, NO LONGER A SUNLIT prominence in this flattened city of New York. His recent trade to the Cincinnati Reds in return for a few journeyman players and untested rookies was a shocking and mystifying affair, but the feelings we are left with seem much deeper than disappointment or aggrieved sporting loyalty. Tom Seaver cried when he cleared out his locker at Shea Stadium and talked to some reporters there about the Mets fans. A woman I know told me that when she called up a friend of hers the other afternoon, the telephone was answered by her friend's eleven-year-old son, who was in tears; when the boy's mother came on the phone, she said that her son had been crying about Tom Seaver for two days. A man I know—not much of a Mets fan, or even much of a baseball fan—told me that ever since the trade he had been waking up in the middle of the night thinking about Tom Seaver; one time, he said, he woke up crying. The sporting press, to be sure, has listed the unhappy circumstances that probably made the trade inevitable: a prolonged salary dispute; serious differences of opinion between Seaver and the Mets board chairman, M. Donald Grant, about the inviolability of Seaver's contract; charges by Mr. Grant that Tom Seaver was ungrateful; charges by Tom Seaver that the Mets' front office had shown persistent ineptitude in building or sustaining a competent ball team; charges of disloyalty; charges of greed; charges of a scurrilous vendetta against Seaver conducted by a local sports columnist. Taken together, these almost seem to add up to a reasonable explanation for the unreasonable event. But they come nowhere near accounting for the sense of loss that so many of us feel, or for the clear suggestion of corporate self-loathing in the Mets' decision to disown their one true star, Tom Seaver, the best pitcher in baseball.

When emotions run deep, images sometimes take the place of arguments or ideas. One of the images I have before me now is that of Tom Seaver pitching; the motionless assessing pause on the hill while the sign is delivered, the easy, rocking shift of weight onto the back leg, the upraised arms, and then the left shoulder coming forward as the whole body drives forward and drops suddenly downward—down so low that the right knee scrapes the sloping dirt of the mound—in an immense thrusting stride, and the right arm coming over blurrily and still flailing, even as the ball, the famous fastball, flashes across the plate, chest-high on the batter and already past his low, late swing. Another image is that of M. Donald Grant, the chairman of the board. A tall, spare, erect, white-haired man who wears dark business suits, Mr. Grant almost never speaks or acts unguardedly. Publicly, he has said that his actions in the Seaver case were impelled by his wish to maintain ticket prices at a reasonable level, and were thus in the interests of the fans. "The contract," he said, "is the fundamental cornerstone in our country." In a half-unguarded moment, he has referred to the players on his team as boys. Privately, he has told Tom Seaver that it is not good for him to be making so much money while he is still a young man. The image that Mr. Grant has chosen for himself is that of a father. Shining young athletes have all the best of it, of course, when it comes to images, but most of us—it is hard to admit it—can see something of ourselves in Mr. Grant, too.

Our national preoccupation with the images and performances of great athletes is not a simple matter. The obsessive intensity with which we watch their beautiful movements, their careless energy, their noisy, narcissistic joy in their own accomplishments is remarkably close to the emotions we feel when we observe very young children at play. While their games last, we smile with pleasure—but not for long, not forever. Rising from the park bench at last, we look at our watch and begin to gather up the scattered toys. That's enough, boys and girls. Time to go in now. Our stiff face and pursy smile slowly break in on their attention. That's *enough,* now! You know what happens when you get overtired. The procession home begins, in despair and relief. The children have been patronized, and we are released from our envy of them.

Off the field, Tom Seaver is not a child, of course, but an articulate and outspoken young man, with strong opinions about the business side of baseball, the relations between professional athletes and their employers, and the nuances of his difficult profession. He is one of the special, lucky few, a child and a man together, the true Tom Terrific, and it is scarcely any wonder that Mr. Grant wanted him gone. Tom Seaver has escaped, and the punishment meant for him has descended on us, the fans. Our joy in him was unstinted. Yelling at the last fastball of the day, watching Tom walk off the mound after still another extraordinary pitching performance, we would rise and shout and clap our hands for his skill, for his good looks, for his sweaty, smiling joy over another famous victory. Savoring the victory, loving him, we suddenly became younger, for we had surely glimpsed ourselves out there, if only for an instant—ourselves at some glowing, youthful best. We had become children, too, and this could not be permitted to last.

4

Several Stories with Sudden Endings

OCTOBER 1977

IT WAS QUITE A SUMMER. THIS WAS THE SUMMER IN WHICH THE Chicago White Sox and the Chicago Cubs led their divisions at the beginning of August. It was the summer when Rod Carew, of the Minnesota Twins, batted .486 for the month of June and finished the season at .388, winning his sixth American League batting title and attaining the highest individual batting average since Ted Williams also batted .388, in 1957. It was the summer in which the Texas Rangers played under four different managers in a single week, and in which four different clubs—the Rangers, the White Sox, the Twins, and the Kansas City Royals—took turns leading the American League West in a single week. It was the summer in which the Red Sox hitters bashed out thirty-three home runs in the space of ten games, and in which the Red Sox pitchers gave up sixty hits to the Milwaukee Brewers in the space of four games: a perfect summary of the Boston season. This was the summer when Pete Rose wound up with two hundred and four hits, tying Ty Cobb's all-time record of nine two-hundred-hit seasons, and when Lou Brock, at the age of thirty-eight, stole thirty-five bases, running his stolen-base total to an even nine hundred—eight more than Cobb's famous lifetime record. Tom

Seaver, traded to the Reds early this summer, finished with a 21–6 record and an earned-run average of 2.59. Without their hero, the Mets finished last in their division, thirty-seven games behind the winning Phillies, and divested themselves of 406,322 former fans. This was also the summer when Ted Turner, the owner of the Atlanta Braves, sent a yacht-load of his ballplayers to sea off Newport, Rhode Island, so that they could watch him competing in the America's Cup trials at the helm of his 12-metre sloop *Courageous;* Turner went on to defend the Cup successfully for the United States, but his Braves, despite their fresh understanding of the importance of perfect teamwork on the foredeck during the spinnaker legs, finished last in the National League West.

There was more. This summer, a shy, left-hand-swinging half-Chinese thirty-seven-year-old slugger named Sadaharu Oh struck the seven-hundred-and-fifty-sixth home run of his career, while playing for the Yomiuri Giants, in Japan, and thus surpassed (in a way) Hank Aaron's lifetime mark; the qualifying parenthesis suggests that Japanese ballparks and Japanese pitchers are not all of major-league dimensions—a fact that the wonderful Oh admitted when he politely murmured, "I don't think I would do as well in American baseball." Back home, some foreign-born baseballs—made in Haiti for the Rawlings Company, and perhaps secretly polished there with applications of Haitian ju-ju oil—may have had something to do with a record one-season total of 3,642 home runs and a jump of eight points in the major-league batting averages, to .264. On the afternoon of July 27th, at Wrigley Field, the Cubs defeated the Cincinnati Reds, 16–15, in thirteen innings; eleven home runs flew out of the park during the game, five of them in the first inning. Among the pitchers, Nolan Ryan struck out nineteen batters in a single game—for the fourth time in his career. There were fresh young flowers in many gardens: outfielder Mitchell Page, who hit twenty-one homers and stole forty-two bases for the abysmal Oakland A's; the Cardinals' new short-stop, Garry Templeton, who hit .322, third best in the National League; first baseman Eddie Murray, who hit twenty-seven homers for the resurgent Orioles; Bruce Sutter, a relief pitcher who saved thirty-one games and notched an earned-run average of 1.35 for the Cubs; and Warren Cromartie and Andre Dawson, who hit and ran and caught fly balls with immense élan for the young, and at last interesting, Montreal Expos. None of the newcomers, however, had as satisfying a season as Willie McCovey. Apparently finished at the age of thirty-nine, Stretch won a place for himself with his old team, the Giants, and—delighting everyone with his customary calm and class, and his familiar, infinitely pleasing scythelike swing—hit twenty-eight homers, including the seventeenth grand-slammer of his career. Another famous favorite, Brooks Robinson, retired after twenty years with the Orioles; one of the most graceful and accomplished defensive players in the history of the game, he won sixteen consecutive Gold Glove awards as the best third baseman in his league. The immensely strong Cincinnati out-fielder George Foster led all the sluggers with fifty-two homers and a hundred and forty-nine runs batted in, while the im-mensely strong Jim Rice and the ditto ditto Greg Luzinski hit thirty-nine homers apiece, for the Red Sox and the Phillies, respectively.

The triumphs of Foster, who once belonged to the Giants, and of Seaver, who once (sob!) belonged to the Mets, permitted me to play some riveting midnight ballgames in my private stadium, Insomnia Park, between all-star nines made up of notable active players who, for one foolish reason or another, have been severed from the Giants and the Mets. At first glance, the Giant Erstwhiles seem to have all the best of it, since their starting outfield includes Foster, Bobby Bonds, and Garry Mad-dox (with Willie Montanez, Bobby Murcer, and Gary Matthews fretting on the bench), but the return of McCovey to the Giants from his brief exile in San Diego leaves a bad hole at first base; in any case, all that power isn't much use against the first two starting pitchers for the Mets Alumni—Seaver and Nolan Ryan, who are heartened by the presence of Tug McGraw in the bullpen, and by *their* outfield of Amos Otis, Ken Singleton, and Rusty Staub. A late-inning pinch-hitter often turns out to be Dave Kingman (a new Padre this year), who, of course, plays for both teams. Just the other night, batting for the Met-vets, he was fanned by Old Giant Gaylord Perry, who got him on a spitter.

Three of the four pennant races remained close and inter-esting until the last few days of August. The exception was in the National League West, where the Los Angeles Dodgers selfishly won seventeen of their first twenty games of the season and by May 30th led the defending two-time-champion Cincinnati Reds by ten games, and thenceforth glided to their half-pennant. The Reds, who had been considered the prime club of this era, never mounted a sustained challenge but competed fiercely among themselves in self-abasement at the end of their disappointing season. "I put these players on an ego trip last spring," cried manager Sparky Anderson. "I sacrificed self-discipline for aggressiveness," wailed George Foster. "I didn't drive in any runs," whimpered Dave Concepcion. "None of us can say he isn't to blame," blurted Johnny Bench. In truth, the Reds lost because of frail pitching (their staff had the tenth-best E.R.A. among twelve clubs), which was partly attributable to a Cincinnati front-office decision last fall to cut loose some of their best pitchers (including the redoubtable Don Gullett) when they threatened to become free agents, and a concomitant high moral resolve to stand aloof from the free-agent market altogether.

The free agents, whose historic arrival in the marketplace of baseball last autumn became the occasion for so much apprehension, speculation, and (in some cases) unbridled disbursement of the owners' money, fared unevenly in their first summer. Rollie Fingers saved thirty-five games for his new team, the Padres, which otherwise had little to show for its heavy plunge into the free-agent pool; another lavish spender, the California Angels, ran into bad luck when two of its expensive new stars, Bobby Grich and Joe Rudi, were drydocked for most of the season with serious injuries. Don Gullett won fourteen games and lost four for the Yankees. (Ah, there, high moral resolve!) And so it went—a mixed return, which will surely encourage some previously hesitant owners to speculate heavily in this year's upcoming free-agent market and others utterly but anxiously to avoid it. In the minds of all of them now, and in the minds of baseball fans and baseball people everywhere, are the vivid summer adventures of the most expensive free agent of them all, Reggie Jackson, who came to the Yankees last year for two million nine hundred thousand dollars (payable, in various forms, over a period of several years). Some of the owners will recall that Reggie's notorious new fame and fortune seemed to contribute heavily to the internal turmoil and clubhouse dissension that nearly shattered the club, and that Reggie's sometimes indifferent play in the outfield was the cause of bitter derision in the stands and, once, of a near fistfight with his manager in the dugout. Others may have noticed that when the Yankees finally did get untracked and mounted their splendid late-summer and early-autumn offensive, it was Reggie Jackson who often contributed the telling hit or the telling catch in another crucial victory. But no matter: all of them—and all of us who share in the game—will remember what he did on the very last night of this long baseball year, when he alone transformed everything and made this season finally famous.

My first glimpse of Chicago's marvellous festival of baseball came early in June, when chance took me to that city just in time to catch a Yankees–White Sox game on a steamy Saturday night at Comiskey Park. The Pale Hose were in second place in the A. L. West, a bare two games back of the Twins, and the picturesque South Side bathhouse was stuffed to its iron rafters with sweating, beery, shirted and unshirted roarers. I sat in the stands and yelled cheerfully and almost neutrally, and tried to suppress my critical misgivings when the home side surrendered seven runs to the Yankees in the second inning, on four singles, a bases-loaded walk, a triple, a ghastly error by center fielder Chet Lemon, and two separate and distinct doubles by Reggie Jackson. However, I had not begun to grasp the White Sox' cunning 1977 strategy, which was, from first to last, to ignore every defensive nuance of the game, thus leaving their players entirely free to concentrate on knocking the cover off the ball. Richie Zisk, the Sox' right fielder and big stick (and, by a consensus of Chicago Poles, a very prince of players), led off the bottom of the same inning with his fifteenth homer of the year, setting off the scoreboard rockets, and Chet Lemon ignited further airborne salutes and flowerpots with a homer in the fourth and another in the sixth. In the seventh, we all rose and, in accordance with local custom, bawled an earsplitting chorus of "Take Me Out to the Ball Game," under the spirited leadership of Harry Caray, the celebrated Sox broadcaster, from his booth. There was barely time to sit down again before Oscar Gamble, pinch-hitting, socked *another* Chicago home run, thus moving the Sox up to within reach of a tie, 8–6. It ended that way, but with two out in the bottom of the ninth the headlong White Sox rapped out two singles, thus bringing up Zisk again, who concluded things with a terrific line clout off Sparky Lyle that was barely pulled down by Roy White in left field. The Chicago fans rewarded their losing heroes with a cacophonous round of applause, and I filed out with the hot and almost happy hordes, all of us exchanging excited glances and exclaiming "Great game!" "Wonderful game!" over and over again.

I could not get back to Chicago until the first weekend in August—at the very end of the party. The Cubs had held first place in the National League East since May 28th, at one time leading by a margin of eight and a half games, but now they were at last running out of pitchers and had slipped toward the onrushing Phillies and Pirates and Cardinals; the White Sox, who stood at the top of their division through the entire month of July, had just dropped four straight, and their cushion was down to two and a half games. The joy-ravished Chicago citizenry, who had not been given a White Sox pennant since 1959 or a Cubs pennant since 1945, had almost stopped talking about a glorious "el" series in the fall. I went back to Comiskey Park on a damp evening, and saw the White Sox beat Bert Blyleven and the tough Texas Rangers, 5–4, in an anxious, gnawing sort of game that was settled in the top of the eighth, when White Sox first baseman Jim Spencer made a fine play on a squeeze bunt by Bert Campaneris and threw out the tying runner at the plate. The crowd had been thinned a bit by the threat of rain, but the fans sustained a full-house din from start to finish, beating on drums, waving bedsheet banners ("THE SOX ARE BETTER THAN SEX"), and, at two- or three-minute intervals, roaring out the inane, marvellous chorus from a 1969 rock song called "Kiss Him Good-bye": "Na-na-na-na—Hey-hey! Good *bye!*" The seventh-inning-stretch concert, under Harry Caray's baton, now picked up the Mickey Mouse Club theme song, and at every opportunity—including several that were almost invisible to me—the fans treated some fresh Sox hero to another standing ovation. Joy had deepened into ritual.

I watched all this in good company, sitting in the press box next to Bill Veeck, the White Sox president, who had acquired the venerable but shaky franchise last year, by dint of some hairbreadth last-minute financing, and then kept it alive, mostly on his own enthusiasm, through a dreary, losing, last-place first summer. Chicago is probably a Cubs town at heart, but the startling White Sox outdrew the surprising Cubs this summer, and everyone in town was happy for Bill Veeck. On this evening, he drank six glasses of iced tea and smoked two packs of Salems and incessantly praised his lightly talented players ("A good kid, a wonderful kid...No one takes more pleasure in the game than he does"), while admitting their failings ("We can't catch the ball very well. We hit a little. We *get* hit a lot. They've been killing us in the late innings"). Veeck seemed awed by the crowd ("They cheer for *everything*—we're leading the league in standing ovations"), and when it was over at last, and the Sox had won, he stood up and coughed happily and murmured what I had come to recognize as his own baseball credo: "Well, that was fun, wasn't it? It's meant to be fun, you know." The White Sox didn't win this summer, finishing third in the A.L. West, twelve games behind the Kansas City Royals, but Bill Veeck had fun right to the end. When the season was over, he mailed out World Series tickets—Comiskey Park World Series tickets—to his season subscribers, with a note that said, "Well, we blew it. No, that's not true—not exactly. Kansas City won it. But, as you can see by the enclosed tickets, we were ready!"

The end of the Cubs' brief reign was much nearer at hand. On the very next afternoon, I went to Wrigley Field and saw them lose to the Padres by 11–8—a defeat that took them out of first place at last and dropped them a half-game behind the Phillies. The Cubs fell a long way after that, finishing in fourth place, with a record of 81–81, but their decline was probably ordained from the moment, on the very day of my visit, when it was announced that Bruce Sutter, their extraordinary reliever, had been placed on the disabled list with an ailing shoulder, and when it became known that Rick Reuschel, their ace starter, would miss a few turns because of a sore back. Up to that point, Sutter, a forkballer, had won five games and saved twenty-four for the North Siders, and Reuschel, who was the best starting pitcher in the National League in the first half of the season, stood at 15–3. Nothing could replace them. In the game against the Padres, the earnest, semi-anonymous Cub regulars—Ivan DeJesus, Larry Bittner, Steve Ontiveros, Manny Trillo, Bill Buckner, and the rest—struggled manfully, but the Chicago pitching was frightful; the Padres blew them away with four homers, including a grand slam and a three-run shot, both by Dave Kingman. The cheering seemed thinner and shriller than it had at Comiskey Park, but that was because the afternoon crowd was mostly children; they remained hopeful to the very end, as kids will, but it was a sad day, and I wished I had come out to beautiful Wrigley Field when the going was good. Later in the summer, I received a letter from a Cubs fan named Tim Rinehart, who told me what it had been like there during the best time of all, which was that terrific thirteen-inning, eleven-homer 16–15 victory over the Reds in July. He wrote:

I was there in the bleachers from noon batting practice until the final run scored at 6:20 P.M.—beer money in my pocket, shirt off, pants rolled up, smack in the special land and time of baseball, the only place to be.... It was 10–7 almost before we knew it, and then the game became one of Reds' surge and Cubs' catch-up, each one less probable and therefore more exciting than the last. Reds 10–7; Reds 10–8; 10–10 tie! Reds 11–10, then 13–10, then 14–10 (great game, but this Cincinnati team is just too much). Reds 14–13 (my God, we are back in this!); 14–14, in the ninth! Reds 15–14 in the top of the twelfth (that damned Rosello never could make the big play under pressure); 15–15 (George Mitterwald, the Baron, hits another homer!) in the bottom of the twelfth; and the Cubs 16–15 at the end (Rosello, of course, comes through with the big hit, a single). In the bleachers, we fans took on a shared, historic, "we were there" spirit. We were high on the game and not on the beer, which ran out in the ninth inning anyway. It was the game that took over.

Tom Seaver went to the Reds in the middle of June, and it was more than two months before the schedule brought him back to pitch against his old teammates, on a beautiful Sunday at Shea Stadium. The fans came back for that one, and Tom received a shattering ovation when the lineups were announced, but the Mets drew heavy mitting, too, and few boos. The Sign Man held up "SEAVER LIVES!" but the emotional contretemps seemed to be beyond the creative powers of the banner artisans. The game, in fact, was a vivid little summer pageant illustrating not only the painfully tested affiliations of true fans but the even more subtle and intertwined virtues and ironies of friendship, loyalty, and competitive pride that all professional athletes have to sort out somehow. Manager Joe Torre started Eddie Kranepool and Bud Harrelson and, of course, Jerry Koosman— all boyish and sun-dappled Mets when all the world was young. It was a fine game, with Cincinnati ahead by 2–1 through the seventh, and with Harrelson and young Steve Henderson and good old Eddie Kranepool combining for the Mets' run. Koosman pitched beautifully, but Tom was even better—eleven strikeouts—and the Reds broke it open in the eighth, after a throwing error by Harrelson, and won it, 5–1. Everyone seemed drained in the end, and it was plain in the clubhouses that Seaver and the Mets had both badly wanted to win.

"I thought we had a real shot," Kranepool said. "If you stay close against Tom, you have a shot. He'll never beat himself. I don't care if a pitcher has been on your team for thirty years, he'll still want to get you out. That's the way it is."

Harrelson was disconsolate. "From the noise, Tom had more fans than we did," he said. "That made it hard out there."

"I'm glad it's over," Tom Seaver said.

M. Donald Grant did not attend.

In the pennant campaigns, the Phillies rewarded their clamorous followers with sixteen consecutive midsummer wins in their home park; the team was never headed after early August, in spite of a brief sag near the end of the month which allowed the Pirates to creep within three and a half games. The Kansas City Royals, helped at last by terrific pitching and some invigorating late-inning rallies, settled the four-team dogfight in the A.L. West with a ten-game streak and then, in September, with an uninterrupted sixteen in a row—the longest run of victories in the majors in twenty-four years. The strangest summer of all was that of the Boston Red Sox, whose season's record bears close resemblance to the temperature chart of a first-stage malaria victim. After the burning fever of that ten-game, thirty-three-homer splurge, which took them to first place in mid-June, the team dropped nine in a row, and then staggered through July, sometimes in first place in the A.L. East and sometimes out of it. Early in August, the Bosox threw off the covers again, winning eleven straight and seventeen of nineteen. Then they lost seven games in a row (and along with them their lead once again), and *then* won ten of eleven, to draw within a game and a half of the Yankees in mid-September. (These symptoms are perfectly familiar to any reliable baseball diagnostician; the anopheles responsible for the chronic and debilitating Fenway blackwater fever is always insufficient pitching.) The Bosox' much steadier and more robust rival through most of these disorders was the Baltimore Orioles, a pleasing and surprising amalgam of veterans (Lee May, Ken Singleton, Al Bumbry, Jim Palmer) and utter unknowns (Eddie Murray, Billy Smith, Rich Dauer), who responded uncannily to the direction of the Merlin-like Earl Weaver and came home at last with ninety-seven victories—good enough for a pennant in a less excessive year.

The Yankees, it may be recalled, had a little trouble along the way. Their relentlessly publicized off-the-field sulks and tiffs and rumorings and squabbles will not be reëxamined here, if only because the daily turns of plot of a soap opera—"Churls' Way," perhaps—lose their edge when seen from a little distance. The trouble, of course, was a violent multiple clash of personalities, brought on by owner George Steinbrenner's intense ambition and his impatient, meddlesome need for total success; by Billy Martin's insecure ego, his dangerous temper and occasional deviousness, and his capacity for martyrdom; by Reggie Jackson's money and display of money, his love of the hottest part of the spotlight, and his actorish ways with the press; by Thurman Munson's brooding silences, his injured pride as a challenged leader, and his distaste for big-city maneuverings; and by the various and equally urgent wants and responses of a dozen other well-paid but fame-frazzled and (in the end) exhausted professional athletes, whose every word and gesture was recorded, from April to October, by enormous squads of local and national reporters and media people. I visited the Yankees after many games last summer, but I rarely stayed long, because it was the most joyless clubhouse I had ever been in. In time, I became sorry for them all, and it even occurred to me that this rich and favored team was terribly unlucky, because it didn't seem to have a true leader—one carefree or charismatic veteran star who could laugh at all this once in a while and thus suggest to the other players that they were young, after all, and that what they were engaged in was, for them if not their glum employers, still a game.

On the field, the Yanks never bored me. In hindsight any

champion team acquires an aura of brilliance and inexorable success, but these Yankees did favor a highly melodramatic style of baseball, often seeming to wait for the big game, attended by the largest and most expectant audience, before coming up with the sudden astounding performance, the impossible play, the killing blow. In June, playing before a gigantic weekend home audience against the Red Sox, just a week after the Sox had humiliated them by belting out sixteen homers during a three-game sweep at Fenway Park, the Yankees took the opener when Roy White tied the game with a two-run, two-out homer in the ninth and Reggie Jackson hit a game-winning single in the eleventh. They won the next game, too, and the one after that—on a ninth-inning single by Paul Blair—to cut the Boston lead from five games to two. The Yankees probably began their pennant move on August 10th, when Reggie Jackson was at last moved to the cleanup spot in the order, but the upward path was a long and bumpy one. On August 16th, at the Stadium, the free-swinging White Sox, trailing by 9–4, erupted for six runs in the top half of the ninth against Ron Guidry and Sparky Lyle—and were immediately beaten in the bottom half on a two-run homer by Chris Chambliss. A couple of weeks later, with the club finally in first place, Chambliss came off the bench and hit a three-run homer in the eighth that whipped the Royals by 5–3. The Yankees won the next day, against the Mariners, on Mickey Rivers' homer in the eleventh, and the day after that on Graig Nettles' homer in the ninth. This kind of momentum, which requires a deep and talented lineup, makes everyone, including the manager, look nine feet tall, but once the Yankees began to make their headlines on the field instead of in the clubhouse, one could see at last that most of these expensive athletes were performing at superlative levels—not only the dangerous Jackson and Munson and Graig Nettles but outfielders Lou Piniella and Mickey Rivers (who batted .330 and .326 this year) and Willie Randolph, who had established himself as the best young second baseman in the league. Sparky Lyle won thirteen games and saved twenty-six more with his down-ducking slider; and Ron Guidry, an unknown left-hander, finished with an earned-run average of 2.82—fourth best among the league's starting pitchers. The manager of such a club might seem to have the same responsibilities as a private chauffeur, but it is my conviction that Billy Martin in the late weeks of this season was the best on-the-field manager I have ever seen. From mid-August to mid-October, his shifts of the batting order, his selections from a roster of often ailing or unsound pitchers, his late-inning picks of pinch-hitters or relief hurlers (or his almost mystifying patience with an incumbent) must have left rival teams and managers at times with the feeling that they had been not only beaten up by the big-city slickers but somehow bamboozled as well. The pilot of a squad like the 1977 Yankees is often disparaged as a "push-button manager," but anyone who knows this game understands that there are a hundred different ways to push those buttons in every game, and many thousands of ways over the course of a season. The piano may be an easier instrument. Away from the field, Billy Martin often seems indifferent or depressed, and unable to shake off the pain of a lost game, which he takes as a deadly personal defeat. He also appears to be distracted by the office work of baseball—scouting reports, statistics, public relations—and this may be the real source of his difficulties with George Steinbrenner, who is a driving and unrelenting businessman. But up on the dugout step Martin is someone else altogether. His intensity is unique. Under the cap, his face is pale and tight, and he looks almost ill with concentration and hostility. His eyes are cold, moving constantly about the field and across the dark inner ranges of stratagem and intuition, in search of the sudden edge, the flicker of advantage, that will win again. It is the face of a man in a street fight, a man up an alley when the knives have just come out. It is win or die.

The Yankees won their pennant, we now know, by taking the first two games of a classic three-game series from the Red Sox at the Stadium in the middle of September. I think that many fans who were there may remember those games even more vividly than the Yanks' later triumphs in the playoffs and the World Series—the enormous crowds (the total of 164,852 spectators was the biggest three-game baseball audience since 1958), the oceans of sound, the weight of the ancient rivalry, the claustrophobic tension of the games themselves. The visitors, who came into the series a game and a half behind and only one game down in the lost column, were frightening at the plate. Their sluggers—Jim Rice, Carlton Fisk, Carl Yastrzemski, George Scott, Butch Hobson, and the rest—set or tied eighteen major-league home-run records this year. (Hobson alone hit thirty homers and batted in a hundred and twelve runs—fair work for an eighth-place hitter.) Against the Pinstripes now, they attacked the ball violently, as always, but the Yankee pitchers and the Yankee ballpark broke their hearts. Fisk and Rice and Hobson and Scott all whacked enormous drives that were pulled in at the last moment just in front of the distant fences. Carlton Fisk, I imagine, will sometimes start up in bed in the middle of the night this winter with the vision of Mickey Rivers at the base of some faraway blue wall gathering in yet another of his four-hundred-foot fly balls, firing the ball back, and then finishing the play with that odd little shiver of his arms and shoulders, like a man ridding himself of a bad thought. In the first game, Rivers also poled a first-pitch drive into the low bleachers, and skinny Ron Guidry fanned nine of the Sox' big swingers and won it, 4–2. In the next, Reggie Cleveland nailed Mickey Rivers in the back with his first delivery of the night (let's see you pull *that* pitch, Mick!) and then set down rows of Yankee hitters in disorderly but effective fashion while his teammates tried frantically to get on the scoreboard. But Reggie Jackson made two marvellous catches in right field, and in the fifth the Sox loaded the bases off Ed Figueroa with none out but failed to score (Lynn bounced into a home-to-first double play; Yaz ripped a sure single up the middle that collided with Figueroa's hip, and was thrown out), and the current of the game, one sensed, reversed direction. No ballplayer is more inflammable in this sort of situation than Reggie Jackson, who, with Thurman Munson aboard in the ninth inning, hit a splendid three-and-two slider by Reggie Cleveland deep into the right-field bleachers for the only runs of the game. The win put the Yankees ahead of the Red Sox by three and a half games (and two and a half ahead of the Orioles), and although the Sox won the following night and subsequently beat the Yankees twice more, up at Fenway Park, they were never able to close the gap. Boston and Baltimore ended the season in a tie for second place, two and a half games behind.

Two postludes, to close this September:

The Red Sox won the third game of the notable series at the Stadium, 7–3, but most of us who were there were not able to give much attention to the baseball. The Yankee rooters (young men, most of them) in the upper deck lost interest in the game when their team fell behind, and gave themselves up instead to showering everyone near them and below them with oceans of beer, to throwing pennies and darts and fruit and bottles and other objects onto the field, to fighting one another, and to waging violent near riots with the equally violent Stadium special police. There was nothing fresh or surprising about this; it happened all the time this summer at Yankee Stadium— a place where I no longer feel comfortable watching baseball in company with my wife or my young son. It seems to me that George Steinbrenner, who throws himself with such energy into every aspect of his business, should now address himself to this one. Perhaps he will recall that a few years ago the Los Angeles Dodgers were troubled by rowdy eruptions in their outfield pavilions and solved the problem in the quickest fashion possible. They stopped selling beer.

Up in green Fenway Park, the Red Sox beat the Yankees, 6–3, on the night of September 19th, and after the game was over a lot of reporters in the Boston clubhouse crowded around a tan young Boston player named Ted Cox, who, as the designated hitter for Boston that night, had singled in his first two times at bat. He had played in his first major-league game the day before, against the Orioles, and had gone four-for-four at the plate, which meant that he had batted safely in his first six official trips to the plate—a miracle: the greatest beginning in the history of the game. Cox, who looked more boyish than any other big-leaguer I had ever seen, was flushed with pleasure. "I never *dreamed* of anything like this," he said two or three times, and I noticed that the writers around him were smiling.* After a while, we drifted over toward Carl Yastrzemski, who had hit his twenty-fifth homer that night—a long drive into the center-field bleachers—and who, at the age of thirty-eight, was coming to the close of another remarkable year. (He played an entire season, one hundred and fifty games, without committing an error.) Yastrzemski, who, like so many great hitters, has oddly protuberant eyes, was still in his long-

---

* Nothing notable or particularly cheerful has happened to Ted Cox in baseball since this day; he is now a reserve infielder with the Seattle Mariners. Sometimes the best comes first—a miserable arrangement.

sleeved undershirt, and he was smoking a cigarette. He was unshaven, and there were deep wrinkles in his neck. He answered some questions about the homer and asked how the Orioles had done that night, and then somebody asked him how he would like it if he were Ted Cox's age and just starting out in baseball.

"Oh, no," he said at once. "No, thanks. I'm glad to be my age."

He lit another cigarette from the first, and a reporter asked him to compare this season with 1967, when he batted .522 in the last two weeks and carried the Red Sox to a pennant. Yastrzemski shook his head, dismissing the question. "I've always hit well in September," he said at last. "I don't know why. Maybe the fans make a difference—I don't know." There was a silence, and then he said, "This is a strange game." We waited in a circle around him, with our pencils and notebooks poised, wanting more. But there was no more. Nobody knows all about this game—not even Yaz.

The roily and momentous events of the two championship play-offs and the World Series have left such vivid pictures on our baseball consciousness that probably only the lightest burnishing is required to bring back the colors. The Yankees' six-game triumph over the Dodgers in the World Series, and Reggie Jackson's epochal feat (in this case, perhaps, hyperbole may be forgiven) of smashing those three successive home runs in the final game, should not let us forget how very close the Yankees came to missing the World Series altogether. Reggie saved baseball's crown jewels. Without him, this would have been another year in which the more brilliant and emotional October baseball came in the preliminary series. It is my guess that the Phillies and the Royals were great public favorites to win their playoffs, if only because both these attractive teams had been losers in the same event last fall and then had made the long summer journey back to win their divisional titles again, each of them with a deeper and far more confident lineup than in the year before. This time, each was eliminated on its own home turf, where it had every expectation of winning at last, and each was beaten under bitter and extraordinary circumstances. I cannot remember such a painful week of baseball.

The Yankees and the Royals began at Yankee Stadium, taking up their business, it seemed, exactly where they had left off last fall, when Chris Chambliss's ninth-inning homer broke up a tied game and a tied series. This time, however, the power hitting was by the team in the dusty-blue road uniforms: Kansas City, which had altered some batting strokes and batting attitudes this year to beef up its attack, racked up six runs in the first three innings and whipped the Yanks, 7–2, on homers by Hal McRae, John Mayberry, and Al Cowens. McRae's attack the next night was on the person of Willie Randolph, whom he upended violently at second base while breaking up a double play; the two ended up in a tangle, yards beyond the bag, with the ball on the ground and McRae, as he peered through the dust, waving urgently and then triumphantly to Freddie Patek, the base runner ahead of him, who scored the run that tied the game at 2–2. McRae's body block seemed legal but ill-advised; it affronted the Yankee hitters, who immediately responded with three runs in the bottom half of the inning. Their pitcher, Ron Guidry, allowed but one subsequent K.C. runner to reach first, and won by 6–2, on a three-hitter.

Pitching is nearly everything in a short series, and the Royals' admirable Dennis Leonard, a twenty-game winner this year, proved this adage in Game Three, with an effortless four-hit, 6–2 victory on his home field, to the ecstatic pleasure of the Kansas City rooters. I watched the game on television, enjoying (via some wonderful NBC camerawork) Leonard's laserlike deliveries and the Royals' eager, contact-hitting style of ball. By my calculation, the Yankees were now out of sound pitchers and out of luck, but I had somehow forgotten about the ever-available Sparky Lyle, who entered the next day's doings in the fourth inning—very early for him—and, bearing down on the batters and on his gigantic chaw of tobacco, threw shutout two-hit ball for sixteen outs and the ballgame, which the Yanks won, 6–4.

Game Five: It began with a fistfight at third base between George Brett and Graig Nettles, and ended with Freddie Patek alone and in tears in the empty Kansas City dugout. The Yankees' comeback, last-inning victory, it might be noted, was the first break in a pattern of nine consecutive alternate wins and losses by these two courageous and uncompromising teams, beginning with their first playoff game last year. The rarity and satisfaction of this kind of competition can best be suggested in diagram:

NY KC NY KC NY KC NY KC NY NY

Here in Game Five (or Game Ten) Billy Martin, stretching his luck and risking his job, benched Reggie Jackson (who had looked bad at the plate and in the field) and put Paul Blair in his spot in right field, and got an essential hit out of both men—Jackson's was a pinch-hit single—late in the game. That's *managing!* The Royals led early, 3–1, but could not widen that lead. Looking back on it all now, I can't be sure whether it was the Yankees' resolution in putting their leadoff batters aboard in both the eighth and ninth innings that really won this game, or whether it was Mike Torrez's dogged work in relief of Ron Guidry, or whether Kansas City manager Whitey Herzog's somewhat precipitate derricking of Paul Splittorff lost it, or whether it wasn't really the Yankee's obstinate defense in the middle innings that made it all happen: a very deep running catch by Mickey Rivers in the fourth and, in the fifth, two dazzling plays by Willie Randolph and a great peg, nailing a base runner, by Thurman Munson. But never mind. The Kansas City fans, who fell into a shocked, incredulous silence in the eighth and ninth, as the Yankees caught up and then went ahead at last, will have all winter and all next summer to think about these doleful issues. Rivers tied it with a single, and Randolph hit the gamer—a sacrifice fly—and the Yankees won, 5–3. When it was over, I was nearly in despair myself, there in front of the set. I couldn't bear to have either team lose.

The pressure of the playoffs had quite a different effect on the National League finalists, causing them both to suffer through several patches of abysmal baseball. In Dodger Stadium, Ron Cey hit a grand-slam home run for the Dodgers in the first game, and Dusty Baker did the same thing the next day (Cey and Baker and Reggie Smith and Steve Garvey all wound up with thirty or more homers for the club this year), but the Dodgers still lost the opener, 7–5, giving back five runs on three frightful misplays by their shortstop, Bill Russell, who sometimes resembles a hunted ruffed grouse afield: steady under pressure until suddenly not. The second encounter was an easy 7–1 ride for the Dodgers' Don Sutton, who has proved to be unbeatable and very nearly untouchable in postseason play, and another hard October loss for the Phillies' estimable Jim Lonborg. The teams repaired to Philadelphia even up. The third game, while undeniably historic, is one that should be expunged from the annals of the sport. In retrospect, it appears that the only participants who could remember the fundamentals were the grizzled Dodger pinch-hitters Vic Davalillo and Manny Mota, each of whom was sent up to bat with two out in the Dodger ninth, and who, in effect, won the game—Davalillo with a picture-book drag bunt and Mota with a double off the left-field fence, which was gloved but then not held by Greg Luzinski. Prior to that, the game had been distinguished by two debatable umpire's calls at home plate; by the suddenly vanished cool of Dodger Burt Hooton, who walked in three runs in the second, to the accompaniment of jungle screechings from the stands; and by successive wild heaves by Reggie Smith and Ron Cey in the eighth, which helped the Phils move to a 5–3 lead. Mota's hit was followed by a fielding error on the ensuing peg, and in a bare few minutes after that the Phillies lost the lead and the game and (it turned out) the pennant on a burning one-hop smash by Davey Lopes that was not held by the third baseman, Mike Schmidt; a very close but (I think) mistaken umpire's call at first on the same play; a wild pick-off throw by a pitcher; and, at last, an undisputed run-scoring single by Bill Russell. The concluding mistake was the league's decision to play the fourth game on schedule the next evening, in spite of a drenching local downpour that perfectly confirmed a Weather Service forecast and the continuing power of network television over common sense and good baseball. The Phillies, still dazed by the sudden unravelling of their fortunes, lost by 4–1. The winning pitcher was the left-handed sinkerball artist Tommy John, who won twenty games this year for the Dodgers. *Partly* left-handed: three years ago, John's severely damaged pitching arm was rebuilt by surgeons, who replaced a ruptured ligament in his left elbow with a transplanted tendon from his right forearm.

After that wild third game, the two clubhouses seemed almost equally subdued, and several players on each team told me that the strain of these short playoffs seemed almost unbearable. "It doesn't seem right," said Ron Cey. "You come through that whole long season, and then you can get wiped out in just a couple of bad innings. I think a longer playoff would be fairer for the players and better for the fans."

I see the point, but I do not agree. Of all our games, baseball most tries the nerves and the composure of its players, and a safer, statelier stretch of games is not necessarily a better show. Serious fans forgive bad baseball in the end, for they know how hard this game really is, and a shocking error or a poor game or series only whets our appreciation of its opposite: the clutch play, the big hit—courage and triumph in the unfair presence of danger.

Even before Reggie Jackson took matters in hand, this was a rousing World Series. The Dodgers hit nine home runs, setting a National League Series record, and if they had somehow been able to carry the action into a seventh game there is good reason to think they could have won it. By far the best game, it turned out, was the first, at Yankee Stadium, and the Yankees' coup was undoubtedly the three runs they scored off the suave and redoubtable Don Sutton. The visitors, it will be recalled, bravely tied the game with a run in the ninth, but then ran smack into Sparky Lyle; deep in the unstilly night, the Yanks won it, 4–3, on a twelfth-inning double by Randolph and a single by Paul Blair. The next evening, Catfish Hunter, who had suffered through a dreary season of injuries and illness, was badly manhandled by the Dodgers, who whacked four homers and won, 6–1. Hunter, a lighthearted hero of many previous Octobers, smiled and shrugged in response to the postgame questions. "The sun don't shine on the same dog's ass all the time," he said.

Out West, within the vast pastel conch of Dodger Stadium, the Yanks now captured two fine, extremely grudging games behind some stout pitching by Torrez and Guidry, who both went the full distance. The Dodgers, apparently determined to win on pure muscle, excited their multitudes with more downtowners, but the Yankees took the first game, 5–3, on two deflected infield singles, and the second, 4–2, on some modest wrong-field hits and a solo homer by Reggie Jackson. Thurman Munson hit a homer in Game Five, and so did Jackson (a homer to be more noticed later on), but only after the Dodgers had whanged out thirteen hits for Don Sutton, who coasted home in a 10–4 laugher.

With the Yankees leading the Series by three games to two, we came back to New York for the extraordinary conclusion. In this game, the Dodgers took an early 3–2 lead on Reggie Smith's home run off Mike Torrez; it was the third round-tripper for Smith, who was beginning to look like the dominant figure in the Series. The other Reggie came up to bat in the fourth inning (he had walked in the second) and instantly pulled Burt Hooton's first delivery into the right-field stands on a low, long parabola, scoring Munson ahead of him and putting the Yankees ahead for the rest of the game and the rest of the year. Jackson stepped up to the plate again in the next inning (Elias Sosa was now pitching for the Dodgers), with two out and Willie Randolph on first, and this time I called the shot. "He's going to hit it out of here on the first pitch," I announced to my neighbors in the press rows, and so he did. It was a lower drive than the first and carried only four or five rows into the same right-field sector, but it was much more resoundingly hit; at first it looked like a double, or even a loud single, but it stayed up there—a swift white message flying out on an invisible wire—and vanished into the turbulent darkness of the crowd.

My call was not pure divination. With the strange insect gaze of his shining eyeglasses, with his ominous Boche-like helmet pulled low, with his massive shoulders, his gauntleted wrists, his high-held bat, and his enormously muscled legs spread wide, Reggie Jaskson makes a frightening figure at bat. But he is not a great hitter. Perhaps he is not even a good one. A chronic overstrider and overswinger, he swings through a lot of pitches, and the unchecked flailing power of his immense cut causes his whole body to drop down a foot or more. He often concludes a trip to the plate (and a Yankee inning) with his legs grotesquely twisted and his batting helmet falling over his eyes—and with the ball, flipped underhand by the departing catcher, rolling gently out to the mound. It is this image, taken in conjunction with his salary and his unending publicity in the sports pages, that seems to enrage so many fans. "Munson!" they cry, like classicists citing Aeschylus. "Now, you take Munson—*there's* a hitter!" And they are right. But Reggie

Jackson is streaky and excitable. I have an inexpungeable memory of the two violent doubles he hit for the Oakland A's against Tom Seaver in the sixth game of the 1973 World Series, and of the homer he hit the next day against Jon Matlack to destroy the Mets. I remember the gargantuan, into-the-lights home run he hit in the All-Star Game of 1971 in Detroit. And so on. Reggie Jackson is the most emotional slugger I have ever seen. Late in a close big game—and with the deep, baying cries from the stands rolling across the field: "Reg-gie! Reg-gie! Reg-gie!"—he strides to the plate and taps it with his bat and settles his batting helmet and gets his feet right and turns his glittery regard toward the pitcher, and we suddenly know that it is a different hitter we are watching now, and a different man. Get *ready*, everybody—it's show time. And, besides, Reggie had been crushing the ball in batting practice and he had hit a homer in each of the last two games against the Dodgers. Hence (to sound very much like Howard Cosell) my call.

I did not call the third homer. One does not predict miracles. This one also came on the first ball pitched—a low and much more difficult pitch, I thought, from knuckleballer Charlie Hough. The ball flew out on a higher and slower trajectory— inviting wonder and incredulity—this time toward the unoccupied sector in faraway center field that forms the black background for the hitters at the plate, and even before it struck and caromed once out there and before the showers of paper and the explosions of shouting came out of the crowd, one could almost begin to realize how many things Reggie Jackson had altered on this night. The game was won, of course (it was 8–4 in the end), and the Yankees were world champions once again. It was their first championship since 1962, and their twenty-first in all. Jackson's five homers for the Series was a new record, and so were his ten runs and twenty-five total bases. The three home runs in a single Series game had been done before—by Babe Ruth, in 1926 and again in 1928, but neither of Ruth's splurges had come on consecutive at-bats, and neither had been conclusive. Reggie Jackson's homer in the previous game had been hit on his last trip to the plate, and his base on balls in the second inning had been on four straight pitches. This meant that he had hit four home runs on four consecutive swings of the bat—a deed apparently unique in the annals of the game. But Jackson's achievement, to be sure, cannot properly be measured against any of the famous *sustained* one-man performances in World Series history—by Brooks Robinson in 1970, for instance, or by Roberto Clemente in 1971. Reggie's night—a thunderclap—was both less and more. It was *hors concours*. Jackson, in any case, had won this game and this World Series, and he had also, in some extraordinary confirming fashion, won this entire season, reminding us all of its multiple themes and moods and pleasures, which were now culminated in one resounding and unimaginable final chord.

Beyond this—or to one side of it, perhaps—Reggie had at last secured his own fame. He had justified his gigantic salary, if it *could* be justified, and in all probability he had suddenly increased the number of players who will now decide to seek their fortunes as free agents in the next few years. More than that, he had arranged for them all to receive a great deal more money for their services. Even the flintiest traditionalists among the owners—and among the fans, too—must sense that a new time has arrived in baseball. We are in the Jacksonian Era.

This World Series was famous at the very end, but it was notorious all the time. Even while they were winning, the Yankees continued their off-the-field bickerings and grudges and complaints. During the Series, clubhouse reporters wrote that Thurman Munson hoped to play for Cleveland next year, that Mickey Rivers and Graig Nettles were also eager to be traded, that Ed Figueroa had almost jumped the team, and that Reggie Jackson was bitterly critical of Martin's use of Catfish Hunter in the second game. A news-magazine story claimed that in the middle of the season two Yankee players had asked George Steinbrenner to fire Billy Martin; Thurman Munson said that the story was a lie. A press conference was convened by the Yankees at which it was announced that the club was giving Billy Martin a new car and a bonus. Reggie Jackson, who is never at a loss for words, continued to grant startling interviews to great masses of media people. "I couldn't quit this summer, because of all the kids and the blacks and the little people who are pulling for me," he said at one point. "I represent both the underdog and the overdog in our society."

In the Dodger camp, the tone of the news, at least, was

different. Manager Tom Lasorda, who did a remarkable job on the field this summer and this fall, attracted hundreds of reporters to pregame interviews, during which he told a lot of Vegas-style standup-comic jokes, and also declared his love for his country and his family and the Dodger organization. "During the national anthem," he said at one point, "a tear came to my eye—I'm not ashamed to admit that. It's the kind of guy I *am*." He made frequent mention of the Big Dodger in the Sky. One day, he confirmed to reporters that he and his wife had had dinner the night before with his good friend Frank Sinatra and *his* wife. Lasorda said that his friend Don Rickles had come to the clubhouse before the fourth game to invigorate his players with insults. "Our team is a big family," he said. "I *love* my players. They've got manners, they've got morals. They're outstanding human beings." The Dodger players, who are clean-shaven and neatly dressed and youthful in appearance, were friendly and cheerful with the press. (The Dodgers are instructed in public relations during spring training, and many of them who live in and around Los Angeles appear at community dinners and other Dodger-boosting functions during the off-season.) Steve Garvey, asked by a reporter what he thought about the Yankee Stadium fans, paused for a moment and then said, "Well, throwing things on the field is not my idea of a well-rounded human being."

I think I prefer the sour Yankee style to the Dodgers' sweetness, since it may bear a closer resemblance to the true state of morale on a professional ball team during the interminable season. It probably doesn't matter much either way. The outcome of this World Series suggests that neither of these contrasting public images had anything to do with what happened on the field. What we can be certain of is that none of this will go away. We live in an unprivate time, and the roar of personality and celebrity has almost drowned out the cheering in the stands. The ironic and most remarkable aspect of Reggie Jackson's feat is that for a moment there, on that littered, brilliant field, he—he, of all people—almost made us forget this. Suddenly he confirmed all our old, secret hopes. He reminded us why we had come there in the first place—for the game and not the news of the game, for the feat and not the feature. What he had done was so difficult and yet was done so well that it was inexplicable. He had become a hero.

5

Voices of Spring

MARCH 1978

Each year, it becomes clearer to me that my first purpose in touring the spring-training camps is not to deepen my appreciation of the sport, or to report on teams and trades, phenoms and veterans. It is to rid myself of the aftertaste of winter baseball news—the bitter flavor of money, litigation, and failed imagination. In the off-season just past we again witnessed the ritual engilding of a handful of ballplayers— there were thirty-two of them, out of a population of six hundred and thirty-eight now on major league rosters—who took up new uniforms and loyalties after declaring themselves free agents. Among them were Larry Hisle, a lifetime .272 batter with the Twins, who moved along to the Milwaukee Brewers for a six-year package (salary, bonus, and deferred compensations) totalling $3,155,000; Mike Torrez, who went from the Yankees to the Red Sox for a seven-year contract totalling two and a half million dollars; and Rich Gossage (he saved twenty-six games for the Pirates last summer), who joined the Yankees for six years and $2,748,000. Most fans still claim not to understand the workings of the free-agent market, which I take as a sign of their continuing deep dislike of the process, but I think that at least a few of them are beginning to notice that it

61

is not the players—the *greedy* players, in barroom jargon—but the club owners and executives who are bidding the salary levels up to their present levels. Big money and shifting player affiliations are distracting and emotional issues, and Commissioner Bowie Kuhn further roiled the baseball seas in January, when he nullified a major deal that would have sent Vida Blue from the Oakland A's to the Cincinnati Reds in return for an infielder named Dave Revering and a cash payment of $1,750,000. The Commissioner declared that the deal was "not in the best interests of baseball," because it could affect the competitive balance of the National League West (in which the Reds finished second last year, ten games behind the Dodgers), and would worsen the competitive ability of Oakland (at the bottom of the American League West last year). There is a dazzling, Zeno-like obscurity in a ruling that prohibits one club from damaging "competitive balance" for the same reason that another is enjoined from getting a chance to improve it, but never mind; the preservation of pure lawyerly thinking may be why sports commissioners were born. In the summer of 1976, it may be remembered, Mr. Kuhn similarly barred Charles O. Finley, the owner of the A's, from selling Vida Blue to the Yankees for one million five hundred thousand dollars while dealing Blue's teammates Joe Rudi and Rollie Fingers to the Boston Red Sox for one million dollars each, in straight cash transactions. The Commissioner also cited competitive balance on that occasion, but a good many baseball cynics (including this cynic) felt that the greater good of baseball was being served just then by discouraging owners from tying million-dollar price tags on star players only a few months before the opening of the very first free-agent bidding season.

These and other dull entanglements of blame and money were swiftly forgotten by me in the clubhouses and grandstands and dugouts of Arizona and Florida this year, where I was repeatedly struck by the humor and eloquence of the players and coaches (and fans and writers) whom I talked with, and by the immense variety of their attachments to this complex game. Once again, it came to me that the gentle, and nearly meaningless competition in the Cactus and Grapefruit Leagues provides a wonderful quiet space in which we can listen to the true voices of baseball, which are silent in winter and are not always heard in the heat and roar of the summer races. On my first afternoon in Arizona, I drove straight from the Phoenix Airport to the Phoenix Municipal Stadium, where the Giants were entertaining the Brewers, and the first spring baseball voice I heard was my own—an inner "Ahh!" as I settled into a piping-hot grandstand seat, squinted out at the shimmering distant mesas and the nearer sunlit lawns, and watched Willie McCovey unfurl his famous tiptilted stance as he came around on a pitch and nailed the ball on a high line to center, where it was pulled down, after a long run, by a distant outfielder. Sunshine and some fly balls were more than enough for starters, but I was also rewarded by the presence of Larry Hisle, the fresh-minted Milwaukee capitalist, who rapped out three solid singles and, forestalling invidiousness, ran them out hard.

The next day, at the Cubs' little wooden ballyard in Scottsdale, I found Oscar Gamble beside the batting cage, similarly clad in unfamiliar colors (the San Diego Padres' road uniform of gold and chocolate-brown) and in fresh celebrity. A year earlier, Gamble had been a spare outfielder with the Yankees, but he had been traded to the White Sox just before the season began, in the deal that brought Bucky Dent to New York.* Playing for Bill Veeck's tatterdemalion free-swingers in Chicago, Gamble enjoyed the best summer of his career. Used almost exclusively against right-handed pitching, he batted .297 and rapped out thirty-one homers—homering, in fact, at a ratio of one downtowner for every thirteen at-bats, which is phenomenal. "Never *did* have so much fun playin' ball," Oscar said to me. "I could hardly wait to get to the park each day. Those Chicago fans, those nice close stands, all that noise..." Gamble became a free agent when the season ended, and was signed by the Padres to a six-year contract, worth two million eight hundred fifty thousand dollars. "I just had no *idea* I'd wind up with that kind of money," he said. In this particular case, I believe, everyone in baseball was delighted by the news of a free agent's good fortune, for Oscar is remembered in

* Well-endowed ballclubs try to look after their old grads. Gamble moved along to the Texas Rangers after a single summer with the Padres, and the Yankees reacquired the peripatetic Oscar in the middle of the 1979 season, in a deal that sent Mickey Rivers to the Rangers. A few weeks earlier, the Yankees had welcomed back another Bronx favorite, Bobby Murcer, after his five-year exile in the National League.

many dugouts as one of the most enjoyable teammates in the game. Encountering him here, I had a sudden flashback to the unhappy, gossip-haunted Yankee clubhouse in Fort Lauderdale last spring, where reporters and television people clustered every day around the cubicles of Reggie Jackson and Ken Holtzman and Thurman Munson and other high-priced, long-faced celebrities. One day, Gamble began to yell and wave a towel. "Hey!" he called out. "When some of you writers goin' to talk to *me?* Who wants the Oscar Gamble Story? No crowds down here. Plenty of room to talk to old Oscar today!" Everybody laughed, because, of course, we just had no *idea.* . . .

Another newcomer with the Padres was Mickey Lolich, the veteran lefty and large-belly, who retired from baseball two years ago after a dispiriting eight-and-thirteen summer with the Mets. His previous thirteen seasons had been spent with the Tigers, for whom he won two hundred and seven regular-season games, plus three famous victories in the World Series of 1968. His lifetime record of 2,799 strikeouts is the sixth-highest in baseball. He is thirty-seven years old.

I asked Lolich if his comeback was attributable to his missing his old profession.

"No, I don't know why I'm doing this," he said. "Oh, they made me an offer, all right, but I never expected I'd be back." Lolich has a high-pitched laugh, almost a giggle—a surprising sound to come out of a large, cello-shaped man—and he laughed now. "I didn't miss baseball at all last year," he went on. "Never thought about it. On the Fourth of July, I was up at our cottage at Greenville, Michigan. I was out on the lake in the morning with my kids, and when we came in for lunch my wife had the radio on, and suddenly I thought, Hey, some people have to go out and play *baseball* on a day like this! I didn't pitch any last year—well, that's not quite true. Al Kaline and I have a sports camp for kids that goes two weeks every year, and I played in the games there. I always pitched for both sides, so I was eight-and-eight for the year—sixteen complete games." He laughed again. "Now I'm back here, trying to make this club as a relief pitcher, maybe. Back to all the old pains and trouble. Don't ask me why."

Lolich pitched one inning against he Cubs that afternoon, retiring his three batters on ten pitches. One of them was a super, down-darting slider that Gene Clines swung at and missed.

Lolich then went to the sidelines, where he threw hard to a catcher for a few more minutes, and retired for the day. I found him in the ancient, splintery visiting-team clubhouse, with his shirt off and an ice bag taped to his shoulder.

"I can't figure it out," he said. "I'm not throwing good but I'm getting everybody out. Maybe I was doing it wrong all this time. Well, it's different now. I used to be a high-recognition pitcher, and I had to do things. Win twenty games, strike everybody out. Now it's just a question of seeing what I can do. If I make it, all right. If not, that's all right, too. The first day here, I didn't know what to expect. But the first time I threw the ball—*boong!*—it was right there. I could hardly believe it. I threw hard, because I had to find out, and they were all right around the knees. Then I knew I could still get people out, still be a pitcher."

Lolich had stopped laughing, and I had stopped wondering why he had come back to baseball.

The next day, back in Phoenix, I looked up John Curtis, a baseball friend of mine who pitches for the Giants. I wanted to know what he thought about the immense Oakland-San Francisco trade, announced the previous day, that had brought Vida Blue to his club but had taken away seven of his teammates. I also wanted to hear him talk about his own career, for I knew he had renewed his contract with the Giants during the off-season. Curtis, a left-hander, is a marginal major-leaguer—the kind of middle-level performer who watches a great many more games than he plays. His lifetime record is fifty-three wins and sixty losses, and he was three-and-three with the Giants last year. Curtis is introspective and complicated, as well as cheerful, and he loves to talk about his profession. I think of him as the Thinking Man's Left-Hander.

"I'm still getting used to the trade," Curtis said after we had greeted each other. "Vida hasn't turned up yet. I think we just traded outselves into contention. Now a team coming in for a series with us has to look at Blue and Halicki and Montefusco, and then at Jim Barr or Lynn McGlothen. We won't have many losing streaks now. But I can't get over so many of us going away. I've been traded twice myself, so I know the short-term nature of baseball friendships, but that doesn't make it any easier. I was really close to Gary Thomasson and Gary Alexander, who are gone now, and also to our young right-hander Alan Wirth, who's gone, too. I think it's basic nature to look for something permanent, and when it's interrupted you feel this—this deep sense of loss. Going over to Gary Thomasson's house in the evening. Going to the movies together on the road. You need your friends in this business."

We were on the Giants bench, in the dugout, and now Hank Sauer, a large Giants coach who was sitting on my right, leaned over and said, "You never make a trade for nothing. But those boys we gave up—Alexander and Wirth and Huffman and the rest—I had every one of them in the Instructional Leagues when they were just starting out. I saw Al Wirth when he was seventeen years old." He spat some tobacco juice on the dugout floor. "It's like losing somebody in your family," he said. "It's like sending a son off to college—you don't see him anymore."

I asked Curtis about his new contract.

"I signed a two-year contract last fall," he said. "I had a chance to become a free agent, you know, and Spec"—Spec Richardson, the Giants' general manager—"told me I could get more money if I went that way. He even promised me the Giants would make a bid for me, because they knew me and they needed left-handed pitchers. My wife and I really like the San Francisco area, and we bought a house there last year, only a few months after I came over to the Giants from the Cardinals in a trade. And I can't forget how the Giants stayed with me last June when I was pitching real bad and I was low man on the roster. I thought about this for a long time, and I finally decided the only way I could prove my attachment was to bargain with them while I was still a Giant. I know that sounds strange, but it's the way I feel."

He leaned back a little and stretched his legs. "You know, maybe part of this was that I've always been a Giants fan," he said. "When I was growing up in Great Neck, on Long Island, all my friends in school were Yankee fans or Dodger fans, but I was always for the Giants. I can still hear Russ Hodges doing those re-creations of the Giants' road games over the radio. The first big-league game I ever saw was at the Polo Grounds. My father took me. I remember it so well—the green grass and the green stands. It was like seeing Oz. And I can remember my first sight of number 24"—Willie Mays—"that day. I was only five or six years old, but there was something about the way he moved and ran that was absolutely different. After that, in all my stickball games and rock-hitting games at home I *was* Willie Mays. When I was traded here from the Cardinals, it was like coming home."

Spring training is so cheerful and disarming that most of the time one is able to overlook the imperfect nature of the action on the field. On another afternoon, however—my last in Arizona—my critical faculties were cruelly reawakened as I watched the Cubs and the A's in action at Scottsdale. Facing several deservedly anonymous Oakland pitchers, the Cubbies put ten runners aboard before they could score their first run, in the sixth, on an error. Another Oakland miscue led to another run in the seventh, and successive butcheries by the Oakland pitcher, second baseman, and right fielder accounted for four more in the eighth. I was sorry for the ex-Giants in the Oakland lineup—Gary Thomasson and Gary Alexander (whose names had not yet been stitched onto the backs of their gold uniform shirts)—because it was plain that the once splendid A's have been allowed to deteriorate to the level of a minor-league club: perhaps a weak minor-league club. The team's best ballplayer, a big young outfielder named Mitchell Page, who lashed out four hits, looked like Tris Speaker in this company. The Cubs, who needed pitchers, have instead added Dave Kingman to their roster; he came aboard as a free agent, and is expected to hit a great many enormous home runs in the friendly afternoon winds of Wrigley Field. In the Cub seventh, I watched Kingman, a lifetime .227 hitter, pop up weakly and characteristically, when he tried to pull a low, outside pitch, and it occurred to me that the Wrigley Field crowd, which is mostly made up of screeching and eternally optimistic schoolchildren, may be the only baseball audience tolerant enough to put up with such embarrassing deficiencies.

During my flight to Florida, I thought again about the Chicago fans, who experienced such a vivid summer last year, when both of their teams unexpectedly distinguished themselves, and I thought about the less fortunate fans around San Francisco, who may even end up losing both of their teams next year, since they cannot quite bring themselves to support either of them now. It happens that I am the fortunate recipient of a small but steady flow of baseball letters, which come to me, winter and summer, from around the country, and "the voice of the fan" has become real to me. My correspondents are mostly strangers, but they write with the intimacy of a shared passion. I have been hearing for several years, for instance, from Chris Haft, of Menlo Park, California, who is now eighteen years old. Last January, he wrote:

> My preseason excitement is not pure, for I am troubled by my Giants' financial woes. I would not be reassured even by Willie McCovey, with his comforting smile, because I know that if the Giants don't draw well this year they will not remain in San Francisco for the 1979 season. I must conclude that this is the most important season in the history of the team. I have suffered over Giant losses in the past, as a good fan should, but with each defeat this season I will watch my heroes go farther and farther away into the hands of a richer owner and a more populous community, where others will perhaps appreciate them as I have for the past nine years. I have also endured the pathetic and unlucky trades that the Giants front office has made since I became a fan, but when Chris Speier was dealt to the Expos last April, I went into a profound gloom. I am past the hero-worshipping stage of my life, but Chris Speier was the one person I would have wanted to visit me on my sickbed. I treasure his penned response to a fan letter I sent him. "We need more fans like you in 1977," he wrote. He will always be the classy Giant shortstop in my heart.

From Donald B. Kenah, of Chicago:

> Last summer, when the Cubs and White Sox were both going so great, I really missed my friend Jimmy, who died about a year ago. Jimmy was a bartender, and the first one in our crowd to own a copy of *The Baseball Encyclopedia*—not that he really needed it. Ninety per cent of us were Sox fans, but it was always suspected that he secretly preferred the Cubbies. Between the two ballparks, he used to get to about a hundred games every year. Jimmy was the inventor of the "Who Don't Fit?" game, which used to while away the late hours in his bar. Here's one I remember: "Who

Don't Fit—Koufax, Holtzman, Rogovin, Rotblatt?" This is easy for a good fan. They're all pitchers and all co-religionists, so Rogovin don't fit: he's a righty. You've won a drink. But wait a minute. Rotblatt was the only switch-hitter! You've won *another* drink. Too many evenings with too many drinks went by like this, talking about the grand game.

From James T. Farrell, the novelist, once of Chicago, now of New York:

There was a time when ballplayers wore diamond-horseshoe tiepins. This was their way of keeping their money, as if in a savings account. In those days, when foul balls were hit into the stands the ushers and special police would retrieve them and return them to the field. A fan could even be thrown out of the park for not giving back a foul ball. And when we boys got a ball—and few of us did—we didn't save it as a souvenir or try to get it autographed, we used it in our own games. . . . My uncle was a travelling salesman and met many ballplayers. He met Rube Waddell in Minneapolis, when Waddell was on the way down, and Waddell gave him a ball for me—unautographed. He met Stuffy McInnis, Wade Killefer, Grover Cleveland Alexander, and others, and they gave me baseballs. Once in 1911, on a cold day, Jimmy Austin wrapped me in a gray sweater and let me sit on the visiting St. Louis Browns' bench at Comiskey Park during the entire game. Change in baseball runs parallel with other changes in American life.

Bill Veeck was also talking about Chicago fans. I found the White Sox owner sitting in the home dugout in Sarasota's Payne Park, the boxy old steel-post stadium where the Sox cavort in the spring. He was drinking coffee out of a plastic cup and watching batting practice. "There was so much pleasure in those games at Comiskey Park last summer," he said, pushing his heavy horn-rimmed glasses up on his nose. "Who can forget it? Our audience was all ages, from fifteen and sixteen to sixty-five or seventy, and they were joyful. I'd almost despaired of ever using the word 'joy' again. You only see it in shopping centers, during the week before Christmas. You know, we're a gregarious people, and we like to get together to savor something. You can't *savor* a basketball game or a football game, can you?

"Did I tell you about the last day of our season? It was the best single experience of my entire life in baseball. We were playing the Seattle Mariners—not a great draw, let's admit it—and it rained all through the game. Not just a sprinkle but a real downpour. But we had a lot of people there—about twenty thousand—and they stayed there to the end, even though we lost. And then they stayed some more. About ten or twelve thousand of them just wouldn't go home. They stayed on, sitting in their seats in the rain, for another hour. They were all singing—'Take Me Out to the Ball Game' and that 'Na-Na-Na' song of ours, and some others. They didn't want the season to end."

Veeck had also arranged to surround himself with crowds this spring—in this case, crowds of aspiring and largely anonymous ballplayers whom he had invited to camp, along with his regulars, with the promise of a full trial and a shot at big-time ball. There were fifty-nine players in camp, which is fifteen or twenty more than most clubs look at in the spring, and the squad included seamy-necked journeymen who had already put in ten or twelve years in the minors, and some friendly, extremely quick aspirants from the Mexican League, and a carefree nomad catcher who was asking for an advance on his meal money one day in Sarasota because he was down to his last thirty-seven cents, and several near-phenoms whose careers had been cut short by severe injury, and a pitcher who had once come within one out of a major-league no-hit game, and a catcher named Larry Doby Johnson, who was making his fifth attempt at a major-league job, and who may have found cause for hope in the fact that his namesake, Larry Doby, was there, too—teaching batting and coaching at first base. Bill Veeck (who had found several of these hopefuls by drafting them in the free-agent market last fall and then signing them to temporary minor-league contracts) outfitted everybody in full White Sox uniforms and then scheduled an inordinate number of intra-squad games and exhibition doubleheaders in order to try to sort things out. It was all a little like a high-school field day, but it was joyful, all right, and I stayed on in Sarasota for several days and savored it.

One of these non-roster players who made the White Sox team was Mike Eden, a small, solidly built infielder, who had somehow been overlooked by the Giants and Braves and A's in his six years in organized ball. "I was about ready to pack it in if I had to go back to Richmond again," he told me one morning. "I was thinking of going to play in Japan or Mexico, just for the money. I mean, I got a family to think about— *sort* of a family. There's my wife and our three German shepherds. Now I'm hopeful again. I got more respect for Bill Veeck than anybody in baseball. He sits out there under the light pole on the practice field every day, and he calls you by your first name—he knows everybody's name—and asks if you're *enjoying* yourself." He shook his head. "I'll go anywhere Bill Veeck wants to send me now."

Another find was a swift, ebullient outfielder named Art James, who was on his way up in the Detroit system when he suffered a freak accident two years ago (trotting with a bat in his hand, he struck the back of his left leg with the bat knob and ruptured the Achilles tendon), which apparently ended everything. But Bill Veeck enrolled him in the Nautilus physical-training program in Deland, Florida, last winter, and James came into camp running freely and eventually won a job on the Sox' AAA farm club.

"It's a blessing being here," he said to me. "Ballplayers never used to have a chance to change organizations if they'd met up with bad luck. The old way, you'd be buried for life. So I'm grateful to Bill Veeck, and I'm grateful to Marvin Miller and the Players Association, because I got free. This is a great day for the players."

Veeck's Irregulars had considerable difficulties afield during my stay in Sarasota, dropping one-sided contests to the Phillies and the Royals and just barely beating the Mets. The chief entertainment of that game was the rustic two-man dumbshow staged by Sox pitcher Wilbur Wood and Sox catcher Jim Essian with their hilarious comedy prop, which was Wood's knuckleball. During Wood's four-inning stint, the pair were together or separately responsible for six hits (nubbers, for the most part), five runs, four walks, three balks, four passed balls, one wild pitch, and one stolen base. The Mets, however, seemed to have *no* pitching, comical or otherwise, and they eventually lost, by 9–8, when the Chisox jumped all over a rookie pitcher named Juan Berenguer, sometimes billed as the Panamanian Nolan Ryan. Art James hit a homer, and Mike Eden had three hits for the afternoon.

The audience at Payne Park didn't seem to care much about who won the games. There was applause for almost everything that happened on the field, good or bad. The place was jam-packed, and very cheerful. This was Easter week, and the bleachers were full of kids and teen-agers on vacation—a lot of them down to visit their grandparents, probably. The old folks—the Sarasota regulars—sat in the comfortable, shaded seats in the grandstand, and they did most of the real cheering for the White Sox. There is always a lot of distraction at a spring-training game—people moving around, a college kid coming up the rows balancing three or four brimming containers of beer, B-squad players in the bleachers yelling to their buddies on the field, public-address announcements ("We have a large crowd here today, folks, and more still coming in, and we wonder if you could please slide a little closer to your neighbor. Thank you"), couples taking turns rubbing suntan lotion on each other's back, and, even during the games, the sight of distant groups of players running wind-sprints in the outfield. (Pitchers walking back to the foul lines after a sprint to center field look like lava moving; an experienced senior moundsman can get himself into shape running toward center and walk himself out of condition again coming back.)

The most talented player in the White Sox' camp this spring was Bobby Bonds, who had been picked up from the Angels for this, his final season before achieving free-agency. Bill Veeck, who inherited an impoverished and depleted organization when he took control of the Chisox in 1976, had become adept at such stratagems, and Bonds, an extraordinarily graceful athlete who has hit thirty or more homers and stolen thirty or more bases in four different seasons in his career, was a replacement for last year's departed Rent-a-Stars, Oscar Gamble and Richie Zisk. Before the Phillies game, Bonds and Veeck and Garry Maddox, the Philadelphia center fielder, were in the Chicago dugout talking about the Giants teams of 1973 and 1974, on which Bonds and Maddox had joined up with Gary Matthews (now with the Braves) in what is widely considered to have been the fastest outfield of all time.

"You guys should have gone in the N.C.A.A. relays, or something," Veeck said. "Or the Olympics."

"We'd of *won*," Maddox said firmly.

"How many balls got between us in that first summer?" Bonds asked.

"Maybe five," Maddox said. "Maybe three."

"And none of them on the ground," Bonds added.

Somebody pointed out that the Giants might have had a pretty solid squad of outfielders if they had held on to the three and kept an earlier departee named George Foster, who hit fifty-two home runs for the Reds last summer and was named Most Valuable Player in the National League.

"Oh-oh," said Bonds. "If you keep George out there, I got to play first base or something."

"Keep George, and I'm on the *bench*," Maddox said.

The Phillies looked good at Sarasota that afternoon, whipping the Chisox by 10–5. It was my first glimpse of them since their frightful collapse in the Championship Series against the Dodgers last fall—their second consecutive failure in postseason play. Last winter, I received a six-page letter from a Phillies fan named Bill Murphy, who dwelt at length upon these and other indignities that his team has inflicted upon him over the years, including a famous ten-game losing streak in September of 1964, which blew a pennant that the club had seemed to have safely in hand. Re-creating the events of October 7, 1977 (the date of the third playoff game last fall), with a careful, masochistic hand, Mr. Murphy wrote:

Never mind the throw inexplicably squirting past Sizemore, allowing Mota to take third, or that near-miss great recovery by Bowa and the questionable call at first, or the errant pick-off attempt.... The game was really over the moment Mota's drive reached the wall, and we all knew it. We knew it as surely as we knew (or should have known) that it was over back in 1964 when Chico Ruiz stole home against us and won the game that was to be the first of our ten consecutive losses.... Once more we were shown that to be a Phillies fan is to suffer. Indeed, a Phillies fan has never suffered enough, and the only question is, Can I take it, year after year? Just thinking about last October causes me pain, and such pain will prepare me for the future.

I have received similar letters over the years from heartbroken adherents of various teams (although the sound of grinding molars in Mr. Murphy's prose is unmistakably Eastern Pennsylvanian), but I don't think I have ever heard a player talk about past defeats in quite those terms. Before the game, I asked Garry Maddox if he still brooded about his club's recent October failures.

Maddox is a reserved, gazellelike man, with very long arms and legs and a small black beard; his uniform fits him like a coat of paint. "No, not really," he said after he'd thought about my question for a moment. "I really would have liked to go all the way last year—won the championship, won the World Series. But—well, we didn't. I'll tell you the truth: I was glad when it was all over. Sure, we'd lost, but it was over, and I got the chance of bein' with my family. You get asked these questions, and you sound like you don't care when you say it didn't bother you. I keep saying I wanted to win as much as anybody. Maybe more than anybody. But when it's gone it doesn't bother you. With the fans, there's all this second-guessing that goes on. I think losing is especially hard on the fans. Our fans really took it to heart. If there's any reason I feel sorry about what happened, it's because of the fans."

The next day's visitors at Payne Park were the Royals, who have also fared unhappily in the playoffs in the past two seasons. The anguish of Kansas City fans may exceed even Mr. Murphy's pain, for in both years their team lost the American League championship in the ninth inning of the fifth and final game. I asked the Royals' wonderfully talented second baseman, Frank White, if he was still suffering over these events.

"I feel sorry about what happened, and everything," he said, "but other than that . . . A day or so after it was over, I forgot about it. When you give all you got—a hundred and ten per cent—that's about all you can do. You can't bring it back. You can't change it. It's happened, and it's over. I think the worst part was that we were ahead in the Series. The people who'd paid to see us all summer, they'd been waiting for revenge over the Yankees for a year. And then here we are, up two games to one, and they think, Hey, we've *got* it! Actually, we had two chances to win the doggone thing, but we didn't do it."

The Royals beat the White Sox that afternoon by 14–3, administering a frightful pounding to several Chicago pitchers. Al Cowens and Tom Poquette hit homers for the visitors. The Royals didn't play George Brett or Freddie Patek or Hal McRae, but they did play an enormous twenty-year-old first baseman named Clint Hurdle, who whacked out a line single and a double off the wall, and a lean, fast outfielder named Willie Wilson, who stole a base in the first inning and kicked the throw out of Mike Eden's glove, and a backup shortstop named U.L. (U.L. for nothing: just U.L.) Washington, who went five for five, and a young blond relief pitcher named Randy McGilberry, with strong legs and a moving fastball. It made me sad, for I had seen no one in the White Sox' immense corps of hopefuls who resembled these future stars. Kind hearts are more than coronets, but what Bill Veeck deserves now is a Hurdle.

I get more baseball mail from Red Sox supporters than from anyone else, and the most surprising Red Sox letter that turned up last winter was a one-hundred-and-sixty-two-stanza epic poem from Mr. Joseph W. Stokvis, who lives in New York City but follows the Bosox *closely*. The number of stanzas—they are quatrains—was determined, of course, by the length of the season: one stanza, that is, for each game of the 1977 Red Sox season. (Actually, the Sox were rained out of their last game of the year, but Mr. Stokvis wrote four lines about that, too.) His poem begins:

APRIL 7TH
Opening Day: the wind really blew.
We led in the ninth, 4 to 2;
Bell's two-run homer ties the score:
Cleveland in eleven: 5 to 4.

Things improve, however:

MAY 28TH
Today's game thrilled every rooter:
We jammed the scoreboard—get a computer!

Homers soared, hits were splattered:
17–12, K.C. was battered.

But sombre, late-summer themes are heard:

AUGUST 29TH
We've lost tough ones, we've lost bad ones.
But this was really one of the sad ones.
8–7 to the Oakland A's!
One of the season's darker says.

And the inexorable end approaches:

SEPTEMBER 13TH
In a series that could well decide
Who'll be bridesmaid and who the bride,
A well-played opener, but when it was through
The Yankees had beat us, 4 to 2.

I felt the need of Mr. Stokvis's gifts for synopsis and classical detachment the following afternoon in St. Petersburg, as eight consecutive St. Louis Cardinal batters safely reached base against the Red Sox in the first inning—seven of them with ringing base hits. The Cards, who looked like world-beaters on this day, went on to bury the Red Sox, 10–4, with seventeen hits. The Bosox are considered to have improved themselves over the winter in two critical areas by picking up Jerry Remy, a quick and experienced second baseman, from the Angels, and by signing free agent Mike Torrez, but I sensed that their pitching staff was still not quite watertight. After their starter, Rick Wise, had departed the premises in the fourth, a Boston scribe in the press box did some quick calculating and announced that the Sox' starting hurlers, in their seventy and one-third innings of spring work, had yielded ninety-seven hits and sixty-seven runs. He also told me that a Red Sox intrasquad game on March 7th, at their camp in Winter Haven, had matched the Sox' awesome front-line hitters against some of their journeymen backup pitchers—a nightmare confrontation that had been sometimes conjured up in Beantown taverns. The hitters won, 26–5.

My informant was Peter Gammons, a young sportswriter

with the Boston *Globe,* whom I have come to rely on for just this kind of entertaining and nutritious baseball data. This spring, after an exile of a year and a half in New York, where he worked for *Sports Illustrated,* Mr. Gammons returned to the *Globe* and the Red Sox. He is a newspaper-beat man at heart, and he found that he missed the urgency of a big sports-attuned daily paper, and a sense of closeness to his readers. In a passionate baseball community like Boston, a Peter Gammons matters scarcely less than Yaz.

"I thought about the Red Sox a lot while I was away," Gammons told me in St. Pete. "I kept finding excuses to go off and see them. They had a game in Detroit early last summer, and I called up Bill Lee, who was going to pitch for us, and I said, 'There'll be fifty thousand people there yelling for Fidrych, but I'll be the one there yelling for *you.*' But it was the baseball itself that I missed, really. Covering baseball in New England is one of the great jobs in the world. During the season, I write about twenty-five stories a week, counting the A.M. and P.M. editions and the Sunday stuff. The New England fans' interest in baseball is sophisticated and consuming, and it never lets up. There's nothing like it anywhere else in the country. I agree with something Mike Barnicle wrote in the *Globe* last winter. He said, 'Baseball isn't a life-and-death matter, but the Red Sox are.' And baseball is the best sport for a writer to cover, because it's *daily.* It's ongoing. You have to fill the need, write the daily soap opera. Listen, even down here in Winter Haven, where we train, there are ten or fifteen places that sell the *Globe* every day. The players can get mad at you even before the season starts." He laughed uproariously.

"I know you're not supposed to get close to the players, but you do," he went on. "You can't help it. You get attached to individuals and you wish them well. But I don't think I ever hold back if I think someone has messed up out there. I've got good friends on the Red Sox, and on other teams, too. Carlton Fisk and Jim Willoughby. John Curtis, who used to be here. Jim Spencer, who's with the Yankees now. Jim Colborn, who pitches for the Royals. I guess Fisk is my best friend in baseball. Whenever I'm off with the team on the road, I go out to early batting practice and shag flies with the guys in the outfield. I've always done that.

"Your fortunes are tied to the team, I think. It helps all of us writers when the team wins. Interest deepens, and you get read more. When the Red Sox won in 1967, it saved two newspapers in Boston. It's best of all when your team goes into the World Series. Being a home writer then is like being in the World Series yourself."

I mentioned his account in the *Globe* of the famous sixth game of the famous 1975 Series, which I clipped at the time and still have somewhere. It is a classic piece of baseball reporting under pressure.

Gammons laughed. "You know," he said, "I have absolutely no memory of writing that piece. I picked up the paper the next morning, and it was all brand-new to me. And the next night, after the seventh game, I finished the last stuff I had to write at about six in the morning—a couple of pieces for a special post-Series section—and then I went out on the roof of a parking garage that's next to the *Globe* and looked around. I was drinking a beer, and Leigh Montville, who works with me, came out and said, 'Do you know you've only had about three hours' sleep in the past week?' It was true. I'd been so involved, so excited, that I couldn't sleep. I went home and went to bed and slept for three days."

What about *this* year, I asked him.

"We'll see," Gammons said expectantly. "I just don't know about the pitching. It's going to be an interesting season. I have one problem, though. My wife's sister is getting married on June 24th, and we're playing Baltimore that day. I wonder if it would be all right if I missed the wedding."

He was perfectly serious.

My preseason tour was running out. It had gone too quickly, as it always does, and once again I sensed in myself the wish to slow down each of the last few games I attended, so that springtime might last longer. At Pompano Beach, I watched the visiting Orioles beat the Rangers, 8–4, as Ken Singleton whacked a single and two doubles for the O's. Most of the names in the Oriole lineup—Bumbry, Dauer, Mora, Roenicke, Smith, Skaggs—still have a tavern-league obscurity, but these are the same nobodies who tied the famous Red Sox for second place in the A.L. East last year, and they are still directed by Earl Weaver, the Bismarck of Baltimore, now beginning his eleventh year as manager. It's unprovable, but I always think

Earl Weaver wins ten or a dozen extra games for his club every year on pure cogitation. The Rangers are loaded with names and money and expectation, having added Richie Zisk and Al Oliver and Jon Matlack over the winter. As sometimes happens with a suddenly respectable team like this, the addition of new stars also made me aware of the talents of the holdovers, and my eye was caught by Mike Hargrove, the Texas first baseman, a solidly built, aggressive left-handed hitter. Hargrove is upwardly mobile, having begun his career in baseball as the five-hundred-and-seventy-seventh selection in the 1972 player draft. Now, after four years with the Rangers, he is a lifetime .303 hitter. Last summer, he prospered mightily at the plate when his manager, Billy Hunter, took a tip from a friend and moved him up to the leadoff spot in the Texas batting order. The tip came from Earl Weaver.

As the game at Pompano Beach slipped along to its last few outs, I gazed around and bade an inner farewell to the Rangers' unassuming park, Municipal Field, which is due for major refurbishing before next spring. It is a country fairgrounds sort of place—a lumpy infield and a rawboned little grandstand behind home, with a few faded banners set about on the roof. Big-leaguers in the outfield are sometimes back to back with local ten-year-olds playing Little League ball on adjacent diamonds. The bleachers come down almost to the foul lines, and the rows of seats out there always seem to be full of children. It is great autograph country. A perspiring rookie Ranger pitcher comes off the field after his last-inning stint (he has been rapped hard), and he stops for a minute by the bleachers to speak to his wife. She steps down out of the stand as he walks through a little gate in the low chainlink fence, and she tips her dark glasses up onto her hair (they are very young, both of them) and looks at him inquiringly, and he shrugs and murmurs something and touches his pitching shoulder, and then heads for the clubhouse (and perhaps Asheville), followed by three or four kids with pencils and programs outstretched.

It was altogether different at Fort Lauderdale that night— an immense traffic jam before the game (the Reds and the Yankees) and, before that, long lines of standees waiting for the bleacher-ticket windows to open. The world-champion Yankees were a powerful draw this spring, selling out most of their home games and all their games on the road. Fort Lauderdale Stadium, which has a capacity of about seven thousand, is trimmed and painted and suburban, and the noise of the crowd during the game is louder and more insistent than elsewhere—the noise of city baseball. In the Cincinnati dugout, Sparky Anderson was meeting with a few reporters. Like many contemporary skippers, he has a smooth, unhesitant way of talking. Managers are interviewed by sports reporters every day, in city after city, and after a time their talk takes on the polish and air of easy performance, and perhaps some of the repetitions of a good repertory actor's delivery.

"Yes, we have one serious problem this year—the Dodgers," Anderson said. "We had no shot at them last year, really. They beat us wire to wire. They gave us a real licking. Never mind what I said then. I was just being a con man, trying to talk us into it. Now we'll try again. And don't nobody ask me about our being a 'hungry' ball team now. You're never motivated by that, no matter what you hear. Professionals don't play that way. Our pitching is much better. Never mind Mr. Blue—I have Tom Seaver all summer this year. You know, even when we won everything—five first places in seven years—we never had the pitching. We'd win, but I'd be out there visiting the mound all night, every game. I was *exhausted*. My idea of managing is giving the ball to Tom Seaver and sitting down and watching him work. We're like Boston in their league—we have the best eight men on the field. You give us the pitching some of these clubs have and no one could touch us. But God has a way of not arranging that, because it isn't as much fun."

The Reds won the game, 5–4, on a three-run homer by Johnny Bench, off Ed Figueroa. It was just another spring game, but it was exciting, because of the noise of the crowd and the familiar, unmistakable movements of so many famous players on the field. Sparky Lyle, the new Cy Young Award winner, came on and pitched the eighth, shifting his tobacco lump in his cheek and throwing almost impatiently and retiring batters, for the most part, with two or three pitches. Rich Gossage, the Yanks' expensive new reliever, pitched in the ninth—a big, fireballing right-hander. He cocks his arm high at the top of his motion and then slams it across his body as he delivers. The arm almost blurs as it comes down, like a swung bat. He fanned the last two Cincinnati batters. Rival teams who hope to catch the Yankees this summer should probably plan on scoring their runs in the first four or five innings.

Rich Gossage came to the Yankees for $2,748,000, and his every appearance this summer will inflame Yankee-haters everywhere (there are millions of them) and again arouse the cry that the Yankees are buying another pennant. Even if the champions win again, the charge will not be proved. To me, the major difference in the Yankees' camp this spring was not the arrival of Gossage and Rawly Eastwick, or the departure of Torrez; it was the absence of Gabe Paul, the team's president and chief architect, who moved along to a similar post with the Cleveland Indians this year. Mr. Paul, to be sure, spent eight and a half million dollars (provided by George Steinbrenner) to acquire Reggie Jackson and Catfish Hunter and Don Gullett. But during his four years as the team's top baseball man he gave most of his attention to trading, and picked up Mickey Rivers, Chris Chambliss, Willie Randolph, Bucky Dent, Paul Blair, Cliff Johnson, Ed Figueroa, Dick Tidrow, Ken Holtzman, and Mike Torrez by that ancient method. The Yankees are Gabe Paul's team and George Steinbrenner's team, and they did not just buy it; they built it.

The next day was my last—Easter Sunday, and the Mets against the Yanks. There was a little spattering of rain during batting practice, and I caught sight of Eddie Kranepool politely holding a woman reporter's umbrella over her head while she asked questions and wrote in her notebook: another clear Baseball First. Later, I talked to Kranepool, too—without an umbrella. Ed Kranepool signed with the Mets out of James Monroe High School, in the Bronx, and he has a good, solid I.R.T.-tinged accent. He has been with the Mets since the team's first summer. He and Jerry Koosman are the only Mets left from the glory days of 1969 and 1973; everyone else is gone. Kranepool is thirty-three, but he looks older than that. Or perhaps he only seems older to me, because I have been watching him play ball since he was seventeen. In many ways, he is a holdover from an earlier era in baseball—a dependable, intelligent hitter who hits the ball to all fields, a player celebrated only for his accomplishments on the field, a fixture: Steady Eddie. He will pinch-hit this year, and back up at first and in the outfield. He has a picture swing—one of the prettiest in baseball.

Kranepool counted the years on the fingers of his big hands. "Yes, this is my sixteenth spring training," he said. "I can't believe it. I think there are only about a dozen of us who have that many years in the game—Stargell, Gaylord Perry, Mota, and some like that. There have been a million changes on this club in the last couple of years. When I first came into the clubhouse last month, I had to look at the names over the lockers to see who was who. I never thought I'd have to go through another rebuilding stage—starting out from the cellar again. There's been a lot of criticism, but I like the organization. They must know what they're doing. I think Donald Grant might be more of a fan than any of us. He wants to win. He's been caught in the free-agency situation, and with some guys who wanted to leave the club. But I think there should be some responsibility on both sides when a contract has been signed. That's how I look at it."

I asked what he thought about former teammates like Tom Seaver and Jon Matlack, who had bitterly criticized the Mets after they left the club last year.

"Tom was very well paid until the crazy new numbers began to come along," he said. "Sure, Tom talked, but he also went out and won. He was the best pitcher in baseball while he was here. He had the right to speak his mind. The question is: How much did you contribute? John Matlack was given the ball every five days for six years with us, and you look at his record and he was a .500 pitcher. That makes a difference, for me. What affects me now, living in New York, is the Yankees' winning so big. Everybody says something about that, and it really shines the light in your face. Nobody ever said anything about them when we were on top. Sure, I want to play with a winner again. It's a lot more fun. But I still like the game. I like to play a game of baseball."

Then I talked to Reggie Jackson. He was leaning against the metal framework at the back of the cage and watching the Mets batters take their cuts. He kept twisting a bat in his hands as we talked. He has been interviewed so often in the last year that a lot of what he said sounded familiar to both of us. He said he was often misunderstood, because people rarely take time to listen to other people, because people don't care to talk honestly about things or talk about them in depth. Most people, he said, wanted to talk to him not because they were interested in him but because he was famous. "You don't want to talk to *me*," he said. "You're here because it's part of your job. Everybody is complex—I'm sure you're complex—but it takes a lot of time to find that out, and no one has time."

I had an impression that I often come away with when I talk to Jackson—that he is telling the truth, but that part of him is watching himself as he talks and judging his performance. The private Reggie is watching the public man, and sometimes vice versa. It's an unsettling business, but it is not artificial, not a show. He is an unsettled sort of man. Reggietalk is sometimes startling in its shifts of mood and character. Last season, Jackson was being interviewed by a knot of reporters on the field before a game and he made some reference to Christian values (I have forgotten the exact matter at hand) in a tone and manner of such spirituality that the scribes felt obliged to remain silent for a brief cathedral-like moment or two before asking their next questions. I wandered off in search of some other player, but when I came back to Reggie's circle, not three minutes later, he was entertaining his audience with a brash, comic comparison of himself and Lee May, the veteran Baltimore outfielder. "He's a little older than me, but we have just about the same lifetime figures, if you look them up," he said. "So how come Lee gets paid maybe one-eighty or two hundred thousand, and I'm the best damned paid player in the game? Why is that? I'll tell you why. It's because *I put the asses in the seats!*"

Here in Florida, Reggie and I got around to baseball at last. He said he was working hard on his fielding this spring, because he had done so poorly in the field last year. I asked if the tricky light in the Yankee Stadium outfield had bothered him.

"No, it didn't," he said. "That's all bull. Everybody looks for excuses. I had no excuse. There was a lot of pressure on me every where I went last year. I was isolated. Everywhere I went—on the field, in the clubhouse, away from the ballpark—I wasn't just Reggie Jackson, I was the three-million-dollar ballplayer. I was the famous free agent. I was the man who had walked out on Baltimore. I was a selfish egotist. Because I was a money-grabber, I was disturbing society. I was proving that inflation was a fact. So all these things affected me. I was alone here on the team. I was a newcomer. I was an *invader*. And I broke. My whole game broke. I wasn't comfortable at the plate. I wasn't comfortable in the field or on the bases, and my game showed it, in every aspect. I didn't even begin to get into the groove of hitting home runs until the middle of August. Just because of my brute strength, I was able to survive at the plate. But I wasn't hitting. I was dissociated from my game. I even tried using different bat models. I never did that before. The hardest thing I ever went through in my whole life was last summer."

He paused, and we could both hear the young fans calling to him from the first couple of rows in the stands. "Reggie!" they pleaded. "Hey, Reggie! Reg-gie, come over here, will ya? Reggie, *please!*" It is a sound that follows him everywhere.

"And now?" I said.

He twisted the bat again and then smiled—his flashing, charming smile. "Now," he said, "everything is different. All that is behind me this spring. I'm glad to be here, glad to work out, glad to play. I won't say I'm *happy*. I don't know if I even like the word 'happy.' I understand the word 'glad' better. That's what I am. I'm glad to be here, and it wasn't like that in a lot of years before this one."

A little later, the Yanks and the Mets played their game. Kranepool had a single and Jackson went hitless for the day, and the Mets jumped on Ron Guidry in the sixth and seventh innings for five runs. It was a pretty bad game, with lots of errors and other mistakes on both sides, so there was some booing and laughter in the stands, as well as some yells. The fans seemed to be about evenly divided: half were for the Yankees and half for the Mets. All afternoon, there was the ceaseless, murmuring undercurrent of people talking and exclaiming—people taking in a game. These were the voices of baseball I like best of all. I left in the bottom of the ninth, when the Yankees were down by 6–3, with two out and a man on base. A rookie named Mardie Cornejo was pitching for the Mets—a forkballer. I went out to the parking lot just behind the stands (I was going to beat the traffic) and stood beside my car and listened for the special sound of the ballpark when the last out comes and the game is over. But what I heard was more yells and then still more, then a silence and then another long burst of shouting. It went on, with pauses interspersed, and I grew apprehensive, because I wanted the Mets to win this special, trifling game, since they won't win many other games this year. And then the voices roared one more time and the noise went on and on, and the first fans came bursting out of the park, and a lot of kids up ahead, yelling and sprinting down the ramps, and I knew the Yankees had rallied and won again after all.

6

City Lights: Heartthrobs, Prodigies, Winners, Lost Children

OCTOBER 1978

Not much new happened in baseball this year. Two thousand one hundred and sixteen major-league games were played, from April to October, to establish the New York Yankees once again as champions of the world. It was their second consecutive championship, their twenty-second in all. For the second straight year, the Dodgers won the National League pennant and then fell to the Yankees in a six-game Series. It was their eighth Series loss to the Yankees in ten tries. For the third consecutive year, the Phillies and the Kansas City Royals won their divisional championships—in the National League East and the American League West—and were then beaten in the playoffs. For the second summer in a row, the Boston Red Sox just failed to catch the Yankees in the American League East. Last year, they lost out on the final Saturday of the regular season (and tied for second place with the Baltimore Orioles); this year, they tied the Yankees on the final Sunday, and then lost an excruciating one-game playoff the following afternoon. Dave Parker, of the Pirates, and Rod Carew, of the Twins, batted .334 and .333, respectively, this summer, thus repeating as batting champions in their leagues, and George Foster, of the Reds, and Jim Rice, of the Red Sox, struck forty and forty-six homers each, thus succeeding themselves as home-run champions. The New York Mets, the Atlanta Braves, and the Toronto Blue Jays all finished in the cellar of their divisions in 1978, exactly as they did last year; the Oakland A's finished in the cellar of the American League West last year, just behind the Seattle Mariners, but this year the two teams *reversed positions*. Finally, attendance in the major leagues set a new all-time record this year, rising by nearly two million to a total of 40,636,886. It was baseball's third consecutive record-breaking year at the gate. Nothing new all down the line. It's too bad.

This is a joke, of course, but perhaps one that can be appreciated only by fans. The season just past was in fact one of the most absorbing, surprising, and painful—painful, above all—baseball campaigns ever, and its ultimate repetitions have only deepened my admiration for the various champions and my sorrow for the almost countless losers, and have reconfirmed the game's capacity for searching out and certifying quality over the long passage of another summer. Yes, the Yankees did it again, but this year's winning campaign—in which the team came from fourteen games behind to capture the pennant, came from two runs behind to capture the thrilling playoff game with the Red Sox, and came from two games behind to win the World Series—was infinitely more difficult and more impressive than last year's. Doing it all over again is the hardest test in sports, and if the reappearance of the same teams and names on the top of the standings in September and October seems unsurprising, and even boring, to the casual follower of the pastime, it is a cause for wonder to those of us who do follow the game that this most difficult and unpredictable of all team sports should so often yield itself in the end to the same rare few, to the best. All through this summer, I heard friends and fans exclaim, "Oh, I hope the Red Sox are going to do it this year! And the Giants, too. I'd love to see some new faces in the World Series." I felt exactly the same way, and I was disconsolate when these two admirable clubs, both passionate favorites of mine, died at the end of this wonderful, hope-filled summer. But then in October, after other, equally worthy players had all failed or fallen short, my appreciation of Reggie Jackson and Thurman Munson and Catfish Hunter and Graig Nettles and Lou Piniella and the rest of the

Yankee veterans, and of Dave Parker and Rod Carew and the other familiar title-winning stars, was suddenly quickened, and I realized that the opposite outcome—a fresh roster of champion batters and sluggers each year, and a new matchup of teams and heroes in almost every playoff or World Series—would soon breed in me the suspicion that baseball was too capricious, too easy, and too much subject to luck or chance for anyone to care about it very long. Dynasties can be loved only after they have been overthrown, but they add zest and danger and seriousness of purpose to each day during which they remain in power. Wait till next year.

This year, in any case, did not lack for divertissements. Earl Weaver, the Bismarck of Baltimore, finding his club down by a score of 19–6 in the fifth inning of a game against the Blue Jays, and facing a doubleheader the next day with the same club, called upon an outfielder, Larry Harlow, and then a catcher, Elrod Hendricks, to pitch, thereby simultaneously resting his embattled pitching staff, enraging traditionalists in the Toronto front office and the Baltimore press corps, and vastly entertaining everyone else on the scene; the Blue Jays won the game, 24–10. The Dodgers, that self-proclaimed court of parfit, gentil knights, were shaken by a violent clubhouse fistfight between their first baseman and Lancelot, Steve Garvey, and their longtime star pitcher, Don Sutton, after Sutton delivered various Modred-like criticisms of Garvey in an interview; the joust seemed to vivify the team, which became nearly unbeatable in the last weeks of pennant competition. Another shining hero, Jim Palmer, won twenty-one games and lost twelve for the Orioles (it was his eighth twenty-game season) but indulged himself in some publicly expressed doubts about the Baltimore outfielders' eagerness to catch fly balls. Protecting a 1–0 lead in a game against the Indians, Palmer saw his left fielder, Pat Kelly, fail to hold a long drive by Jim Norris, which was ruled a double. Palmer threw one more pitch and then announced himself unable to continue; the Orioles lost, 2–1. Tom Seaver suffered an indifferent (for him) season with the Reds, finishing at 16–14, but finally achieved his first no-hitter, against the Cardinals; previously he had pitched five lifetime one-hit games. National League batters report that the famous Tom Seaver fastball at last may have lost an inch or two, but Tom once again struck out more than two hundred batters, for the tenth time in eleven years. Seaver's one-season National League record for most strikeouts by a right-handed pitcher (two hundred and eighty-nine) was broken this summer by James Rodney Richard, of the Houston Astros, who fanned three hundred and three batters. Richard is six feet eight inches tall, and his delivery—a gigantic, leggy stride down the mound—makes him look like a man falling out of a tree. The San Diego Padres received sterling pitching performances from two veterans—Rollie Fingers, who saved thirty-seven games, and Gaylord Perry, who won twenty-one games and lost only six, and was voted the Cy Young Award in his league. Perry, who is forty years old, now has three thousand and one strikeouts, and trails only Walter Johnson and Bob Gibson in lifetime whiffs. Phil Niekro, a thirty-nine-year-old pitcher, won nineteen games for the Atlanta Braves with his knuckleball, and was startled by team owner Ted Turner with an unnegotiated and unexpected bonus of one hundred thousand dollars.

The year's most enjoyable one-man show was Pete Rose's mid-summer assault on Joe DiMaggio's famous hitting streak of fifty-six consecutive games, which came in 1941. Rose was finally stopped after hitting safely in forty-four straight games and during the latter stages of the streak he attracted immense crowds of fans in Philadelphia and New York and Atlanta, almost all of whom, in their wish to participate, however distantly, in baseball history, seemed to be cheering for him, and against the home-team pitchers. Pete himself seemed worn down by this carnival thirst for new records, because when the streak ended, in Atlanta, on August 1st, he groused bitterly about the last pitcher he faced, Gene Garber, who had struck him out on a change-up pitch. "Most pitchers in baseball just challenge a guy in that situation," Rose said. Garber, an experienced relief pitcher, said, "I wanted his streak to continue, but I wanted to get him out, too. That's what I get paid to do." I think Gene Garber has this right, but never mind; no clubhouse forensics can diminish Pete Rose's achievement. In retrospect, it is easy to understand that Rose's special attributes—he is a leadoff man, a switch-hitter, a fine bunter, an assiduous student of pitchers, and (crouched at the plate, glaring out at the pitcher over his upraised front shoulder) the most confident batter in baseball—made him the ideal man to mount a serious assault on DiMaggio's record. Rose's string wiped out the modern

National League hitting record of thirty-seven consecutive games, which was set by Tommy Holmes, of the Boston Braves, in 1945, and it tied him with Willie Keeler's ancient record of forty-four games, set in 1897—a record that must be discounted, since the rules of that day did not count foul balls as strikes. Because of its prolonged and cumulative day-to-day pressure on the athlete, the DiMaggio record continues to stand as the greatest individual batting feat in the history of the game. (My selection for the greatest *team* record, which I bring up here only because it seems absolutely unlikely that any modern club will come close to challenging it, is the nearly forgotten mark established by the New York Yankees between August 3rd, 1931, and August 2nd, 1933, when they played three hundred and eight consecutive games without once being shut out.) Pete Rose fell two short of his customary two-hundred-hit level this year, but his lifetime base-hit total now stands at 3,164, which puts him ninth on that all-time list. Rose has just become a free agent, having failed to come to terms with the Reds, for whom he has played throughout his sixteen-year career. The bidding for his services and the eventual terms of his new contract now offer an opportunity for some ambitious club owner to set a record of his own in an other-wise unpromising free-agent year.

Off-the-field news was mercifully scarce this year. The club owners and the Players Association are bracing themselves for another round of baseball SALT talks next year, when the basic agreement between the two great powers comes up for renegotiation. The owners have hired a new and aggressive labor representative, and there is a growing conviction among them that some form of serious recompense to owners who lose stars in the free-agent market must be written into the compact. In another area, which does not come under the basic agreement, several owners are pressing for a switch to an entirely new system of leagues and of post-season play after the 1979 season. This would entail the establishment of three geographical divisions within each league, and a playoff season that would stretch over several weeks, involving three regional winners in each league plus a "wild card" team. This package—the same kind of television-inspired scheduling that now interminably stretches out the professional basketball and hockey seasons and vitiates their ultimate championships—is being offered to the three networks as a device that would "heighten baseball fever."

The defects of this shabby scheme are too numerous and too evident to be examined in detail. Can it be that the owners have failed to notice that their game is booming, on a roll, with attendance rising each season and national interest deepening almost every day? This abundance, this green growth everywhere, springs from the natural resources of the sport—close competition, a sustained high quality of play, and some remarkable individual performances by the old and new stars of the game: all the feats and figures I have enumerated here. As every real fan knows, baseball's long, gruelling schedule is ideally suited to the searching out of deserving pennant-winning clubs, for the multiple difficulties of the game will inexorably wear down lesser teams *in due course*—which is to say not before mid-September at the earliest and, very often, not before the last weekend of the season. This is fever enough, and it depresses (but no longer surprises) me to see how the proprietors of the pastime continue to ignore its evident truths. I don't know: maybe they don't go to the games.

Onward. One more shower of statistics is inescapable. The violent head-to-head competition between the Red Sox and the Yankees for the American League East title this year was made possible by the simultaneous achievements of two great young stars, Jim Rice and Ron Guidry. Rice led the batters in both leagues in hits, triples, homers, runs batted in, total bases, and slugging percentage. His four hundred and six total bases were the most in the league since 1937. Thirty of his forty-six homers either tied the score or put the Red Sox ahead. And so forth. Ron Guidry's twenty-five wins and three losses for the Yankees this year constituted the highest winning percentage (.893) of any twenty-game winner in baseball history. His earned-run average of 1.74 ties him with Sandy Koufax for the lowest E.R.A. posted by any left-hander since Carl Hubbell's 1.66 in 1933. (Bob Gibson's 1.12 in 1968 is the lowest for all modern-era pitchers.) Guidry won his first thirteen decisions without a defeat, and threw nine shutouts in all—the most for a left-hander in his league since 1916, when Babe Ruth had the same total. Guidry's record since the All-Star break last year stands at thirty-nine wins and five defeats, including two Series and two playoff victories. And so on. In postseason balloting among the members of the Baseball Writers Association, Guidry was the unanimous choice for the Cy Young Award in his league and Jim Rice was selected Most Valuable Player. The members of the selection committee for the latter award were forced to make a choice between Rice and Guidry, which is like being asked to award a prize to a novel or to a concerto.

Both men are immensely strong, of course, but their appearance could not be more different. Rice's power is always visible—he is six feet two and weighs two hundred and five pounds and is a picture of the ideally proportioned athlete— but never more, perhaps, than when he is fooled by a pitch and manages to get only a bit of the bat handle on it and still somehow muscles the ball out over the infield on a line. With Guidry, one wonders always where all that heat is coming from. He is skinny and bowlegged, and weighs about a hundred and sixty pounds. His motion is quick and economical, and the secret of his superior fastball may lie in his upper-body movement, led by his right shoulder, which at the last instant drives forward and the downward toward the batter with a sudden, pistonlike swiftness, releasing the power in his left arm. American League batters have told me that Guidry's fastball is too quick to be attacked, because one can simply lose sight of it while striding; one must lie back and shorten stroke and hope for a piece of the ball at the last instant—a maneuver that makes the hitter terribly vulnerable to Guidry's other main weapon, a swift down-ducking slider that sometimes seems to cross the plate at shoe-top level. This was only Guidry's second full season in the majors—"He's still just a green pea," his manager, Bob Lemon, said recently, in a tone of wonder— but his pitching intelligence is mature and subtle. He is not a thrower, and his every pitch, including the slider, contributes to an eloquent major theme built around the keynote, which is the fastball. Strangely enough, the Yankees have had very few great strikeout pitchers over the years, and the Stadium crowds this year fell into the delightful habit of rising to their feet whenever the Cajun Conjurer got two strikes on a batter, and screaming in unison for the almost inevitable coming K. When it came, Guidry would settle his cap with a swift double-touch, fore and aft, as he does after every pitch, and then walk up the mound to the rubber in four jerky backward steps, looking like a figure in some backward-running comedy footage from an old silent movie. Here, to be sure, there was no silence; in showers of noise, Guidry would put up his glove for the ball and wait, motionless and composed, for the next batter to step in.

There were no such moments over at Shea Stadium this summer, where the Mets again finished dead last in their division, on merit. Doug Flynn fielded elegantly, and John Stearns improved a lot behind the plate, and Pat Zachry pitched a two-hitter (and also broke a toe while kicking irritably at the dugout steps), and Craig Swan somehow led all the National League's pitchers with an earned-run average of 2.43, and Joe Torre managed his young, thinly talented troupe with patience and class, but the club's chronic hopelessness at the plate made even these attainments seem sad. "I thought we stunk this year," Stearns said when it was all over. "We were just horrendous." Attendance barely came to a million—a gate loss of sixty-three per cent since 1970, when the club drew 2,697,479 customers and was considered one of the prime franchises in the game. There are some good young Mets arms in the minors, but no bats, and it looks as if the main entertainment at Shea Stadium next year will again turn out to be Willie Montanez's all too rare homerun trot—a slow, four-cornered dance, during which he approaches each base with a dozen tiny steps and then a large leap, like a show hunter clearing a fence.

Other teams had more fun and more company. The Dodgers drew the first three-million gate ever—3,347,845 fans in all—and the Giants, who unexpectedly led the Dodgers and the rest of the N.L. West for thirteen weeks of the summer, picked up more than a million new customers; it was only the fourth time any club had pulled *that* off. The big gainer in the American League was Milwaukee, which broke its previous highest home attendance by more than four hundred thousand. This, too, was done on merit. The Brewers finished third in the demanding American League East, behind the Yanks and the Red Sox, but they won ninety-three games—enough for a pennant in some years. The Brewers led both leagues in home runs, hits, and club batting—and perhaps in sheer pleasure. Their astounding pickup of twenty-six games over their 1977 record is attributable to thirty-four homers off the bat of Larry Hisle, a free agent who signed last winter for more than three million dollars, and to outstanding seasons by an erstwhile part-time outfielder, Gorman Thomas (thirty-two homers), an erstwhile bad-arm hurler, Mike Caldwell (twenty-two wins), and a couple of dashing twenty-two-year-olds, pitcher Lary Sorensen and infielder Paul Molitor, but most of all, surely, to the arrival of George Bamberger, a longtime pitching coach with the Orioles who was signed on to pilot the team by the Brewers' new general manager, Harry Dalton.

I made it out to Milwaukee in the middle of July and visited Bamberger in his office at Milwaukee County Stadium just before a night game with the visiting Red Sox, who were then leading the second-place Brewers by eight games.

"I guess everybody in the state is surprised by us," Bamberger told me. He is a round-faced, rumply sort of man, with a half-moon smile. "I know I am. I thought this team could play about .500 ball this year. We've had some eyeopeners all right, but the best thing this club has going for it is our mixture of youth and experience. You hear a lot of talk about leadership on a ball team, but it isn't always so easy to find it. But the leaders here are people like Larry Hisle and Sal Bando and Don Money, and they *lead*. They are men, and the kids really look up to them. I look up to them, too. I don't know if you know it, but I didn't want this job. I'd never managed, and I was all set in Baltimore. I just wanted to stay in baseball a couple more years. I let Harry Dalton talk me into coming. But before I said yes I asked about what kind of people there were here—the kids and the rest of them, too. If they were going to be a pain in the ass, I sure wouldn't have taken the job. I'm no dope."

It was Sheboygan Night that night at County Stadium, and an hour before game time there were hundreds of cookouts going on in the jam-packed parking lots, and the evening air was delicious with the smell of kielbasa. The incoming traffic on the East-West Freeway was backed up all the way to the Schlitz plant. It was a family crowd, by the looks of it— parents, boys and girls, grandparents—and when the game began the roomy, smoky old steelpost grandstands were stuffed with optimism and clapping and repeated, thunderously bawled choruses of "Roll Out the Barrel." There was a full moon over the left-field bleachers. Lary Sorensen pitched, and held the Bosox hitless for the first four innings, and Larry Hisle hit a two-run homer in the third, bringing the screeching home-towners to their feet and setting off the modest but live home-run show up above the scoreboard: zip! came "Bernie Brewer" down a chute from the balcony of his Tyrolean chalet, ker-splash! into a mammoth beer stein, which emitted balloon bub-bles into the night sky.

The dangerous Red Sox began to come on in the middle innings. Brewer second baseman Paul Molitor made a won-derful play in the seventh, fielding a high looper way over behind first base and then turning a hundred and eighty degrees in midair to throw out Yastrzemski on a force at second. But George Scott singled after that, and so did Butch Hobson, and so did Frank Duffy, and when Scott was signalled safe at the plate after a peg from the outfield, catcher Charlie Moore was so incensed at the call that he allowed the ball to roll unnoticed out of his mitt while he argued it, and Hobson, who had never stopped running, scored another run. He came all the way around from first base completely unseen by Moore or by any of us (who was *that?*), because we were so intent on the rhu-barb. The Sox broke the game open in the eighth—two singles, a balk, a walk, a three-run homer by Carlton Fisk—and won it by 8–2. Too bad, of course, but quite a midsummer evening, all in all, for Sheboygan, and for the rest of us, too.

A deadly smugness descended on me at this point in the baseball summer. After that night game in Milwaukee, the record of the Red Sox—*my* Red Sox—stood at sixty-two wins and twenty-eight losses, and the pennant race in the American League East looked almost over. The Boston batting was awesome. Fred Lynn was hitting .327, Rice was at .322 (with twenty-three homers), Yastrzemski was at .311, and Dwight Evans had eighteen homers. Only nine pinch-hitters had come up to bat for the team all season. On the mound, Dennis Eckersley—the young power pitcher acquired from Cleveland just before the season started—was eleven and two, Bill Lee was ten and three, Mike Torrez was twelve and five, and Luis Tiant was seven and two: forty wins and twelve losses for the four starters. The defense—with Lynn's range and Evans's incomparable arm and glove in the outfield, and with the harelike new second baseman, Jerry Remy, meshing impeccably with shortstop Rick Burleson in the infield—looked impregnable. Carl Yastrzemski said that this club had the best pitching and the best defense of any Boston team he had played on. In the previous month, I had watched the Bosox overwhelm the Yankees, winning four out of six clamorous games in Boston and New York. Eckersley, who had never beaten the Yankees before, whipped them three times in twelve days. The defending champions seemed broken by injuries and dissension. Mickey Rivers, Bucky Dent, Willie Randolph, and Thurman Munson had been sidelined or had gone on the disabled list for various periods; Reggie Jackson was having trouble with his eyes and his psyche. The champions' pitchers, once overabundant in depth and skill, were in the worst shape of all. Don Gullett, Andy Messersmith, Catfish Hunter, and Ken Clay had all been shelved with arm miseries; young Jim Beattie had been shipped back to Tacoma; Ed Figueroa was struggling. Up in Boston, Catfish Hunter was tried again in late-inning relief and instantly gave up four hits, two of them homers, before Yastrzemski struck out—perhaps intentionally, in order to save the Cat further humiliation. Young and utterly anonymous pitchers—Dave Rajsich, Bob Kammeyer—were hastily called up from the minors and thrown into combat, like Eton boys at Passchendaele. The famous rivals looked so ill-matched that when their July 4th game at Fenway was rained out, after a one-sided Boston win the night before, I had a commiserating, condescending feeling of relief. It would be fairer and more fun for the two teams to play later on, when the odds were better. The Yankees went off to Texas and then to Milwaukee, where they were swept by the Brewers in three straight. By the time of my visit there, the Yankees were fourteen games behind, and, by their own admission, out of it.

In baseball, Yogi Berra once said, you don't know *nothing*. One thing I didn't know was that the Red Sox would lose the next night in Milwaukee, and would continue that road trip by dropping six of their next seven games. Rick Burleson's absence with a damaged ankle for twelve games was the first check to the team's Mercedes-like passage through the summer landscape. The Yankees, meanwhile, began to motor in the opposite direction, moving from fourteen games behind to eight behind in the space of eight days. Another thing I didn't know was that Catfish Hunter's fortunes were undergoing a dramatic alteration. Immediately after his appalling outing in Boston, he had been treated by the Yankee physician, Dr. Maurice Cowen, who put him under anesthesia and manipulated his damaged pitching arm; the doctor said later that the popping noise when he broke the adhesions in Hunter's shoulder was so startling that for a moment he thought he had broken the pitcher's arm. Hunter played catch with his son the next day and reported that he had thrown without pain for the first time in two years. A little later, he had a very poor outing against the Indians, but again felt no pain. He then won his next six decisions in a row, and the Yankees' pitching was restored.

Another thing I didn't know was that Billy Martin would resign his job, on July 24th (after some alcoholic and ill-considered words about his employer, George Steinbrenner), and that Bob Lemon, who had been released earlier in the summer as manager of the White Sox, would take his place. No autopsy will be attempted here on this celebrated but moldering cadaver of sports news, or its startling sequel—the announcement by Steinbrenner that Billy Martin would return as the Yankee manager in 1980, with Bob Lemon moving up to the general manager's office. Speculation cannot determine what effect the change of managers had on the Yankees' triumphal course through the rest of the season; for that matter, no one has been able to prove that a *manager* was ever responsible for winning or losing a single ballgame. What is clear is that the difference between the two men in outward (and perhaps inward) manner is antipodal—a contrast that is perhaps best illustrated by the manner in which each comported himself upon being removed from office. Martin, it will be recalled, broke down before the cameras and reporters during an extempore press conference on the mezzanine of a Kansas City hotel and was led away in tears. Bob Lemon, after being relieved by White Sox owner Bill Veeck, because the club had gone sour on the field and at the gate, asked his boss if he could speak in private to the Chicago players before he departed. One of those players, the veteran shortstop Don Kessinger, later said to a local writer, "It was something. All he did was talk about *us*. He thanked us, and told us how good we were. He never mentioned himself once." This seems typical of the man. Bob Lemon is the only contemporary manager I have encountered who always refers to his players as "they," instead of the currently obligatory, Scoutmasterish 'we." He also never makes critical comments or jokes about a player in front of his teammates or to members of the press. He is soft-spoken and outwardly gentle and consistently humorous, and since he has moved into his office there, the Yankee clubhouse has become a cheerful and much more youthful place, and a pleasure to visit. In Martin's defense, it should be pointed out that the Yankees won for him last year, when the clubhouse atmosphere was tainted from April until October, and that this year's team had just run off five straight wins when Billy quit. Martin is a tough and resourceful field director, and there is no evidence that sweetness and laughter in the locker room or on the team bus are translated into winning habits on the ball field. I have no idea if he will be in pinstripes next year, but he will be back somewhere.

The last traces of my baseball neutrality disappeared during the month of August, which I passed on vacation in Maine, deep in Red Sox country. Far from any ballpark and without a television set, I went to bed early on most nights and lay there semi-comatose, stunned by another day of sunshine and salt air but kept awake, or almost awake, by the murmurous running thread of Bosox baseball from my bedside radio. I felt very close to the game then—perhaps because I grew up listening to baseball over the radio, or perhaps because the familiar quiet tones and effortless precision of the veteran Red Sox announcers, Ned Martin and Jim Woods, invited me to share with them the profound New England seriousness of Following the Sox. Sometimes, I must confess, I did fall asleep, usually when the team was playing on the West Coast—well past midnight on Penobscot Bay—and when I awoke in the morning to the lap of water under my windows (or, at low tide, to the conversation of gulls and crows on the stony beach) I would spring up, scoreless and anxious, and twirl the dial in search of the news. Whatever the result, the previous night's game was then replayed during the morning and afternoon with my friends and co-religionists at the general store, the post office, and the boatyard, and then again over drinks at the end of the day on somebody's porch overlooking Eggemoggin Reach and, behind Isle au Haut, Fenway Park. I have spent many summers in this part of the world, but this was the first year I could remember when the Red Sox were in first place all through August—a development that seemed only to deepen the sense of foreboding that always afflicts the Red Sox faithful as the summer wanes. First place, I suddenly understood, means responsibility. We Red Sox fans were like a young couple who for years had rented a nice little apartment on the second floor, dreaming and saving in the hope that someday they could afford a house of their own. Now, at last, we had it—Top o' the Hill Cottage—and for the first time we realized that the place was mortgaged, that it had to be painted and kept up and looked after, and that it could be lost. It was almost better the other way.

The Sox entered August five games ahead of the second-place Brewers and finished it six and a half ahead of the second-place Yankees, but it was—in truth as well as in our imagining—an anxious sort of month. Against the Yankees, Boston won a two-day game in which they had once trailed by 5–0, before tying it up in the eighth. Postponed after fourteen innings by rain, the game was resumed the next night, with the Sox winning it by 7–5 in the seventeenth; then they won the other game that night, by 8–1. The team fared less well against easier foes, and one began to notice that several Boston victories were attributable to plain luck. They beat the Indians in the thirteenth inning when one Cleveland infielder dropped a little pop fly and another threw the ball past third base, giving Butch Hobson a hitless inside-the-park homer. They beat the A's when Jerry Remy hit a three-run homer in Oakland just after the home-plate ump had called a foul tip on an apparent third strike—a magical foul tip that Remy himself could not detect. Down a run with two out in the twelfth inning, they beat the Angels when the California third baseman threw wildly past first on a routine play and Jerry Remy was ruled safe at home on a frightful call by the ump. (A lot of American League umpires had hard days at the office this summer.) Luckily, too, the Yankees ran into repeated difficulties with the last-place Mariners. But the Yanks kept coming on now, and a lot of Red Sox regulars were aching or were mired in slumps. George Scott struck out again and again. Bill Lee lost seven straight games and was taken out of the rotation. Lynn and Fisk and Hobson were injured. The bone chips in the elbow of Hobson's throwing arm were so painful at times that he fell into the habit of sprinting toward first base before getting off a peg; he also made a great many errors. Dwight Evans was beaned, and Jerry

Remy cracked his wrist. Carl Yastrzemski had an agonizing back-pull and a sore right wrist. (Corseted and bandaged, Yaz came off the bench and went four for six against the Angels.) Somehow, the team won six in a row at home, and it looked as if the mortgage might be safe after all.

I came home tanned and confident, but my real troubles were just beginning, for the Red Sox now fell into a corpselike stillness at the plate. In one game at Baltimore, after Jim Rice hit a three-run homer in the first inning the next twenty-three Boston batters went out in order, as the Orioles won by 5–3. When the Yankees came into Fenway Park on September 7th, to begin a pair of critical home-and-home series on successive weekends, the Bosox had lost six of their last eight games, while the Yankees had won twelve of their last fourteen. The Boston lead was down to four games. Then it was down to three, as the defending champions thrashed the Sox, 15–3, scoring twelve runs in the first four innings. (This game, by the way, was the rescheduled Fourth of July rainout that I had so magnanimously and insanely wished to see played when the teams were more evenly matched.) The following evening, the Sox committed four atrocious errors in the first two innings while the Yankees were scoring eight runs; eighteen Boston batters went down in order against Jim Beattie, the Yanks' big freshman right-hander, and the Yankees won by 13–2. There were seven Boston errors all told. The Sox had now committed twenty-two errors and given up nineteen unearned runs in their last nine games. Keeping score, I had begun to feel like an accountant for a Wall Street brokerage firm in the fall of 1929. The cabdriver who took me home from Fenway Park that night said, "I turned that game off three different times on the radio."

The game on Saturday—Eckersley vs. Guidry on a glazy, windy, sharp-shadow day at the Fens—was better, at least for a while. In the fourth, Yastrzemski made a diving, rolling catch of Jackson's drive at the foot of the wall in left, and the relay doubled Munson off first base—the kind of play that sometimes turns a series and a ball team around. A moment or two later, however, with two Yankee base runners aboard, five Boston fielders (not including Remy, who was still benched with his injury) circled and stared and paused and pulled back under

Piniella's high, wind-bent fly in short right-center field, allowing it to drop untouched for a double. At once, there came a little flurry of hits and walks, a wild pitch, and a passed ball, and the Yankees had seven runs—and this game, too, was gone. Guidry pitched a two-hitter, so perhaps none of the rest of it mattered. I left after seven innings—my earliest departure ever from Fenway Park, I think. I didn't have the heart to come back the next day, when the Yankees won again, 7–4, and moved into a tie for first place. In the four games, the Yankees had scored forty-two runs on sixty-seven hits, as against the Red Sox' nine runs on twenty-one. Boston had also committed twelve errors, and "The Boston Massacre" had gone into the baseball lexicon.

They resumed the next Friday in New York, with the Yankees now up by a game and a half and the Stadium hordes yowling into the night like coyotes. Once again, the Red Sox made a trifling mistake in the fourth, and once again the Yankees, with two outs, scored all the runs of the game. Rivers was on second and Randolph on first when Piniella rapped into a round-the-horn double play, on which Rivers took third, and a little more; Yastrzemski (who was playing first base) took the peg and, seeing Mickey ten or twelve feet down the line, fired a hasty throw back across the diamond to Hobson, hoping for an incredible triple play. The throw went wild, past the bag, and Rivers scored on the error. Then Jackson walked. Then Chambliss homered. Then Nettles homered. Four runs. Guidry was the Yankee pitcher again, and again he threw a two-hitter. "I'm not sorry for the Red Sox, but I pity them," Sparky Lyle said later.

Saturday afternoon's game was closer—wonderfully close, in fact, until the Yankee ninth, when Mickey Rivers led off with a triple to deep left field and scored on Munson's sacrifice fly, to win it by 3–2. Mike Torrez had been given a 2–0 lead on Jim Rice's first-inning homer, but Catfish Hunter held the Sox scoreless after that. The two big Yankee blows—a homer by Reggie Jackson and Rivers' triple—each came when Torrez had gone ahead on the count by two strikes and no balls and had then come in with a careless, fatal bad pitch. The Boston clubhouse was whispery and tomblike after that loss, and we circling writers eyed each other silently, like volunteers at the site of a catastrophe. The Red Sox won at last the next afternoon, behind Eckersley, but I did not attend. I couldn't stand it anymore.

What happened to the Red Sox? There have been other famous foldups in baseball, of course—the 1951 Dodgers, the 1964 Phillies, the 1974 Red Sox (who led their league at the end of August and then lost twenty of their last twenty-eight games)—but this collapse, particularly during those four games against the Yankees at Fenway Park, appears unique. The Red Sox, to be sure, were suffering from multiple injuries and from coinciding slumps on the mound and at the plate, but their sudden mass inability to catch and throw the ball—sometimes to make even the most routine infield plays—is unparalleled and inexplicable. That week, Carlton Fisk took one of the Boston reporters aside in a hotel lobby and muttered, "Tell me something. *What's the matter with us?*" No one can say. In fairness to the wonderful team that beat them, it can be suggested that the Red Sox failed because in many respects they were exactly the opposite of the Yankees. They were heavy-footed, for instance, and rarely made the exceptional play, in the field or on the bases. They had no one in the lineup like Mickey Rivers, who puts such pressure on pitchers and fielders with his wandlike bat and his quickness around the base paths, and who so often seems to tilt a game with a tiny hit or a long one: I doubt that Yaz would have tried for the impossible triple play against any runner but the anxious-making Rivers. The Red Sox had no bench strength to speak of (how often in September we fans remembered Bernie Carbo, who was sent away in an ill-considered deal back in June), and their batters, through bad stretches as well as good ones, continued to swing from their heels, looking for the long ball that they have lived by all these years. The great green wall at Fenway, which lies three hundred and fifteen feet away from home plate down the left-field line, is traditionally held to bemuse visiting pitchers and hitters, but I have come to believe that it is the Green Wall mentality which so often brings down the apparently indomitable Boston ball teams in the end. In their heart of hearts, I suspect, Boston hitters believe that a single and a hit-and-run and a sacrifice fly constitute a scruffy or demeaning way to score a crucial late-inning run; the proper Bostonian style is two triples off the top of the wall. The team at its best is awesome, but it is slow and luck-prone (good and bad) at other times, and at its worst it resembles wet concrete. The Yankees, by contrast, seem capable of playing four or five different kinds of offensive baseball; in the first game of the Massacre, the 15–3 affair, they hit sixteen singles. Finally, I must observe that the Sox appear too restrained or introverted by nature to turn their troubles into a purging anger on the field. The Yankees are raunchy and disputatious and hard for most of us to cotton to, but their scandals and harsh words somehow translate themselves into a cheerful and extremely dangerous pride when the going is toughest. The Red Sox are a team of watchers and quiet talkers, with a few true eccentrics and emotional zombies among them. The leaders, Carlton Fisk and Carl Yastrzemski (Yaz especially), burn within, and sometimes burst into beautiful, fiery deeds on the field, but their finest feats—the impossible late-season batting outburst, the fabled catch, the historic homer—appear as isolated and hallowed events, almost too painful in their personal cost to be emulated or enjoyed. These are decent, lonely men caught up in a dream of one perfect and thus perfectly unattainable season.

My own September sufferings became so comical and unbearable that I took them to California for a few days, hoping for some help from my other favorites, the Giants. I got there too late. Just before my visit, the Giants had dropped five out of six games on a road trip, to slip four games behind the Dodgers, whom they now had one final crack at in a pair of home games. They lost them both, and eventually finished the season in third place in the National League West, behind both the Dodgers and the Reds, and six games out of first place. It was plain to me that I had become a baseball Typhoid Mary (with me in the park, my two old heart-throbs lost ten consecutive crucial games in the late going), but for some reason I was not much downcast by the Giants' defeats. The happy, bundled-up night crowds at Candlestick Park seemed to bear little resemblance to the shocked and heartbroken multitudes I had just left at Fenway. These San Francisco rooters looked younger, for one thing, and it occurred to me that since the Giants had drawn so poorly for the previous three or four years, most of the fans held an affiliation of much shorter duration than the old Boston bloodlines and were less afflicted by Sophoclean memories. The Giants themselves were young, too, most of them, and now, evidently afflicted at last by self-doubt, they made a lot of boyish mistakes—collisions in the outfield, gratuitous long leads given to the enemy base runners, fatal pauses on the base paths—all of which were seized upon by the alert, opportunistic Dodger veterans, who won by 7–2 and 8–0.

In the stands and in the home-team clubhouse, I got the feeling that almost everyone would look back on this Giants season with gratitude, forgetting its sad ending and keeping instead a picture gallery of its unexpected pleasures: Vida Blue gesticulating and laughing in front of the dugout as he led the roaring midsummer crowds in cheering; Jack Clark, the big, free-swinging young outfielder, tagging up after a fly in San Diego and scoring the winning run against the Padres all the way from second base ("JACK CLARK IS GOD" was the message I saw on an upper-deck banner); Mike Ivie hitting a pinch-hit grand-slam home run against Don Sutton before the biggest crowd in Candlestick Park history (and hitting *another* pinch-hit grand slam in Atlanta); Bill Madlock smashing into Pirate shortstop Frank Taveras to break up a ninth-inning double play in Pittsburgh, in a game that the Giants then won on a squeeze bunt by Rob Andrews in the eleventh ("NEVAH GIVE UP!" is the huge, wavery message painted on the wall of the tunnel between the Giants' clubhouse and the dugout, an exhortation by Winston Churchill daubed there this spring by Rob Andrews); and two successive, brilliant victories at home against the Dodgers in early August—just before two losses to the same team, which first suggested that this might not be a miracle autumn on the bay after all. "All our games have been thrilling," Bill Madlock said to me.

I also talked to the Giants' sachem, Willie McCovey, who passed the five-hundred-homer mark this summer. He is forty years old, and played on the San Francisco Giants' only World Series club, in 1962. He is an enormous and gentle man, with massive hands, an elegant nose, and strange, Oriental eyes.

"When you're younger, you always think there are a lot more years of baseball ahead," he said. "When you get to be my age, you think a little more about what's passing. In 1962, I'd have bet my life's earnings that it wouldn't take this long to get close again. I thought we'd be in it for the next five years, easy. But you don't ever know in baseball. You don't even know if you're going to be there on the same team the next year. So there's a lot more emotion for me this year. I've been more anxious for us to win, because it could be the last time for me."

I said that it seemed to have been a painful season all around, for the fans as well as for the players.

Most ballplayers seem to have almost no awareness of the people in the stands, but McCovey responded at once. "The fans sitting up there are *helpless*," he said. "They can't pick up a bat and come down and do something. Their only involvement is in how well you do. If you strike out or mess up out there, they feel they've done something wrong. You're all they've got. The professional athlete knows there's always another game or another year coming up. If he loses, he swallows the bitter pill and comes back. It's much harder for the fans."

I returned to Candlestick Park once more, for a now almost meaningless game against the Atlanta Braves, which the Giants eventually lost. There were only a few thousand of us there— the smallest crowd of the year—and I sat in the sunlit stands behind first base. My neighbor in the next box was a very thin, elderly gentleman from nearby Santa Rosa, who wore a button-up plaid flannel shirt and two caps—an orange-and-black Giants cap over an old cardboard visor, which he had pulled over to one side of his forehead to keep the sun off his face. He wrote out the Giants' lineup with a pencil on a three-by-five card.

We fell into conversation during the slow, almost eventless innings, and he told me that he and his wife had season tickets but that they came only to the afternoon games. "My wife's out taking a little nap in the parking lot right now," he said.

I asked him how long he had been a Giants fan.

"Oh, a long, long time," he said. "And before that I used to watch the Pacific Coast League teams here. All the DiMaggio brothers played here then. I can't remember if I really saw Joe DiMaggio play for the Seals. I don't remember everything now—not like I should. It used to be that in every vacant lot around here there'd be a baseball game going—people playing ball in every vacant lot in San Francisco. You don't see that anymore. We had the Seals here then, and the Oakland club across the bay. You could watch an Oakland game in the morning and go to see the Seals in the afternoon."

Something happened out on the field, and the crowd began to clap and cheer.

"If only there was some little thing we could do to help them," the old man said, echoing Willie McCovey. "All this hollering don't help none. But I come whether the Giants win or lose. It's good to be at the game. I just like the game, I guess."

In the sixth or seventh inning, I went off to get a hot dog, and when I came back my friend was gone. The Giants lost in the twelfth inning, but I didn't mind at all. It was good to be at the game.

The best part of the baseball year was just ahead. The Red Sox recovered their poise after winning that final game in Yankee Stadium, and picked up a game and a half on the league leaders in the next six days, to cut the lead to a single game, with seven to play. The two teams, which had alternated between strength and frailty throughout the year, now steadied to their duties, each winning on six successive days against lesser clubs in their division. The Red Sox had the closest call, pulling out a fourteen-inning affair at Toronto in which the Blue Jays loaded the bases in the eleventh and again in the thirteenth but could not score. The Yankee margin on the last Sunday morning of the season was still one game.

Unable to decide which park to visit, I stayed home that Sunday and frantically manipulated the dials of my television set, like Captain Kirk at the controls of the Starship Enterprise, as I tried simultaneously to bring in the critical plays from the Indians-Yankees game at the Stadium and the Blue Jays-Red Sox game at Fenway Park. Unsurprisingly, I usually clicked away from each field just before some significant moment, but finally, after I had added a radio to my instrument console, the broad messages began to come through. Rick Waits, a left-handed Cleveland curveballer, stifled the Yankee hitters while his teammates were jumping all over Catfish Hunter and several successors, winning by 9–2. Up at the Fens, Luis Tiant threw a masterly two-hitter against Toronto, in a game that the Bosox finally broke open with late homers by Burleson and Rice, and won 5–0. "THANK YOU, RICK WAITS," The Fenway scoreboard said in lights when it was all over. The two clubs were tied at ninety-nine wins and sixty-three losses apiece, and a one-game playoff at Fenway Park would settle it the next afternoon.

Before I departed for the Hub, I thought at length about the Red Sox, whom I had given up on so often in the times of their worst troubles. Here, at the very last, they had won twelve of their final fourteen games, including the last eight in succession, and not only had achieved the tie but had somehow preserved themselves as a team worth our emotion and attention. Anything less, given their horrible earlier fall from grace, would have stamped them for good as characterless losers—in their own minds as well as in the forever hoping, forever doubting mass unconscious of the New England fans—with bitter and unimaginable consequences. The same result would have come, I believe, if the Red Sox had collapsed in the playoff game. But that didn't happen, either.

By every standard, the playoff was a classic—a game that held us spellbound for every moment of its two hours and fifty-two minutes. Omens and citations hailed its arrival. The Boston *Globe* quoted Dickens ("It was the best of times, it was the worst of times...") in its pregame story that morning. Ron Guidry, the Yankee starter, could pick up his twenty-fifth victory by winning the game. The team that won it would step onto the marble plinth of one hundred wins for the season—and into the East-West playoffs the next day. Mike Torrez, the Red Sox pitcher, had been a Yankee last year but had quit the club, with considerable bitterness, to become a free agent. The only three pitchers to beat Guidry this year (Caldwell, Flanagan, Willis) were all named Mike. Carl Yastrzemski said, "Today is the biggest ballgame of my life."

It all meant such a lot that nobody in the shirtsleeved, sun-drenched crowd seemed to have much fun. The cheering, when it came, was savage but abrupt, quickly terminated again and again by the weight and anxiety of the occasion. It was a game played for the most part in a profound, crowded silence. The first real noise was an ovation for Carl Yastrzemski—the captain, the nonpareil—as he stepped up to bat in the second inning, and the second, and much louder, explosion of sound came an instant later, when he pulled Guidry's second pitch on a low, precise parabola into the right-field stands, *just* fair. Fisk and Lynn followed with hard, long outs to the farther reaches of the park, and it was clear that Guidry on this day was a little below his untouchable best. But the Yankees were attacking Torrez, too—a double by Rivers in the third, a frightening line drive out to right field by Jackson—and the strange waiting silence again fell over the park. No one in the bleachers was moving; in the crowded bullpens, the pitchers and catchers sat immobile in two silent rows, as they stared in, riveted, through the low-lying, glary sunlight. On the mound, Mike Torrez, all emotion, repeatedly kicked the dirt and shook his head as he battled homeplate umpire Don Denkinger for the corners. Then he would heave in a great breath of air and blow it out again, and fire another fastball. When his turn came, Guidry, a little pitching machine, reared and threw, touched his cap, walked backward, did it all over again.

Torrez opened the fifth by walking Roy White, and Brian Doyle, the rookie Yankee second baseman who was filling in for the injured Willie Randolph, rapped the ball to the right side on a hit-and-run, just as he was meant to, moving White to second. Bucky Dent popped up, on a killing Torrez pitch that came in on his fists. Mickey Rivers bounced deep to short, where Rick Burleson, glimpsing Mick flying up the line, wheeled at the last instant and threw instead to Brohamer at third, who tagged White, sliding in, for the third out. Wonderful baseball.

After six innings, Torrez had surrendered only two hits, and in the home half of the sixth Burleson doubled, moved along to third on a bunt by Remy, and came in on Rice's single—hit on sheer muscle off an excellent pitch by Guidry. Rice went to second on Yaz's infield out, and Fisk was passed intentionally. Freddy Lynn worked the count to three and two, and, as the runners flew away, lashed a deep drive to the right-field corner, where Piniella, hunching over and half averting his head against the frightful sunlight, pulled it in on the run—a difficult, crucial chance.

Two runs ahead now, and perhaps feeling more comfortable, Torrez surrendered singles to Chambliss and White. With two out, he threw a high slider on an 0–2 count—only a middling-good pitch at best—to Bucky Dent, the ninth hitter in the Yankee order, and Dent lofted it down the left-field line and just into the netting above the wall, for a three-run homer. The silent, apprehensive crowd had been right after all. Since that day, I have heard some Red Sox fans complain that Dent's minimal wind-lifted blow would have been an easy out at any other park, including Yankee Stadium, but this is unacceptable. Those who live by the wall must die by the wall. And this bitter railing at fate (or at Mike Torrez) does not take into account what the Yankees did next, still with two outs, when Mickey Rivers walked and Thurman Munson, swinging against Bob Stanley, the new Boston pitcher, doubled him home. In the top of the eighth, Reggie Jackson hit a leadoff homer, to make it 5—2 for the Yankees. For me, these deadly secondary shocks are the absolute certifying mark of a champion. You cannot open the door to the Yankees by as much as a centimetre, for they will kick it down.

The Fenway silence after these disasters was blown away for good in the bottom of the eighth, when the Red Sox, down to their last six outs of the year, rallied for two runs. Remy doubled (Gossage was the Yankee pitcher now), and came scooting home on Yaz's single to center. Carlton Fisk battled Gossage interminably, barely fouling off his fastballs again and again, and singled on the tenth pitch. Then Lynn singled, too, to bring it to 5—4. With two out, George Scott stood in ("Boom-ah! Boom-ah! Boom-ah!" the bleachers cried), and struck out, swinging.

I left the press box and went down into the dark, ancient grandstand, standing between home and first among hundreds of clustered, afflicted rooters who had gathered behind the sloping stands for a closer look at the end of it. Peering over shoulders and around heads, I saw Burleson walk, after one out in the ninth. Now Jerry Remy whacked a hard drive to right, and Lou Piniella, paralyzed by the glaring sun, froze in the field with both arms outstretched, unable to see the ball. Suddenly it rematerialized and bounded in front of him, a foot or two to his left but within reach. Backing up, he gloved it on the first big hop—a lucky play, perhaps, but by no means an easy one. Burleson, thundering past second, abruptly threw on the brakes and came back to the base—a final but perhaps fatal bit of Boston conservatism on the base paths. Rice flied out to right, deep enough to send Burleson to third.

Two out, and the tying run on third. Yastrzemski up. A whole season, thousands of innings, had gone into this tableau. My hands were trembling. The faces around me looked haggard. Gossage, the enormous pitcher, reared and threw a fastball: ball one. He flailed and fired again, and Yastrzemski swung and popped the ball into very short left-field foul ground, where Graig Nettles, backing up, made the easy out. It was over.

Afterward, Yaz wept in the training room, away from the reporters. In the biggest ballgame of his life, he had homered and singled and had driven in two runs, but almost no one would remember that. He is thirty-nine years old, and he has never played on a world-championship team; it is the one remaining goal of his career. He emerged after a while, dry-eyed, and sat by his locker and answered our questions quietly. He looked old. He looked fifty.

Later that week, many editorials and sports stories in the Boston papers explained that it was the fate of the Yankees to win always, and the fate of the Red Sox always to wait another year. Emily Vermeule, a professor of classics at Harvard, wrote in the *Globe*, "The hero must go under at last, after prodigious deeds, to be remembered and immortal and to have poets sing his tale." I understand that, and I will sing the tale of Yaz always, but I still don't quite see why it couldn't have been arranged for him to single to right center, or to double off the wall. I'd have sung *that*, too. I think God was shelling a peanut.

Some other good ball teams were valiant participants in their local games of Capture the Flag, and were overlooked by me only because of my all-absorbing love affair with the Red Sox. The Cubs had a brief early-summer tenure at the top, and the rising young Tigers, under the guidance of Ralph Houk (who retired at the end of the season), finished with the best fifth-place record in American League history. In the American League West, the California Angels were in and out of first place all summer but fell to the Royals when their pitching aces, Frank Tanana and Nolan Ryan, both wore down at the end. The club also suffered a shocking blow when outfielder Lyman Bostock, one of the great young hitters in the game, was murdered in an off-the-field shooting incident. In the National League East, the Pirates, behind the formidable Dave Parker, made two separate assaults on the firstplace Phillies in the final month, winning twenty-four straight games at home before succumbing on the last Saturday of September. The satisfaction felt by fans of the Royals and the Phillies upon their teams' attainment of divisional pennants must have been accompanied by a cruel anxiety—a presentiment almost instantly borne out when both clubs were beaten in the playoffs for the third year running. In deference to these bruised and perhaps despairing partisans, I will try to be brisk in my account of the double championships.

I travelled first to Veterans Stadium, in Philadelphia, where the home team appeared to be still trembling over its epochal letdown in the third playoff game last year, when the same visiting Dodgers rallied for three sudden runs and the win in the ninth, after several gruesome Phillies malfeasances. No such outcome was possible this year, since the Phillies quickly fell behind 7–1 in the first game, which they ultimately lost, 9–5, and then died at the plate in the second, losing by 4–0. The opener was more like batting practice than a championship game (Steve Garvey hit two homers and a triple), and the only real pitching to be seen was some exemplary Dodger relief work by a large right-handed fastball-thrower named Bob Welch, who is twenty-two years old. The next day's shutout was a mesmerizing four-hitter by the Dodgers' Tommy John, whose left-handed sinkerball accounted for twenty-one groundball outs. The Phillies fans booed their heroes throughout the evening— a local custom, like scrapple for breakfast—and the elegiac postgame remarks by veteran home-team catcher Tim McCarver summed up the Philadelphia story. "I'm sorry we have to look for reasons for rationalizing the way we play," he said, "but we do."

Out in Los Angeles, the Phillies rallied for a time, winning the ensuing game, 9–4, behind their pitching star, Steve Carlton, who helped himself by hitting a homer and driving in four runs. They performed courageously the next day, too (I was watching these games on the tube), tying the game on a pinch-hit seventh-inning homer by Bake McBride, but then lost it all, in a new and exquisitely painful fashion, when their estimable Gold Glove center fielder, Garry Maddox, made an error on a routine fly ball in the tenth inning, and the Dodgers instantly administered the coup de grâce, winning by 4–3. Nobody—I least of all—can understand what happens to the Phillies in the autumn. Their postseason record, going back to the World Series of 1915, now stands at three wins and seventeen losses.

The Royals, who had taken the Yankees down to the last

inning of the fifth playoff game in each of the last two years, did less well this fall, losing in four. This time, the pennant may have been settled in the very first game. Playing on their home carpet, which suits their fast, singles-hitting team so well, and facing a Yankee pitching staff that was in tatters after so many extended late-season cliffhangers, the Royals managed a bare two hits against Jim Beattie (who was pitching for Dartmouth three years ago) and were blown away, 7–1. The Yankees, clearly flying after their victory in Fenway Park, banged out sixteen hits, including a single, a double, and a three-run homer by Reggie Jackson. The Royals turned things around the next day, routing Yankees starter Ed Figueroa in less than two innings, and coasting to a languid 10–4 win. Now the teams repaired to Yankee Stadium, where they had at each other in a rip-roaring, extraordinarily exciting, sustained baseball entertainment, in which we saw the lead (which never exceeded one run) erased, won back, or reversed seven times in eight innings. George Brett, the blond, square-jawed Kansas City third baseman, who won the American League batting title in 1976, was playing with a damaged right thumb and a torn left shoulder, both of which were due for postseason surgical repairs, but he did not, in truth, seem much handicapped. He opened the game with an upper-deck homer, struck off Catfish Hunter's second pitch of the afternoon. Batting with one out in the third, he hit a homer that restored Kansas City to the lead, by 2–1. Leading off in the fifth, he homered once again (still against Hunter), to tie the game at 3–3. The reciprocating blow, three times repeated, was delivered by Reggie Jackson in the even-numbered innings: a homer, a run-scoring single, and a four-hundred-foot fly ball, caught at the top of the center-field wall, which also scored a run. The cries of wonder and passion in the sunlit stadium became almost continuous—one sustained afternoon shout—and it occurred to me that the old sports-page locution "ding-dong action" should have been kept in its box all these years and then taken out, still fresh in its tissue paper, for this one particular game. There were other chills and thrills: a costly throwing error by Freddy Patek, a violent, almost operatic protest by Lou Piniella after he was called out at the plate by umpire Ron Luciano, and more—so much activity, in fact, that I always seemed to be about a page behind in my notes. In the eighth, the Royals tied the score again, against Goose Gossage, and then retook the lead at 5–4—this time without Brett's help—thus preparing the stage for the grand crescendo, which was Thruman Munson's monstrous four-hundred-and-twenty-foot, two-run homer into the left-field monuments in the bottom of the same inning, which settled it at 6–5, New York. "It seems like we keep winning the exciting games," Lou Piniella said afterward.

My eight-year-old son was watching all this in the upper deck, in the company of his mother and two third-grade classmates. Before the game, I had taken him aside and said, "Don't be too disappointed if nothing much happens there today. Lots of ballgames are sort of dull, you know."

"I know," he said, but I don't think he really believed me. Still doesn't.

Brett started things off the next day with a triple off Ron Guidry, and scored the Royals' first run a moment afterward—the first and also the last, for this was quite another sort of baseball, though scarcely of lesser quality. The Royals' pitcher, Dennis Leonard, looked better than Guidry on this day. He gave up a tying home run to Graig Nettles in the second inning and then disposed of thirteen Yankees in succession before Roy White lofted a short solo homer into the right-field stands—a modest blow, but good enough for the pennant, because the visitors, given several opportunities, could not quite crack Guidry or the Yankee defense. Writhing in the quicksands, they went down before Gossage in the ninth—one, two, three—with the tying run on second base.

Bob Lemon, looking back on his club's dangerous, brilliant week, said that the first game, against the Red Sox, had still been the hardest one of all. "They really drug it through the knothole at the end up there," he said, wincing at the thought of it. "All this has certainly made an older man out of me, but a very happy one."

The Yankees' six-game comeback triumph in the World Series would be unfairly diminished if we were to permit it to seem inevitable in retrospect. Since a baseball game is the most linear of all sporting events, with many hundreds of pitches and plays that can be dissected later and picked over for omens and indices, an autopsy often makes the most elusive patterns or psychologies of a game or a series appear easy. This is where the momentum turned, there was the telling throw, and look here at this tiny rent in the cloth, where the whole fabric of a team began to give way. Yes, of course; we knew it all along. What I knew for certain after four innings of the first World Series game, in Los Angeles, was that the Yankees were finished for the year. By that time, they were trailing in the game by the score of 6–0, after three Dodger home runs (two of them sizable successive clouts by second baseman Davey Lopes), and their long-range prospects were equally glum. Their pitching was worn bare. Figueroa had been routed again here; Hunter had been savaged by George Brett in his last appearance; and Guidry, exhausted by his recent labors, would not be ready until later in the week. New or chronic injuries afflicted many of the regulars. Willie Randolph was out for the season. Rivers and Chambliss were capable only of sporadic appearances, Munson could not swing or throw without evident pain. The Dodgers, by contrast, were mostly fit and entirely confident; in the important games I had seen them play and win against the Giants and the Phillies in the previous weeks they had looked wonderfully efficient, cool, and opportunistic. The Dodgers had matured at last. This was their year. The Dodger fans, of course, shared my conviction, and the immense Chavez Ravine audience, was ravished as the home club coasted to an easy 11–5 victory, in which a home run by Reggie Jackson— a space shot to the back wall of the Yankee bullpen—counted only as added entertainment. Tommy John again was the winning pitcher, and again the Dodger outfielders were almost able to pull up easy chairs during his tenure on the mound. As usual, I took great pleasure in watching John work. His left-handed motion seems stiff and hesitant, and even a bit awkward—a beguiling mannerism in an era of largely characterless rock-and-heave pitching styles. This delivery may be the result of a surgical overhauling he underwent four years ago, when the ruined elbow of his pitching arm was rebuilt by the addition of a bit of tendon removed from his right, or non-throwing, arm, but in any case his pitching style perfectly suits his personality, which is gentle, soft-spoken (he has a faint stammer), and mature.

The next day was even more pleasurable for the California ticket-holders. It was a much more absorbing game, in which Catfish Hunter and the Yankees led until Ron Cey put the home side in front, 4–2, with a three-run shot into the stands in the sixth inning, and its curtain was unsurpassable melodrama: the full-count swinging strikeout of Reggie Jackson by the rookie fastballer Bob Welch, with two out and two on in the ninth. Before that, the Dodgers had nearly come up with a big inning, in the fourth, and only three superior defensive plays by Graig Nettles at third, including a satin-smooth double play that he began with a tag of Steve Garvey in the base path, had kept things close. But no matter; it was better this way, because of the last scene. Reggie Jackson, the October man, had already driven in all three of the Yankee runs and seemed prepared to take charge of the entire pageant once again, as he did last year, with his famous outburst of five homers, three of them in succession in the final game. Bob Welch, his opponent here, looked like a casting director's stroke of genius—a large (six feet three), strong, good-looking blond youngster who seemed a bit overmatched in these straits but who was evidently eager to make up for that with luck and courage. Although he is not yet widely known to fans, Bob Welch is far from being a baseball nonentity. I had first seen him pitch two years ago, during a trip I made with a baseball scout to Eastern Michigan University. Welch was a college junior then, and ineligible for the baseball draft that year, but his size and poise and, most of all, his exploding fastball had the normally impassive scouts in ecstasies of aesthetic pleasure. This year, Eddie Kasko, the director of player procurement for the Red Sox, told me that Bob Welch is considered perhaps the finest pitching prospect to have turned up in the past decade. "Every other young pitcher we scout now is measured in comparison to Welch," Kasko said. "He is the standard." Welch signed with the Dodgers in June of 1977 and was called up to the parent club from their Albuquerque farm team in June of this year. He won seven games in his short National League season, including a critical win over the Giants in early August which began the Dodgers' catch-up.

The wonderful confrontation was executed in broad strokes. With the tying run on second base in the person of Bucky Dent, and with Paul Blair leading off from first, Jackson needed only a single to do his primary task, but his full, staggering foul cut at Welch's third fastball, on the one-and-one count, told us that Reggie was not interested in shortening up. This was all or nothing: the famous millionaire slugger was going to take the kid downtown. Two more burning fastballs were fouled off, with Reggie's lurching swing each time causing him to resemble a dangerously defective drilling machine, and we were all on our feet, yelling and pointing and laughing. Jackson took a ball, fouled off a high pitch, and took another ball, to run the count full. I had been secretly hoping that Welch would attempt a change-up, because it seemed possible that the Jackson machinery would break into several pieces when he swung at it, but Bob Welch, too, wanted this entertainment pure. He stared in, stretched, and reared, the two runners took off, fifty-six thousand fans yelled together, and Reggie cut mightily at a high fastball, swinging through it cleanly, and the game and the marvellous moment were over. Jackson, enraged at his failure, smashed his bat in the dugout, but he calmed down quickly. "The kid beat me," he said in the clubhouse.

Although the Dodgers were now two games to the good, some of the Dodger players seemed less than eager about their upcoming visit to New York. As they dressed after the game, several of them brought up the matter of Yankee Stadium fans, whom they had found to be a difficult and sometimes hostile audience last fall. "New York is very distracting," Ron Cey said, "I don't like all those obscenities. A lot of it is childish, in my opinion." Reggie Smith said, "I'm not going to be intimidated by the New York fans. It would mean a lot to win in front of them."

I found this curious, but I dismissed it as another evidence of the puzzling southern-California style, like the team's endless (and, to me, tasteless) public preoccupation with the death of its longtime first-base coach, Jim Gilliam, who died just before the Series began. The team had dedicated its World Series to him, and Manager Tom Lasorda and several players had made repeated mention of his helping spiritual presence during the first two games. Each Dodger now wore a small black circle on the sleeve of his uniform, with Gilliam's number, 19, in its center. In death, Gilliam had become another Dodger Stadium celebrity.

My own feelings about Yankee Stadium crowds, I should explain, are mixed. I do not enjoy their obscenity, and I detest their widespread drunkenness and the violence of their late-inning upper-deck brawls. On occasion, fans throw things at enemy outfielders, which is criminally dangerous. (The police say, by the way, that most of the troublemakers seem to be suburban youths, who drive to the games and often arrive at the Stadium already half drunk.) These societal disturbances are on the rise in most big-city sports gatherings, and are certainly not an exclusive problem of the Yankees, but I think the Yankee management people could do much more about controlling the young rioters in their audiences than they have attempted so far. None of this, however, has much to do with the Yankee Stadium fans' enthusiasm for their players—a screeching, passionate, hilarious extroversion that, if decibels are a fair gauge, equals, or perhaps surpasses, any other local loyalty in the game. The Yankees are loved, I sometimes think, just as deeply as they are hated; there seems to be no middle ground.

The Yankee-lovers were there in full numbers (56,447) and in full, crazy voice for Game Three. Guidry and Sutton were the pitchers, and the local citizenry screamed expectantly whenever Ron got to two strikes on a batter. But Guidry was having difficulties with his control on this evening, and wound up walking seven batters and striking out a bare four. Roy White hit a solo homer in the Yankee first, but the focus of this game, it turned out, was not the mound or the batter's box but the base paths. In the second inning, with Nettles and Chambliss aboard, Brian Doyle hit a grounder to Bill Russell, the Dodger shortstop, who flipped to Lopes at second to start the double play, but Chambliss, sliding in, tied up Lopes so neatly that he never got off his peg. An instant later, Lopes took Cey's peg for another force, but was wiped out by Doyle's body-block, which also averted a double play and allowed Nettles to score. The same aggressive, McGraw-like style of hardball again victimized Lopes in the seventh, this time with Paul Blair amputating him and forcing a low, poor throw to first—a maneuver that kept alive a three-run flurry that settled the edgy, 5–1 Yankee win. These are routine baserunning plays, of course, but the Yankees executed them vehemently. No Dodger infielder, by the way, distinguished himself in this game, or subsequently.

Even better things were visible around third base, however, for this was the game in which Graig Nettles had his coming-out party. He had plenty of business there, because of Guidry's indifferent stuff, and by subsequent estimation saved as many as seven Dodger runs in the game. In the third, he speared a line drive by Davey Lopes. Then he retired Reggie Smith by diving for his ground shot, collaring it on his knees in the dirt, and scrambling up to throw him out. In the fifth, he knocked down a difficult bouncer by Smith, holding him to a single instead of a double. A moment later, he flashed to his right to seize Steve Garvey's hard grounder; continuing with the momentum of the ball, he spun three-quarters around to his right, with his back to the plate, and got off his throw to second, for an inning-ending force. All this, of course, was done in less time than it takes to write it or read it here, and with perfect smoothness; the progress of the ball into Nettles' glove and, redirected, out of his throwing hand toward second was a single, stitchless movement. Anybody in the stands who was unlucky enough to miss this elegant maneuver was given a second chance in the ensuing inning, when Nettles graciously repeated it, as if on a televised replay; taking Lopes's tough grounder across his body and, spinning around again to his right, he threw out Mota at second, to end the inning and snuff out two Los Angeles runs.

Nettles' display vividly brought to mind Brooks Robinson's extended doctoral thesis on third-base play, which he presented in the otherwise unnotable World Series of 1970, between the Orioles and the Reds. Nettles' work around the bag this fall, like Robinson's then, made plain for a national audience what local watchers had already understood—that he is the great third sacker of his day. It also occasioned a good deal of speculation as to whether Nettles might be Brooks Robinson's superior. (It is certain that Nettles—a left-handed slugger who has averaged twenty-seven home runs per year in his six years with the Yankees—is a more powerful hitter than Robinson was.) Nettles himself seemed to have the best answer to this unanswerable question. "I feel I can play third as well as anybody," he said. "I've played it well for ten years. If I can do it for another ten years, I'll put myself in Brooksie's class."

All this raises the interesting possibility that a few infielders do get better and better as the years go by. Mark Belanger, who played shortstop beside Brooks Robinson for a decade, is now thirty-four but consistently makes plays that his teammates say would have been beyond his abilities a few summers back.

Nettles is also thirty-four, which would seem to be a bit past the prime for a position that calls for instant reactions, but experience and defensive adjustments count for more at the hot corner than some people realize. Like many other third basemen, Nettles almost always knows whether the next pitch will be a curve or a fastball—he receives the message from his shortstop—and adjusts, or leans, accordingly. He also studies batters' eyes as they flick a glance in his direction before stepping in. Although he plays a deep third, he sometimes feints another step back, inviting the bunt.

After the game, Bob Lemon said, "I don't think anyone has ever played third base better than that."

Game Four was the fulcrum; when it was over, the weight of this strange World Series had shifted irreversibly. The game was a long, multi-part affair that ran from mid-afternoon to mid-evening, with a forty-minute delay for rain in the third inning—a humid, draggy entertainment, in truth, until Reggie Smith, the admirable Los Angeles slugger (he had not been himself at the plate so far, probably because of a recent touch of the flu), whacked a three-run homer off Ed Figueroa in the fifth. Tommy John was pitching for the Dodgers, and the Yankees' prospects again appeared dismal. Then, with one out in the sixth, White singled and Munson walked, and Jackson delivered the first New York run of the game with a single. This situated the principals for the notorious events to follow: Munson on second, Jackson on first, Piniella at bat. Lou hit a soft, low liner to the left of shortstop Bill Russell, who had it in his glove for a moment and then dropped it. (Some press-box watchers felt that Russell had misplayed the ball on purpose, in order to go for two outs instead of one, but I was not convinced.) Recapturing the ball quickly, Russell crossed the bag, forcing Jackson, and threw toward Garvey for the D.P. But Reggie, who had stopped in his tracks when Russell caught the ball, was nearly in the path of the throw, perhaps fifteen feet in front of first base, and at the last instant he appeared to twitch his right hip slightly. The ball struck him and deflected past Garvey and into foul ground, and Munson, who had retreated toward second, reversed course and scored easily. The Dodgers—roaring, pointing, pleading—cried interference, but the first- and second-base umps (who were in proper position but in the wrong line to see Jackson in relation to the flight of the thrown ball) said no. The case was over, though not its endless rehearings in the moot court of the clubhouse.

The game went on. The Dodgers still led, 3–2, and Tommy John retired the Yankees harmlessly in the seventh. Dick Tidrow had come in to pitch for the Yanks. It was night now, and the air was fresher and suddenly much colder. The day and the weather had turned, and, with them, the pace and feeling of the game. The immense throngs packed into the long sweep of the lower stands were transformed into blackness and faces—thousands of pale oval dots, row upon row. The grass lightened, and the infield dirt, now illuminated, had turned from brown to gray. Summer was over.

Paul Blair, leading off the Yankee eighth, singled through the left side. Terry Forster came in to pitch for the Dodgers. Roy White, bunting on Forster's first pitch, sacrificed Blair to second, and Munson, his bat flashing, pulled a sudden double that bounced just inside the white foul line behind third, two inches fair. The game was tied. Bob Welch came on and struck out Graig Nettles for the last out in the eighth. Sailing through the ninth, he fanned Chris Chambliss and Jim Spencer. Gossage was the Yankee pitcher now, and he, too, looked to be entirely in control of things: two big, overpowering fastballers going head to head, throwing nothing but heat. It was riveting. With one out in the tenth, Roy White walked. After Munson popped up, Reggie Jackson, swinging less recklessly this time, nudged a single to right that moved White along. Lou Piniella cut at Welch's first fastball and missed (his helmet, as always, half toppling off, and his empty swing, as always, concluding in a little one-footed double hop on his back leg). Enveloped in noise ("Lou! Lou! Louuuu!"), Piniella took a ball and then drove Welch's next delivery—a high, outside fastball—quickly and cleanly into right center, for a hit and a run and the game. A few minutes later, in the interview room, Piniella said that Welch reminded him of Jim Palmer. "But we're all professional hitters here," he went on. "If you get nothing but fastballs, sooner or later you're going to hit one."

Of the deflection, Jackson said, "It was in my road and it hit me." He smiled slightly and enigmatically, relishing the moment. Tom Lasorda was loud and adjectival: it was interference, but nothing could be done about it.

Steve Garvey's testimony was significant, for he had been closest to the scene of the accident. He claimed that the throw would have hit Jackson in any case, and that Reggie's rumba step had been not into the ball but a bit away from it.

I asked him if he thought Jackson's move toward the ball—if in fact he *did* move—constituted cheating.

He thought about it for a moment. Garvey, of course, is baseball's most celebrated straight arrow; his probity and his spotless image have brought him much celebrity. There is even a school in California named in his honor: Steve Garvey Junior High.

"I think maybe it comes under a subcategory of cheating," he said at last smiling. "How does that go—you're only cheating if you get caught, otherwise it's a heads-up play?"

I asked him if he would have done the same thing in Jackson's place.

Again he paused. "I don't think so," he said at last.

The Jackson ricochet, in spite of its consequences in the game, was a trifle, possibly only an accident, but reactions to it diverge and are perhaps irreconcilable. Yankee-haters (there are millions of them) will seize upon it as another example of the team's unlovable, coldhearted, big-city ways—its attention to the main chance, its weakness for success at any price. I tend to the other view. Baseball, in its immense variety, offers sudden, glimmering opportunities for victory—sometimes an opportunity never seen before in the history of the game—and many of these lie in the outer fringes of legality. I don't think the purpose of sport is to build purity of character, and I have a sneaky fondness for the quick-eyed player who walks in this borderland searching intently for the minute gleam of advantage at his feet, the prize among the weeds. Jackson's twitch, an almost unconscious reaction, was the same kind of baseball instinct that he and his quarrelsome, brilliant teammates on the Oakland A's demonstrated again and again during their three-year tenure as world champions in the early nineteen-seventies. They thought always about winning, and, one way or another, they almost always did win. Like the A's, these Yankees have street-smarts. They win.

* * *

After that the baseball was less rewarding. The Yankees won the next day, 12–2, in a terrible ballgame. The Dodgers made three errors and a wild pitch, and gave up two passed balls, and several of the Yankees' eighteen hits caromed off or zipped past Dodger infielders. Brian Doyle and Bucky Dent, the bottom two batters in the Yankee order, were six for nine for the day. Jim Beattie went all the way, permitting no Dodger runs after the third inning. It was embarrassing.

The finale, back in Los Angeles (which I watched on television), was mercifully better, but the Yankees, behind Catfish Hunter, led from the second inning on, and won by 7–2. Doyle and Dent, enjoying themselves like kids at a picnic, went six for *eight* this time. (After the game was over, Bucky Dent was voted the Most Valuable Player of the Series, but several other Yankees were scarcely less splendid. Brian Doyle, for instance, played solid, impeccable ball as a fill-in at second base and batted .438; he had begun this season, incidentally, as a utility infielder in Tacoma.) The final two Yankee runs of the year came on a very long home run by Reggie Jackson in the seventh inning, struck off a first-pitch fastball by Bob Welch. Reggie tipped his hat to the Dodger fans as he crossed the plate. Everything had been settled in the end, it seemed.

As the Dodgers began to lose, they began to complain. Before they headed back to Los Angeles after the fifth game, with their two-game lead demolished and their hopes almost gone, some of them seemed to give way altogether. Tom Lasorda suggested that the heavy infield grass at the Stadium explained Graig Nettles' brilliance. Bill Russell blamed the New York sportswriters and the New York fans for his team's bad showing. "With fifty-six thousand screaming people out there, it's hard to concentrate," he said. "It's tough to play here. [The writers] are the worst. The fans are the worst. The city is the worst." Rick Monday said, "I don't like the park, I don't like the town. I don't understand their way of life."

It was not the grass or the press or the fans who beat the Dodgers, of course; it was the Yankees. The Dodgers contributed to their own downfall with their consistently poor defensive play, and they suffered at the plate because Reggie Smith was not in full health and because their other prime offensive star, Steve Garvey, fell into a sudden and uncharacteristic batting slump. The Dodgers have now lost all three World Series in which they have appeared in the past five years, and its young veterans may secretly think of themselves as losers. This is debilitating, of course, but it does not quite explain the whining of Russell and Monday, which is not at all characteristic of professional athletes. It seems to me that these malcontents, and perhaps a good many other Dodger players as well, have been distracting themselves in a significant and frightful way. This is more than a matter of style; it is a true delusion. I think the Dodgers have begun to believe in their carefully nurtured, highly publicized image, which is that of an exceptionally attractive family of modest, friendly, good-looking young citizens; they seem to feel that in some way they embody a preserved American innocence, and thus represent a higher and more valuable element of our society than their rivals do. The team has reached a moral conclusion about itself, which is rarely a useful idea, in sports or elsewhere. This narcissism is the result of a bedazzling mix of money, youthful success, good luck, good looks, sunshine, public adulation, and ceaseless self-congratulatory public relations. It is a deeply provincial mind-set, endemic to southern California, and it explains why the Dodgers—some of them, anyway—settled so readily and unquestioningly into a currently popular attitude about New York City, which is to look at the place as if it were all one piece, and to despise it. New York residents—most of them, I think—tend toward the opposite mode, which is to see their city as being made up of several thousand or several million different ideas and forces, problems and losses, horrors and triumphs, each one of which must be subjected to scrutiny and to a separate conclusion. This takes time, but it avoids dreadful mistakes. The Dodgers got the Yankees mixed up with New York City itself. No wonder they sounded like children. No wonder they lost.

The process of selectivity and judgment, the big-city shake-out, must now be applied to the big-city champions, the Yankees, if we are to see the team for what it is and to appreciate what kind of a baseball year it was in the end. The Yankees are the most distracting sports phenomenon of our time—even more complex and emotive than Muhammad Ali—and it is difficult to think about them without falling victim to one's feelings or conclusions about George Steinbrenner and Billy

Martin, or Reggie Jackson and Joe DiMaggio, or free agents and inconceivably large sports salaries, or dirty-mouthed fans and drinking in the stands and infields being torn to bits by souvenir hunters at the end of the season. These are disturbing issues and people, but it is sad and diminishing if we can't manage to put them to one side and press on to the team itself, to the baseball.

A friend of mine from Santa Monica dropped into my office a few days after the Series was over, and railed at length against his Dodgers. "They were terrible," he said. "They just went to pieces." I suggested that the Yankees themselves had done pretty well this year, but he would have none of it. "I can't stand them," he exclaimed bitterly. "Reggie Jackson and all the rest of them. That Jackson—nobody can convince me *he's* a ballplayer!"

Just the same, I will try. In 1977, Reggie Jackson established nine new slugging records in the World Series and tied five others. In eleven postseason games last year, he batted .306, hit five homers, and batted in nine runs. This year, Jackson was much less spectacular, but in his eleven 1978 postseason games (including the playoff at Fenway Park) he batted .400, hit five homers, and drove in fifteen runs. He was better than last year. The Yankees were better, too—so good, in fact, that there is immense pleasure for me (and I am not a Yankee fan, as someone may have guessed by now) in looking back once more at what they did. After August 24th, they won thirty-seven games and lost twelve, in the most gruelling circumstances imaginable. No other American League team has ever made up a fourteen-game deficit, and no other team has ever lost the first two games of a World Series and then won it in four straight games.* The Yankees will be different next year, because the free-agent market now requires a winning team to change its personnel more rapidly from year to year. They may win again next year, but it is unlikely that they will be better. The people who most appreciated the 1978 Yankees were the 1978 Red Sox, and I will always remember the flood of compliments one heard in both clubhouses after the great playoff game in Fenway Park—all the Yankees expressing their ad-

*The Dodgers matched this latter achievement in their comeback six-game victory over the Yankees in the 1981 World Series.

miration for the Red Sox players who had so nearly beaten them, all the heartbroken Boston players saying wonderful things about the Yankees. Jerry Remy, the Red Sox second baseman, said, "They're a great ball team. As far as I'm concerned, this was the World Series this year. One run at the end of the year deciding it all. . . . They're a hell of a ball team." Then he said it again. "A hell of a team."

7

Sharing the Beat

MARCH 1979

EARLY THIS MONTH, A FEW WEEKS BEFORE THE BEGINNING OF the new baseball season, Commissioner Bowie Kuhn sent an advisory memorandum to the twenty-six major-league clubs suggesting new regulations to govern the admission of female reporters to the teams' clubhouses this year. He said that the matter would be largely left to the discretion of the individual teams (as it is in professional basketball, hockey, and football), and urged all the clubs to do what they could to "minimize problems in this area" and to take steps "to afford identical access, in one way or another, to all reporters, regardless of sex." The initial response from the clubs suggests that in about half of the twenty-six ballparks women reporters will now have some form of postgame access to the clubhouses, at least for a time. The practical effects of Mr. Kuhn's dictum remain to be seen—specifically, whether male and female reporters will be able to talk to the players on a truly equal basis, and whether access to the clubhouses for all reporters will be more restricted than it has been in the past. On the surface, however, the new plan does seem to represent a change of direction for the Commissioner, who was taken to court last year in a celebrated case for his refusal to allow women reporters to enter the home-team and visitors clubhouses at Yankee Stadium. The plaintiffs—Melissa Ludtke, a young reporter for *Sports Illustrated*, and her employer, Time, Inc.—said that Miss Ludtke had been excluded from the clubhouse during the 1977 World Series (between the Yankees and the Dodgers), and claimed that the exclusion had been based solely on her sex, thus violating Miss Ludtke's right to pursue her profession under the equal-protection and due-process clauses of the Fourteenth Amendment. Mr. Kuhn, speaking for his sport and his co-defendants (the Yankees, the president of the American League, and the Mayor and other officials of the City of New York, which owns Yankee Stadium), responded in an affidavit that he had ordered women reporters kept out of all major-league clubhouses in order to protect the "sexual privacy" of players who were undressing and showering, to protect the image of baseball as a family sport, and to preserve traditional notions of decency and propriety. His tone suggested that the suit posed a threat to the game almost equal to the Black Sox scandal. He stated that the American public accepts baseball as "emblematic of the highest standards of integrity and morality in professional sports," and that the "standards of conduct and the attitudes and behavior of people in the 'big leagues' often serve as role models for millions of children." He said that "to permit members of the opposite sex into this place of privacy, where players, who are, of course, men, are in a state of undress, would be to undermine the basic dignity of the game."

The case was first heard last April before Judge Constance Baker Motley, in Federal District Court in New York, who found for the plaintiffs. She enjoined the Yankees from further exclusion of women from the Stadium clubhouses unless men were also excluded, and said that the privacy of the players could be adequately assured by installing a curtain or a swinging door in front of each player's dressing cubicle, or simply by instructing the players to wear towels. The Stadium locker rooms become officially heterosexual on September 26th, during the last week of the 1978 regular season. Because the Commissioner had said that the court's edict would not apply to any other major-league clubhouses, women reporters were still barred from the players' quarters at Veterans Stadium, in Philadelphia, and at Dodger Stadium, in Los Angeles, during the National League playoffs, and also at the Kansas City

Royals' stadium during the American League playoff games there, between the Royals and the Yankees. During the World Series, no women reporters were admitted to either clubhouse in Dodger Stadium, but they did come into both clubhouses at Yankee Stadium during the three Series games there.

Bowie Kuhn did not have a very happy time of it in the courts last fall. His concern for the privacy of his players and for the protection of baseball as a family sport was dismissed by Judge Motley as being "clearly too insubstantial to merit serious consideration." The Commissioner then requested Judge Motley to stay her order while his attorneys prepared an appeal, but was denied. Persisting, he did win a clarifying order from Judge Motley, in which she explained that the Yankees' options included the right to ban all reporters, male and female, from their clubhouses for a period long enough to permit the players to dress, and to ban them altogether if a separate interview room were provided. During the World Series, Mr. Kuhn moved along to the Second Circuit Court of Appeals in search of a stay of action while baseball's official appeal was polished up. *This* motion was denied almost immediately by a three-judge panel. The presiding jurist, Judge Walter Mansfield, commenting on the "baseball is a family game" argument, said, "The last I heard, the family includes women as well as men." On February 8th of this year, Mr. Kuhn and his attorneys dropped their appeal. The matter is out of the courts, at least for the present.

In recent weeks, Mr. Kuhn seems to have moved away from his obdurate, arms-akimbo stance at the clubhouse door. He consulted at length with editors and lawyers at Time, Inc., before issuing his memorandum to the clubs. This is commendable, I guess, but no memorandum can wipe out the injuries and strong feelings that have arisen from this conflict, whose meanings may go deeper into American sport and the American unconscious than most of us would admit.

Women in the clubhouse is an emotional issue—almost a parade float of classical postures in which noble-visaged representations of Propriety, Wholesome Sports, and the Innocence of the American Family are seen to be under attack by similarly admirable figures representing Social Mobility, Equal Opportunity, and Freedom of the Press. Evaluating public response to this crowded tableau is extremely difficult, and even among professional journalists there appears to be a wide swing between public and private attitudes, between conscious scruples and unconscious fears and wishes. Many male reporters I have talked to support their female colleagues' claim that any ban or limitation on their admission to the clubhouse is discriminatory and places them at an impossible disadvantage in their trade. Other male reporters admit all this but still oppose the change, because it offends their sense of propriety or chivalry, or because it seems to violate the players' right to privacy within their den, or simply because it shatters tradition. All the male sportswriters, however, are concerned about the evident possibility that Commissioner Kuhn's recent ruling will lead to severe limitations on their own rights and long habits of access to the ballplayers—specifically, on their being able to talk to them in the clubhouse immediately after the last out, when the sweaty, beer-gulping young participants are fresh in their memories of the game, and their reactions (exultant or despondent, bitter or comical or evasive) may be taken down or taped and translated at once into the heart of the next edition's story or column or sidebar on the game. Women sportswriters, who as yet make up a very small percentage of the total, have the same concern about any limitation of access, but they have sharper and more personal feelings of anxiety. Almost all of them have encountered the closed lockerroom door, in baseball and in other sports, and the professional leagues that have reversed themselves and opened some of their clubhouses—notably the National Basketball Association and the National Hockey League—have done so only after prolonged skirmishing with a few vehement pioneering women writers and their editors. For the most part, women reporters have had to cajole individual players into emerging, half-dressed or clutching a towel, for a fragmentary interview in a corridor or an equipment room, or have had to wait outside the door interminably, dying by inches as a deadline crept closer, until the players emerged—combed and dressed, homeward- or hotelward-bound, and often sucked dry of news by multiple interviews—and then have had to beg them to summon up again the now receding contest. One alternative to the open locker room is a separate, formal interview room, to which the rival managers and a few individual stars or goats may be summoned, to testify into a battery of microphones, like some visiting rock star or foreign minister. Interview rooms are now customary at championship games or all-star games in most major sports, for they offer an alternative to the noise and crush of the locker rooms, where several hundred newspaper and magazine and TV and radio reporters are trying to get at a handful of bewildered athletes. The interview room, however, usually yields a guarded, statesmanlike form of sports news, or a succession of wrenching one-liners by athletes and coaches who secretly envision themselves as television personalities. Other variations suggested in the wake of the Motley decision—the closing of the locker rooms until all the players are dressed, or a fifteen- or twenty-minute interview period inside the clubhouse, followed by the departure of all media people—seem inadequate or stifling in comparison with an open clubhouse, in which a quick and questing sportswriter can search out conflicting game stories, rumors, whispers of team feuds, hidden injuries, managerial pomposities, salary discontents, or incipient trades, all in a day's or a night's work. Reporters are endlessly harassed by bureaucratic obstacles to their labors, and the smallest hint of some fresh restraint to their freedom elicits instant outrage and cries for redress. Women sportswriters find a clanging irony in all this, for the real or threatened limitations to the male reporters' working customs in baseball as a result of Ludtke v. Kuhn are exactly the same handicaps that women on the sports beat have had to put up with all along. These women, who have never received much public support from their colleagues, are concerned now that any rules imposed by the various clubs in response to their presence on the baseball scene will cause fresh bitterness among their male adversaries, and will even turn their supporters against them in the end. The women sportswriters—and many of the men, too—suspect that this may be the secret hope of not a few sports executives.

Notoriety pursues the Yankees everywhere, and vice versa, and the arrival of the first female reporters in the Yankee clubhouse last September had perfectly predictable results. On the night that Judge Motley's order took effect, the Yankee clubhouse was suddenly crowded with strangers, male and female, who had come to report on the new socio-journalistic phenomenon. Most of the women, I have been told (I was not there), were local television reporters, and they smilingly asked the players what they thought about the presence of women in the locker room, while the cameras caught it all. This, by the way, was the last Tuesday of the regular season, and the Yankees, who were playing the Toronto Blue Jays that night, were then leading the Boston Red Sox by a single game. Reggie Jackson, after delivering his opinion about the admission of women to the clubhouse (for, with reservations) to Carol Jenkins, of WNBC News, finally said, "Aren't you going to ask about this pennant race we're in?" An Associated Press photographer snapped a picture of Willie Randolph, who was naked, talking to a female reporter; Randolph was furious—not about the interview but about the photo. Clyde King, a Yankee coach, came out of the shower room with no clothes on and jumped back in. Goose Gossage pulled off a towel worn by Coach Art Fowler. Still another coach, Gene Michael, delivered an angry harangue about women reporters and their motives. So did some of the players, the two loudest being reserve outfielder Jay Johnstone and backup catcher Cliff Johnson. Most of the other players seemed calm. A day or two later, Johnstone tacked up an obscene message about Judge Motley over his cubicle, and relief pitcher Sparky Lyle brought in a cake in the shape of a phallus with the message "For Women Sportswriters Only" on it.

After the first night, however, the clubhouse was a much quieter place, and the players, caught up in their excruciating race, talked mostly baseball. On Friday night, the Yankees, now in possession of Judge Motley's clarifying order, announced that the clubhouse would be closed to all reporters for forty-five minutes after the game, to permit the players to shower and dress. The reporters—most of them regulars who had been covering the club all summer—were badly upset. There was some angry shouting in the press elevator between writers and club executives; during the game, Yankee owner George Steinbrenner conferred with several local newspapermen at the back of the press box, and a compromise was worked out: the clubhouse would remain open for fifteen minutes immediately after the game, to accommodate writers for the morning papers and late-news TV reporters, and then would close for thirty minutes. A week later, when the Royals came to town for the playoff games at the Stadium, the clubhouse remained open for an initial forty-five minutes, and this period was extended to an hour during the subsequent World Series games in New York. Several women reporters and photographers came into the clubhouse during the Series games, but no one seemed to pay any special attention to them.

I had begun to pay attention, however. I missed the first-night sideshow at the Stadium—fortunately, I thought—and my subsequent visits (I was there as a reporter) indicated only that scandal and innovation were giving way to acceptance and custom, which was all right with me. It was not all right, I had begun to notice, with a lot of other people. Sports columnists across the country took up the Ludtke decision, and a great many of them suggested that women sportswriters had fought and struggled and finally gone to the courts to get into the clubhouse mostly because they wanted to ogle naked athletes. This was generally put in the form of a joke. "Folks, I'm all for equal rights for gals," it went, "but what about *my* equal rights? When do I get into a locker room to interview Chrissie Evert with her clothes off?" A lot of my friends— male friends—got off this same joke, and I think I may have smiled at it the first eight or ten times I heard it. (The question it poses, although the question is not its point, is easily answered: in women's professional tennis—and in most other women's sports—the athletes are interviewed immediately after the match is over, at courtside or in some neutral area; the locker rooms are closed to all reporters.) I was not much startled by the columns I read, but the names of some of the columnists did surprise me—surprised me both ways. Dick Young, the conservative, enormously popular sports columnist for the *News* (he is also its sports editor), accepted the arrival of women reporters in the clubhouse as being no less than their due; he suggested that all professional teams might do well to follow the example set three or four years ago by the New York Cosmos, of the North American Soccer League, who had issued bathrobes to their players and then welcomed all reporters. (More recently, during an appearance on "The Dick Cavett Show," Mr. Young revived the women-tennis-players joke and then went on to suggest by innuendo that women sportswriters give sexual favors to athletes as a means of getting news.) Red Smith, in a column that appeared in the *Times* shortly after the

Ludtke suit was instituted, came out on the side of player privacy and the interview room—thus allying himself, almost for the first time ever, with Bowie Kuhn. Writing with his customary lightness and civility, he said that Melissa Ludtke would be much better off in an interview room than she would be being "buffeted, elbowed, and trampled" in the winning locker room after the last game of the World Series. "Had she been thus occupied," he concluded, "she would have missed the gathering in another room [the interview room, that is] down the hall, where managers of both teams and key players on both sides were present to answer all her questions." This was the last line of Mr. Smith's column in the *Times*, but when the syndicated piece appeared in many out-of-town papers it terminated with one more sentence: "Still, she might have got to see Reggie in the buff."

Other things happened in the lively and familiar settings of autumn baseball that began to make me owlish. In the crowded pressrooms and hospitality rooms of the playoffs and the World Series, where hundreds of reporters—almost all of them men, of course—gathered, as usual, to talk shop and to drink and pass the time of day, the Ludtke case and its rulings were frequently discussed, and in the course of the conversations I often heard Melissa Ludtke defamed by people in her own profession. Her reportorial abilities, her seriousness, her motives for bringing the suit , her appearance, and her private life were snickered at and vilified. Only some of the writers talked this way, and none of the remarks came from members of the New York press corps, who know Melissa Ludtke, as I do, as a hardworking young professional and as a friend. (Her name, by the way, is now Melissa Ludtke Lincoln. She was married last year to Eric Lincoln, who is an editor and reporter with the sports department of the *Times*.) I was startled by the slanders, not just because I know Miss Ludtke but because the worst of them were delivered with a perceptible, barely concealed rage—verbal hate mail. Something was going on here.

After the last out of the first game of the World Series, which the Dodgers won, 11–5, in their home park (they won the next game, too, it will be recalled, and then dropped four straight games and the Series to the Yankees), I took an elevator down to the clubhouse level of Dodger Stadium and hurried to the interview room, where, in company with scores of other reporters, I heard Ron Cey and Tommy John and Dodger manager Tom Lasorda and others describe their cheerful recent adventures. I left before the interviews were over, heading for the locker rooms, and on the way out I nodded to another woman sportswriter I know, B. J. Phillips, who was taking notes for her story; she is an associate editor of *Time* and is its chief writer on sports. Thirty or forty minutes later, emerging from the Yankee dressing rooms, I came into a sort of rotunda that lies between the two locker rooms and is open to the public, and there I saw B. J. Phillips again. She was leaning against a railing and was bent over in an odd posture and clutching her notebook. She was still wearing her press credentials—a large printed blue ticket, which was fastened by its string to her blouse. I went over and asked rather casually if something was wrong (she was a recent acquaintance, whom I had met for the first time the previous week, at the National League playoffs in Philadelphia), and when she looked up I saw that her eyes were swimming. She glared at me, and in a strangled voice she said, "I won't cry! I *won't!* I won't let the bastards make me cry!"

She told me that when she had left the interview room, in company with many other writers, she had started down the corridor leading to the rotunda and had been met there by two public-relations men, representing the Commissioner, who barred her path, even though she told them that she was not heading for the Dodger locker room, which she knew was closed to women. One of the men politely explained that she had been issued the wrong credentials; he proffered her a yellow credential card, on which someone's name had been crossed out and hers written in. "There's been a mistake," the P.R. man said. "*These* are your credentials." B. J. Phillips—aware, of course, that a yellow credential card did not entitle its bearer to enter the clubhouses—said that she was keeping the credentials she had been mailed. Again she said to the men that she had no intention of going into the locker room. She told them that lawyers for Time, Inc., had undertaken negotiations with the Commissioner's office, before the World Series, to have her admitted there, but had failed. She told the men that she did not believe in confrontation. She said, however, that she would not give up her blue credential card. "I treated that yellow card like a dead rat," she told me. The men still would not allow her to go down the corridor and ordered her to leave via a tunnel leading to the Dodger dugout and then out onto the field. "You even have a servants' entrance for us, don't you?" she said, giving up at last. When she reached the field, she discovered that the only way she could return to the rotunda and the elevators to the parking lot was through the lower grandstands. There were loiterers and drunks still in the stands, who saw her credential card and offered loud suggestions about why she had been in the Dodger clubhouse and what she had seen there.

B. J. Phillips had stopped crying by the time she told me all this, but then she looked up and noticed several TV reporters and camera crews approaching, and again she looked stricken. "I'm the wrong person for this," she murmured. "I *hate* this. I want anonymity. It's the only way for a reporter to work." (She and her story did subsequently appear on national television, though.) I said something encouraging to her, and then I left, promising that I would bring her any interesting comments I could pick up in the Dodger locker room, where I was listening to the players, I kept thinking about her, and then, uneasily, I remembered making the same kind of promise to Melissa Ludtke in previous years, at previous important games or Series games in New York and Boston and Philadelphia and Cincinnati and other cities, when I had glimpsed her outside the doors of different clubhouses, standing among the pushing, jammed-together fans and hangers-on and guards and kids and policemen while she waited for some ballplayer to come out and answer her questions. Sometimes I remembered my promise to Melissa, and sometimes I forgot it, because the truth is that I hardly thought about the matter. I was always sure I was doing her a favor, or was about to.

Since last October, I have tried to think about this a little more, and I have asked a lot of people about women in the clubhouse. I have talked to athletes and sports executives and male sportswriters, but most of all I have tried to listen to the women sportswriters themselves. Their voices seemed to be charged with a special resonance. They spoke as if they represented some foreign constituency within us all that has been waiting and wondering if it would ever be remembered or dealt with. Sports, I keep reminding myself, mean a lot in this country.

Women sports reporters and announcers have been turning up in increasing numbers on television screens and on the radio; some of the TV reporters, like their male counterparts, seem to have been hired mostly for their looks. It is extremely difficult to find out how many women are now employed as working sportswriters on newspapers. I talked about this not long ago with Le Anne Schreiber, who is the sports editor of the *Times* and at the moment is the only woman journalist on its sports staff. "Women sportswriters are still a very small minority," she told me. "Newspaper sports departments all around the country are beginning to hire women, but in a pretty gingerly way. I lost an experienced reporter, Robin Herman, to our Metropolitan Desk this year, and I'm looking for qualified women right now—and qualified men, too. The Washington *Post* just hired its third woman for sports. Any paper that has taken on a second or third woman in its sports department has probably moved beyond tokenism."

Women sportswriters are not a perfectly new phenomenon. Some years ago, I remember, the *Times* had a former champion golfer named Maureen Orcutt on its staff, who covered women's golf. Another woman, Jeane Hoffman, used to write about baseball and other sports for the *Journal-American*—stories about Edna Stengel and that sort of thing. Mary Garber, who is in her sixties, has been covering tennis, track, football, and basketball—Atlantic Coast Conference college games, for the most part—for the Winston-Salem *Journal* ever since 1944. But these have been rarities, like women surgeons or women railroad conductors, and only in the past seven or eight years have greater numbers of young women who were starting careers in journalism begun to give serious consideration to the sports beat. In many newspaper sports departments, they are still looked upon as oddities. Several male sportswriters I know have told me that they have never met or worked with a woman who seemed to know anything about sports, and others were dubious about women's motives or sports experience. Speculating on this subject in the Boston *Globe* last fall, Leigh Montville ("Leigh," in this case, is a man's name) wrote,

I have only a few questions. . . . I ask them because I am serious and I wonder if the lady is serious. . . . That is all I would want to know about anyone in this business. . . . Did she grow up on sports? Was her life absolutely dominated by sports when she was a kid? . . . Has she ever held a hockey stick in her hands? Has she ever shot a basketball from behind a pick? Has she ever set a pick? Was she ever given a subscription to the *Sporting News* for Christmas? Did she ever spit in a baseball glove?

And so on. Some of the women in sports I have talked to would pass Mr. Montville's test, and others might not. There doesn't seem to be any pattern to it.

B. J. Phillips: (*She is of medium height, with pale, wide-set eyes and a humorous, combative expression. She attended the University of Georgia in the mid-sixties and then dropped out. There is a faint trace of Georgia in her speech. She has been a news reporter with the Atlanta* Constitution *and the Washington* Post. *She joined the staff of* Time *in 1970, and wrote national news. She won an Alicia Patterson Fellowship in 1973, and went to Vietnam and Ireland and the Middle East. When she returned to* Time, *she began to cover sports. What "B. J." stands for is a secret; no one except her family knows. Thirty-five years old.*)

"I think if I'd been a guy I'd have been a sportswriter from the start. I've always thought sports was a poorly reported and misunderstood phenomenon. I took the chance when it came. I think I was tired of writing about dead people. I like sports. I like to get into things. I played short center on the *Time* softball team two years ago, when we won our championship. I won a Gold Glove for my fielding, and I batted over .400 for the season.

"I think I have a reputation as being a pretty tough lady. I've been around. I was a marcher in the sixties. When I was with the *Post*, I covered Woodstock, the Apollo 13 space shot, Capitol Hill—everything. I've picked up a severed leg outside a blown-out pub in Northern Ireland, I've interviewed women terrorists, I've heard a President of the United States lie at a press conference. But the first time in twelve years I've been forced to tears in public was there in Dodger Stadium. To think it was the World Series that did it—it's ludicrous. It's like that line 'It's so sad it makes you want to laugh; it's so sad it makes you want to cry.' I've been treated worse in sports than anywhere else. I've never felt that resentment anywhere else. I covered a series of games between the Royals and the White Sox in Chicago three years ago, and nobody in the press box spoke to me for three days. Nobody. I'm bitter about what happens to women sportswriters. I can't accept it.

"You know, after I was on television that time, I heard a lot of people say, 'Some people will do anything for publicity.' Jesus Christ! I can get all the publicity I want, from my own work. I wrote the first cover story *Time* ever ran on Jimmy Carter. Last year, I wrote four cover stories and won a Page One Award for a sports piece. But that doesn't matter to some people. What hurts is that so much of this comes from my professional colleagues, who know why access is essential in our business. It *kills* me that my peers treat women writers with an attitude that says they're something between a pariah and a sex-crazed thrill seeker. It hurts privately. I don't think anybody knows the price we're paying.

"It confuses me when I realize that there are men who really can't see that what we care about in the locker room is not the naked bodies but our work. They can't seem to grasp that. I'm treated like a pervert for trying to do my work. It's clear that something has these people terrified. I don't understand what's behind it. I don't understand the social dynamic. Maybe I'm dense. I just don't get it."

Robin Herman: *(She is tall, with dark hair. She graduated summa cum laude from Princeton in 1973—the first Princeton class to admit women as freshmen. In college, she joined the* Daily Princetonian, *the undergraduate newspaper, and eventually became its sports co-editor. She was a member of Phi Beta Kappa. She joined the* Times *in 1973, and was quickly assigned to cover the New York Islanders, in the National Hockey League. Later, she became the* Times *writer covering the New York Rangers. She has also covered professional basketball. She is now on general assignment for the Metropolitan Desk. Twenty-seven years old.)*

"I didn't get deeply interested in sports until I was sent to the Islanders. A professional curiosity sets in, and you realize that if you're going to do it right you have to learn everything. You've got to be right. I was sent to the Islanders because they were an expansion team, way out in the boonies, and nobody else wanted to cover them.

"I was one of the first women to get into a National Hockey League locker room, but now all the teams except five—Chicago, Buffalo, Toronto, Detroit, and St. Louis—let women in. Each of them has an old-line ownership or an old hockey figure who has stood in the way. Bob Pulford, in Chicago, is a decent man, but he's adamant about this. There was a lot of trouble with the Atlanta Flames. Their coach, Fred Creighton, told me that he was against it, but that he didn't know about the players. I asked if he'd poll them, and when he did they voted unanimously to let us in. So Fred said it was O.K. It always seems easy when it finally happens.

"I was covering the N.H.L. All-Star Game back in 1975, in Montreal, and at a press conference before the game Leo Monahan, of the Boston *Herald American*, asked the two coaches, 'When are you going to let accredited women reporters into your clubhouses?' The coaches were Fred Shero and Bep Guidolin, and they sort of looked at each other and shrugged and said it would be O.K. that night. That was how it all began. It was treated like a joke. Marcelle St. Cyr, who'd been broadcasting Canadiens games for Station CKLM, in Montreal, and I were the first women in. I had no plans to make it happen, or anything. I couldn't believe it. All-star games are sort of boring, and Marcelle and I were the story that night, not the players. There were a lot of jokes and pranks.

"The Rangers didn't let any women in that year. Emile Francis was the general manager, and he said that the players' wives would object. Somebody always says that, but I don't believe it anymore. Once the players get used to you, it never comes up again. When John Ferguson took over at the Rangers in the middle of the 1975–76 season, I asked him if I could get in. Ferguson is a macho, no-nonsense sort of guy, but he has a real sense of fairness. He just waved his arm toward the locker room. I said 'You mean? . . .' and he nodded. Later on, when Lawrie Mifflin had started writing hockey for the *News*, he even offered to try to ban *all* reporters from the visiting-team locker room at Madison Square Garden if a visiting team wouldn't let women in, but we said no, we didn't want that.

Can you imagine how that would have gone over with the other writers? Wow!

"Hockey players are friendly and polite, but basketball players are a lot looser. Most of them are black, of course, and they seem able to treat you like an individual—like a woman as well as like a reporter. They're cooler dudes, or something. They're big-city people, most of them, and almost all of them went to college. They've been around. I think they may be more at ease with their own sexuality. Basketball players are treated like men by their coaches. Nobody watches them or keeps a curfew on the road. Hockey players are treated more like boys.

"It's been tough. It was awful at the beginning. I remember a playoff game in Toronto—I think Philadelphia was playing the Maple Leafs. I'd been through it all so many times, and we were still having trouble with the Flyers then. It was late at night, my time was running out, and I had to write. I was outside the door of the Flyers' dressing room, and there were a lot of people there looking at me and making remarks. Finally, one player came out—I think it was Bob Dailey. I asked him some questions about the game, and when I was finished I had to hurry down a long corridor and then up a flight of stairs to get to the pressroom. I stopped in a stairwell, because I realized I was so angry I couldn't speak. I was like Billy Budd—I was *silenced*. I thought, What am I doing here? Why am I putting up with this? I got my crying out—nobody saw me—and then I went up and wrote my story.

"Getting into the locker room seems like such a foolish thing to waste your energies on. Sixty per cent of my time and effort used to be spent on just trying to get to the players, instead of on what I was writing. It's emotionally draining. It uses you up. Before I left sports, I sometimes wondered about writing baseball someday, but I wouldn't try it now. I just couldn't go through that clubhouse thing all over again, now that I know it doesn't mean anything."

Diane K. Shah: *(She is an associate editor of* Newsweek, *where today she writes mostly for the "Life/Style" department. She grew up in Chicago, and graduated from Indiana University in 1967. She worked as a reporter for the* National Observer *and for the Chicago bureau of United Press International be-*

fore joining Newsweek *in 1977. She has published a novel,*
The Mackin Cover—*a thriller, with a professional-football
setting. She is married but is separated from her husband. She
is very tall, with striking, faintly Oriental-looking eyes. Thirty-
three years old.)*

"Sports has changed in its attitude toward women, but baseball still has a pretty long way to go. Back in September of
1972, I persuaded my editor at the *Observer* to send me up to
Boston to cover some Red Sox games at Fenway Park. The
team was in a close pennant race with the Tigers and Orioles
and Yankees, and everybody was very excited and involved.
It looked like a great story. I got in touch with the Red Sox
public-relations man, Bill Crowley, and he said, 'We don't let
women on the field, and the Baseball Writers Association runs
the press box.' When I called up the man who was running
the Baseball Writers in Boston that year, he sort of stuttered
and put me on hold for a long time, and then he said he couldn't
do it. My editor, Henry Gemmill, and one of the company
attorneys talked with the Red Sox people, but when I got up
there all I'd heard was 'Well, that girl can come in if she
behaves herself,' and I didn't know what that meant. Bill Crowley had told me he'd get me a box seat and said he'd bring
players there for me to interview. I said, 'You mean you'll
bring Carl Yastrzemski to see me in the stands right after a
game?' and he said 'Well, I'll *try*.' Finally, I got my pass to
go out on the field, but when I went out there during batting
practice I found that none of the players would talk to me.
They simply wouldn't answer when I asked them questions.
Then I discovered that there had just been a team meeting,
where they'd been told I was coming and warned to watch
their language. Only two of them talked to me in the end—
Carlton Fisk and that left-handed pitcher John Curtis. The rest
thought they'd been told not to say anything at all.

"Before the game, Dick Bresciani, the assistant public-
relations man, took me up on the roof, where the press box
and the pressroom are. I could see he was terribly uncomfortable about something, and when we got there he explained that
I could come into the press box but that the pressroom was a
social place, for eating and drinking, and no women were
allowed in there. I saw that they'd set up a little ice-cream
table outside the pressroom, with one chair and one place set-

ting, and there was a little folder on it with 'Ladies' Pavilion' written across it. I didn't eat at all that night. I just ignored it.

"During the game, Dick Bresciani sat between me and Bill Crowley in the press box. I think he thought I'd make a terrible scene, or something. Finally, after about four innings, I introduced myself to Mr. Crowley and I said, 'See? Nothing terrible has happened.' He said, 'Well, it will,' and I asked him what could happen. He said, 'Tomorrow, there'll be fifty girls like you here.' I said I didn't think there were fifty women sportswriters in the whole country, and he said, 'Maybe not, but they'll say they are, just so they can get at my players.'

"The next night, I was allowed in the pressroom. Tom Yawkey, the team owner, had told everybody that if I was accredited I was to be let in. I sat all alone. Nobody came near me. But then Mr. Yawkey sent word over to me to come and join him at his table. When I wrote the story, I sort of made it a point of honor not to put any of this stuff in. The strangest thing of all, when I look back on it, is that none of this seemed to have been done with any malice. They were all polite, in a distant sort of way. They just didn't know what to do about me.

"The leadership on a team makes a big difference in how you're treated. Earl Weaver, of the Orioles, is very accommodating and easy, and so are his players. So is Chuck Tanner, of the Pirates. The Red Sox always make you feel sort of uncomfortable, but I think they're an uncomfortable kind of team, even among themselves. The Yankees—well, I rode on a team bus with them in Kansas City a couple of times last year, while I was working on a story, and there was a lot of bad language in the back of the bus. I mean a *lot*. You could tell that most of it was for my benefit. Billy Martin, who was still manager then, was very nervous about it, and Elston Howard was so embarrassed that he offered to take me with him in a cab next time. The Yankees aren't exactly a mature team, to put it mildy.

"I get the feeling that baseball players have always been a pretty special sort of athlete. From an early age, their whole lives have been tied up with the locker room and its intensely male feelings. They usually get married very young, when they're still in the minors, and they talk a lot about protecting their wives. Some of them have never met a woman as an equal—maybe most of them. They have no women as friends. They live together more of the time than other athletes do. It's a long season, with a lot of traveling. They hang out together a lot.

"I always try to meet their wives and talk to them, so I can show them that I'm serious. Hardly any of them have ever met a woman reporter. The players and their wives both seem to think that you're some kind of groupie who's been clever enough to get her hands on a press pass.

"There's nothing I love more than baseball, but every time I walk out onto a baseball field I feel a dread about being there. It upsets me, because I started in with baseball exactly the same way most kids did. My father was a secret Yankee fan in Chicago—an exile—and he began taking me to a lot of games when I was about twelve. He taught me how to keep score. I used to keep Yankee scrapbooks—I cut out all the Yankee stories and Yankee box scores I could find and pasted them up. I was very self-conscious about this, because I knew other girls didn't do it. I used to buy *Sport* magazine, and I'd bring it home inside an envelope, so people couldn't tell. When I grew up, one of the very first stories I got to write for the *Observer* was about an old Yankee hero of mine, who was still in baseball as a coach. I went and talked with him, and when we went out to dinner he got drunk and fell down in the street. He said he was wearing new shoes, or something, but that wasn't it. It was sad. I didn't write that, either."

Betty Cuniberti: (*She covers the University of Maryland football and basketball teams for the Washington* Post, *and fills in on the paper's coverage of the Washington Redskins and Bullets. Previously, she was a sports reporter for the San Bernardino, California,* Sun-Telegram *and then for the San Francisco* Chronicle. *She is twenty-seven years old, with curly brown hair and a quick smile.*)

"Most women in this business don't cover games. Ninety per cent of us don't—not a good balance. The standard idea of a woman sportswriter's story is doing Steve Garvey's wife or writing a feature about Nancy Lopez. The men on the beat are always aware of that. This is why locker-room access is the heart of it all. Access is the key to covering games, and you aren't a sportswriter—you haven't paid your dues—unless you cover games.

"Pro football is just about the last bastion. The N.F.L. leaves it up to the individual teams, but only the Eagles and the Vikings let women into their locker rooms. Tom Landry, of the Cowboys, closed his locker rooms to everybody last fall rather than let women in. Pro football is the prestige beat, the biggest of them all, and sports editors almost never let a woman near it. They think we haven't earned the assignment, or else it just doesn't occur to them. They think it's like sending a dog to do your income-tax return, or something.

"When I was with the *Chronicle* in 1976, I went on a game trip to Kansas City with the Oakland Raiders, and I heard that Al Davis, the Oakland owner, was upset about my presence on the charter flight. I had a feeling that I was being watched, to see if anything would happen. Davis told people that he was also afraid I might be bad luck—like a woman on a ship. The stewardesses didn't count, of course. I used to have real trouble with some of the Raider players. They'd hassle me—hide my typewriter, or hide my car in the parking lot. One of them grabbed me in a hallway. None of that ever happened with the 49ers. I finally spoke up to John Madden, the Raider coach, and it stopped right away. But those were rocky times.

"I hate to say it, but I think it's going to take more court action to change all this. There aren't enough of us, and there aren't enough editors or newspapers like mine, who will make an issue of women. I think more editors and more reporters in the business have to see that this is a writers' issue, not a women's issue. And then, even if you do get some support, at the end of it all you just get bombarded with bad mail. You know, sportswriters aren't very popular anyway. People just don't understand deadlines. The players are always blaming us for what we report—for real quotes or for criticisms of them—and they blame us when they lose. No matter what you do, the image that the public holds on to is of a ravening, fire-eating woman coming in and taking advantage of some poor, shy, tired boys. My name is synonymous with nudity—I think it's the first thing most people think about me.

"I never saw any of this coming when I was growing up. When I was a kid in San Francisco, I always knew I was going to be a writer—I asked Santa Claus for a typewriter when I was five years old—but I thought I was going to be a professional athlete, too. I was a tomboy. I was always the fastest runner on my block. My family had season tickets for the 49ers, and in the summer we went to a lot of the Giants' games. I thought I was going to grow up and pitch for the Giants. I was sure of it. My hero was Mike McCormick, who had won the Cy Young Award. The only thing that worried me about my future was that he was left-handed and I wasn't. I thought that was all there was that stood in my way."

Melissa Ludtke Lincoln: *(She became a reporter on* Sports Illustrated *in 1974, shortly after her graduation from Wellesley. Her byline has appeared occasionally in the magazine, but for the most part she has done legwork and research for writers who are senior to her. She has covered baseball and professional basketball. She has an oval face and brownish-blond hair, which falls to her shoulders. She speaks in a flat, quiet voice. Twenty-seven years old.)*

"I'm politically naïve. I never thought much about discrimination until I saw how women were treated over the locker-room thing. When I tried to get into the locker room back at the 1977 World Series, it was for obvious professional reasons. I went through all the proper steps, asked all the right people, explained my reasons. Then the door was slammed in my face. Literally, I mean. It was Pete Carry, my editor—the baseball editor—who took it up from there and made it all happen. He was the hero. It took a long time, and it was worth it, of course, but things haven't exactly turned around. If I'm sent on a story to Detroit, let's say, this summer, I still won't be able to get into the locker room there. I'm still only one bus stop down the road.

"This crusade has worn me down. I'm a little discouraged by my own situation. I think I was a symbol for Time, Inc. More than fifty per cent of the employees there are women, and some of them filed a complaint about discrimination with the New York Division of Human Rights a few years ago. It was settled by agreement, and my suit was the most convenient way for Time, Inc., to show its support for women. But the basic workings of my magazine haven't changed much.

"I'm tired of the difference between public and private attitudes. When I first tried to get into the clubhouses in 1977, the Dodgers voted to let me in. Billy Martin said I could come into his office. Then the Commissioner stepped in and began collecting affidavits, and suddenly everything was different. Last summer, one of the Yankee executives introduced me to his wife and two daughters, and they congratulated me on what I had done. He looked at me and winked, because he and I knew that his official stand had been one of absolute opposition to me.

"Some of the Yankees were terrific with me last fall. Roy White was super. So was Fred Stanley. Reggie apologized to me for some of the bad scenes in the clubhouse. I think I got that open hostility from players like Jay Johnstone and Cliff Johnson because they hadn't been much involved in the pennant race or the playoffs. They were having trouble with their careers and their egos. It was a way for them to be a star at something—to get the writers around them.

"I hope I'll begin to feel at ease in the Yankee clubhouse, the way I do in the basketball locker rooms. I'm still not anxious to go in there. If I'm afraid, it may be because people there don't know my face yet. If people know me, I'm all right. I can't tell if what I feel is a human nervousness or if it's because I'm a woman. I can't separate them."

There are many hundreds of men who write regularly about sports in this country—most of them for the daily papers. No survey of their opinions about women sportswriters or the admission of those women to the athletes' locker rooms has ever been undertaken. The three sportswriters quoted here were selected not in any attempt to present a balance but because each is a friend of mine and because each, it turned out, was willing to speak his mind in a remarkably candid fashion.

Murray Chass: *(After graduating from the University of Pittsburgh, he worked for ten years as a sportswriter with the Associated Press. He has been with the* Times *since 1969, and is the current chairman of the New York chapter of the Baseball Writers of America. He covers the Yankees, and he has become widely known for his reporting on the financial, legal, and labor aspects of big-time sports. He is married, and has two sons, a daughter, a stepson, and a stepdaughter. He has red-*

dish-brown hair and a small beard. Forty years old.)

"The only thing that bothers me about women sportswriters is when they're dumb or don't know what they're doing. But I feel exactly the same way about male sportswriters. I would guess that some of the women are going to have to work a little harder at it than the men do, because they may not know quite so much in advance. There's a pressure on them to be very good. I think it's the same as it was when Jackie Robinson first came up. He knew he had to excel. I don't like to make the comparison, but it's there.

"There's no question in my mind but that the Yankees tried to turn the male writers against the women after the Ludtke ruling last fall. You could see it happening, and they did it on purpose. If the Commissioner and everyone else had just left the issue alone, it all would have been resolved in three days. It just would have gone away.

"Being kept out of the clubhouse for any reason or taking players into another area for interviews is unacceptable, and I'll scream about it. The issue is perfectly plain. It's freedom of access for all writers. Wherever I have a right to go, a woman has a right to go, as long as she's there to do a job.

"The players' right to privacy is a tricky issue, though. Last spring, in Fort Lauderdale, a woman photographer was allowed into the clubhouse, and some of the Yankee players were genuinely shocked. One of the pitchers was talking to me about it, and I pointed out to him that most of the players—easily ninety per cent of them, married or unmarried—fooled around when they were on the road, so they couldn't be too shy. He said sure, but when he was in bed with a woman they *both* had their clothes off, and he had been—well, consulted about it. I had to think about that. Later on, I asked my daughter Debbie, who is fourteen, what she thought about this business of the players' privacy and the reporters. She said, 'Are men allowed in there to see them?' I said yes, and she said, 'Well, then women should be in, too.' She was right, of course."

Jerome Holtzman: *(He is the senior baseball writer for the Chicago* Sun-Times. *He has been on the baseball beat for twenty-two years, covering the Cubs for half of each season and the White Sox for the other half. He writes a lengthy summary of each baseball year for the* Official Baseball Guide.

He owns a notable collection of baseball books and memorabilia, and he has written three books about baseball. One of them, No Cheering in the Press Box, *is a series of interviews with old-time titans of the press box—men like Richards Vidmer, John Kieran, John Drebinger, and Ford Frick. He is of medium height, with broad shoulders, gray hair, and bushy eyebrows. He smokes cigars. He is married, with four daughters. Fifty-two years old.)*

"The liberal in me says that women reporters are entitled to be in the clubhouse and to get all the courtesies I get. The chauvinist and the realist in me say they don't belong. I feel that by getting their rights—all that they're entitled to—they're abrogating the players' right to privacy. Anyhow, I think clubhouse reporting is overrated. Editors are impressed by it, but players don't always tell the truth in that kind of interview. Clubhouse reporting results in a pretty sloppy kind of work. You can come to the park in the seventh inning and skip the game altogether. I think there's going to be a swing back to the other kind of sportswriting—to game writing. And that macho feeling of the clubhouse isn't a very important part of a team.

"Listen, I know it's a problem. I know women are entitled to be sportswriters. But I feel there's something unwholesome about it all. There's something unwholesome about a woman having to scramble at a World Series or at a big game—having to run after the players. I don't mind men running, the way you and I do, but why should women have to do it? I think I still have something of a romantic attitude toward women.

"Women reporters have certain advantages over men. I've seen it. Athletes open up to women more in a one-on-one situation. Most of the women also have the advantage of their age, and that applies to younger male reporters, of course. I used to be a lot closer to the players than I am today. One of the worst aspects of being a sportswriter is that you get older and the athletes get younger. Jimmy Cannon once said that sportswriters are entombed in a prolonged boyhood. And the Midwest sports editor of the A.P., Jerry Liska—he's retired now—always said that after you got to be thirty-five or forty you shouldn't be a sportswriter anymore.

"The assignment has changed. There's more behind-the-scenes crap. Nobody wants to know who went from first to third. Sports is getting to be just entertainment. I suppose the fact that this was an all-male world was what made it so exciting to me at first. And now that it's being invaded and eroded it's much less attractive. Maybe I am a chauvinist—I don't know. The press box used to be a male preserve—that was its charm. I'd rather not have a woman as a seatmate at a World Series game. It wouldn't be as much fun. I've never met a woman who knew as much baseball as a man. But there was a woman once who was an official scorer. I remember reading about it. It was in some minor league—maybe the Texas League. Isn't that interesting? You could look it up."

Maury Allen: *(He has been a sportswriter with the* Post *for eighteen years, mostly covering the Yankees and the Mets, and is now a columnist. He was one of the original "Chipmunks"— a group of young, iconoclastic sportswriters who became celebrated in the early nineteen-sixties for their questioning, irreverent attitude toward athletes and sports institutions. He has written fifteen baseball books, including a biography of Joe DiMaggio. He is married, with a son and a daughter. He has prematurely white hair and a black mustache. His manner is cheerful. Forty-six years old.)*

"I have a gut feeling that letting women into the clubhouse violates the traditions of baseball. The idea of a girl romping through a clubhouse filled with naked athletes is not going to be good for the game. I am also very concerned that the baseball establishment is going to use the arrival of women as an excuse to cut off the clubhouse altogether. Professional athletes make so much money now that they only just tolerate the press, and Bowie thinks that we only come into the clubhouse to agitate the players and to snoop. But you have to report the clubhouse—the inside environment of baseball. Ever since television began covering the game, the clubhouse has been the writer's beat. The players and the general managers and the Commissioner are agreed on one thing—we are the enemy.

"What will happen to the women reporters on the road? Most of the women writers I've seen are girls I wouldn't cross the street to ask for a date. But there will be some attractive girls among them, and they'll be thrown into compromising situations. There will be a scandal, and it will be bad for all reporters.

"Sex is a very significant aspect of athletes' lives. If you think about it, you realize right away that athletic performance and sexual performance always go hand in hand. Why did Joe Namath become such a national hero? Because he was macho. Because deep down in our hearts *we* wanted all those broads. I think sexual performance is even more important to baseball players, because they have so much time on their hands, being on the road so much. They have all that hotel time. The peer pressure to drink and chase girls and commit adultery is almost impossible for the younger players to resist. This is what's behind the macho, kidding-around atmosphere of the clubhouse—the cursing and that male coquettishness. The players are wary of any mention of the on-the-road part of their lives. It's never written about, and they all cover up for each other. The writers are sworn to secrecy, and they know it. That's why there was such a stink about Jim Bouton's book *Ball Four*—it broke the unwritten rule. Any reporter who wrote about all this might just as well turn in his baseball card. He'd be as good as dead. I don't know if a woman would understand any of that.

"I think most male sportswriters are failed athletes. I was a highschool baseball player at James Madison High, in Brooklyn. But I was never much more than a fringe player, so I could see it wasn't going to happen. I did the next-best thing, which was to become a baseball writer. But what is the psychology of a woman in this business? Is it a misplaced role for her? I'm in terrible conflict about this. I consider myself a political liberal. I have an eleven-year-old daughter, and she wants to be a sportswriter. I want women to be brain surgeons and Supreme Court justices. If Barbara Jordan ran for President, I'd vote for her. But I think that just as I can't become pregnant, women shouldn't become sportswriters. When I was ten years old, my father began taking me to ballgames, and this relationship was very significant to me. It was male. It was something that separated me from my mother. Baseball is our most traditional game, and on an emotional level I don't want to break away from those traditions. I have disagreements with other writers about this. But I think the coverage of baseball is as traditional as the game itself. I see the erosion of all our deepest sports feelings coming. I feel that the romance of the game will be damaged.

"Maybe I don't want this changed because I want to think of sports as being unchanged, still juvenile. I want to go on thinking about baseball as being a part of our life that doesn't have the same values as the rest of it. Something about the joy of the game is going. I trouble in my mind about all this. I wish I weren't presented with it."

Three more women:

Jane Gross: *(She is the daughter of the late Milton Gross, who was a well-known sportswriter and columnist on the* Post. *After graduating from Skidmore, she became a researcher at Sports Illustrated, and in 1975 she joined the sports staff of* Newsday. *That year, she started covering the New York Nets, and she has also covered the Knicks. She has been to Wimbledon for* Newsday, *and she will soon travel to North Korea to cover an international table tennis tournament. She is small and slight, and she speaks in a precise, confident manner. She is thirty-one years old.)*

"I'm an accidental sports reporter. I planned on being a different sort of writer. I didn't play sports as a kid, and I don't much like sports. I never watch sports on TV on my day off. I think I was hired by *S.I.* out of college because they were sure I knew all about sports—on account of my father. All I had was a network of sports connections, and I had to learn a lot of things that Stephanie Salter and Melissa Ludtke knew already. My father almost hysterically discouraged me from going into sports. He wanted me to be in an easier side of journalism, like magazines or TV, where there would be rugs on the floor. I've heard that because of my father some old-time sportswriters get upset at the thought of me in the locker room with a lot of naked athletes. But I'm loyal enough to his intelligence to think that I could convince him it was right. Maybe not, though.

"I was perfectly sure that Melissa was going to win her lawsuit, and I was perfectly sure that the Yankees would respond to it by closing the locker room in some way. They would fulfill the obligation to be equal, but 'equal' would take something away from the men. That's a very worrisome trend, because we women writers have to live in this world and we're so outnumbered. The men are going to be justifiably furious if their prerogatives are taken away from them, and a lot of them are going to take it out on us.

"I think women reporters have a lot of advantages, starting with the advantage of the players' natural chivalry. We women are interested in different things from the men writers, so we ask different questions. When Bob McAdoo gets traded from the Knicks, my first thought is, How is his wife, Brenda, going to finish law school this year? And that may be what's most on *his* mind. I'm very close to the players' wives. Julius Erving's wife, Turquoise, is a good friend of mine. I don't think the wives worry about me or other women writers when the team is on the road. Athletes' wives have very anxious lives. They have a lot to be nervous about, but the only complaint I've ever had from them is that I get to spend more time with their husbands than they do.

"The other advantage of being a woman is that you're perpetually forced to be an outsider. As a rule, you're not invited to come along to dinner with a half-dozen of the players, or to go drinking with them, when maybe they're going to chase girls. This means a lot, because I believe that all reporters should keep a great distance between themselves and the players. It always ought to be an adversary relationship, basically. That's a difficult space to maintain when you're on the road all through a long season. I can remember a trip, when I first started out, when I called room service for my meals for nineteen straight days. It was hard to take, but later I saw it was really an advantage, a strength.

"I've not always been perfectly at ease in a locker room, but I'm comfortable now. It's an earned comfort—it takes a long time. I don't think anybody who hasn't been in a locker room when women are there can believe that it isn't a big deal. Most of the men who have fought so hard to keep women out probably have never seen a locker room with women in it. My presence doesn't change the way the players act or talk. I've begun to see that the pleasure men take in being with each other—playing cards together, being in a bar together—isn't actively anti-female. It isn't against women; it just has nothing to do with them. It seems to come from some point in their lives before they were aware that there *were* women. They have so much fun together. I really have become much more sympathetic to men because of my job.

"I wonder if a lot of the suggestions that men make about women reporters may not have something to do with sexual envy of blacks. I'm sure the black players treat me differently from the way they treat male writers. They don't think I'm a honky—I'm another oppressed minority. They may not have thought this all the way through, but it's there. Male sportswriters all seem to think that the athletes are going to take a shot at us on the road, but it hardly ever happens. In fact, that comes much more from the sportswriters than from the players, and you can tell them I said so."

Stephanie Salter: *(She grew up in Terre Haute, Indiana, where she was a high-school cheerleader. She went to Purdue and became the editor-in-chief of the undergraduate daily, the* Exponent. *Like Jane Gross and Melissa Ludtke Lincoln, she was a researcher and reporter with* Sports Illustrated. *She became a free-lance writer in 1974, and joined the sports staff of the San Francisco* Examiner *the following year. She covered the Golden State Warriors, of the National Basketball Association, for two seasons. Now she covers the Oakland A's and is a backup writer on the San Francisco Giants, which makes her one of the few women in the country with a regular baseball beat. She has light-brown hair. She talks rapidly, with a wry, half-amused smile. Twenty-nine years old.)*

"I sometimes think the whole sports world exists in order to maintain some code of meaningless courtly manners. I used to have these shouting matches with guards or officials who wanted to keep me out of press boxes, and I was always told I couldn't get in because of the bad language in there. Well, as it happens, I curse a lot—I'm not proud of it, or anything, but it's true—so that always made me laugh. It was hysterical. But the way I talk sort of confirmed something for the men, too—the only kind of woman who wants to come into a press box is the kind who talks dirty. With a lot of sports people, women are either revered or despised. There are good girls— the ones they marry—and there are the other ones, the kind they shack up with on the road. We women writers are a challenge to that simple filing system. They just don't know what to make of us. This isn't the majority attitude with the players anymore, but somehow it carries over and becomes the official sports attitude. It's what the front offices hold on to.

The older men in sports almost insist on it, for some reason.

"I'm always amazed at the amount of hostility among the male writers that is directed at the players. Obviously, not all the writers are failed athletes, but there are far too many of them. You hear them asking these smart-aleck questions that are meant to show up the players and prove that the writers know as much about the sport as the players do. It's as if they're fighting over who will be the leader of the pack: Which of us is more virile—me with my pen or you with your bat? At least, we women are free of that.

"I don't think that the presence of women is going to change big-time macho sports in any real way. There are so few of us, and it's all so much bigger than the tiny fists we beat against it. Years ago, I tried to crash the Baseball Writers' annual dinner in New York, and I got thrown out. Now I'm a member of the Baseball Writers, but the invitation to the big New York dinner this year still said it was a stag affair. Men only.

"I'm tired. I don't feel like fighting anymore. The thought of the start of another baseball season is so damned discouraging. I really love baseball, but I don't look forward to standing outside the clubhouse anymore and going through all that crap. Neither the A's nor the Giants are opening their clubhouses this year. When you get these bad feelings, you begin to ask yourself. 'Why *am* I doing this?' I think of myself as a feminist, as somebody who wants to win a cause, but I've begun to wonder about myself. Am I looking for male approval? Am I here because I'm incapable of not trying to please men in some special way? But this is a trap that's sort of been set for me. Maybe I've begun to think there's something wrong with me because so many other people seem to think there is.

"I hate the analogy of women and blacks, but it's there. When you stand outside the clubhouse, you're the perfect symbol of the eternal outsider. I always feel as if my arms were tied to my sides. I have dreams that I'm outside some clubhouse and there are ropes around me. There have been times when I just couldn't do it anymore, because it hurt so much. I had to go away, because they'd made me cry again."

Lawrie Mifflin: *(She graduated from Yale in 1973, worked as a summer trainee at the Philadelphia* Bulletin, *and then attended the Columbia School of Journalism. She was hired by*

the News *as a general-assignment reporter, and then went on
the City Hall beat. After two years, she became the first woman
reporter in the* News *sports department. She covers the New
York Cosmos and the New York Rangers—both of which admit
women to their locker rooms. She is married to an artist,
Richard Raiselis, but has kept her own name. She is five feet
tall, with thick hair, large eyes, and an earnest, eager manner.
Twenty-seven years old.*)

"I'm pretty strange, because I really believe in all the clichés
about sports. I think sports do build character. I believe that
sports allow you to channel your aggressions and to use them
in a specific, controlled way. Men have always been brought
up with that advantage, but women have been taught to hang
back, not to sweat too much. If I had my way, I'd rather be a
professional athlete than a sportswriter. If I could get paid
enough for it, I'd be a professional field-hockey player. I play
every Sunday in the fall. I get up at six in the morning and
take a train out to the middle of New Jersey and then change
to another train and then walk a mile to the field. I play left
wing with the Essex team, in the New Jersey women's league.
I grew up in Swarthmore, outside Philadelphia. That's always
been a great center for women's sports, for some reason. I was
the oldest of five children—I have two brothers and two sisters—so the locker room has never been a surprise to me. At
Swarthmore High, the girls' field-hockey team was just as
important as the boys' football team. The school had *six* competitive hockey teams for the girls. Everybody always called
it 'hockey'—the other kind was 'ice hockey.' It wasn't until
I was about eighteen, at Yale, that I realized that most people
thought that only big ugly girls were supposed to take sports
seriously.

"Not enough sportswriters have been trained as journalists.
They don't seem to have learned to ask the right questions,
and they don't challenge the answers they get. A lot of them
grew up knowing all the names and rules and stats in sports,
and they seem to think that's enough. There isn't an analogy
to this anywhere else in newspaper work.

"I think that to the players all of us reporters are aliens.
They tend to lump women into the same group of aliens, and
that really disturbs some of the regular writers. These men are
suddenly forced to realize that they're strangers in the locker

room, too, and not part of the team at all. They're forced to see that they're really much closer to any woman reporter there—even someone brand-new on the job—than they are to the players, because they and the women are both in the same business. It almost drives them crazy. But this is true only of some of the older writers. Most of the younger men think of us as being the same as they are—of the same ilk. They haven't reached the stage of feeling bitter about sports.

"I've never wanted to be part of the hanging-out side of sports. I never go into the locker room when the Rangers have a practice, because I don't have a deadline then. Women can't be part of all that, and I don't miss it at all. My husband has nothing to do with sports. Most of our friends are painters and sculptors, and we never talk about sports. I think I'd be sort of depressed about the whole sports scene if I never could get away from it.

"I don't think there's any advantage to being a woman in my business. The real advantage for me is my age. The Rangers are a very young team, and the players relate to me because we're about the same age. We can be friends. I've always been able to get along with men in an easy, non-sexual way. The younger people are, the less they worry about sex differences."

Men and women, sports and sex, tradition and privacy, young people and older people—that parade float has become still more crowded with symbols and overtones, and still more, I believe, we on the sidewalk should resist looking for a moral or an easy summary as it creaks past us. I am upset by the cruelties that men in sports have inflicted on the women who have recently come into their world, hoping to share its pleasures and complexities and rewards. I pull back instinctively from these cuts and slights, and I suspect that I have hoped to purge myself of my own complicity in them by writing about the subject. But nothing is easy here, and, like Stephanie Salter, I must also ask myself why I was so attracted to sports in the first place, and (in my own case) why I have continued to watch sports and to write about sports now that I am well past the age when, according to Jerome Holtzman, I should have left them. I am not persuaded by Maury Allen's arguments about the sexual implications of our adulation of athletes, but I can't quite say they are a lie. I have always sensed a covert resentment of the players among men in the front office and in the press box, who spend their adult lives in pursuit of these gifted, golden creatures. The players are fawned upon and also bullied and patronized, it seems to me, because out there on the field, in the light and the noise, they can actually do that beautiful thing that all of us once wished so deeply to be able to do. Perhaps we can now guess also that our mixed envy and hatred of them persists—not just in the stadium but on the road and in their hotels—because they are at some peak of youth and physical power and freedom and sexuality that all the rest of us men have longed for and still long for. Maybe this is what sports are all about.

It seems to me that the people who run sports and who claim to be most concerned about the "sexual privacy" of their athletes in the clubhouse—surely one of the most sexless and joyless surroundings in which men and women can meet—are men who want to keep both sports and sex in some safe, special place where they first locked them up when they were adolescents. The new presence of capable, complicated women in the inner places of sports means that relations between the sexes cannot be relegated just to marriage, or just to hotel rooms, either. When women are not easy to sum up or dismiss, traditional male responses to them suddenly begin to look pathetic. The mass male preening of the locker room and the foul-mouthed aggressiveness of the team bus lose their purpose when grown-ups fail to pay attention, and most mothers I know would probably just as soon be spared the fussy, hypocritical anxieties that beset front-office elders who wish to preserve the innocence of American children by presenting them with an image of sports as a place of infantile sexual purity. Sex becomes a lot simpler and happier when it is freed from these old obsessions, and in time it may become even more significant than the athletes perceive it to be. If men discover that the company of men does not equal the company of men and women together, they may decide that sports can be a common property, a great dream or pageant or drama to be shared among us all, and that its idealization as a male ritual and religion is part of a national neurosis—a form of infantilism that degrades its players and watchers and feeds childish anxieties and delusions, which we can all begin to outgrow now, at long last.

One missing voice here, it will be noticed, is that of the

players. This is a considerable omission. In the past week, I did ask a good many baseball players and basketball players and hockey players what they thought about the arrival of women reporters in their locker rooms, and many of them showed an awareness of the conflicting issues involved. But they also expressed strong feelings about their own privacy, their wives' anxieties, and the importance of a clubhouse in maintaining team morale. "That's where you *become* a team," said Vida Blue—who, by the way, favors the admission of women reporters to his own San Francisco Giants clubhouse. Players have a difficult sort of life, all in all, and their customary attitude of irritation or sullen patience or cynicism about the habitual cajoling and bullying and meddling they must put up with at the hands of the front office and the writers and the fans has not been improved by the news that some *court* has now ruled that their own privacy can be taken care of with a robe or a towel. It is my own belief, however, that the players' privacy has already been fatally compromised by the presence of the scrambling, questioning, rumor-hunting male reporters in the clubhouse. At the same time, I think the reporters are demeaned when they are forced to kneel or crane or shove one another for a better position beside the cubicle of some naked, sweating sports hero, or to follow him to the door of the shower room or the training room in hope of the favor of one more muttered quote. I think we should ask the athletes to keep their uniforms on for as long as seems necessary for the press to do its job, and to let everyone in to talk to them. In time, it may be hoped, newspaper readers will diminish their demand that athletes be transformed into mere celebrities; when that happens, we can close the clubhouse altogether and give our attention, as writers and fans, to watching the players when they are at their splendid best, which is on the field.

On a weekend in late February, I went to Madison Square Garden, where I watched New York's two pairs of local professional winter teams have at each other on successive nights. On Saturday, the Knicks beat the Nets by 111 to 107; on Sunday the Rangers upset the powerful Islanders, 3–2. Both games were noisy, exciting affairs, with the doubly partisan crowds in wild voice. I visited the locker rooms after both games, and found many other male reporters there, of course, and a few women. A basketball locker room is a good deal smaller and scruffier than a baseball clubhouse, and the extremely tall undressing or towel-clad or naked or getting-dressed basketball players in the quiet Nets' room and in the somewhat happier Knicks' quarters were—well, close together. Nobody minded, that I could see—or if anyone minded he kept quiet about it. Nobody *looked*, and then, because I was looking to see if anyone was looking, I began to feel embarrassed at being there on such an odd errand. I talked to a few players, and ended up in conversation with Phil Jackson, a bony, bearded six-foot-eight forward and center, who used to play for the Knicks and is now a player-coach with the Nets. He was towelling himself after his shower and chatting with Eric and Melissa Ludtke Lincoln. I told him what I was there for, and Jackson said, "Nobody thinks about it anymore. Oh, we had some rookies on the Knicks last year who were a little tight about it—a few guys ran into the training room—but we told them to shape up, and they did. I don't know why baseball makes so much of it all. Nobody cares or notices. Nobody looks—except for Melissa here. Melissa is a peeker, a regular Peeping Thomasina."

He laughed, and we laughed, and he put on his underpants.

The next night, in the Rangers' locker room, I talked to Dave Maloney, the team's twenty-two-year-old captain, who is a defenseman. I had heard that hockey players were generally more modest than basketball players, but my impression that night was almost the opposite. Maybe it was because there were more women there—four or five of them, at least, including a photographer and a member of a TV crew—or maybe it was because there are so many more people on a hockey squad than on a basketball squad that the cumulative nakedness seemed both more noticeable and less noticed. I had seen Lawrie Mifflin talking to Maloney about the slambang game we had just watched, and when she moved along to interview another player (she had a preoccupied, near-deadline expression) I introduced myself to Maloney. He had a freshly skinned patch on the bridge of his already battered nose, and he seemed almost terminally exhausted. "Boy, I'm glad I don't have to play eight games like that one!" he said, in an "o"-accenting Canadian voice.

I asked him what he thought of Lawrie Mifflin.

"Lawrie is—well, I *like* Lawrie," Maloney said. "She shoots straight. She's friendly. When she's in here asking questions it's just two people talking together—not a man and a woman but friends. She's patient, and patient people are better at that job, I think. Lawrie is just like a sister."

I told him that these were almost exactly the words she had used when she talked about her feelings about the Rangers. Then I asked him if he had ever felt anxious about the presence of women in the Ranger locker room.

"I guess I was sort of surprised by it when I first came up, three years ago," Maloney said, "but I got used to it. This is the big city, and you learn to go along with things. But I'll tell you, we never had anything like this back home. I come from a small city in Canada—Kitchener—and it's different there. I thought about it when I first saw Lawrie and the other girls in here, and I realized that the last woman I'd seen in a hockey-team locker room was my mother. I was about seven years old then, and she was in there to lace up my skates."

Afterword: Three years have passed since this story was written, and some alterations are visible on the troubled landscape it describes. The baseball commissioner's office has continued to encourage equal clubhouse access to all accredited reporters, regardless of sex, and there has been no restriction on women reporters at the Championship Series and World Series games. At the same time, a few clubs—among them the Reds, the Indians, the Cubs, and the Expos—continued to ban women from their clubhouses as recently as last summer. This local option appears to depend on the private preference of an incumbent manager or general manager, and has often altered when that job changed hands.

Many of the women quoted in the article have moved along to other journalistic undertakings. Diane K. Shah writes a thrice-weekly sports column for the Los Angeles *Herald-Examiner*. Melissa Ludtke Lincoln is a researcher/reporter with *Time*, whose range of assignments includes medicine and the press. Betty Cuniberti became a Washington feature and cityside correspondent for the Los Angeles *Times* after her own paper, the Washington *Star*, ceased publication last year. B. J. Phillips is a correspondent with the Atlanta bureau of *Time*. Jane Gross is a sportswriter with the New York *Times;* she was on the baseball beat last summer, doing backup coverage on both the Yankees and Mets, as well as other assignments. Stephanie Salter still covers the San Francisco Giants and the Oakland A's for the San Francisco *Examiner*. Lawrie Mifflin is a writer and associate producer with the ABC "Sports-Beat" television show.

"The women who have quit writing sports in the last couple of years have done it of their own accord," Stephanie Salter said not long ago. "It was time for them to move on to something else—maybe something better. There still aren't many women on the baseball beat, but that's because it's such a plum. Most women sportswriters still get stuck with high-school sports or tennis, so things haven't changed all *that* much, I guess. There's been one breakthrough: my membership card in the Baseball Writers Association no longer has a 'Mr.' printed on it. I hope that's not what this whole struggle was for."

B. J. Phillips said, "I did five long years on the sports beat. It was a great ride, but now I want something different. I think I may know too much about sports now. There are a lot more women in the business today than there were when I came along. Almost every little paper in the South seems to have at least one woman writing sports. The biggest change has been in peer respect. So many women have done a good professional job in sports that we're accepted and admired by our colleagues now. That's what it's all about. The athletes never were a problem.

"My last assignment writing sports for *Time* was the Thomas Hearns—Sugar Ray Leonard fight in Las Vegas last summer. I was riding on the press bus there one day and some old troglodyte sportswriter peeked at the press card on my shirt and saw who I worked for. 'Say, what do you do for them, honey?' he said. 'Are you one of their leg-girls?' So it ended for me just the way it started—with an insult."

She laughed.

8

Walking into the Picture

MARCH-APRIL 1979

SPRING AGAIN. THE OAKLAND A'S ARE LEADING THE SAN DIEGO Padres, 2–0, in the fifth inning at Scottsdale Stadium, in Arizona, and nobody is paying much attention. There's a new Oakland pitcher in the game, a left-hander, but none of the sportswriters can figure out who it is. Maybe it's Dave Hamilton—it *looks* like Dave Hamilton—but there is no Hamilton listed in the A's press guide. Yes, it must be Hamilton; he's a non-roster player this spring, trying to hook on for another year in the majors. Let's go, Dave. Gene Richards, of the Padres, dips his bat suddenly, bunts past the mound, and beats it out. The sun is shining, and four or five writers have moved out of the press box and down into some unoccupied box seats behind the visiting-team dugout to work on their tans. Chub Feeney, the president of the National League, in slacks and a pale-beige T-shirt, is sitting with them, and there are a lot of rumors and jokes flying around. Chub is an agreeable man. The Giants have just signed Billy North, a free agent who was with the Dodgers last year. Good move for the Giants, everyone agrees: North will help in center field, and will give them some real speed in the leadoff position. All that the Giants need now is better catching. Nobody has enough catching this

162

year. . . . The A's, it seems, are about to be sold by Charlie Finley; the deal will go through any minute now. This particular rumor must be left over from last spring; Charlie is always about to unload the A's. No, I am told, this is a *different* sale: a group of East Bay businessmen—from the San Francisco East Bay area, that is—are serious about it, and they have the money. Commissioner Bowie Kuhn feels very optimistic. Old Bowie must be dying to see Charlie leave the game.

There is an infield hit, and then a close play at first, where the runner has turned the base and had to dart back; the ump hesitates and then calls the runner safe. The Oakland first baseman, Dell Alston, stares at the ump in disbelief. The umpire turns away. He is small and young, with long, bushy hair—a startling sight on an ump. Chub Feeney is asked about the play. "Greatest first-base call I ever saw," Feeney says instantly. Everybody laughs. The major-league umpires are out on strike, demanding more money, and when Chub Feeney is not watching a game he is usually on the phone with the umpires' lawyer or with the National League's lawyers. The negotiations are not going well. The umpires working the spring games this year are local volunteers and fill-ins, rustled up by the home clubs. "The man at first is a great arbiter," Feeney announces. "He's going to be another Bill Klem."

Dave Winfield, the tall, stork-legged outfielder and slugger, stands in for the Padres and waggles his bat menacingly. He whacks a long sacrifice fly, driving in the first San Diego run of the day, and there is a spatter of applause from the old folks and kids in the stands. Partisanship doesn't run very deep here. Last year, the Cubs played in this old board-fence park, and the Oakland team did its training over in Mesa, a few miles to the south; this year, the teams have switched camps, and the Scottsdale fans may still be a little unhappy about it. Maybe not; it's hard to tell.

Another Oakland pitcher comes into the game, and the baseball talk goes on. Rod Carew, somebody says, has hit safely in every game he has played for the Angels this spring. He is killing the ball. Since the Angels signed him (he used to play for the Twins, of course), their season-ticket sales have gone off the charts. But the Angels, too, have catching troubles: Brian Downing has a sore arm. It is said that he hurt it weight-lifting during the winter. It is said that, over in Florida, Carlton

Fisk's arm is so bad that he hasn't thrown a ball or swung a bat this spring. The Phillies, it is said, are looking to trade Richie Hebner to the White Sox for Francisco Barrios before the interleague trading period ends, tomorrow night. And has anybody heard that Scott McGregor may have tendinitis? The Orioles' doctors have told him not to touch a ball for a *week*. . . . What about Bob Welch? Bob did something strange to his arm just fooling around in the infield. Terry Forster had that operation, you know, and if he doesn't come around fast the Dodgers may be in real pitching trouble. But Messersmith has been looking good for them. . . . When does Gaylord Perry pitch again for these guys—tomorrow?. . . . I don't know, but he's here. I saw him before the game. He looks great. . . . I know. He's been around so long that he's beginning to look like somebody out of the history of baseball. He looks like Grover Cleveland Alexander. Somebody like that. . . . Hey, you hear this one? Name the two active pitchers who have beaten all the clubs in both leagues—who have decisions against every major-league team. . . . Well, Gaylord has to be one of them. . . . Sure, but who's the other?. . . Wait, now. Don't tell me. Just a minute, now. . . .

In the game, the Padres have gone up by 4–3, but now Glenn Burke nails a home run over the left-field fence for the A's, to tie it up. There is some real noise in the stands this time. Burke does not look particularly happy as he trots back to the Oakland dugout; last year at this time, he was playing for the Dodgers. . . . The sun is terrific. The writers stretch and yawn. Birds are twittering. A young woman in cutoff jeans comes down the aisle lugging a bucket full of ice and beer. She is very tan. "Beer?" she says, almost shyly. "Any folks care for a beer?" The new batter for the A's, an outfielder named Joe Wallis, is sporting a full beard. "Say," Chub Feeney says suddenly, "Look at his batting helmet." Wallis is batting left-handed, but his batting helmet is meant for a right-handed batter and is protecting the wrong side of his head. Maybe he's expecting a sweeping curveball, somebody says.

Wallis singles, scoring Miguel Dilone, and the A's go back in front by 5–4, or 4–3. Something like that, anyway. I yawn and yawn. A terrible wave of sleepiness has come over me. This sun is too much. I begin to think about a nap in my motel room, followed by a dip in the pool. Spring training is hard on writers. I pick up my scorecard and stats, and start up the aisle. Then I stop and announce that I have figured out the other pitcher who has beaten all the other major-league clubs. It must be Ferguson Jenkins.

Wrong, two or three writers tell me in unison. Everybody picks Fergie, but he never beat the Cubs, because he was pitching for them all those years when he was in the National League. They are delighted.

I give up.

It's Rick Wise.

Rick Wise? Rick Wise, *of course!* Damn.

I sat in the stands again at my next spring-training game—a morning affair at Sun City, between a B squad of the Milwaukee Brewers and a touring Japanese team, the Yakult Swallows. The game was already in progress when I got there, and just as I slipped into the sun-warmed seat in the second row, near home, a smallish, bespectacled Milwaukee batter hit a drive that skipped between the Swallow left fielder and center fielder and rolled all the way out to the wall. As the batter scampered around first, a young woman just to my right jumped to her feet and cried, "Lennie! Lennie! Lennie! Lennie! Yay! Oh, *Lennie!*"

The base runner rounded second, then put on the brakes and returned to the bag. The young woman sat down, still clapping her hands, and gave me a dazzling smile. She had pale reddish hair and freckles.

"Are you—" I began.

"Yes, that's him," she said. "I'm her. That's my husband. I'm Darren—Darren Sakata. Hi."

I said hi, and then I stole a look at my Milwaukee press guide and discovered that Lenn Sakata is an infielder who spent most of last season with the Brewers' farm team in Spokane, where he batted .269. I also noticed that his middle name is Haruki, and that he was born in Hawaii. Dazed with coincidence, I realized that I had just sat down in a ballpark next to the wife of the man up at bat, and that the first batter I had ever seen swing against a Japanese pitcher was himself of Japanese descent. Baseball is full of surprises.

"Where did you two—" I said to Darren.

"In Albuquerque, last summer," she said instantly. "We met

in this Howard Johnson's—on *Lomas* Street? He was playing there. In Albuquerque, I mean. Albuquerque and Spokane are both in this Triple-A League, see, and Spokane was *visiting?* I'm from Aztec, New Mexico, myself, but I was going to the U.N.M., in Albuquerque. The University of New Mexico, I mean. We—"

She stopped because the Swallow's pitcher—a right-hander, with "Kurata" on the back of his uniform—had suddenly whirled and thrown to his shortstop, who tagged Lenn Sakata out at second. Sakata got up slowly and trotted in to his bench, with his head down.

"He was dead, boy," Darren announced. She shook her head disconsolately. "Oh, Lenn, that was so *stupid!*"

A few minutes later, the Swallows' catcher, Yaebashi, picked another Milwaukee runner off second, with a fine peg.

"Damned tricky, these Japanese," Darren said.

The Yakult Swallows (who won the Nihon Series—the Japanese World Series—last fall) were not just tricky. They beat the Brewer B team by 8–4, in a seven-inning game, and looked extremely competent in the process. Their pitchers—Kurata, who was a curveballer, and his successor, Tetsuo Nichi—weren't exactly overpowering, but they mixed up their pitches, and everything they threw seemed to be around the edge of the strike zone. The Swallows' infield play was crisp, and they attacked the ball eagerly at the plate, although without much sock; the largest player on the squad, an outfielder named Suiguru, did crack a two-run, wrong-field triple off the left-field wall. Their baserunning seemed a step or two slower than our American big-league level. Most of all, the Swallows looked trim; I have never seen an entire baseball club in such terrific shape. The moment the game ended, most of the Swallows went out into the field, broke up into pairs, and began punishing each other with frightful ground exercises. A few of the visitors, though, came over and shook hands with Frank Howard, the Brewers' first-base coach. Then they produced cameras and took turns posing for pictures with him. Frank Howard is six feet seven inches tall and weighs three hundred pounds, and sometimes he had to bend his knees a little in order to get his arm comfortably around the shoulders of one of the visitors while they smiled at the camera together. Great snaps.

In the afternoon game, the Brewers and the visiting California Angels took turns whacking the ball to the far corners of the Sun City ballpark—a strange, hollowed-out green moon crater, entirely surrounded by golf carts and senior citizens—in a game that the Brewers eventually captured by 8–6. Cecil Cooper had four hits, including a two-run homer, for the Brewers, and Willie Mays Aikens went three for three for the visitors. Only one man now stands between Aikens and a regular job at first base for the Angels: Rod Carew.* As almost everyone knows, Carew won his seventh American League batting title last year, hitting .333 for the Minnesota Twins; two years ago, he batted .388. Carew was one season away from attaining free-agent status, and the Twins, who cannot afford star salaries at the present intergalactic levels, traded him to the Angels during the winter, after extensive negotiations with several other teams, including the Giants and the Yankees. Carew's new five-year-package contract with the Angels will pay him about nine hundred thousand dollars per year. (The Angels, who are owned by a group headed by Gene Autry, now have the fourth-highest payroll in baseball, topped only by the Yankees, the Phillies, and the Red Sox. Because he is not a power hitter and because he played for a team that has enjoyed very little success in the past few years, Carew has always received less appreciation and celebrity than seem his due. Now, thanks to his new money and his new team—the Angels are aflame with expectations this year—he will begin to belong to fans everywhere. Before his visit to Sun City, he had played in six of the Angels' eight spring games, and was batting .474—a pretty good excuse for taking the afternoon off, though it broke the hearts of the locals.

I was more disappointed by the absence of another Angel—Ron Fairly, an old favorite of mine, who had retired a few weeks earlier to become a "color man" with the club's television crew. Fairly, an aggressive red-headed first baseman and outfielder, with a lovely left-handed swing, had played twenty-one years for the Dodgers, the Expos, the Cardinals, the A's, the Blue Jays, and the Angels. He first came up to the Dodgers in the summer of 1958, which means that two more seasons' play would have qualified him as one of the very few players

*Aikens was traded to the Kansas City Royals at the end of this 1979 season.

who have played major-league ball in four calendar decades—
Ted Williams, Mickey Vernon, Bobo Newsom, Minnie Mi-
noso, and a handful of other durable statistical marvels. The
Class of 1980 is thus reduced to three eligibles: Willie Mc-
Covey, Tim McCarver, and Jim Kaat. Hang in there, gentle-
men.

After the game in Sun City, I had a few words with the
oldest rookie on the field that day, the home-plate umpire.
Major-league umps are so miserably paid and so casually treated
that my sympathy has been with them in their strike, but my
eye was caught by the brisk and stylish work of the substitute
plate arbiter, who turned out to be a sixty-one-year-old retired
fireman named Gene Downing. "I was a tillerman and an engineer with the St. Louis Fire Department, but I always worked
as an umpire or a ref back there, too, in my spare time," Mr.
Downing told me. "I did softball games, soccer games, basketball, hardball—you name it. I was a baseball umpire for
high-school and college games, in American Legion ball, and
for a semipro group called the Heinie Meine League. I played
Class D ball years ago, with the Cardinal chain, and after I
hurt my arm I went into the umpiring line. It keeps you out-
doors."

I told Mr. Downing, who had called balls and strikes for
the Swallows game as well, that he looked perfectly ready to
work another doubleheader.

"Well, I'm getting back in shape," he said. "I was sure
pleased when the Brewers people came and asked me to help
out. I'd kept my uniform as a souvenir when I retired and came
out here. Well, no, that's not true. The truth is I couldn't give
it away. But all I had to do was dust off my black shoes, and
I was ready."

I asked him whether he had considered umpiring during the
regular season if the umpires' strike was not settled by then.

"Hell, no," he said. "Do I look crazy? There isn't enough
money in the world to make me leave Sun City. This is one
great place to live."

Spring training has often been a period of convalescence for
me—the time of year when I try to recover from the foolish
and dispiriting winter baseball news inflicted on us by the
owners and the Commissioner and the agents and other busy

non-players of the game. This year, there were fewer causes for discontent, which permitted me to concentrate my irritation and incredulity on a new scheduling proposal that has been enthusiastically supported by Bowie Kuhn and most of the owners. Under the new plan, which it was once hoped might be enacted in time for the 1980 season, each league would be arranged into three regional groups—East, Midwest, and West—which would mean three four-team divisions in the National League and two five-team and one four-team divisions in the American League. Mr. Kuhn has pointed out that this would keep more teams in pennant contention, with a resulting higher September attendance in several cities—not a burning consideration, one might suppose, in view of the fact that both leagues established all-time gate records last year. The real purpose of the shakeup is to make possible an additional set of playoff games, which could be sold to television as an immensely profitable package. Three levels of postseason play would also permit baseball, for the first time, to include all three networks in its champion-event television scheduling— another triumph for Mr. Kuhn, whose continuing abject excitement about the medium resembles that displayed by members of the audience at the "Let's Make a Deal" game show, who wear baby clothes and other outlandish costumes in hopes of pleasing the M.C. and thus being rewarded and horribly patronized before an audience of millions. The preliminary round of play of the Kuhnshow would involve the three divisional winners in each league, plus a fourth, "wild card" team— the second-place club with the highest winning percentage in regular-season play. The survivors would then move into another elimination to determine the participants in the World Series. Similar schemes, of course, already dominate the latter part of the professional football, basketball, and hockey seasons. Next year in the National Hockey League, for instance, only five teams will be eliminated after the regular eighty-game season; the remaining sixteen will then begin their almost interminable spring and early-summer playoffs.

Baseball, it seems to me, is singularly unsuited to this kind of tinkering. The long season, which already begins and ends in frigid weather in many cities, would be stretched by another week. The pennant races, which are the heart of this slow and searching sport, and which so often seem to conclude in riveting late-summer competition that sustains itself right down to the last weekend of the season, would be cheapened and devalued, and a sudden natural miracle, like the Yankees-Red Sox tie and one-game playoff last fall, would go almost unnoticed. The double playoff would further water down the World Series, and would increase the possibility that the ultimate champions might be a plainly inferior team—the club with the most pitching and the most luck during the endless eliminations. It takes only a little pencil work to reveal what shabby matchups we fans would be asked to give our passions to, and to pay for at premium ticket prices. The wild-card teams qualifying for the playoffs, of course, would all be non-winners in the present alignment. Some of them would be an embarrassment to the game. I have jotted down the regional winners and the wild-card teams that would have emerged during the present decade if Mr. Kuhn's Prefab Playoff had gone into effect in 1970, and I find that the wild-card team in the National League would have finished an average of eleven and a half games behind the best club; in the American League, it would have finished thirteen games behind.*

Luckily, this foolish prospectus is not about to be ratified—at least, not in the next season or two. It does appear to have strong support in the American League, where a vote passed by three-quarters of the clubs is sufficient to permit structural alterations to the game. The National League, however, requires unanimity, and the opposition there is known to be so large and powerful (the Dodgers, the Reds, the Phillies, and the Cubs are against the plan) that the matter has never been put to a formal vote. But keeping bad ideas out of baseball is like protecting democracies in Latin America; the juntas and reschedulers are always hovering in the shadows, waiting for the next crisis or the next election, and when at last their shiny, reasonable, progressive new regime is given a trial term in office one somehow knows that it will be forever.

* * *

*The owners got their chance to try out this sort of artificial scheduling and an additional round of postseason play in 1981, when they divided that season into two parts after the seven-week cessation of play brought about by the players' strike—with exactly the same resulting mismatches and ironies that I have outlined here. See page 389 *et seq.,* for the sad details.

One little blaze of news that warmed me in midwinter was the election of Willie Mays to the Baseball Hall of Fame. The apotheosis, which came five years after his retirement and in the first year of his eligibility for the honor, was no surprise to anyone (the surprise was that twenty-three members of the Baseball Writers Association of America, which selects the immortals, left Mays off their ballots altogether), but I was startled at the amount of pleasure it brought me. I suspect that his enshrinement allowed me to remember Mays as he had been in his wonderful youth—the brilliant boy gliding across the long meadows of the Polo Grounds, or running the bases in a cloud of speed and dust and excitement—and to forget the old, uncertain, querulous Willie Mays who came to the Mets in his final few seasons and who had so clearly stayed too long in the game. The shift in my feelings was like the change that sometimes comes when we remember a close relative or a friend who has died in old age or after a long illness; suddenly one morning, our sad last view of that person fades away and we are left instead with an earlier and more vivid picture—the one that stays with us. It is a miracle of sorts. When this happens with one's feelings about a ballplayer, the shift becomes the final scene of the ultimate baseball drama—the little life that a few great athletes live out for us on the field, from birth to death, all in the span of a few decades.

One afternoon in Arizona, I talked about Willie Mays with Bill Rigney, who played with him on the old New York Giants and later became his manager. Rigney, who has also managed the Angels and the Twins, is now on special assignment with the Angels. He is sixty years old—a tall, trim man with straight white hair, a humorous, intelligent face, a sun-wrinkled neck, and expansively gesturing hands. He has an infielder's look and an eager, singles-hitting way of talking and thinking. We sat by the side of a deserted pool and sipped a little whiskey and talked about Willie, while a late-afternoon breeze nudged a beach ball to and fro in the water near our feet.

"What I remember most was the strength he had," Rigney said. "Besides the great plays and the hitting, I mean. He never got hurt. He played every inning, played every game, and he played hard all the time. I was still with the Giants when he came up, and you could see that right away. There never was any Cadillac-ing in Willie. Another thing I marvelled at—

beyond the ability, to one side of it—was the instinct he had for the game. Mostly, you have to teach players a lot—even the ones who are tremendous athletes. But Willie seemed to have it all. Even in his first year, he'd get on second base, say, and right away he'd steal the catcher's signals—within a minute he'd see the combination. He *knew*. No matter what was going on, he knew what it would take to win the game. I couldn't get over that. I was thirty-two or thirty-three when he came up and joined us in '51, and I was already thinking I'd like to manage someday, and it impressed me that there could be a player so young who seemed to know everything. I thought that maybe that was all there was to being a manager—just sitting back and watching a man like Willie Mays play ball for me.

"I remember the day he arrived. We were in Shibe Park, getting ready to play the Phillies, and he turned up late but still in time for batting practice. We'd all heard what he had done out in Minnesota that spring, in the minors—I think he'd batted about .480 over two months out there—but none of us was ready for the sight of him. He got into the batting cage, and all the Phillies and all the Giants stopped what they were doing to watch him. He hit balls up on the roof and balls off the wall—balls ricocheting everywhere. Even in batting practice on his first day in a major-league uniform, at the age of nineteen, he caught your eye.

"I think I saw almost all the great catches. The Vic Wertz catch in the '54 Series. The catch off Bobby Morgan at Ebbets Field, when he ran and dived horizontally and grabbed the ball—it was a *shot*—and hit his head against that low concrete wall they had along the fence in left field there, and still held on to the ball. I saw the Clemente catch in Pittsburgh, when he caught up with the ball running with his back to the plate and grabbed it off barehanded. I can still see him trotting back in with the ball in his hand and dropping it on the mound. The one I liked best, I guess, was the play he made once in the early season at the Polo Grounds. The grass out there had been resodded—Horace [Horace Stoneham, the Giants' owner at the time] had to do that every year, because the football Giants had always chewed it up pretty good—and we'd had rain. There was a routine fly ball hit to left, and Bobby Thomson made a move for it and slipped and fell down flat. Willie had drifted over near him—you know, just in a routine way to cover—and when Bobby slipped and fell, Willie made the catch with one hand, and with the other hand he reached down and pulled Bobby to his feet, all in the same motion. I can still see it.

"What a hitter he was! He *destroyed* pitchers. They all threw at him—there was a lot more of that in those days. Down he'd go, but he'd jump back up again and dig in, with that determined, surprised look of his. When I was his manager, back in the late fifties, when we'd moved out to San Francisco, there was a pitcher with the Reds named Bob Purkey, who threw at Willie every single time. Willie would step in and—bang!—here came the pitch at Willie's cap, and he'd be in the dirt. After a while, Willie wasn't hitting much more than about .150 against him. I wasn't exactly pleased by this, you understand, and at the All-Star Game that year—I think it was at Forbes Field, in Pittsburgh—I saw Warren Giles, the president of the National League, and the Commissioner, Ford Frick, sitting together, and I went over and complained about it. I'd had a couple of Bloody Marys in the pressroom, and I figured the hell with it—let it come out. So after I told them about Mr. Purkey knocking my center fielder on the seat of his pants every time, they both sort of smiled, and Mr. Giles said, 'Well, Rig, we all know that isn't in the rules, but it's part of the game, isn't it? It's part of the game of baseball.' I said, 'I'm glad to hear you say that, sir, because now I know how to solve the problem. I've promised Willie that the next time Bob Purkey comes up to bat in a game against us I'm going to switch my pitcher and my center fielder and let Willie Mays pitch against Purkey. It's all taken care of. Thank you.'

"Well, you can imagine what happened. They both said, 'Hold *on*, now, Rig! You can't do *that*! We're not going to have a race riot on our hands because of you.' And a couple of days later there came a flood of directives out from the league office and the Commissioner's office to Horace and to me, telling us to lay off. It was too bad. Willie had really been looking forward to knocking Bob Purkey's hat off, for a change. Purkey never did stop throwing at him, of course, but some of our pitchers had taken notice, and they found ways of showing Mr. Purkey that we really cared about our center fielder."

* * *

In Phoenix, in the third inning of a game between the Giants and the Padres, Willie McCovey singled sharply up the middle, lashing at the ball like a gigantic umbrella being opened; he moved to third base on an error by the San Diego center fielder, and came in to score on a single. McCovey got a big hand from the fans—too much applause, really, for a single; there was a memorial tone to it. McCovey was in extraordinary condition this spring, but he is forty-one years old now, and his movements afield (he is a first baseman) had become dogged and thoughtful. Nobody wanted to talk about it, but it was clear almost from the beginning of spring training that the Giants' first baseman this year would be Mike Ivie, a blond, twenty-six-year-old right-handed slugger, who hit two pinch-hit grand-slam homers last year. Ivie took off twenty-five pounds during the winter, in preparation for his new responsibilities. McCovey has five hundred and five lifetime homers and is the most popular figure ever to play in Candlestick Park; anyone who has ever had secret dreams of being a major-league manager should reflect for a moment or two on the feelings of Joe Altobelli, the San Francisco skipper, when he walks past McCovey in the Giants' dugout this summer. In Phoenix, one of the Giants players murmured to me, "Nobody likes to take down a monument and replace it with a K-Mart, but sometimes it has to be done."

With McCovey on the bench, the main thing the Giants may lack this year is the daily presence on the field of a charismatic hitter—a Rod Carew, that is. I watched Carew in a game between the Angels and the Cubs in Ho-Ho-Kam Park Stadium, in Mesa. Playing before a sellout crowd of 4,251 old folks who were wearing 4,251 different shades of pastel sun hats. Rod singled sharply in the very first inning, to drive in a run; a moment later he stole second. Carew is tall and elegantly slim, with long, wristy hands, long legs, and narrow pants. He is coffee-colored—light coffee, half-and-half—and good-looking, if you don't mind the bulge of tobacco in his cheek. Watching him up at bat is a treat. He hits left-handed, with the bat flattened a little and held loosely in his hands, almost as if he were trying to guess its weight, until the instant he begins his swing. He moves around in the box, and in relation to the plate, depending on the pitcher he is facing, but with each pitch his lead foot, the right, lifts and pauses delicately, with only the toe of his spikes touching the dirt; the ensuing stride is minimal, and the shoulders and hips open smoothly and beautifully. The swing looks like a golf-instruction film played in slow motion; you sense there is time to study every part of it.

Later, I asked Bill Rigney about this feeling I had about Carew—the impression that he had more time than other batters in which to swing at a pitch. Rigney had managed Carew for three seasons on the Twins, and now they were together again with the Angels.

"He doesn't remind you of anybody else out there, does he?" Rigney said. "I used to think Stan Musial was the best hitter I ever saw. Well, Rod isn't anything like Stanley at the plate, except that he hits the ball with the same consistency. He hits it everywhere, and he hits it *often*. He hardly ever pops out, and even when he grounds out he does it with authority. He gets the good part of the bat on the ball about two-thirds of the time. The theory and secret of hitting is waiting. The longer you wait, the better chance you have. You never see Rod in a bad position up at bat. He has more time to take a good swing than anyone else I've ever seen. Think how often you've seen a catcher put his glove up for a pitch on the outside corner and then Rod reaches out and seems to hit it right out of the glove and on a line down into the left-field corner. The man is *late*. If you leave power out of it, he's the best hitter in the league. He's the best in baseball.

"I think he's going to draw big this year. He's going to help the other hitters around him in the lineup. It looks like Rick Miller will lead off for us this year and Carney Lansford will be second. They're not going to let Rod Carew hit alone— hey, let's have somebody on base when *this* man is up! It was just the same when Willie came along with the Giants: he excited the other hitters. I can hardly wait to see it happen again."

During the late innings of another game—the Mariners and the Giants this time—I moved out to a lightly populated stretch of left-field bleacher seats in Phoenix Municipal Stadium and began to watch a rookie San Francisco pitcher named Mike Glinatsis warming up on the sidelines. He was a tall, strongly built right-hander with long arms, and his fastball was making satisfactory popping noises in the glove of Tom Haller, the Giants' catching coach. Haller is six feet four, but he had furled himself close to the ground behind the plate to give Glinatsis a good low target, and from time to time he nodded encouragingly when he straightened up and fired the ball back. At the other end, Glinatsis was being observed by Larry Shepard, the Giants' pitching coach, who stood about three feet behind him and a little to one side. Shepard, a small, gray-haired man, stood motionless, with his legs wide apart and his hands plunged deep into his black Giants warmup jacket. His cap was cocked forward against the late sunlight, with its bill almost touching the bridge of his nose, so that his whole face was in shadow; only an occasional reflected gleam showed that he was wearing sunglasses. Now and then, he would murmur something to Glinatsis. An inning ended; Glinatsis threw one more pitch to Haller and then came over and picked up his jacket from a bench before hurrying in to the mound to take his warmup pitches as the Seattle batter moved out of the dugout. Another San Francisco pitcher—Gary Lavelle, a left-hander who is the Giants' best reliever—took Glinatsis's place on the bullpen mound and began throwing to Haller. Glinatsis (now a small, distant figure) gave up an instant double to Julio Cruz—a solidly hit blow that rolled all the way to the left-field fence. Then he was hit for a line single by Willie Horton. Then he gave up a single to Larry Milbourne. Shepard and Haller paid no attention to the game. Shepard talked to Lavelle and then took his hands out of his pockets and made a pitching gesture with his left arm, ending it with an exaggerated waggling motion of the wrist. Lavelle wound up and threw, and the pitch dropped off a little just before it disappeared into Haller's glove. Shepard waggled his wrist again. "Keep it loose," I heard him say. Lavelle threw, and again the ball seemed to drop and die as it crossed the plate. Shepard had resumed his motionless posture, with his hands in his jacket pockets, but he nodded to Lavelle as Haller stood up once again and fired the ball back.

All this seemed to be happening with unusual clarity—Shepard's stance and Haller's crouch, and the sound of the ball hitting the glove, and the low slant of the afternoon sun, and the odd look of batted balls and infield throws when they are seen almost from ground level about three hundred feet away—and for a brief moment I had the feeling that I could also see myself within this scene, with my feet up on the row just below me and my elbows on my knees: I was watching myself watching baseball. This was peculiar, to say the least. I knew that I had observed almost exactly this same scene dozens of times, or perhaps hundreds of times: some young pitcher warming up on the sidelines with a coach beside him, and then the pitcher walking into the game with his large strides and with his warm-up jacket over his arm, and then (usually, not always) the kid getting his ears knocked off in there. This time, it had seemed to be waiting for me, so to speak, and all I had to do was to walk into the picture and sit down in order to make it fresh again, and also to make it old—to bring it back just as it had always been.

The next day, in Tempe, before a game between the Mariners and the Milwaukee Brewers, George Bamberger, the Milwaukee manager, was talking about getting out of baseball. Bamberger was a minor-league pitcher for eighteen years, playing for Class AA and AAA teams in places like Jersey City, Oakland, Vancouver, and Ottawa. Along the way, he appeared in ten major-league games, for the Giants and then the Orioles, pitching a total of fourteen innings, with no decisions and an earned-run average of 9.65. He retired after the 1963 season and became the minor-league pitching instructor for the Baltimore Orioles organization. He moved up to the parent club in 1968, and for the next decade he coached the distinguished Baltimore pitching corps. Last year, with some reluctance, he accepted an offer to manage the Brewers. He did brilliantly in his very first year, steering the heretofore docile Brewers to a third-place finish in the dangerous American League East and the fourth-best won-lost record in the majors—accomplishments that caused him to be named the Major League Manager of the Year. Bamberger is an informal and cheerful man, with large ears and a large smile, and honors rest lightly on him. "If I wasn't managing, this would be my last year," he said to me. "Sometimes I wish I *wasn't* managing. Anyway, I think 1980 will probably be it for me. It's about fifty-fifty I'll quit after that. I'm not going to get out of baseball. It's just that I'm sick of all this goddam travel. I look to get myself a job somewhere as an instructor. Maybe I can help some club with their pitchers during spring training. I just like to work with kids. That's the best part of this game."

I was a little embarrassed by Bamberger's remarks, because I have heard a great many coaches and managers, in baseball and in other sports, say the same thing. "I just like to work with kids" is a frightful sports cliché. I climbed up in the stands, and the game started—a dour, windblown sort of game, with a fine, chilly rain after the fourth or fifth inning. I drank a cup of coffee, warming my hands around the plastic cup, and then I remembered Mike Glinatsis and Larry Shepard working in the sunlight over at the Giants' park the day before, and it was suddenly clear to me that I had no business feeling superior about what George Bamberger had said, because he was telling the truth, and because I felt exactly the same way. I'm still not entirely sure why the sight of some young pitcher warming up in spring training means so much to me, but I would almost rather watch and write about that than see Reggie Jackson or Pete Rose come up with men on base in some jam-packed, roaring stadium in October. The old coach with his hands in his pockets watching the young man pitching is the same sports cliché—it's almost a recruiting poster for baseball—but I'm not sure that it should be resisted for that reason. Its suggestions are classical. A mystery is being elucidated before our eyes; something is being handed on. The young man may fail (probably he will), but in time he may do better. One day, he may surprise his tutors, and they will turn and begin to take note of him when he is in the game. He will become better known, possibly famous; he might even become one of the best pitchers ever. It could happen; probably it won't. Either way, it touches something in us. Because baseball changes so little, it renews itself each year without effort, but always with feeling.

The Brewers' starting pitcher in that drizzly game against the Mariners was a blond right-hander named Lary Sorensen, who was struggling with his control and was knocked about for six hits and four runs in the first two innings. He will have better days. Last year, in his second season in the majors, at the age of twenty-two, he won eighteen games and lost twelve. The sports pages often misspell his first name. Sorensen grew up near Detroit, and his parents are lifelong, diehard Tiger fans; they named him after Frank Lary, a Detroit pitcher of the nineteen-fifties and sixties, who specialized in beating the Yankees. Last June, while the Brewers were visiting Tiger Stadium,

Lary Sorensen heard about a forthcoming sportscasters' luncheon honoring the 1968 Tigers, who won the World Championship in a famous comeback World Series victory over the Cardinals. Sorensen invited himself to the affair, and when he got there he asked if he might be allowed to say a few words. When he was introduced, he stood up and looked about at some of the recent Tiger immortals seated near him and said, "Uh, Mr. Kaline, Mr. Cash, I suppose you remember the end of the game here ten years ago in September—the night you beat the Yankees, 2–1, and won the pennant, and all those kids ran out on the field and began to tear up the infield. There was a lot of talk afterward about what happened. I guess it shouldn't have happened. But I was one of those kids. I was *there,* and I ran out on the field and tore up a piece of turf from right behind the pitcher's mound. In fact—" And here Lary Sorensen reached under the table and produced a plastic bag containing a chunk of something green. "In fact—well, here it is. It's been in my mother's refrigerator ever since."

I came in out of the rain in the middle innings of the game at Tempe and headed for the press box, and on the way I ran into an acquaintance of mine, Jim Colborn, who was out of uniform because he was scheduled to pitch for the Mariners the next afternoon. He greeted me cheerfully and introduced me to his pregnant, red-haired wife, Jennie, and to their three young, blond daughters, Daisy, Rosie, and Holly. Jim Colborn, who is thirty-two, is a sociologist as well as a pitcher, and has done graduate work at the University of Washington and the University of Edinburgh. He suffered through a miserable season last year, being traded in May from Kansas City to Seattle and then losing his first six starts for the Mariners. He got better late in the year, however, and during the winter he was signed to a new two-year contract by the Mariners, for about ninety thousand dollars a year. (A hundred thousand dollars is now the average major-league salary.) "The best part is being back in Seattle," he said. 'We have a great house up on Lake Washington, and it's the best city to live in if you have a family. Nearly everything you can think of to do there is free."

Colborn told me that he thought he had suffered from a sore arm most of last year without knowing it. "It hurt some in spring training," he said, "and I guess I began to throw a little wrong then, to favor it. My arm was finishing in a different place with every pitch, so the results weren't exactly surprising. But then about three weeks ago here I began to throw without any pain or strain, and suddenly it was there again. I'd throw a pitch and look at it, and I'd think, 'Hey!' It was like saying hello to an old friend."

I left the game before it was over—the Mariners won, 8–3, and the rain continued to the end—but before I departed I fell into conversation with a little knot of Mariners fans, who were standing together under the covered part of the stands, out of the rain, and peering down an aisle to watch the action on the wet green grass below us. (*Devoted* fans, I should say: the Mariners finished with a 56–104 record last year, the worst in baseball.) On the field, Julio Cruz, the small and ebullient Mariner second baseman, helped turn a neat 5–4–3 double play, and a woman next to me clapped her hands delightedly and cried, "Beautiful, Julio baby!" She was wearing a Mariners T-shirt. I remarked to her that I had been relishing watching Cruz play ball, which was true: he and Ozzie Smith, the Padre shortstop, were the best young infielders I saw all spring. The woman said, "I've seen him play ever since the first day he came up. I remember the very first day he ever got into a major-league game, two years ago. I was sitting out in the right-field bleachers at the Kingdome. A ball was hit to him, and he made a terrible play on it, but it was only because he had been so busy looking at his own uniform out there— admiring his shirtfront and how he looked—that he messed up. I could see it all through my binoculars. Everybody around me was disgusted, but I knew he'd get better. Last year, he was the best-fielding second baseman in the league—did you know that? And he stole all those bases. I just hope they'll let him bunt more this year. He's still only twenty-three or twenty-four years old. He's just a baby. I love Ruppert Jones, but I think Julio is the best player we have, don't you? He's going to be our first big star."

Listening to her, I recalled what it had been like to root for the Mets back in the nineteen-sixties, when *they* were the worst team in baseball. We all used the possessive pronoun when we talked about the young players on the team, and we talked about the better times to come. It was wonderful being there at the confused, wildly hopeful beginning of things, like that; it was like the first weeks of a great love affair.

Baseball, however, is a business first of all, and it can be a hard one. Ten days after the rainy afternoon in Tempe, just before the beginning of the regular season, the Mariners, who are said to be in financial straits, dropped three veteran pitchers from their roster, including Jim Colborn. The current high level of player salaries makes headlines whenever a superstar is signed to a golden multi-year contract, but it has not been much noticed that many clubs are economizing in the off-season by cutting loose experienced middle-level players who have comfortable but non-guaranteed salaries and keeping rookies in their place. Jim Colborn's new contract was not guaranteed. Because he was cut so late in the spring, he was not able to find an opening with another team, and he has gone into the house-building business in Ventura, California. He seems to be out of baseball.

I flew to Florida from Phoenix and drove to Lakeland for a night game between the visiting Red Sox and the Detroit Tigers—a sellout affair also observed by about two dozen members of the enormous Boston press corps, which was getting itself ready for another summer of Euripidean despair. *Everything*, I was told at once, had gone wrong with the Bosox this spring, but it seemed to me that the Tigers had almost more to whimper about, for Mark Fidrych's damaged wing had not come around, and Rusty Staub, the best designated hitter in the league, had apparently retired after a long salary wrangle with the front office. The game was a brisk one, with almost everybody first-ball hitting, and the young Detroit lineup whacking Dennis Eckersley repeatedly and stealing bases like peanuts. The Tigers went ahead for good in the fourth on a two-run homer hit into the outer darkness by a large, left-handed rookie phenom named Kirk Gibson, who has begun a career in baseball in spite of many blandishments and cajoleries from the National Football League. It was his second hit of the spring season—both hits being two-run homers against the Red Sox. All this seemed sufficient entertainment for one evening, but we were given a double bill. Early in the game, a trombone-voiced Tiger fan took up a stance at the back of the grandstand, behind home plate and directly in front of the low press box, from where he commenced a non-stop, mind-bending baiting of the Red Sox batters. His reviews were strongminded but lacking in variety. When Jim Rice stood in at one point, the critic yelled, "Hey, Rice! Hey, *Rice!* You know what you are, Rice? You're a rice pudding, Rice! You hear that, Rice? You're a rice pudding, Rice, that's all you are! Hey, Rice! Why don't you send your accountant up to bat for you Rice? Send your accountant up to bat for you, you big rice pudding! Hey, Rice! *Rice!* You know what you are, Rice?..." Similarly inventive metaphors and suggestions were offered to each Boston batter in turn. There were cries for mercy from fans and scribes alike, but the man was adamant in the exercise of his rights and his tonsils. After four or five innings of this, a gentle Fenway transcendentalist seated just to my right in the first row of the press box arose, muttering, and then returned carrying a medium-sized beer cup filled with water. He balanced this with exquisite care on the lip of the press-box parapet, directly in front of me and perhaps eight inches above the scalp of the Lakeland Demosthenes, who had gone silent for the moment, while his Tigers were at bat. The inning ended, the teams changed sides, the Tiger pitcher warmed up, and the next Red Sox batter stepped up to the plate.

"Hey, Scott" we heard. (It was indeed the Boomer.) "Hey, *Scott!* Hey—"

Fatigued, my companion yawned and stretched, and by mischance the fingers of his left hand just nudged the paper cup. The ensuing roar of pleasure and gratitude from the stands in front of us far outdid the welcome previously given to Kirk Gibson's homer. Then there was a further and extremely cruel second burst of cheering, almost as loud as the first, when a responding, upwardbound refreshment—beer, this time, I discovered—suddenly drenched an innocent press-box bystander, or bysitter, recently off a plane from Phoenix.

Well before nine o'clock the next morning, sizable lines of fans began to form up in the bright sunshine outside the ticket windows at Chain O' Lakes Park, in Winter Haven. This is Red Sox country, and the Yankees were coming to town. The Red Sox' multiple anxieties—Carlton Fisk's arm, Bill Campbell's shoulder, Jim Rice's new salary, Carl Yastrzemski's old salary, Butch Hobson's elbow operation, George Scott's age and waistline, the loss of Luis Tiant, the loss of Bill Lee, the team's collapse last September, the loss of the playoff game to the Yankees in October—had made for a distressing, almost panicky sort of spring in their camp, but on this morning there was a new taste of expectation in the warm, orangey air. Reporters holding paper cups of coffee stood together outside the batting nets and watched George Scott take special batting practice. The Boomer looked thin and serious. He was wearing a rubber shirt and swinging again and again at balls that were being tossed underhand by coach Walk Hriniak, who was kneeling behind a low screen about six feet away. Hriniak would flip up a ball, and Scott would cut at it instantly, swinging only from the waist up—a maneuver designed to improve his bat speed. Scott gave an explosive grunt each time he swung, which merged at once with the crack of the bat and then the whisper of the ball as it skinned along the rope netting off to his left: "Hunh!" *Crack! Shhhh . . .* "Hunh!" *Crack! Shhhh . . .*

An hour or two later, after the morning workouts, Red Sox vice president Haywood Sullivan and Carl Yastrzemski held a brief press conference to announce that Yaz's present contract had been extended to run through 1981, at a level later estimated at about six hundred thousand dollars a year. From the moment that Jim Rice signed a seven-year, $4.9-million-dollar contract last winter, it had been plain that Carl's salary would have to be brought up to Rice's neighborhood (Yastrzemski had been getting three hundred and seventy-five thousand dollars a year), in spite of the Red Sox' profound reluctance to begin breaking open existing contracts—a feeling shared by every front office in baseball. Rice led both leagues last season in hits, homers (forty-six of them), and runs batted in, and was voted the American League's Most Valuable Player, but Yastrzemski, of course, is Yaz. Captain Carl, in any case, was in wonderful good humor, and an hour after the press conference he held a more informal talk with a small group of reporters out by the bullpen pitching mounds. He was shirtless and bareheaded in the sun, with a towel around his neck. He talked most about his hitting. "I can't hold my bat up here now, the way I always did," he said, in his Boston-tinged accents. "I've dropped my hands down, for more speed, and I've stopped trying to muscle the ball. I have to flip the bat. I talk to myself in the batter's box. The main thing I've had trouble with over the years is dropping my back shoulder—trying to loft the ball, instead of staying down and driving it. You can loft it after you make contact, but if you do it too soon you pop up. Maybe you've noticed I've been leaning forward in the box more, to keep my front shoulder down."

In all our minds, of course, was the image of Carl Yastrzemski leaning forward in the box in the ninth inning of the playoff game against the Yankees at Fenway Park last October 2nd, with two outs and the tying run at third base, and Boston down by a run, and the pennant and the year in the balance. Goose Gossage fired, and Carl swung and popped up weakly to third, in foul ground, to end the Red Sox' season. Now somebody asked, "Your last swing last year—was that a good swing?"

"It was horseshit," he said, and we all laughed. "No," he went on, "I can't say that. It wasn't a good swing, but the guy made a hell of a pitch. The ball sailed in on me, and at the speed he throws, you know, there isn't much time for correction."

Someone asked if he had thought about the pitch and the swing afterward, during the winter.

"I'll always think about that swing," he said.

But Yaz, who had died for New England last October, was alive and smiling here in the spring sunshine. He looked like a young hero. Sometime next August, he will knock out his three-thousandth base hit; along about the same week, if statistical projections hold up, he will hit his four-hundredth homer. The two blows might be the same blow; it might even happen in Minnesota on August 22nd, on Carl Yastrzemski's fortieth birthday. I wouldn't bet against it.

Both managers—Bob Lemon, of the Yankees, and Don Zimmer, of the Red Sox—kept saying that the game that afternoon was just another meaningless spring affair. "Try and find it in the records," Zim muttered. But the fans knew better, and so did the Red Sox, I think. The starting pitchers, by wonderful accident, were Ron Guidry and Mike Torrez, who had been the two starters in the playoff game, and the second Yankee pitcher would be Luis Tiant, the grand stylist and stopper of the Boston mound corps in this decade, who had gone over to the enemy as a free agent after the Boston front office mortally offended him by never talking money last summer. Long before game time, every seat in the park was gone and there were people sitting and standing all around the jam-packed new bleacher seats on the grassy outfield banks. Somebody out there in left-center had the best seat of all, it turned out: somebody who was one bounce beyond the first landing place of the ball that Jim Rice hit there in the third inning—an immense, three-run downtowner struck off Guidry, which set the festive tone for the entire afternoon. There were other causes for celebration—Rice's five runs batted in, a homer (off Tiant) by rookie catcher Gary Allenson, and a marvellous peg from the deep-right-field corner by Dwight Evans, which overtook Graig Nettles, churning up the base path to second, and nailed him at the uttermost tip of his slide. Chambliss homered for the Yankees, and so did Reggie Jackson, the latter blow clearing the right-field wall and then bounding over a high wire fence and into an orange grove, where it was pursued eagerly by a small boy—the boy and the ball going over the fence together like a fox after a rabbit. Tiant, looking like some mercenary-army brigadier in his gray New York road uniform, gave up three runs in his first inning of work, thus further troubling the mixed allegiance of the watching hordes. By the seventh, however, with the Sox holding their ultimate winning margin of 7–3, everybody there, in the stands and on the field, began to remember that this was spring training, after all, and that nothing sad or serious could happen on this day. Tiant trotted out some of his famous mound mannerisms against Jim Rice—the Low-Flying Plane, the Slipper Kick—and Jim, leaping out of the box in alarm, laughed and gestured "C'mon, Louie, throw the ball!" Yaz, in his turn, ran up a few steps, faking a bunt, and when he popped out at last he came back in past the mound and lifted his batting helmet in a comical and courtly salute. All in all, it was quite an afternoon. Carlton Fisk, who had taken some careful, stretching practice pegs in the outfield, reported that his painful elbow was a little better (he played fifty games with a broken rib last year, and extended a nerve or tendon by throwing when hurt); Butch Hobson had played in his first game of the year; Bill Campbell had thrown batting practice, and said afterward that *his* arm—his shoulder, to be exact—felt almost alive again. Right to the end, it was a day of good news.

In St. Petersburg the next night, the Yankees whipped the Mets, 9–3, on a wet and windy field. Tommy John, still another free agent now happily enslaved by a lucrative Yankee contract, worked six innings and notched fifteen ground-ball outs with his skulking slider. John, a battle-tested left-hander, seems likely to win fifteen or eighteen games for the champions this year—an event guaranteed to cause more trembling and groaning among the countless Yankee-haters across the land. Perversely, I was depressed that evening only by the sight of the thinly talented, semi-anonymous Mets making their earnest preparations for another season of losing baseball. Having failed to make any significant improvements in the last-place club over the winter, the Mets front office has evidently decided upon cheese-paring as a prime tactic with which to win back the lost affection of millions of Gotham fans: manager Joe Torre has been told to make do without a bullpen coach this season. The Charles Shipman Payson family, which owns the Mets and easily has the means to match George Steinbrenner in the winter money wars, no longer seems to care for the business or sport of baseball; I wish it would sell the club to somebody who does.

The game that night at St. Petersburg was another sellout. The Yankees, in fact, played to sellout crowds at all thirteen of their road games in Florida this year, and came within a few dozen tickets of selling out all their home games at Fort Lauderdale, too. Many other clubs also reported record-breaking attendance figures. Baseball is currently enjoying the greatest national popularity in its long history, but I think other forces and factors may explain the big turnouts in the Grapefruit and Cactus League exhibitions. Last month, Bob Lemon complained that he could not get a real look at his rookies and second-line players during the spring games, because fans everywhere expressed outrage if they did not get to see his famous regulars—Reggie Jackson, Thurman Munson, Mickey Rivers, Graig Nettles, Lou Piniella, and the rest—in the starting lineup. Lemon was under pressure to play them every day, and George Steinbrenner once criticized him when he did not. Giving the manager an opportunity to take a long look at his organization's youngsters and substitutes is mostly what the spring-training games are *for;* he already knows what his stars can do, and they, for their part, are experienced enough to know when they should play and when they should rest, as they get themselves ready for the long season ahead. More and more now, it seems, fans come to these games not for the rare chance they give to watch baseball quietly and at close range, played in something like a manner of its casual and rural past, but to ogle the new millionaires and celebrities on the field. The gigantic sums of money that ballplayers are able to command seem to distract the attention of the fans, shifting it away from the athletes' wonderful feats afield—the very thing that made them suddenly worth so much money—and toward the commonplace attractions of personality and celebrity. This can happen very quickly. Bucky Dent, a handsome but unremarkable shortstop for the Yankees, hit the winning three-run homer in the playoff against the Red Sox last year and then sustained a wonderful October hot streak at the plate and in the field, which won him the Most Valuable Player award in the World Series. Dent's name and smile are now visible everywhere, and he is said to have earned more than a hundred and fifty thousand dollars for his endorsements and appearances during the winter. The ultimate baseball celebrity of 1979, of course, is Pete Rose, who played out his tenure with the Cincinnati Reds last summer and then signed a four-year contract with the Phillies worth almost three million dollars. Reporters and friends of mine who visited the Phillies camp this spring told me that the fans who came to Clearwater to see Rose often could barely pick out the top of his cap as he went about in the midst of a daily crowd of newspaper and magazine reporters and television interviewers and photographers and TV-commercial directors (including people making commercials for Japanese television) and network camera crews. Pete Rose is an engaging and talkative fellow, a pleasure to interview, and he is a vivid, exemplary player on the field. I had planned to pay a call on him and his teammates this spring, but after I heard what the Phillies entourage was like I changed my itinerary. One way or another, I figured, Pete Rose would be coming my way. I was right, too; there he was on my television set just the other afternoon—not playing ball, to be sure, but wearing a tuxedo and a ruffled shirt and grinning in response to jokes by Milton Berle and Phyllis Diller and some others on a nationally televised special called "The Pete Rose Roast."

Baseball is a durable and resilient phenomenon, and I think it will survive even its new status as a fad. I was encouraged in this notion by a talk I had with Ted Simmons, the veteran St. Louis catcher, whom I ran into before a Cardinals-Pirates game in St. Petersburg, on the last day of my tour. Simmons, who is twenty-nine, is beginning his twelfth season with the Cards; he is tough and efficient, almost always playing between a hundred and fifty and a hundred and sixty games every year. He bats from both sides of the plate, and his lifetime average is .298, which makes him the second-best switch-hitter in baseball—second only to Pete Rose. Simmons has a surprising off-the-field career as a serious collector of antiques—a field of expert interest that has won him a post on the board of trustees of the St. Louis Art Museum. I started to ask him how he had become involved with antiques, and he immediately held up a hand and said, "I'm sorry, but I don't want to go in that direction. If you and I had dinner together, or had a whole evening together, or had time to spend two or three days together, and if you happened to have a particular interest in antiques, then we might both get around to saying some things that might be useful and interesting. But just talking like this for a few minutes before a ballgame, you can't ask me a question that would let me say anything about it that would make any sense. O.K.?"

I said O.K. Then I said it again, in a startled sort of way, for it is not often that I meet people—ballplayers or anybody else—who are simultaneously articulate and private. It turned out, however, that Ted Simmons and I did have a subject in common—baseball. This is not a joke: a great many men who play the game—a majority, easily—seem to take only a minimal interest in its nuances and complexities. Ted Simmons, however, is a fan—a fanatic.

"I played all sports when I was younger," Simmons said (he was a football, basketball, and baseball star in high school at Southfield, Michigan), "but I always loved baseball most. I really think I love it more all the time. All you have to do is think about Abner Doubleday or that other man—that Alexander Cartwright, the mathematician—sitting down and deciding that the bases ought to be ninety feet apart. That was more than a hundred years ago, and it's never been necessary to change that, or change the other distances in baseball—not even by an inch. I can't get *over* that. Just think about it: the fastest man in the game today can hit the ball to deep short, and if the shortstop makes the play he'll still get him out—by an inch. There is no better game—I don't care if it's bridge or hockey or basketball or backgammon. Baseball has the ingredients to satisfy everybody. There's strategy, subtlety, tactics, beauty—everything. Unfortunately, not nearly enough people get a chance to experience the game at all levels, the way players do, but you don't really have to play baseball to understand its finesse and grace. All through a game, there are plays that result from a ball being hit to a certain place, and the patterns they follow tell you what's really going on and how the game is really played. If a fan is paying close attention, instead of just watching the flight of the ball, he can begin to pick this up.

"Let's say there are base runners on first and third, with one out or none out. The batter pops the ball up into foul territory behind the plate but deep—close to the fence and on the first-base side. I go back for the ball—I mean, the catcher goes back for the ball. Everybody sees that, but not everybody notices that the shortstop has moved directly to second base and the second baseman has moved directly to a spot well inside second base but on a straight line between the ball and the bag. Every infielder knows this. It's automatic—one, two, three. If you don't defense in that way, then the man on first takes off as soon as the ball is caught, the catcher throws to second, and the runner on third just cakewalks home, because of the long throw the catcher has to make. But if the defense is right, the second baseman cuts off the throw and gets the man at the plate easily. Then most people in the stands only think, 'Oh, how could that base runner be so slow?' They haven't seen the play. If the ball is hit to the other side, of course—on the third-base side—then the two infielders just flip-flop, with the second baseman going to the bag and the shortstop into the cutoff spot. There's no *news* about this— I'm not telling you anything you don't know. But I always wonder if the fans are seeing enough. If you stay with this game and really watch it, your appreciation goes much deeper. It rewards you."

Ted Simmons, batting right-handed, singled in the first inning and again in the third inning of the game against the Pirates that afternoon, driving in a run each time. But the Pirates were hitting, too. Dave Parker, their gigantic batting champion and M.V.P., whacked two line-drive singles and came around to score each time. Almost everybody was hitting the ball, in fact—fourteen hits for the two teams in the first five innings.

I had to leave before it was over, but I stopped and stood in an exit behind first base and watched one more inning from there. My hotel in St. Pete, the Bay Front Concourse, is right across the street from Al Lang Field, and when I went up to my room, on the fifth floor, before my late checkout—I was going to drive to Tampa for an evening flight to New York—I finished my packing and then I stood by my window and watched the game again for a little while. The players were too far away to be recognized, but I could see the bright colors of their uniforms and caps, and their shadows on the infield dirt, and sometimes a sudden flurry of movement by the fielders and base runners allowed me to pick up the white speck of the ball in its flight. Even from there, you could make out the patterns of the game.

_9_

Wilver's Way

OCTOBER 1979

Baseball, so various and voluminous are its possibilities, often gives the impression that it will always arrange the thrilling complexity, the obligatory challenge and response, at the summit of every important game or series. Sometimes it does. Reggie Jackson, gigantic with fame and pride and secret self-doubt, silences all his critics with a sudden Olympian gesture—the greatest October batting feat of all—in the final game of the World Series. An entire summer of lineups and innings, batters and pitchers, hits and outs clicks away in order to bring Carl Yastrzemski up to bat for the Red Sox against the Yankees at Fenway Park, with the tying and winning runs aboard, in the ninth inning of the single playoff game that must do away with one of these two exhausted, anxious, and courageous teams. These cathartic fires of two recent seasons were not quite equalled this year, which concluded with bitterly contested but one-sided league playoffs and a seven-game World Series, between the Pirates and the Orioles, that was notable above all for the refreshing and attractive personalities of the two new pennant-winning teams and for the triumph of Wilver Stargell, who has emerged as the most admired and admirable player of his time. The Series, which ended on a rising note

191

of excitement as the Pirates came back from the brink to win the last three games and the championship, produced some vivid moments and engrossing tactical maneuvers along the way, but it will also be remembered for its abominable weather, its poor defensive play (the two were connected, of course), and a nagging sense of letdown. Before we proceed to these matters, however, I want to suggest that the baseball season just past also presented us with a most unusual pattern of events, which was, in its own somewhat slower fashion, just as rewarding as the stirring moments I have cited. This summer, at the end of a baseball decade, an abrupt upheaval of form threw down all the famous, much publicized championship teams and habitual challengers of the recent past—the Yankees, the Dodgers, the Phillies, the Red Sox, the Royals, and (near the end) the Reds—and produced in their place a pushing, eager crowd of young teams that will struggle to dominate the arena of the nineteen-eighties: the California Angels, the Montreal Expos, the Houston Astros, the Milwaukee Brewers, the Orioles, and the new world-champion Pirates. And then, with classic propriety, the sport balanced all this greening and upspringing with a burst of brilliant performances by some of the oldest and best-known players of our era. It was a wonderful summer for fans, but a hard one, too, and my scorecards and unkempt baseball notebooks became filled with complaints and elegies and exclamation points as I tried to keep up with it all.

Splendors and Good Nights

Manny Mota, as ardent and elegant as ever, bowed out of baseball at the age of forty-one with a .357 season and fifteen pinch hits, establishing himself as the most productive pinch-hitter on record. He will stay on with the Dodgers as a coach and exemplar. The Niekro brothers—Joe, of the Astros, who is thirty-five, and Phil, of the Braves, who is forty—between them sailed about ten thousand knuckleballs through the soft summer air and ended up winning twenty-one games apiece. Phil's feat was the rarer one, for he also lost twenty games—an egalitarianism most recently achieved by Wilbur Wood, in 1973. Pete Rose, who is thirty-eight, moved along to the Phillies as a free agent this year, but he was not able to prevent his new teammates from slipping to a disastrous fourth-place finish, fourteen games behind the Pirates. This was not for lack of trying, however. Rose batted .331, and his two hundred and eight hits marked his tenth two-hundred-hit season, which broke the old record for two-hundred-hit years that he had shared with Ty Cobb. His one hundred and fifty-nine singles also put him past Honus Wagner as the best lifetime National League singles hitter. If these figures require any emphasis, it could be pointed out that at the beginning of September Rose was batting .310, with one hundred and fifty-seven hits. He batted .421 for the month of September and at one stretch went thirty for fifty at the plate, which is a .600 average, and, within that, twenty-eight for forty-five, which is .622, and twenty-three for thirty-four, which is .676. As Lou Brock said about Rose, "He seems to have an *obligation* to hit."

Brock himself this summer became the fourteenth player to attain the plateau of three thousand lifetime hits. He also stole twenty-one bases, putting his lifetime total at nine hundred and thirty-eight, and obliterating an old, tainted mark established by one Bill Hamilton at the turn of the century, when a base runner who moved from first to third on a single was credited with a stolen base. Brock now stands alone as the premier base-stealer in baseball history. For all that, his finest achievement this year was to sustain a batting average that kept him up among the league leaders all summer and faded a bit only near the end, to .304. Brock, who is forty, had announced last year that this would be his final season; he was coming off a dismal .221 record in 1978, and everyone expected that he would appear at most Cardinal games only as a benchwarmer and a famous local landmark—everyone but Lou Brock, that is. Carl Yastrzemski, who is also forty now—Yaz *forty?*—struck *his* three-thousandth hit in September, after suffering through an excruciating dry spell at the plate; earlier in the summer, he had bashed his four-hundredth lifetime homer. Hank Aaron, Willie Mays, and Stan Musial had previously achieved this double, but Yaz is the first to turn the trick in the American League. He will return, by the way, for at least one more season at the Fens.

Some old favorites of mine took their leave during the summer, or at the end of it, and some others will probably disappear during the winter. Eddie Kranepool, who is thirty-five, left the Mets and is trying his luck on the free-agent market.* He was

---

*He found no takers there and retired from baseball.

signed by the Mets at the age of seventeen, just after he graduated from James Monroe High School, in the Bronx, and he
has played in every season of the club's history. He led the
Mets in lifetime hits, homers, extra-base hits, and runs batted
in, but the club did not see fit to give him a trophy or a "day"—
a chance for the fans to say goodbye—at the end of his long
tour. Jim Lonborg was cut loose by the Phillies in July, and
his batterymate Tim McCarver retired at the end of the year—
one season shy of his fourth calendar decade in the majors. I
think I will miss Catfish Hunter most of all. He had announced
that this was to be his final season, and although he badly
wanted to depart as a winner, he could not get the batters out
at the end, and finished with a 2–9 record. He went home
without complaint, for he is a man of imperturbable style and
good humor. His last five years were spent with the Yankees,
during the team's notorious era of clubhouse gossip, scandal,
and moneyed nonsense, but none of it ever seemed to touch
or discompose him. One of the great right-handed pitchers of
his time, he won more than twenty games for five straight
seasons, from 1971 to 1975—his last four years with the Oakland A's and his first year with the Yanks. He pitched a perfect
game—no hits, no runs, nobody on base—at the age of twenty-
two, against the Minnesota Twins, and people who were there
say that his teammates didn't have a difficult chance in the
field all day. In his later years, his fastball wasn't much, but,
as I have written on more than one occasion, watching him
work was a true aesthetic experience, because each pitch was
so clearly and intelligently related to the one just before it and
to the one next to come: slider up and in, curveball down and
away, change-up just off the plate, fastball in on the batter's
fists, and so on—a tapestry of deceit and experience and ef-
ficiency; a lesson in pitching. Even his mannerisms were ed-
ucational. Hunter's outsized cap, which he resettled after each
pitch, was a reminder to him not to twist his head during his
delivery—a bad habit that afflicts many hurlers; if the cap was
askew at the end of his motion he knew he was overthrowing.
And there was an added edge of anxiety and pleasure to Hunter's work, because sometimes one of his unfrightening deliveries would catch an inch or two too much of the plate and
would depart, noisily and suddenly, toward some distant upper-
tier grandstand or faraway parking lot. I remember an epochal
blast that Dave Kingman hit against him in a spring-training
game at Fort Lauderdale a few years ago—easily the longest

homer I have ever seen anywhere—and a World Series game against the Dodgers in 1974, which Hunter won in spite of two deep downtowners, whacked by Bill Buckner and Willie Crawford. Hunter seemed to enjoy these surprises almost as much as the batters did. After that Series game, Hunter winked at the reporters clustered around his locker and murmured, "Well, I had some friends here from North Carolina who'd never seen a homer, so I gave them a couple."

DIGITS

It was a hitters' year, all in all, for geezers and youngsters alike, with the two leagues combining for a .265 batting average and just under nine runs per game—the highest in eighteen years. (Could there have been an extra drop or two of *élixir de lapin* in the ball this year? Go ask Ralph Nader.) Keith Hernandez, of the Cardinals, batted .344 to lead the National League, while his teammate Garry Templeton, a switch-hitter, pulled off a curious first by rapping a hundred safe blows from each side of the plate. Dave Kingman struck forty-eight homers for the Cubs, and Gorman Thomas wafted forty-five for the Brewers, to lead their leagues, while Don Baylor, of the Angels, and the enormous Dave Winfield, of the Padres, batted in the most runs—one hundred and thirty-nine and one hundred and eighteen, respectively. Fred Lynn and Jim Rice, of the Red Sox, continued their unconscionable bullying of American League pitchers, with Lynn's eventual .333 winning the A.L. batting crown. Rice's .325 , thirty-nine homers, and one hundred and thirty runs batted in were only a whisper below the figures that won him the Most Valuable Player award last year. The Pirates' Dave Parker, who is Rice's perennial rival in barroom Comparative Literature seminars, wound up with .310, twenty-five homers, and ninety-four R.B.I.s—a disappointing year for nobody in the world except him. Special mention should also be made of George Foster, who missed forty games because of an injury but still drove in ninety-eight runs for the Reds. Because I happen to enjoy crisp line drives even more than towering shots over the bullpen, my private Batter of the Year award (an old Al Weis bubble-gum card) goes to George Brett, of the Kansas City Royals, whose two hundred and twelve hits this summer included twenty-three homers, forty-two doubles, and twenty triples. The last American League player to rap at least twenty doubles, twenty triples, and twenty home runs in one season was Jeff Heath, who did it in 1941; the last National Leaguer was Willie Mays, in 1957. George Brett can *play*. During a do-or-die game against the Angels in mid-September, he bunted safely and then stole second on the next pitch; the catcher's throw went through to the outfield, and Brett got up and scored from second base—home to home on two pitches.

The pitchers, as I have noted, had a harder time of it this year. Ron Guidry, of the Yankees, slipped from his astounding twenty-five wins and three losses of last year to 18–8, but his earned-run average of 2.78 was again the best in his league. His teammate Tommy John won twenty-one games, and Mike Flanagan, of the Orioles, won twenty-three. In the other circuit, James Rodney Richard, of the Astros, wound up with an E.R.A. of 2.71, three hundred and thirteen strikeouts, and a new four-year contract worth two and a half million dollars. One more twenty-game winner, please: Jerry Koosman, now of the Minnesota Twins and formerly of the New York Mets, for which hapless crew he had gone 8–20 and 3–15 over the previous two seasons. Koosman, who is an amiable man, won his twentieth by shutting out the Brewers on the last day of the season—the only time anyone kept that team off the scoreboard all summer.

Umps Walk

The strike called by the fifty-two major-league umpires during spring training dragged on until the middle of May—further dispiriting evidence of the belligerence and suspicion that characterize baseball's labor relations. The issue was money. The umps had been earning between seventeen and a half and thirty-nine and a half thousand dollars per year (from rookies to senior solons), which seemed a penurious recompense for a physically and emotionally demanding line of business that kept a man on the road without cease from April to October. The settlement calls for wage levels from twenty-two to fifty thousand dollars, an increase in per-diem allowances, and, for the first time, a two-week vacation during the season—altogether not much strain on a business in which quarter-million-dollar salaries have become a commonplace and in which the average player now earns over a hundred thousand dollars per annum. Unnecessary damage was inflicted on the sport. The fill-in arbiters did their best, but they weren't very good. Anyone who watched them at work over a span of games developed a much deeper appreciation of the quickness, fluidity, and precision of the old pros—the technicians of the great machine. Over the decades, baseball had endeavored to surround its umpires with an aura of professionalism and impregnable integrity, even to the extent of forcing them to travel on trains or planes different from those the teams have booked, and to put up at different hotels, but this year it was willing to forget all that because of a trifling squabble over dollars and per-diems. There is an unavoidable suspicion that the unpleasantness was allowed to drag on as long as it did because the leagues and the owners wished to present a posture of determination and unity on the eve of the much larger labor negotiations that will precede the signing (or non-signing) of the new basic agreement between the owners and players, which comes up for renewal at the end of this year. The strike also left some very hard feelings among the umpires themselves. Before the season started, the leagues invited a number of minor-league umpires to fill in during the walkout. Higher pay and a chance to break into the top level of their small profession were tempting, and eight young umpires accepted the offer. These eight—four in each league— were subsequently kept on to fill the enlarged roster of umps required by the new vacation agreement. The rookies were scattered among veteran crews, and they passed a frightful summer, hated and held in Coventry and sometimes hazed by their seniors. It is a miserable situation.

MIDWAY

Thursday afternoon, May 17th, and fair stood the breeze for France! Also for Port Moresby, Murmansk, Maracaibo, and other distant ports of call. The breeze in this case was the infamous north-Chicago williwaw that sometimes blows outward and bleacherward at Wrigley Field, causing pitchers to shrivel in horrid anticipation of the voyage to come. The visiting Phillies drove the Cubs' starting pitcher to cover after one out and scored an apparently terminal seven runs in the first inning—only to sustain a countering six-run broadside by the Cubs in the bottom half. Another Philadelphia task force was launched, putting the visitors ahead by 17–6 and then, in the middle of the fifth inning, by 21–9. The second part of this horrendous engagement, however, went to the Cubs, who tied the score in the eighth at 22–22; Mike Schmidt, the Philadelphia slugger, then concluded matters in the tenth, with his second home run of the afternoon, and the Phillies won by 23–22. There were eleven homers in all—including three by Dave Kingman—plus a trifling ten doubles, two triples, and twenty-seven singles: fifty hits. Among the casualties was the Philadelphia pitching corps' earned-run average, which went from 2.91 to 3.37 during the day. The combined total of runs did not set a record, for the Phillies were only avenging an earlier loss they had suffered on the same field—the game of August 25, 1922, when the Cubs beat them, 26–23, in the highest-scoring game on the books.

This year's bloodletting seemed to enfeeble the winners. The Phillies, who were leading their division after the game with a solid 24–10 record, thereupon lost seventeen of their next twenty-three, to slip to fourth, and they never recovered. Visiting their clubhouse during a pair of games in their home park in mid-June, I noticed that they were unusually subdued; they seemed almost dazed. "Well, we've had a lot of rain and a lot of injuries," Larry Bowa said when I asked him about this, "but I think all our troubles began on that crazy afternoon out at Wrigley Field."

HARD TIMES

Further troubles the Phillies encountered after the game at Wrigley Field included the sidelining of three of their pitchers on the same day—July 4th, when Dick Ruthven hurt his elbow, Larry Christenson pulled a muscle, and Randy Lerch broke a bone in his right hand when he was mugged outside a restaurant. The Kansas City Royals, too, were laid low in a single night, when a scatter-armed young fireballer named Ed Farmer, of the Texas Rangers, hit Frank White, the Royals' second baseman, with a pitch in the first inning, breaking a bone in his right hand, and then hit outfielder Al Cowens with a pitch in the fifth, shattering his jaw. The Dodgers—who collapsed in the first half of the season, falling seventeen and a half games behind the leaders by the All-Star interval—could blame some of their frightful season on serious injuries to Rick Monday, Terry Forster, Doug Rau, and Reggie Smith. The team did better near the end, climbing to third place in its division, but there were mutterings and harsh words in the clubhouse, which suggests that some of the ageless golden youths may not be wearing Dodger Blue next year. The Red Sox got limited service from their bullpen ace, Bill Campbell, and lost their second baseman, Jerry Remy, for much of the season. Worst of all, they had to do without Carlton Fisk behind the plate; he reinjured the ailing elbow of his throwing arm three times, and may be finished as a catcher. The longest and most painful fall, of course, was suffered by the two-time-champion Yankees, who finished fourth in their division, thirteen and a half games behind the Orioles. (The Brewers and the Red Sox came in second and third.) No team ever had a more miserable summer. Goose Gossage tore ligaments in his thumb during a shower-room scuffle and was lost for three months. Al Rosen, the club president, resigned and manager Bob Lemon was dismissed, and Billy Martin (who was fired last year) was rehired. Ed Figueroa underwent surgery on his pitching arm, and Mickey Rivers, who was sidelined repeatedly by injuries, was traded to the Rangers. Yankee-haters abound in the land, and many of them may have drawn some perverse comfort from these misadventures, but all that was silenced or swept away on August 2nd, when the Yankees' captain, Thurman Munson, was killed in a crash of his private plane near Akron, Ohio.

I was on vacation in New England that week, and we got the news at dinnertime, when a visiting friend received a telephone call from his fifteen-year-old son in New York, who had heard about Munson's death on the radio. At breakfast the next morning, the friend shook his head and said, "I can't get over it. I don't understand why it upsets me so much." I felt the same way. I had never really known Thurman Munson. Like other occasional visitors to the Yankee clubhouse, I had kept my distance, because he had made it clear that he distrusted strangers and writers. He seemed to be a rough customer— silent and scowling, possibly dangerous. I gave him a wide berth, although a few reporters had told me that he could be wonderful to listen to if you got him talking about hitting. Most of his teammates, it seems, had had the same difficulty with him at first; he could be tough and harsh, they said, but once they broke through they found that he was a shy and sensitive man and a loyal friend. The grief of Munson's teammates was open and moving. Graig Nettles said that he had counted on talking to Thurman Munson for the rest of his life. None of this applied to me; I knew only that I would miss watching Munson on the field, where he had always been one of the most vivid and aggressive players of his time. Yet his death kept coming back as a shock and a loss. I was startled, because I was certain that my admiration for the many hundreds of gifted or brilliant players I have watched was based almost entirely on how they played the game; I had always tried to concentrate more on what they did on the field than on what they said or who they seemed to be away from the diamond. It was all right, or almost all right, to be a middle-aged fan as long as I had this sorted out. But now I am beginning to suspect that athletes may play a larger part in our lives than we are willing to admit. Without our quite being aware of it, they may have begun to seem like members of our family, or like trusted friends. My own circle of intimates seems smaller than it used to be, and there have been moments when I have realized that I seem to know more about twenty or thirty baseball players than I do about some friends I have had for many years. I can only conclude that these adopted, seasonal relatives have filled a real need for me, and perhaps for other fans as well. The lives of most baseball players may be trifling, but there is always fresh news of them; something is happening to them every day, which is more than we can say with certainty about ourselves. This is not just a wish for gossip or vicarious adventure. Belonging anywhere now is terribly difficult, I think, and the old childhood dream of *really* belonging will not go away. Nothing comes closer to a band of brothers than a team, and the knowledge that athletes' attachments to one another are transitory, sentimental, possibly homosexual, and surely motivated above all by hopes of the team's success on the field does not quite drive out the dream. We want to know all about ballplayers, because then somehow they will know about *us*, and then we will belong, too. Ballplayers are more vivid than we are, and, thinking about them, we wonder what it feels like to hit an enormous homer, to throw out a base runner, to weep openly for a brother, to belong, to die.

Thurman Munson, in any case, was a special kind of player. The catcher is the physical and emotional focus of every base-ball game; he faces outward, surveying and guiding it all, and everyone else on the team looks in at him. The rock-hard catcher is the jewel of the movement, and Munson was the center bearing of every Yankee team of his era. Rick Dempsey, who played behind him on the Yankees and then moved over to become the Orioles' regular catcher, said at the end of the summer, "After Thurman had gone, it was like baseball was finished in New York. Playing against the Yankees had lost its lustre. Thurman was a battler. What every fan thinks is thrilling about the game, Thurman was part of, some way—a ninth-inning hit to win the ballgame, a slide in to beat somebody up. Knock them over, knock the ball loose, block the plate, throw somebody out! Thurman was always in the middle of it."

A VERY REMOTE AREA

"You always have to know your purpose in playing. You have to have a premise, and the premise can change. Think about all the money ballplayers are making now. The money is asking for a Superman performance. The player can't reach that level, and he's in anguish. Every error he makes feels worse to him now, because of the money. But you can't be afraid to make errors! You can't be afraid to be naked before the crowd, because no one can ever master the game of baseball, or conquer it. You can only challenge it."

Lou Brock was talking baseball in the coffee shop of the Cardinals' team hotel in New York, toward the end of a September afternoon. From our table we could watch sheets of rain sweeping across Seventh Avenue; that night's game against the Mets had already been called. Never mind. This was the last road trip of Lou Brock's nineteenth year in the majors, and there was absolutely nothing left for him to prove as a player. Brock talks in the same cheerful, alert style he has always displayed on the field. He is narrow and sinewy, without a sag or a seam on him. At a glance, you might take him for an up-and-coming young infielder, probably a pure singles hitter, and you would be wrong three times. He is a forty-year-old outfielder, and he used to swing from his heels and strike out a lot. But he is also one of the three players (along with Joe Adcock and Hank Aaron) ever to hit a ball into the centerfield bleachers at the old Polo Grounds. In the middle of his career, he began to cut down his swing, so that he could get to first base more often. Then he would steal second. In 1974, when he was thirty-five, he stole a hundred and eighteen bases.

"That record meant the most, because it was the only one where I challenged," Brock said. "All the other records I just caught up with, because of time. They were milestones. Learning how to steal bases is like anything else you set yourself to do. There's a lot to it that's technical, but first of all you have to go to the faraway wonders and explore them. You have to go into the unknown. A three- or four-step lead off first was my comfort zone, and we all like to stay on solid ground. But what would happen, I used to wonder, if I took a *ten*-step lead off first? What could a pitcher do to stop me? Sure, he could make me look foolish sometimes, if he got me, but what was going to happen to *him* when I took that extra step or two? Now I was outside of his solid ground, and suddenly he was so uncomfortable that he had become an entirely different kind of pitcher. He had never given such a thing much thought, and probably he couldn't deal with it. It's the same with catchers. With some of them, like Bob Boone, I always tried to move so as to keep the first baseman between me and him if I was leading away. He wouldn't know quite *where* I was, and that would give me a little edge. Or I'd yell 'Hey!' or 'There he goes!' just as the pitch was released, and he'd come up ready to throw—only I hadn't gone yet! That's wordology. Every time there's an unexpected sound on the field—a yell, a noise, anything—people snap around. They're used to playing the game from sight. They have to see before they can react. They're not used to sound, so you use that."

I murmured that this sounded almost like school-yard base-ball, and Brock said, "Yes, that's *just* what a kid might do! After all, it's a kid's game. That's what I mean! Are you afraid to act like a kid out there? That's one of the wonders to me. It sounds childish, but you make it professional. Have you ever noticed the kind of games that go on between a catcher and a good base-stealer when the base-stealer comes up to bat? The catcher will stand up tall and try to stare down at you—most catchers are big and most base-stealers are small. Johnny Bench always tried that with me. But I wouldn't look at him until he'd gone down into his crouch, and then I'd turn and stare down at *him*. Then I'd tap the head of my bat in the dirt just in front of his shoes, and maybe a little particle of dust would go on them." He laughed delightedly. "You always want that edge, the little one-up. It can create a kind of madness in them."

I asked Brock about his three-thousandth hit, which had come off Dennis Lamp, of the Chicago Cubs, before a full-house home crowd at Busch Memorial Stadium, in St. Louis, on August 13th. Brock had singled in the first inning, for Hit No. 2,999.

"I knew I was within touching distance then," Brock said, "but you can't grab for a record, so you never know when it's going to come. You have to *touch* it at the end." He touched my wrist lightly with his forefinger. "In the fourth, the first two pitches to me were sliders, for strikes, and then there was a change-up, away. Then, lo and behold, he threw a pitch up under my chin that put me down in the dirt. It jolted me awake, I'll tell you. It drove away any dreams of a home run, or anything like that, so it was the best thing that could have happened to me. When you get knocked down like that, what you want to do is hit the next pitch through the pitcher's box on a line. All my life I've wanted to do that, and I think this was the first time I ever did it. It was the hardest ball I hit all year. I thought it was a line drive into the outfield, only the pitcher got in the way of it. Maybe you heard about it."

I had heard about it. Brock's three-thousandth hit was a bullet that struck Dennis Lamp on the leg and then caromed off his pitching hand with such force that the ball rolled into foul territory near third base. Brock wound up on first, where he was mobbed by his teammates. Lamp's bruised hand forced him to leave the game.

"I was probably as big a fan of the event as anyone else there," Brock said, smiling. "After all, I'd never seen anybody get three thousand hits, either."

SEPTEMBER SONG

I am a Red Sox fan, with all the psychic scars to prove my membership in that ancient company, and this summer I continued to participate in the obligatory Yankee-Red Sox wars, although there was evidence almost from the outset that they would decide nothing this season. Over the last two days of June and the first two days of July, I watched Lancaster and York split four thunderous games at Yankee Stadium before immense audiences—a perfect standoff, one might suppose, except for the fact that the second-place Sox and the fourth-place Yankees each lost a game and a half to the league-leading Orioles in the process, to slip five and a half and eleven games behind, respectively. Even before the first inning of the first game had been played, I saw on the scoreboard that the Orioles had already won their game for the day, which meant that the best the local winner could do was to hold his rung on the ladder, and I had sudden vision of Earl Weaver, the Oriole skipper, enjoying the news from New York by radio or television, with his feet up and a couple of beers at hand. Nobody could quite believe what was happening. After one of the games a New York reporter asked Reggie Jackson if he took the Orioles seriously. "I take them as seriously as *death*," he said gloomily.

When I saw the two teams again, on Labor Day and the following evening, the news was plain enough. The Red Sox, who had lost ten of their last thirteen games, had slipped to third place, nine and a half games behind Baltimore, and the shattered Yankees were fourteen and a half out. It was odd to watch these two famous opponents play a truly meaningless series ("This is just like playing *Toronto*," Ron Davis, the Yankees' rookie reliever, said), and odder still to discover the newcomers and erstwhiles who now filled out the Yankees' lineup as a result of their midsummer disasters—Oscar Gamble and Bobby Murcer (both back in pinstripes after late trades), George Scott, and a baby-faced catcher named Brad Gulden. The Yankees won both games, again before the customary screaming multitudes, but after an inning or two of the opener I became aware of an unusual inner lightheartedness as I watched the two old rivals have at each other. The awful weight of success had been lifted from us all, and for once we were free simply to enjoy the baseball.

I went up to Boston the next weekend, and saw the Red Sox lose three straight games to the soon-to-be-champion Orioles, to fall fourteen and a half behind. The Orioles, who always play with élan in September, had the best record and the best pitching in baseball, and their per-game margin over the rest of the teams in their league was an awesome 1.1 runs. The Boston pitching, by contrast, was nearly a shambles, and the team, which hadn't won two games in succession since August 16th, was approaching the kind of September catatonia that had done it in just a year earlier. Watching the team's repeated failures when running the bases or trying to move up base runners, I was reminded of the words of Bill Lee, the intensely opinionated left-hander who had toiled on the mound for the Bosox for many summers before departing the team last winter, and who was currently enjoying a splendid year with the Expos. Talking with me in Montreal a few weeks earlier, he had said, "There's nothing in the world like the fatalism of the Red Sox fans, which has been bred into them for generations by that little green ballpark, and by the Wall, and by a team that keeps trying to win by hitting everything out of sight and just out-bombarding everyone else in the league. But late in the year, every year, when the regulars get tired and the onshore September breeze begins to blow in Boston, suddenly the long ball doesn't work anymore. All year long, the hitters make the headlines, and then when they can't hit anymore they turn around and start blaming the pitchers, and the writers start blaming everybody. All this makes the Boston fans a little crazy. I'm sorry for them."

On Sunday—a dazzling New England early-fall after-noon—the Orioles batted around in the fifth and again in the sixth, scoring eleven runs in the process, and a slow, unchar-acteristic reality began to infuse my own special craziness as I came to understand, at long last, that this famous local band of hitters and heroes—Fred and Jim and Yaz, Pudge and Butch and Dewey and the rest, most of them warriors of the mar-vellous 1975 World Series—had just about come to the end of the line. Probably they would be broken up—I suddenly hoped they would be—but in any case the team would be best left out of my expectations until someone in charge in Boston began to think about speed and defense and pitching, which are the quieter and more sustaining philosophies of the game. In the bottom of the eighth inning, with his team down by 14–4, Carl Yastrzemski led off with a searing line-drive single up the middle, for his 2,999th lifetime hit—a perfect symbol of something or other—and I rose and said goodbye again to Fenway Park.

Waiting for Yastrzemski's three-thousandth hit—the "Yaz Watch," as the Boston papers had named it—became a cruelly slow business, for Carl, apparently worn down by the exigen-cies of the occasion, had fallen into a stiff parody of his normal swing, and also seemed intent on marking the occasion with a homer. The achievement had made him into less of a hitter, instead of the other way around, and as I watched his taut, exhausted expression at the plate while he repeatedly popped up or bounced into easy infield outs (I was seeing this by television, from New York), it came to me once again that almost nothing in Yastrzemski's long and triumphant career had been easy for him, or even much fun. When the hit did come (a modest eighth-inning roller past second base, against the Yankees, after twelve successive fruitless trips to the plate), the milestone was celebrated, in crushing anticlimax, with a full quarter hour of on-the-spot ceremonials, speeches, and photographs. The game was stopped in its tracks—an offensive and inexcusable recent custom in baseball—while functionaries attempted to deepen our appreciation of the man and the moment. All this wiped away something that had come along earlier in the game: the sudden, heartfelt burst of applause given to Catfish Hunter in the fifth inning, when he was again knocked out of the box. As he left the field, and the splendid Boston fans began to understand that they would probably never see this redoubtable enemy pitcher in action again, everyone in Fenway Park rose to his feet, and the applause swelled and deepened until Hunter came back to the dugout step and raised his cap in farewell. Something had really happened—an event instead of an Event.

THE NEW WAVE

Surprising things kept taking place in the other league, where the Montreal Expos and the Houston Astros, both relentless losers in the past, stubbornly clung to the top of their divisions for most of the summer; both fell in the very last week, but their new hordes of fans must have recovered from their disappointment by now and can think back upon their heroes' ardent efforts with pleasure and gratitude. Most of the Astro players are exceptionally tall and thin; when seen at play, in their astounding orange-and-red-and-yellow-swatched uniforms (on which numerals appear at groin level), they sometimes suggest a troupe of gazelles depicted by a Balkan corps de ballet. Often there was a Sylphide-like quality to their games as well, which can be understood after a glance at their team statistics. Although they finished only a game and a half out of first place, and a full ten games ahead of the third-place Dodgers, the Astros scored fewer runs than anyone else in the National League—five hundred and eighty-three, which is only one run more than their pitchers gave up, over all, to their opponents. The Astros hit forty-nine homers for the year—one more than Dave Kingman's personal total—and whacked more triples (fifty-two) than homers. Jeff Leonard, who batted cleanup for the Astros most of the time, did not hit one homer. None of this, it should be understood, is easy to do. Speed and pitching made up for a lot. Five of the Astro regulars stole

more than twenty bases apiece, and three Houston pitchers—
James Rodney Richard, Joe Niekro, and Ken Forsch—finished
in the top ten in the league, and threw forty complete games
among them. *Close* games, we may assume.

Montreal, whose pitching was even better than the Astros'—
the best in the league, in fact—moved out to a six-game lead
in its division early in July, after winning twenty-six of its first
thirty-two home games. Rapturous crowds at the Stade Olympique delivered a standing ovation for every Expo maneuver,
including sacrifice bunts and discerning bases on balls. Winning at home is the traditional sign of a young team, and most
of the screaming of *les Exponents* (as the Montreal rooters call
themselves) centered upon the vivid play of the three dashing
outfielders, Warren Cromartie, Andre Dawson, and Ellis Valentine; the estimable catcher, Gary Carter; the immense, bearded
third baseman, Larry Parrish; and an infielder named Rodney
Scott, who were all twenty-five years old this summer. I visited
the Stade at the very end of July—almost too late for the party,
I realized, for on the day of my arrival the sports section of
Montreal's *La Presse* bore sombre headlines: "PIED DE NEZ DES
PIRATES—*Double Défaite des Expos Devant une Foule Record.*" The onrushing Pirates (the team had been aroused by
the recent acquisition of Bill Madlock, a two-time National
League batting champion, who came over from the Giants in
a stunning trade) had swept a doubleheader the previous night,
before 59,260 *Exponents effrayés*, to cut the Expos' lead to a
bare half game. This margin vanished, too, after three or four
minutes of the next game, when Dave Parker swatted a two-
run homer toward the "BUVEZ 7UP" sign in right field in the top
of the first inning, to put the visitors ahead for the night. There
were brave ovations even after the Expos had dropped behind
by 5–0, but the audience was plainly miserable about the loss
of first place, which its team had occupied since the middle of
June. (Bill Lee had told me that the pressures of the pennant
race had begun to show during the previous week, when the
first fistfights of the year broke out in the stands.) During the
game, a glowering *amateur* just in front of me (I was sitting
in the lower-deck *corbeille*, behind third base) kept up a hoarse
nine-inning stream of muttered and sometimes shouted criticism
and commentary, which I listened to yearningly, as if at a
performance by the Comédie-Française; the burden of the message was clear enough, but I missed all the nuances.

Happiness and first place were restored on the following

afternoon, a Sunday, when Andre Dawson hit a providential checked-swing, wrong-field triple to drive in three runs, in a game that Montreal won by 5–3. The hero of the day, however, was Rusty Staub, the Expo first baseman. Staub, who as *le grand Orange* was the most popular member of the team a decade ago, during its tottering first seasons as an expansion club, had been purchased from the Detroit Tigers a few days earlier, and his return to the lineup was acclaimed in the papers in terms *("un merveilleux talent allié au charisme")* previously reserved for Maurice Richard, the hockey immortal. Staub, a serious chef off the field, had evidently not been getting much exercise as a designated hitter for the Tigers, and his movements afield caused one press-box observer to murmur, "It's like having Julia Child playing first." Mrs. Child, however, can't hit. Rusty rapped out two singles during the afternoon—each accompanied by another standing o. and a curious, rolling volley of sound that I could not quite identify. Then I noticed that the bottoms of the plastic seats in the grandstand of the Stade Olympique—an immense and truly ugly concrete egg, built for the Olympic Games of 1976—were hinged and spring-operated, like theatre seats; when forty thousand Expo fans jump to their feet in ecstasy, one instantly hears Montcalm and Nelson Eddy and the Northwest Mounted Police galloping out of the forests to save the day.

The Pirates won back first place early in August, and began to win important games in the sudden-accident style that often characterizes pennant-bound clubs—a pinch-hit grand-slam homer by John Milner, a tenth-inning three-run homer by Phil Garner, and so on. The Expos slipped slowly backward, exactly as I had expected they would, and trailed by three games at the end of the month. Then, without my expecting it at all, Montreal won ten straight games, and then seventeen out of eighteen games, and squeezed back into first by a sliver of a percentage point on September 11th. In the ensuing ten days, the two clubs exchanged the lead four times. The history of this year's Pirates is now secure in the records and in our memories, but attention should still be given to the courage and tenacity of the young Montrealers and the skill of their manager, Dick Williams, which together very nearly unmade the whole story before it began. The club slipped out of first place for good in the last week, by which time they looked worn and jumpy (the Expos were not, in truth, a very good defensive team), but they were still in the race on the final

Sunday, the very last day of the season, when they were shut out in Montreal by Steve Carlton and the Phillies, before fifty thousand cheering, standing, heartbroken *Exponents*.

FAMILY MATTERS

"O!" *(hands in a circle over the head)*—"R!" *(left arm forms semicircle, with fingers at rib level; left leg extends)*—"I!" *(feet together; hands together over head)*—"O!" *(as above)*—"L!" *(right arm is raised, left arm extends)*—"E!" *(left leg extends; right and left arms extend to left, parallel to each other)*—"S!" *(body turns left; left arm is pointed away from forehead in Egyptian-frieze style, and right arm points astern)*, followed by banner-wavings and tumultuous cries.

Hundreds of thousands of Baltimore and other Maryland citizens know this ceremonial by heart, and they roared out the message on every imaginable occasion this summer at Memorial Stadium. Their shaman was Wild Bill Hagy, a large, bearded, gap-toothed cab-driver from the Dundalk area of Baltimore, who instituted the letter-cheer two years ago in Section 34 of the upper deck; this year, it swept the park and the city, and Hagy, in his well-stuffed orange T-shirt and straw cowboy hat, became a Baltimore institution, like white stone stoops. (Near the end of the last home game of the regular season, manager Earl Weaver and the rest of the Orioles came out on the grass in front of the dugout and went through the spelling dance together, in honor of the fans.) The Orioles succeeded this year not only in their league but at the gate, which has been a much more difficult challenge for them over the years. They drew 1,680,561 fans—almost three-quarters of a million above their average attendance in the past two decades, during which time they were winning more games than any other team in baseball. The youthful, hopeful, extremely informal Baltimore multitudes who screeched and sang during the local play-off games and then through the World Series were a delightful addition to the autumn scene, for they perfectly matched the young, informal, optimistic Orioles. The new fans came just in time. The Orioles were sold this summer to the Washington attorney Edward Bennett Williams, and there was talk that the team would be moved to the capital within a couple of seasons. Not now, though. Who wants to body-spell "W-A-S-H-I-N-G-T-O-N"?

The American League playoffs started briskly in Baltimore, with the Angels' Dan Ford smashing a first-inning home run off Jim Palmer, and with Nolan Ryan fanning seven Orioles in the first three innings. The home side achieved a pair of unearned runs in the third, however, and held on, at 3–3, until Ryan departed the premises in the eighth, suffering from a tightened calf muscle. This was a pure gift for the Hagy hordes, because Ryan, whose fastball is a liquid streak of white, habitually throws harder in the later innings than in the early ones—often going from timed speeds of about ninety-two or ninety-three miles per hour up to the nearly invisible environs of ninety-six and ninety-eight. His successor, John Montague, sustained the tension until the bottom of the tenth inning, when, with two Orioles on base, he threw two admirable forkballs to a left-handed pinch-hitter, John Lowenstein, and unwisely followed them with a third, which Lowenstein banked into the left-field stands, for the game.

The next evening, the Orioles pitched their ace, Mike Flanagan (who later received the Cy Young Award as the best pitcher in his league this year), and handed him a helpful 9—1 lead after three innings—a laugher, in short. But the Angels, who averaged more than five runs per game this season, scored another in the sixth, another in the seventh, three more in the eighth, and two more in the ninth, and now suddenly had the bases loaded. Like everyone else in the park, I kept running down my scorecard and counting the dots in the crowded Angel boxes. Could it be? Six, seven . . . yes, *eight* runs. The donor of the last two California counters was Don Stanhouse, the best reliever on the deep Oriole staff, and Earl Weaver, the veteran Baltimore logical positivist, now elected to stay with him a bit longer. Stanhouse thrives on crises, and often seems to invent them in order to inspire himself: a firebug fireman. Deluged with disbelieving screams, he cranked and threw only a fairish pitch, a slider, to the extremely dangerous Brian Downing, the California catcher, who slapped the ball directly at Doug DeCinces, the Baltimore third baseman. DeCinces seized it on the base path and stood there like a traffic cop to tag the oncoming Dan Ford for the last out. "It wasn't pretty by no means," Stanhouse said of his performance after the game. Still, I admired Earl Weaver for his patience, if only because he would have been unmercifully criticized if the Angels had gone on to tie or win the game against Stanhouse. Weaver doesn't give a damn what anybody will think later, which makes him a pearl among managers and men.

No team has ever come back from a two-game initial deficit in the playoffs, and the Angels came to the brink of expiring in three when they trailed by 3–2 in the ninth inning of the next game, which was played on their own rock-hard turf, in Anaheim. I was watching on television, and I was startled but pleased when the Angels suddenly rallied and won it in the ninth on two hits and a walk (Rod Carew cracked a double to start it all) and a frightful error by Oriole fielder Al Bumbry, who dropped an easy, series-ending fly ball in short center. Even before this gift, it was a thrilling game for the local rooters, with some sprinting, sliding catches in the outfield, an enemy base runner cut down at the plate, and a home run by their slugger and favorite, Don Baylor. More than two and a half million Angels fans turned out this summer, benumbing the local freeways, and friends who were at the Anaheim play-off games told me that the Californians' decibel level outdid even the Baltimore roarers'. Game Three was the reward that every Angels fan deserved. The summer ended for them the next afternoon, when Scott McGregor shut them out, 8—0, in a game illuminated by a diving, airborne catch over third base by Doug DeCinces that expunged the only California rally of the day.

The Cincinnati Reds showed grit in the first two games of their playoffs against the Pirates, forcing each of them into extra innings before succumbing by 5–2 in eleven and 3–2 in ten. (The Reds, by the way, won their division this year with a new manager, John McNamara, and a new third baseman, Ray Knight; their immediate predecessors were Sparky Anderson and Pete Rose. Unawed by his burdens, Knight batted .318. The club also got some useful work from Tom Seaver, who won eleven straight games in mid-summer.) The opener was an austere, tautly played game, with thoughtful, excellent pitching by Seaver and John Candelaria, and two behemoth home runs, by George Foster and Willie Stargell; the latter's, a three-run shot against Tom Hume, won the game. Game Two was much less rewarding, thanks to some ghastly base-running on both sides. I was watching these encounters on television, and neither game aroused me as much as it should have, given the close scores. Perhaps the trouble had to do with the prim, doubt-stricken Cincinnati fans, who maintained a disapproving silence whenever their team fell behind. At one moment, while the NBC cameras panned across the silent, staring thousands,

Joe Garagiola murmured, "This is not a painting."

The third game, an afternoon affair at Pittsburgh, which I attended, was delayed by a heavy rainstorm (a gruesome meteorological omen, had I only known it) but then began in lively fashion, when the Pirates got a run in the first inning on pure zeal. The lead-off man, Omar Moreno, walked, and stole second on the very next delivery by the Cincinnati pitcher, Mike LaCoss. Tim Foli then hit a high bounder to Dave Concepcion, on which Moreno unexpectedly proceeded to third, slithering under the startled shortstop's peg. Then he scored on a fly. In the third, Phil Garner, the dandy Pittsburgh second baseman, saved a run by diving on his belly to knock down Concepcion's single behind the bag, and in the bottom of that inning Stargell and Bill Madlock each hit home runs. The Reds, by contrast, looked corpselike at the end, as Bert Blyleven went the distance for the Pirates, who won by 7–1, to take the pennant. All year at Three Rivers Stadium, the field loudspeakers blasted out the Pirates' theme song during the seventh-inning stretch—a thumping, catchy disco-rock number, "We Are Family," by the Sister Sledge group. This time, with the late-summer shadows deepening and the championship at last in hand, the wives of the Pirate players suddenly moved forward from their seats, just behind the screen, and clambered up onto a low, curving shelf that rims the field behind home plate. At first, there were only a few of them, but more and more of the young women ran down the aisles and were pulled up onto the sudden stage, and then they were all dancing together there arm in arm, jiving and boogieing and high-kicking in rhythm, in their slacks and black-and-gold scarves and long, ballplayer-wife's fur coats, all waving and laughing and hugging and shaking their banners in time to the loud music. It was terrific. Since then, I have heard cynical comments about this party, and wry suggestions from writers and fans that the much repeated and much reported Pittsburgh theme song and the players' evident closeness and joy in one another were nothing more than a publicity device, and reminders that *all* winning teams are families, for as long as they win. I don't agree. It is true that the smallest flutter of a spontaneous incident—in sports, or anywhere else in public life in this country—is now seized upon and transformed at once into a mass-produced imitation or a slogan or an advertising gimmick. Bill Hagy was appearing on a television commercial in Baltimore during the playoffs and showed up repeatedly on local TV interviews and game shows. I have no doubt that by next summer two or three major-league teams will come up with organized fans' cheering sections and letter-cheers, in imitation of the Orioles, or even a wives' cheering-and-dancing group, in imitation of the Pirates. It is dispiriting, but we can't let ourselves miss the moment of humor and exultation when it does come along, or deny its pleasure. I thought about the Pirates' family when I visited the Cincinnati clubhouse after the last playoff game and saw the Reds preparing to depart for the winter. Joe Morgan was taking off his Reds uniform for the last time. He will venture into the free agent market this year, but he is thirty-six now, and he had had a disappointing season, batting .250 and looking much slower afield; he had gone hitless in the playoffs. Just three years ago, Morgan and his teammates destroyed the Yankees in the World Series, for their second World Championship in a row, and Joe Morgan was named the Most Valuable Player in the National League for the second straight year. That team was a family, too—the Big Red Machine— and now there was almost nothing left of it. But surely nobody understands all this better than the ballplayers themselves— the players and their wives—for that is the nature of their business. Injured, traded, slumping, benched, or simply playing for the wrong team, they are forever, or nearly forever, falling short of their best expectations, while their youth and their skills inexorably fade. Most big-league players never get to play in a World Series at all. When it does happen, then— the unexpected great year, when a whole team comes together, against all the odds, and wins—it should be celebrated, for the good times almost surely will not last. Why not dance?

CLASS

Whatever its drawbacks in weather and fielding, this World Series restored some credibility to the wall sampler which proclaims that sports build character. I have no idea how much of this came through on television, but those of us who were on the scene and in the clubhouses remarked again and again on the poise and generosity and intelligence of the players on both teams. This was a refreshing and surprising change from the demeanor of several more famous clubs and better-paid athletes in recent Octobers. The tone of the occasion—the absence of moneyed cool or aggrieved silence—was struck by

Phil Garner, who said one day, "Yes, of course there's pressure. I feel anxiety about these games—why deny it? If you don't feel anything, a thump of the heart, about playing in the World Series, then I don't want you on my team. I'm excited. I get to the ballpark very early every day. I can hardly wait for the games to begin."

Both teams seemed to have this eagerness of spirit, and both of them, I believe, had absorbed it in great part from their managers. Earl Weaver and Chuck Tanner, the Pirates' skipper, are exceptionally good company, because at every moment of the season they appear to be caught up in the intellectual and emotional challenges and pleasures of their calling. Ask either one of them a question, and you get back instant strategy and history, example and perception, psychology and comedy and (in Tanner's case) homily, all in a rush. It is a treat and an education. Both of the pennant-winning teams were known in their leagues for the looseness and high spirits of their club-houses. The Orioles' den often suggested a high-school or college locker room, full of euphoria and flying towels. The Pirates' quarters, by contrast, were an overcrowded city block in some ethnically confused but exuberant neighborhood—people eating, people drinking, people playing cards, people playing backgammon, people urging the game-players to come and do something else, knots of people shouting at one another in apparent rage and then collapsing in laughter, somebody sleeping and somebody else preparing to wake up the sleeper in a singularly frightful or comical fashion, several people deep in mysterious conversation with visiting strangers, people playing quietly with their young children or with their neighbors' children, people getting dressed and talking at length about one another's clothes and jewelry and hats, people bursting into song, and, over and through it all, the pounding, ear-wrenching noise of music—rock and disco and salsa—blasting out from enormous stereos and tape decks, and filling every corner of the room and the mind. All this was delightful, but in the end I was more impressed and convinced by the way the players and the coaches on both teams talked about themselves and each other, showing a pervasive tone of modesty and common sense that is often notably missing on clubs where money or public relations or consuming ambition tinges the entire operation.

Ray Miller, the Orioles' pitching coach, discussing the teams' apparently endless supply of extraordinary young pitchers: "We try to simplify a simple game. You listen to some coaches and managers and they make baseball sound like chess or something. The idea of pitching is to keep ahead of the batter, to make him hit your pitch. Never give him the chance to look for a good pitch. Don't walk him. Don't fall behind. We emphasize teaching the change-up to every pitcher, starting at the rookie level. Get in the habit of using your defense to get outs. Most of all, we try to take care of our young arms. We watch for the right spots for them, and we watch their mistakes. We never just throw them in the fire. If you look back two or three years, you'd see that pitchers like Dennis Martinez and Mike Flanagan were kept back and brought out of the bullpen only in long-relief situations or for spot starts. That's how you get to learn the league. Now they're regulars, and Mike may be the best in the business. You have to be patient."

Frank Robinson, the great Reds and Orioles slugger, who later managed the Indians and is now an Orioles coach: "When we're filling out the roster at the end of spring training, we spend a lot of time on the last four or five names that come up. We weigh this against that—left-hand and right-hand, can he throw, can he run, and all the rest—but in the end you pick because of character. You take a Terry Crowley because he's a pinch-hitter and he knows it, and he can sit week after week and then jump off the bench and do the job. You pick a Dave Skaggs because he's got a good personality. He doesn't play every day, but he'll sit there for months with no complaints and be *ready*. We're all in this, all twenty-five. That and Earl. Earl has always believed in himself, and he's always prepared. He's almost never caught short. That's why the players believe in him. He wins."

Earl Weaver (he always seems to enter a conversation at a full sprint, and his voice is hoarse with cigarettes and intensity): "I don't care about all that looseness and laughing in our clubhouse. That don't mean a thing. The only thing that matters is what happens on that little hump out in the middle of the field. Or if the pitcher isn't doing it, it's what the hitters are doing. Nothing else matters. We want to make a man believe in what he's doing. We tell the pitchers if you can get a batter out with your fastball, then stick to the fastball. Don't get beat fooling around out there with four or five different pitches. And the man at the plate is the one you want to get out. If you've got men on base, still concentrate on the man up there at bat. If you get him out, then you can work on the *next* man up there. It's all basic, but"—his voice drops to a whisper—"it ain't so damned easy to do it."

Chuck Tanner (his face is pleasant and lightly lined, with a bulge of Red Man in one corner): "I don't think a manager should be judged by whether he wins a pennant but by whether he gets the most out of the twenty-five men he's been given. There are third- or fourth-place managers who have done as well or better than the fellow who finishes up on top. It's easy to manage a team with no problems: everybody drinks milkshakes and hits .325. Nowadays, a lot of young ballplayers come up who have been hitting way over .300 in the minors, but when they get here they look around and suddenly baseball becomes a job for them, because they're trying so hard. The manager's real work, as I see it, is to reach the kid who's sitting over in the corner of the dugout and get him to play with the same attitude he had back in American Legion ball."

Phil Garner, on the racial composition of the Pirates—a club that included fifteen black or Hispanic players on its twenty-five-man roster this fall: "There really is no distinction between black and white on this club. If I didn't honestly believe that, I wouldn't say it. To keep factions from developing, you have to have someone that the blacks respect and someone that the whites respect, and the guy who puts that all together for us is Will Stargell. You know, I've heard it said that one reason we've never drawn very well here in Pittsburgh is that we have too many blacks on the club. I'm not saying that it's true, but it's sad if it *is* true, because we have such great talent. Why, you look at a Stargell, a Dave Parker, a Bill Madlock, a Manny Sanguillen, a Grant Jackson—you can't *find* better players than that. If you play good ball, you deserve to be cheered."

Tim Foli, the Pirate shortstop (who joined the club in April, coming from the Mets in a trade; he had been known in the league as an angry ballplayer, a hard rock): "There's none of the jealousy you find with other teams—not with Stargell here. Every time somebody on the team does something in a game to help, he'll notice it and say something about it and emphasize it. You can't help being influenced. Nobody ever understood what kind of a player I was until I got here. But everything I did here was *noticed*. It gives you a different feeling."

Phil Garner, on Tim Foli, his second-base partner (the two are a little below average size and perhaps not better than average in range, but they both throw well, and they play together elegantly; they both have mustaches, and in the Pirates' boxy, old-fashioned baseball caps they suggest a pair of pugnacious bartender-infielders in a saloon league at the turn of the century): "When Timmy came, we started to turn things around on this club. We knew he was an exceptionally intelligent player, but I don't think anybody knew how good he was. He's been batting second, behind Omar Moreno, who can steal bases, and ahead of Dave Parker, who can drive in a lot of runs, and the man sure knows how to use that bat. He has changed his personality here. It just took him a little longer than it takes some others. He's grown up."

Dave Parker, on a gift he had presented to Willie Stargell during spring training last March, on Stargell's thirty-eighth birthday: "Well, it was a gold baseball. I handed it to him and I said 'Happy birthday, Pops.' He said 'What's this?' and I said it was a present to him from his favorite son. He said 'Yes, but what *is* it?' He kept looking at it and studying it. So I told him I'd taken it off the Gold Glove award I'd got for last year—the ball was part of the trophy, I mean, and I just pulled it off. Then he said 'Aw, you shouldn't have done *that*, man,' and I said 'I never could have got the award without you.' Then we hugged each other."

Willie Stargell, at various times, on the ballplayer's life (he was born in Oklahoma, and his voice is unhurried and buttery): "We go out to have fun, but we work hard, too. It's supposed to be fun. The man says 'Play ball,' not 'Work ball,' you know.... You only have a few years to play this game, and you can't play it if you're all tied up in knots.... There was such a closeness this year. We were all so proud of ourselves. I said we worked hard, and I also mean the wives, who had to stay up so late so many nights because of us, or go to meet a late plane, and who had to look after the children when we were away so much, and try to be a father to them as well as a mother. It wasn't easy for anyone. I feel so grateful when I look back on this year. Oh, my, there was a day in San Diego, when Dave Roberts came in to pitch in a game we was losing. The bases were loaded for them, and a three-and-oh count on the batter, and Dave came in and made these three *outstanding* pitches and struck the man out, and we came back, caught up, and won. That was a moment when we knew what this team was like. Or, you know about the time the Hammer come up to pinch-hit, and . . ."

THE WINTER GAMES

The weather was appalling. The opening game of the Series was postponed for a day, and the next morning it snowed considerably in Baltimore and then rained all afternoon. At game time, the temperature stood at forty-one, and it went down from there. The next night was a bit warmer at first, but a late-inning drizzle turned the field to slime—the worst conditions, several players said, they had ever encountered. Game Three, in Pittsburgh, was suspended for more than an hour by a third-inning deluge, and Game Four, played in the afternoon, under scudding wintry clouds, was the coldest baseball I have ever sat through. Only in the last two games was the weather not a factor. During World Series week, there was a run on long johns and scarves and mittens in Baltimore department stores, and brave jokes were made in the press rows during the games ("If you're going inside to warm up, would you leave me your socks and shoes?" "Isn't drowsiness a symptom of freezing to death?"), but there was nothing jolly about what went on out on the field, where six errors were committed in the first game; Bruce Kison, the Pittsburgh starter, injured his arm in the cold and was finished for the year. No extended editorial comment on this weather report will be offered, since it would serve no purpose. This year's playing conditions were the worst in World Series history, but in recent years a considerable number of Series games have been played in icy winds or daunting storms, because these are perfectly normal mid-evening mid-autumn conditions in much of the country. For years, baseball has been vulnerable to this chronic disaster, because the commissioner and the owners insist on maintaining a season that runs a week or ten days too late into the fall, and because they are willing captives of network television, which wants the Series games to be played at night during the week and very early or very late in the afternoon on weekends (before or after football games, that is), since this schedule will draw the highest audience ratings. The nabobs of baseball could alter all this in a moment, if they had the wish to do so, by scheduling

World Series games on afternoons in early October, but they are not so inclined, and it clearly doesn't matter to them that their famous showcase now offers a truly inferior version of the pastime, played under conditions that demean and endanger the contestants and punish the local fans. Every baseball player I have consulted on this matter is indignant about it—not so much because of the discomforts involved as because of the damage inflicted on the sport—and thousands of fans keep asking why something isn't done about it. But nothing will be done, because the ratings are right. They want it this way.

The Orioles scored five runs in the first inning of the opener, after Phil Garner threw a routine double-play ball six feet to Foli's left and into left field; later, Garner said that handling the wet ball was like trying to throw a bar of soap. Kison could not grip the ball in the cold, and gave up two walks, a wild pitch, and a two-run homer, to Doug DeCinces. The Pirates almost climbed back, but Mike Flanagan held on and won it, 5–4. Throughout the game, each player on the field was accompanied by the hovering, visible vapor clouds of his own breath, and DeCinces—who made two errors at third base and was lucky not to be charged with a third—said afterward that he had tried to blow out his breath just before each of Flanagan's pitches, so that he would have a view of the play.

The second meeting produced a tangled, tense, eventful game, stuffed with accidents and eventualities, which the Pirates won by 3–2 in the wet, with the field at the end resembling a winter salient at Verdun. Jim Palmer, the Orioles' grand master, surrendered two early runs, but then wisely shelved his fastball for the rest of the evening and did much better. The Birds caught up on two blows by their young switch-hitting slugger, Eddie Murray—a monster homer off Bert Blyleven, almost over the right-field bleachers, and then a whistling double to left, which scored Ken Singleton all the way from first. This World Series produced an amazing dossier of discussable baseball tactics and problems, and the remaining topics of the evening can be presented in a spot quiz, to which I append my own tentative answers.

Q: (a) With one out in the bottom of the sixth, was Eddie Murray (a fast man) right in trying to score from third base after Lowenstein's fly to Dave Parker in medium right field? And (b) since he did go, should he not have tried to collide with or discommode catcher Ed Ott, in the hope of jarring the ball loose?

A: (a) Sure—why not? (b) Well, Parker's throw was a laser beam, reaching the plate when Murray was still discouragingly far up the line. But yes, Eddie should have crashed.

Q: In the eighth, with the game tied, and with Murray leading off second and DeCinces off first, why didn't Earl Weaver instruct Lowenstein to bunt the runners along?

A: I still don't know. Weaver said after the game that the bunt is not his style, which is plain enough but non-responsive. As it was, Earl was cruelly punished for his flouting of classic strategy. Pirate shortstop Tim Foli was so convinced that the bunt *was* on that he broke with the pitch to cover third base as third baseman Bill Madlock charged the plate, and thus found himself perfectly positioned to field the grounder that Lowenstein bounced to the left side. Foli tried to tag Murray on the base path and missed, but threw to second for the force, and Murray was then doubled up in a rundown. (For a glimmering moment, Foli believed he even had a triple play in front of him.)

Q: Two out, top of the ninth, still a tie game. Ed Ott (a slow runner) is on second when Manny Sanguillen, pinch-hitting, singles to right against Don Stanhouse. Does hindsight offer any excuse or exoneration for Eddie Murray's impulsive decision to cut off Singleton's gentle but perhaps adequate peg home, in order to wheel and zip a faster throw to the same spot—too late, it turned out, to cut down Ott, who slid in with the winning run?

A: No.

Back home at Three Rivers Stadium and comforted by the roars of fifty thousand encircling supporters, the Pirates moved away confidently to an early lead in each of the next two games, and lost them both. They whacked the Baltimore starter, Scott McGregor, for three runs in the first two innings of Game Three, and might have dispatched him altogether if they had not damaged their own cause with some overeager baserunning. The Orioles were mysteriously succored by a third-inning cloudburst that held things up for more than an hour, because McGregor was an indomitable pitcher after the intermission, while John Candelaria, the Pittsburgh flinger, was suddenly no pitcher at all, being abruptly dispatched when the Orioles blew the game open with five runs. The key blows in their 8–4 victory were a two-run homer by Benny Ayala and a bases-clearing triple by Kiko Garcia, who wound up with four hits for the evening. These yeomen were in the lineup—Ayala in left field and Garcia at short—because both are right-handed batters, and Earl Weaver wanted an all-righty lineup swinging against Candelaria, who is a southpaw. This is a routine baseball strategy, not quite Einsteinian in its difficulty, but the tactic says a good deal about the Baltimore machine, which is made up of an unusual number of movable parts. Garcia is an uncertain fielder, to put it charitably, but he hits better than Mark Belanger, his alternate at short, who is impeccable afield but no use at all at the plate. The Orioles, it should be added, were strained for hitting all through these games, because of the different rules that govern the World Series in alternate years; this year, there was no designated hitter, which meant that the Orioles, deprived of their d.h., who is Lee May, had to make continual gingerly alterations at the plate or in the field as they tried to take up the slack. During the season, Weaver often boasted cheerfully about his club's "deep depth," but the Pirates, it turned out, were deeper.

Earl Weaver made all the right moves the next afternoon, waiting imperturbably (well, *almost* imperturbably) while the Pirates banged out fourteen hits in six innings and ran up a 6–3 lead. What he was waiting for was Kent Tekulve, the skinny, spidery, side-arming Pittsburgh relief pitcher, who now, in the eighth, came into the game during a Baltimore rally that had suddenly loaded the bases. Tekulve, a right-hander who led the élite Pittsburgh bullpen crew this summer with thirty-one saves, had been untouchable in two previous Series outings, and he had particularly embarrassed the right-handed Baltimore batters, who sometimes appeared to be wielding boathooks as they reached feebly for his dipping serves. Weaver, now beginning to play his hand, sent up the lefthanded John Lowenstein to pinch-hit, and Lowenstein pulled a startling double into the right-field corner, scoring two runs. Another left-handed pinch-hitter, Billy Smith, was walked intentionally, thus reloading the bases and preparing the table for Earl Weaver's hole card, Terry Crowley, *another* left-handed pinch-hitter, who also smashed a two-run double to right, putting the Orioles ahead for keeps in the game, which they won by 9–6.

"This was the first time we've been able to keep the gun loaded right to the end," Earl said after the game. He looked like a cat with a mouthful of feathers, and who could blame him? The strategic maneuvers available to a manager are, in fact, extremely limited, and only rarely do they produce such swift and visible rewards. They are also unprovable. Tekulve, who discussed his disaster with perfect aplomb, said that, for his part, he hadn't pitched especially well, because he was releasing the balls a fraction too late, causing it to rise too much into the strike zone. Maybe he was right, at that; just after Crowley's double, Tekulve yielded a run-scoring single to Tim Stoddard, the Baltimore pitcher, who was making his very first appearance at the plate in the major leagues.

Down three games to one, the Pirates now seemed to be plucking at the coverlet. Only three teams had ever come back to win a World Series after finding themselves in such a predicament. The Pirates were whacking the ball, to be sure—the club was batting .329—but they were also playing at something less than their best, having committed eight official errors and a number of other omissions and malfeasances on the field and on the base paths. (The Orioles' six-run eighth inning had begun when Dave Parker lost track of a short fly ball by Kiko Garcia, which dropped in for a single.) Worst of all, they now faced the utter necessity of defeating Mike Flanagan, Jim Palmer, and Scott McGregor in three successive games, at a time when their own pitching was suddenly worn thin. The burden of all this kept the Pirate fans in a frenzy of apprehension during the early part of the next game—a late-Sunday-afternoon affair, and the last baseball of the year at Three Rivres Stadium no matter who won it. They shuddered and "ooh"ed at every pitch to a Baltimore batter, and then yowled and clapped and twitched their front-row bedsheet banners ("THE BIRDS WILL DIE," "FOLI'S FIENDS," "WILVER," and a heroic likeness of a rearing cobra, with Dave Parker's number, 39, under it) imploringly as each Pirate batter stepped up and dug in and stared out at the enemy pitcher under the billows of noise. Somehow, it all worked and these vespers brought surcease and joy at the end. Chuck Tanner solved his pitching problem by giving the ball to Jim Rooker, a thirty-seven-year-old left-hander who had been twice disabled by arm miseries during the season. Holding nothing in reserve, Rooker threw fast and then faster, dismissing twelve of the first thirteen Oriole batters he faced, and departed in the middle of the fifth, after he had surrendered a lone run. He was succeeded by Bert Blyleven, in one of the extremely rare relief appearances of his career, who blew away the Birds, giving up a bare three hits the rest of the way. The final score was 7–1, Pirates, but even comfortable wins can have their hard moments and critical turns. I think the door to this game swung open in the bottom of the sixth, with two out and the score tied at 1–1, when Bill Madlock fought off several excellent Flanagan pitches with his calm, compact stroke and at last rapped a good inside fastball up the middle, to score Dave Parker from third. Madlock had four hits for the day, and afterward Earl Weaver said, "We haven't exactly learned how to pitch to him yet—or to some of the others, either. What've they got now, sixty-five hits?"

It was sixty-one hits, in fact. Sixty-one hits in five games.

PICTURES IN THE FIRE

As we know, the Pirates won the last two games as well, by scores of 4–0 and 4–1, and their sustained aplomb and courage in winning the championship against such unlikely odds made the World Series the most satisfying event of this eventful baseball year, which is as it should be. At the same time, it must be said that the sixth and seventh games, like the fifth, were unsatisfying entertainments. In all these games, the Orioles gave up the eventual winning run in the sixth or seventh inning, and the Pirates then went on and increased their lead in the late going. It should take nothing away from the Pirates' triumphant, unrelenting style of play to recall that the Orioles died at the plate in these three games, scoring two runs in the twenty-seven innings and never really mounting anything that could be called a threat along the way. Their cleanup hitter, Eddie Murray, went hitless in his last twenty-one times at bat. Baltimore was no better afield, making five errors in the three games and, more significantly, repeatedly failing to come up with the big play. True baseball fans are insatiably, and properly, critical in their demands, and most of them, I think (I exempt the Pittsburgh fans, of course), will look back on this Series with a sense of disappointment because of these unexpected Orioles failures. This was a flat spell but certainly not a collapse. The Orioles are a young and wonderfully talented team—Eddie Murray is twenty-three years old and has already hit seventy-nine major-league home runs—and I think we will be watching them again in October in the years just ahead.

What we remember about baseball after the game or the season is over is its marvellous moments—the sudden situation that offers a flashing succession of difficulties and chances and possibilities, all in the space of a second or two, and is then abruptly and sometimes shockingly resolved. That and the players' own moments—the images of the best of them that we carry with us into the coming winter. All of us, of course, will keep hold of our picture of Willie Stargell's home run against Scott McGregor, which won the last game. The Orioles were leading, 1–0, in the sixth, and McGregor had been pitching so well, spotting the ball and throwing a lot of sinkers, that a lot of the now terribly doubtful Baltimore fans must have begun to allow themselves to think that the one run just might be enough. (Tekulve, still waiting in the bullpen and all the more formidable, somehow, because of his brief recent loss of form, meant that there probably wouldn't be more than one run.) Bill Robinson's sixth-inning single was only the fourth Pirate hit of the evening. He led off first base as McGregor delivered the next pitch to Stargell—a low curve (a little *too* low, McGregor said later, for Stargell is a murderous low-ball hitter)—and Wilver hit it to deep right field, a high-sailing fly ball that descended just beyond the fence and just above Ken Singleton's leap and stretch and momentarily arrested empty reach. I have seen Willie Stargell hit so many home runs over the years (so many of them this fall, in fact) that I can run off the reel of this one again and again in my head, like a home movie: the preparatory forward double whirl of the bat, with his shoulders tilting and leaning forward, and with the weight of his body low and evenly placed on his feet but still somehow leaning, too—everything leaning—and then all of it abruptly rotating back in the opposite direction like an immense wheel, as weight and shoulders and arms and bat unwind together on the swing, and the circling, upswooping bat almost negligently intercepts the ball and disposes of it, and the body, finishing up, opens and rises, with the arms flying apart and the broad chest turning and facing out toward the field (as if it were watching the ball, too, along with the rest of us) while the bat, held only in the right hand now, softly finishes the circle and comes to a stop in the air behind the batter.

Willie won it all—the game and the Series, and the Most Valuable Player award for the Series, and a fistful of Series slugging records, and, best of all, something like a permanent place in our national sporting regard—and there is a special pleasure in all that, a thump of the heart, because of his way of doing things, because of the kind of man he is. Stargell's triumphs this fall were a perfect recompense for 1971, when the Pirates also beat the Orioles in a seven-game Series but one in which he played a very small part. Although he had led his league that year in home runs and had batted in one hundred and twenty-five runs, he went hitless in the playoffs and then batted only .208 in the Series, driving in one run. His sufferings at the plate were almost too painful to watch, but, as I wrote later, he endured this stretch of pop-ups and strikeouts and weakly topped grounders with unruffled calm—no bat-tossing, no puzzled head-shaking, not a word of explanation or complaint to the press. Near the end of that Series, I approached him in the clubhouse and asked how an intense, proud competitor like him could endure these disappointments and humiliations with such composure. Stargell's son, Wilver, Jr., who was then about four years old, was playing at his father's feet in the dressing cubicle, and Willie nodded toward the boy and said, "There's a time in life when a man has to decide if he's going to *be* a man."

Perversely, however, I continue to prefer the complexities of baseball to its curative ultimate resolutions and simplifications, no matter how heroic they may be. For me, the best moments of this Series came in the penultimate sixth game. I will not quickly forget Jim Palmer and John Candelaria battling through the first six scoreless innings: the Candy Man again and again firing outside fastball strikes to the Oriole right-handed batters and then running his nearly sidearm slider in under their fists; and Palmer, the tall and handsome hero, in his long white uniform, standing loosely and calmly in the center of things—staring *down* at the game, one always feels—with his glove hand and pitching hand held together high on his chest, almost under his chin, and then his stiff-legged stride and downhill stagger as the ball, delivered almost over the top, descended in a sudden line and flashed dangerously through the top story of the strike zone for another swinging strike.

The situation—the deadly difficulty—began when Omar Moreno singled to right field in the top of the seventh inning (there was still no score in the game), just out of Eddie Murray's reach. Moreno was then dispatched toward second on a hit-and-run play, and Foli hit a soft, high chop over the pitcher's mound that Jim Palmer leaped for and could not quite pull in; the ball, flicking off the tip of his glove, was slightly slowed in its progress, and bounced toward second. Kiko Garcia, who had moved to cover the base when Moreno was released, was in front of the bag, and he simultaneously attempted to field the chance and step on second for the force. He mishandled the ball, which trickled past him for a hit. A more experienced shortstop—a Mark Belanger, say—probably would have made the tiny, instant mental adjustment after Palmer's deflection that would have told him to forget about Moreno and make sure of the out at first. If Palmer had fielded the ball, or if he had not touched it at all, the Orioles would have had a double play.

With first base occupied, Palmer was forced to pitch to Dave Parker, and Parker, unwinding menacingly from his unique, almost cross-footed stance (he is six feet five inches tall, with columnlike legs, and he holds his long bat at the highest possible level behind his left shoulder, like a sledge-hammer in midair), smashed the first pitch toward second base-man Rich Dauer, who in one instant seemed to have the play before him, and in the next fell on his knees as the ball rico-cheted oddly off the infield dirt and over his right shoulder into center field. It happened very quickly, and you could see Dave Parker still only a step or two toward first base at the moment that Dauer, on all fours in the dirt, dropped his head in despair as he understood that the ball was not in his glove, that Moreno was sprinting for the plate, and that the game was forever altered. Parker, it was agreed later, had crushed the pitch, hitting the ball exactly in its middle with the middle of his bat, so that it flew toward Dauer without any spin—a knuckleball, in short, which took a sudden and characteristic knuckleball veer at the last instant and skipped free. Tim Foli, running toward second, was the nearest witness, and he said later, "I could see the seams of the ball, so I knew what had happened. It was so strange to see a ball hit that way, and hit so hard, that I yelled 'Look out!' as it went by me. Dauer never had a chance."

10

Sunshine Semester

APRIL 1980

LAST MONTH, DURING THE MIDDLE INNINGS OF A MORNING B-squad game between the California Angels and the Milwaukee Brewers, I joined sixty or seventy members of the Yankees, Phillies, Mets, Reds, Pirates, and other teams who were attending a baseball clinic in the right-field grandstand at Sun City Stadium, in Arizona. Their presence at the ballpark, it occurred to me, must have made for a sudden jolt in the actuarial tables of this year's spring baseball audiences at Sun City, which is a retirement community, for my fellow-students were all members of the West Side Little League teams, on a visit from Phoenix. A few of the boys had put on their full uniforms, but all of them were wearing their team caps, with various major-league insignia; the caps looked to be all the same size, with adjustable tabs and snaps behind, and if you sat behind one of the smaller ten-year-old players, whose cap seemed about to swallow his ears, you could see that the snaps had been taken up as far as they could go. All the players, from the smallest to the largest, were sitting motionless in the lower three or four rows of seats, riveted with interest. Our professor was Lary Sorensen, a bushy-haired, blond, six-foot-two right-handed pitcher, who won fifteen games and lost fourteen for the Brewers last year—a record he will have to improve on if the Milwaukee club is to realize its burning ambition for a pennant in the American League East this summer. He stood with his back to the field and with his hands in the pockets of his silky blue Milwaukee windbreaker (it was a chilly morning, with low, scudding clouds and occasional spatters of rain, and there was a smell of fresh wet turf everywhere) and talked about his trade. Keep your tail down when fielding the ball, he said, and try to keep the ball in front of you. Keep your eye on the ball. See the ball into your glove. Be comfortable up at the plate, and don't let anyone change your style there if it feels right to you. Make contact. If you're a pitcher, always try to throw with your arm above your shoulder, instead of going sidearm and across the body. Get the ball over the plate. "I strongly advise against throwing the breaking ball," he said. "There may be one or two future major-leaguers sitting right here today"—there was a stir in the grandstand and some exchanged glances at this news—"and you'd hate to think later that you'd ruined your chances by hurting your arm so early. Work on the fastball and a change-up. The whole theory of pitching is to keep the batter off balance. I throw my fastball at about ninety miles an hour"—"Yoww!" said a small Yankee sitting just to my left—"but all I'm after is to get the batter to hit the ball on the ground. Don't try to strike people out. Maybe some of you have heard of Nolan Ryan"—nods, sophisticated chuckles—"who is a great, great pitcher, but his lifetime record is only eight games above .500, because he tries to strike everybody out. *Work* on the batter. Think. Try to pitch up and in and then low and away." Sorensen paused. "Sometimes even that doesn't work," he said, smiling. "Two years ago, in a game against the Twins, I threw a perfect low outside fastball to Rod Carew—he bats left-handed, you know—and he hit it down the left-field line for a double. The next time he came up, I knew I wouldn't give him that pitch again, and I threw the ball up on his hands—a real good pitch—and he hit it down the *right*-field line for a double."

"Yoww!" said the Yankee again.

Sorensen took some questions from the audience ("Do you know the players on the other teams?" one youngster asked. "Are they friends of yours?"), now and then holding up both hands for attention. "One more thing," he said. "Stay in school.

Work on your baseball, but work on your books, too. Somebody made a statistical study that showed that only one in every five hundred thousand Little Leaguers ever makes it to the major leagues. The average major-league career is less than two years. On the whole, I'd recommend becoming a doctor or a lawyer."

The lecture ended, and there was a rush down the aisles for autographs. I went back to my seat behind first base and watched the Angels-Brewers game for a couple of innings, but I kept thinking back to what we had just heard. One or two of the dozens of boys now clustering around Lary Sorensen might make it into baseball someday, as Sorensen had said, but the odds, as he had also said, weren't so hot. Good, complicated advice: both things were true. Keep the ball low, but try never to have to pitch to Rod Carew.

Baseball is simple but never easy. Each year, just before spring comes, I begin to wonder if I shouldn't give up this game. Surely it must be time for me to cut short my abiding, summer-consuming preoccupation with scores and standings and averages, and to put an end to all those evening and weekend hours given to the tube and morning hours given to the sports pages. Is there no cure for this second-hand passion, which makes me a partner, however unwilling, in the blather of publicity, the demeaning emptiness of hero worship, and the inconceivably wasteful outpourings of money and energy that we give to professional sports now? I would happily avoid ever again having to watch the beery rage of a losing crowd in some dirty big-city stadium on a sweltering night in August, or—just as bad—suddenly noticing across the room the patronizing stare of some baseball hater, a certified adult, when he hears me mention Reggie or Yaz or Willie and watches me wave my hands or take up a stance at a make-believe plate while I tell some friends about what I have just seen or once saw, and how they should have been there, too. Every year, I think about such things, often in the middle of the night, and I groan and say to myself, "Yes, all right, this is the last year for me, no more baseball after this." But then, a few days or weeks later, back in the sun in Arizona or Florida in March, I change my mind. None of Lary Sorensen's talk to the West Side Little Leaguers at Sun City was exactly new to me, but it made me feel cheerful and instructed to hear it. I think I am almost too old for baseball, but every year I find that I need to go on learning it. Most of all, I think, baseball disarms us.

That afternoon, it rained off and on during the game between the Brewers' and the Angels' front-line teams, but in between the showers I kept coming back from my car in the parking lot to watch the action, because both of these clubs are stuffed with talent. It was the third time I had seen the Angels this spring, so the faces and mannerisms of their stars were pretty familiar to me—Carew and Joe Rudi and Bobby Grich; the massive, long-legged Don Baylor, who drove in a hundred and thirty-nine runs last year and was named the league's Most Valuable Player; catcher Brian Downing, who stands in the batter's box squarely facing the pitcher, like a man about to kick off at the beginning of a football game; and the lanky, remarkable twenty-three-year-old third baseman Carney Lansford, who, afield, almost touches the infield dirt with his glove and fingertips as he hovers with vampirelike attention over each pitch. Here Grich and Downing hit homers up into the damp, hurrying air, and Lansford had three ringing singles, and Freddie Patek, who came over from the Royals this year to help the Angels at shortstop, rapped out a pair of singles, as the visitors jumped all over a young Milwaukee left-hander named Dave LaPoint and his successors, racking up sixteen hits and eleven runs before another desert downpour mercifully put a stop to things at the end of the seventh. The Angels finally became nationally known during the American League playoffs last fall, which they lost in four games to the Orioles, but the Brewers, who won ninety-five games last year and may be an even better team, are semi-strangers to a lot of fans in their own division, because of the club's geographical isolation from the rest of the American League East and its extremely rare appearances on national television. For me, studying the Brewers' lineup and trying to commit their stars to memory is still a process of agreeable surprises—the slick, angular, left-handed first baseman Cecil Cooper, who has hit .300 or over for the last three seasons and won a Gold Glove at his position last year; Sixto Lezcano, a Gold Glove in right field, who batted .321 last year and hit twenty-eight homers; the brawny, hairy, mustachioed Gorman Thomas in center field, who led the league with forty-five homers in 1979 ("Who the hell is *Gorman Thomas?*" a lot of friends of mine exclaimed last September);

and, far from the least, twenty-three-year-old Paul Molitor, a smooth, classically elegant second baseman, who batted .322 last summer, which was only his second season of professional baseball. The Brewers lost their chance at a pennant last year when their leader and prime slugger, Larry Hisle, tore a shoulder muscle—the "rotator cuff," which currently holds the No. 1 spot on the baseball Hurt Parade—while making a peg in late April, and was out for most of the rest of the campaign. (This spring, shortly before my visit to Sun City, the Brewers had suffered a shocking double blow: their batting instructor, Harvey Kuenn, lost a leg because of complications attending a blood clot, and their esteemed manager, George Bamberger, underwent open-heart surgery. Both are expected back before midseason, and the club is currently in the hands of another coach, Buck Rodgers.) Hisle, who will be limited to the designated hitter's spot this year, did not play in the game against the Angels, but in the clubhouse he told me that he was swinging without pain. "I try to block out what happened, but a thing like this really makes you begin to think," he said, in his soft, quiet voice. "I'm much more aware now of what the game means to me. I'm going to try to achieve more from now on, though they won't let me play defense again—and I love it out there. But even if I have the best year at the plate of my entire career, I'll never get back all the games I missed last year. Every play and every at-bat you don't participate in seems so rare once they've gone by. They'll never come back."

I have been thinking about Larry Hisle's feelings of waste and of loss in the days since the last week of spring training was cancelled by a strike called by the Major League Baseball Players Association. It also voted to walk out again on May 23rd, during the regular season, if its differences with the owners are not resolved. I cannot pretend to any mild neutrality about the issues involved; it has been perfectly plain to me from the start that the twenty-six owners and the league presidents and their advisers have determined that the basic structure of free-agency, which has governed the movement of senior players (players with six years' service in the majors), must be radically altered or they will close down the game. They are serious about this; they have hired a new labor negotiator, Ray Grebey, to represent them, and they have put together a sizable war chest of funds and special insurance policies to sustain them within their fortification if a strike comes. There are several secondary matters, involving pensions and arbitration procedures, under negotiation, but free-agency is at the center of everything. Heretofore, a player has been permitted to sell his services to the highest bidder after he has completed six years of play with a major-league club. (Achieving free-agency can sometimes take a good deal longer than that—up to a dozen years, in fact—because the club owning a given player may choose to employ him in the minors for three years, and then shuttle him back and forth between the majors and the minors as an "option" player for another three years, before his qualifying six-year span begins.) A team losing a free agent to another team is currently recompensed by the award of that team's first pick in the next semiannual draft of young high-school and college players—not much of a reward, let it be said, for the loss of a Reggie Jackson or a Nolan Ryan. The owners propose that each club losing a prime free agent be permitted to replenish its lineup by selecting a player from the roster of the buying team, and that the buying team may protect only fifteen of its present first-line players. The Players Association rejects the entire concept of further recompense for the owners, and now proposes that the qualifying period for free-agency be lowered to five years. This is the hard nut at the center of the impasse.

The other ingredient in the dispute—and the true issue, I believe—is money. Major-league salaries and emoluments, of course, have ascended giddily since the players were freed from the shackles of the reserve clause by an arbitrator's decision in the winter of 1975. Since then, the average salary of major-league players has risen from forty-six thousand to a hundred and twenty-two thousand dollars as of last year, and is expected to go up to about a hundred and fifty thousand dollars this season. The spectacular (or infamous—depends on how you look at it) contracts won by star performers and their agents have led the way; last winter, Nolan Ryan, departing the Angels, signed a three-year contract with the Houston Astros that will bring him one million dollars per year, with bonuses totalling five hundred thousand dollars more. Dave Parker, staying on with the Pirates, signed a five-year contract last year worth about the same sum yearly. Furthermore, a number of plainly middle-level, or even sub-average, players have signed free-agent contracts of astounding generosity. Rennie Stennett, a second baseman who batted .240 as a part-timer with the Pirates for the past two seasons, moved to the Giants last winter for a total of three million dollars over the next five years. John Curtis, a left-handed pitcher whose record in the majors since 1970 stands at sixty-seven wins and seventy-two losses, signed on with the Padres at one million eight hundred thousand dollars for five years. And so on.

Player salaries—and especially these inflated rewards for apparently everyday players—are what the fans seem to fasten on just now, but there are other figures to be taken into account. Baseball is booming in dollars and attendance, and perhaps even in national regard. Last year's total attendance of forty-three and a half million fans was another record—the fourth record year in succession—and eight clubs have announced record advance ticket sales for the 1980 season. In the five years since the reserve clause was annulled (since free-agency, that is), attendance has registered a forty-six per cent gain, while revenues from television have doubled. At the same time, it is refreshingly clear that competition has never been brisker or more invigorating than in the past few years, because of the wider distribution of talent that free-agency has brought about. The owners' much publicized prediction that free-agency would result in a cornering of all the best players by a handful of rich teams hasn't come to pass. Some owners have spent freely and wisely in the open market—George Steinbrenner, for example. Others have poured out as much or more money in search of instant pennants and have had no luck at all—perhaps because they didn't understand baseball very well, or perhaps because "buying a pennant" is much more difficult and chancy a process than it appears. Ray Kroc, of the Padres, and Brad Corbett, who sold his controlling interest in the Texas Rangers last winter, have each parted with millions for free agents since 1975 without ever mounting a real pennant contender. Some very successful clubs—the Reds, for instance—have remained in the thick of competition while passing up free agents almost entirely. On the other hand, the California Angels, who are owned by Gene Autry, spent several millions in the past half-decade for free agents like Rod Carew, Bobby Grich, Joe Rudi, Don Baylor, and the late Lyman Bostock before finally capturing their flag last year. In the pennant races of 1979, the free-spending World Champion Yankees fell to fourth place in their division, which was won by Baltimore—a team that lost Reggie Jackson, Wayne Garland, Bobby Grich, and Ross Grimsley to free-agency in recent years while adding one middle-price pitcher, Steve Stone, and a little-known infielder, Billy Smith, by the same process. In the National League, the Reds lost out to the Pirates, the eventual World Champions, who built their wonderful team from their farms and by astute trading, plus the addition of pitcher Jim Bibby and reserve outfielder Lee Lacy, who came aboard by the free-agent route. The Dodgers, who fell to third place in the National League West after playing in the World Series the two previous autumns, have only recently extended their rather limited previous forays into the free-agent market, with the acquisition of two expensive free-agent pitchers, Don Stanhouse and Dave Goltz, over the winter. The financial and competitive picture is clouded, then, but not all *that* clouded. Free agents have helped some clubs and not others, and the open market has raised players' salaries everywhere, sometimes by enormous margins. Business is terrific.

The owners disagree. It is their claim that very few teams among the twenty-six are making any money—or *enough* money—and that free-agency has driven their salary levels to unconscionable heights and made it impossible for a poor or middling-poor club ever to build a contender. (Baltimore, as noted, is one of the awkward exceptions to this argument.) The owners produce no figures to back up these claims. Most clubs never open their books, which makes it difficult to assess or put much credence in their cries of poverty. Some of them belong to larger entities—the Cardinals to Anheuser-Busch, for instance, and the Braves to Turner Communications—and others have been purchased, or are controlled, by businessmen who have enjoyed great success in other lines of corporate or private endeavor: Mr. Kroc with McDonald's, Mr. Steinbrenner as a shipbuilder, Mr. Autry as Gene Autry, and so forth. In either case, it is hard not to believe that losses on the baseball side of a conglomerate ledger can make for handsome tax savings over on a different page. In addition, the value of a baseball franchise—the capital side of the business—goes up, too, no matter what a given team has done in recent years; the

New York Mets, abysmal last-place finishers for the past three seasons, cost the Payson family less than two million dollars in 1962 and were sold to Doubleday's for some twenty-one million dollars last winter.

Finally, it should be understood that in the opinion of a great many baseball people—including this sideline expert—the owners' idea of allowing a club that loses a free agent to tap the middle levels of the buying team's roster will effectively put an end to the entire free-agent process. Very few clubs—perhaps none—would risk adding a free-agent star if this meant losing a solid current pitcher or a coming star player from their farms or a competent day-to-day pinch-hitter—a Terry Crowley, say—which is the kind of exchange this plan would come down to. The owners' offer does stipulate that only an owner who has lost a "prime" player—that is, a player for whom at least eight other clubs have said they intend to bid—can pick from the signing team's roster, but there is nothing in the proposal to prevent every club from making a token bid for each free agent from now on. The owners, it is plain, wish to turn back the clock. The players, for obvious reasons, refuse to give up the rights they have earned.

The emotions and hopes and darker reasonings that underlie all this are more interesting to think about, it seems to me, than the numbers and issues themselves. There has been a good deal of speculation in recent weeks that the owners now feel, publicly or privately, that they require some kind of "victory" over Marvin Miller, the quiet, efficient economist who has been the executive director of the Players Association since 1966. Mr. Miller's understated manner and his signal achievements in court and at the bargaining table and with the press have sometimes appeared to offer an almost unfair contrast to the owners' blustery and perhaps obtuse approach to labor relations, but if a personal vendetta directed against him is their prime goad this time around, then they are even more masochistic than any of their critics have previously supposed. I believe, rather, that the owners have perceived a public state of mind that may permit them at last to close out the players as partners in and co-owners of their business (which is what free-agency has come to); put some check on the uncontrolled bidding for free agents by a handful of irresponsible or greedy owners, which has knocked the salary structure askew; and restore baseball to the friendly, clublike enclave of sportsmen-nabobs that it remained throughout its first century. What the owners are counting on, I think, is a widespread public notion (one hears it every day on all sides: on the street and in bars-and-grills, in people's homes, in newspaper sports pages and letter columns, on radio and television) that baseball players make too much money, that they are spoiled, greedy babies, and that the salary levels of their sport are wildly disproportionate to their skills. This attitude is so widely and vehemently expressed that it seems plain that the owners have already won the public-relations side of the struggle. It is almost certain that Mr. Grebey and some of the top executives of the game foresaw this as their prime weapon when they adopted their stiff-necked posture.

The idea that ballplayers earn too much money is not really an economic argument or a bargaining point, of course, but, rather, an emotional or ideological concept, and is thus fogged over with wishes and prejudices—the notion that too much money is bad for young people, that it sets a bad example for the rest of us, and, most of all, that there is something out of whack about giving all that loot to *athletes*. I agree absolutely with the last point if it is in fact the owners' intention to take back Nolan Ryan's salary, along with that of his fellow boy capitalists, and give these millions of dollars to deserving schoolteachers, painters, philosophers, and medical students, and to the restoration of the old Pennsylvania Station and the preservation of the humpback whale. This is not their plan, alas; the "too much money" that the players have been earning is part of the owners' money, taken in at the gate and from the networks (which have just negotiated a new four-year, hundred-and-eighty-five-million-dollar contract with the clubs), and whatever the owners get back from the players they will keep for themselves or spend elsewhere, in baseball or in other enterprises. All this is ironic, and even entertaining, to think about (the greatest irony being that it is the spoiled, immature athletes who are being asked to agree to a plan that will rein in owners who are too improvident or impetuous to restrain themselves), but the damage that a long, angry strike could inflict on the game, and on the special feelings that so many of us hold about it, could be grievous indeed. It is the curious nature of this strange industry, or dream factory, that its laborers are not unseen riveters or fitters who piece together some shiny desirable item of merchandise. Rather, it is they themselves who are the product, and if that product is made to seem overpriced or of inferior quality, then the public may not always come back, money in hand, to buy these elusive and glittering wares once again.

Tom Seaver was talking about these issues and values not long ago in Tampa, a few days before the camps were shut down. "I don't understand the owners," he said. "Once again, I can't see what their motives are. If they can't make a profit with the baseball business the way it is, then when will they ever do it? I think they think they've been beaten. Baseball has come so far from the inequities of the old days that they can't help thinking they've lost, instead of thinking that it's someplace where we all *should* be. I believe they want this strike, but if the blame is put on us, the players—and we *are* being blamed—then the strike is going to cost us all a great deal of money and harm, maybe more than anybody can imagine now."

One day in Arizona, before an Indians-Cubs game at Mesa, I talked with Dave Garcia, the Cleveland manager, about the unusual number of wonderfully talented younger players I had begun to notice this spring—and, for that matter, over the last couple of seasons. Garcia, who for more than twenty years was an infielder and then a manager in baseball outposts like Oshkosh, Sioux City, and Danville, later coached for the Padres and the Angels, and then managed the Angels in 1977 and 1978. Last year, he brought the Indians home one game over the .500 level—something of a feat for a sixth-place club. He is cheerful and garrulous, with twinkling eyes, a hooked nose, and a large Adam's apple, somehow suggesting a New England grocer in looks and manner.

"I went about five years without seeing any American League games, but when I joined the Angels I began to notice that a change had come over the two leagues," he said. "The National League had all the best of it for a long time, you know—maybe because they signed so many of the great black ballplayers when they first came into the game—but I think more of the real good young players have been coming into the American League in the past five years. I'm not saying they don't play good ball over there, and we all know who won that World Series last fall, but *we* have the Rices and the Lynns and Ken Singleton and that young Eddie Murray. The Tigers' double-play combination of Whitaker and Trammell is *outstanding*, and I don't think anybody has a better defensive outfielder than our Rick Manning. Then there's the Brewers' Paul Molitor, who reminds me of a young Alvin Dark or a Dick Groat—that kind of infielder. He isn't a great infielder yet, but don't forget he's just beginning, and he's an aggressive sort of hitter, and he runs well, and he knows this game. And that Carney Lansford, with the Angels—well, he's going to be a superstar, that's all. George Brett, Gorman Thomas, Steve Kemp—those are pretty good ballplayers, it seems to me. Everybody puts too much emphasis on the All-Star Game"— the National League has won the last eight All-Star Games— "but that's just an exhibition, just one game, and quality takes longer than that to show itself. It may be dumb of me to say so, but I think this American League East division is the toughest bunch of teams we've had in one league in a long time. Two years ago, I thought there were four teams who could have beaten the Dodgers in the World Series. The Yankees got to do it, but the Red Sox or the Orioles or the Brewers could have got the job done, too."

Garcia and I were sitting on folding chairs beside the Indians' dugout, and a terrific noonday Arizona sun was slowly frying us, like a side order of tortillas. Garcia got rid of a little tobacco juice and recocked his cap over his eyes. "The great thing about baseball," he went on, "is that so much of winning is your state of mind and your pitching. I remember when I was with the Padres back there, and we'd go to play the Cincinnati Reds, who were league champions, you know, and a great team. You'd look down their lineup and figure there was just no *way* we could take a game from them. But if Clay Kirby was in form for us, we'd go in and win a series from them, as often as not. If a couple of your pitchers are going good, you can have the worst team in baseball and still go in and beat the best. That doesn't happen in any other sport. People are always talking about the special things in this game—no clock on the field, and all that—but what makes it really special is that there's always somebody out there, the pitcher or somebody else, who's trying to keep you from doing something in the game. He's trying to keep you from getting on base, or from hitting the ball, or from moving up a runner—and it's always happening right in plain sight. They don't let you get started, and you're going crazy trying to plan how to make it happen. It's all visible, every part of it. Which makes it nothing like football, for one thing."

Garcia said that he had once attended a National Football League exhibition game in San Diego with his friend Don Zimmer, who manages the Red Sox. "Zim *loves* football," Garcia said, giving me his crinkly, V-shaped smile, "and before the game started—it was the Chargers and the Cardinals, I think—I said, 'Zim, I'll tell you what. I got this piece of paper here, and I'm going to keep score.' He said, 'Hell, Dave, there ain't no way to keep score in football,' and I said, 'Well, if a wide receiver is out in the open on the field, and the passer hits him on the hands with the ball and he drops it, isn't that an error?' Zim said yes, he guessed so, and I said, 'All right, now it's the same thing, only this time the passer throws the ball five yards over his head. Isn't *that* an error?' And Zim said sure it was. So I said, 'What about missed open-field tackles, and what about the blockers opening a big hole in the line and the runner running someplace else and getting nailed for a loss?' And Zim said, 'Hell, yes—all errors.' Well, sir, I watched and kept score, and when the game was over I counted up, and there was *twenty-eight* clear errors on my piece of paper. I showed it to Zim, and he said, 'God *damn!* And that doesn't even count all the errors they made there in the line, where you can't see what's happening.' So don't anybody try to tell *me* which is the harder game to play."

Players are what you go to watch in the spring; teams don't begin to emerge until summer. Still, the sense of a team rising or, more often, slipping sometimes breaks through the exuberance and wishful optimism of the training camps, and you get a glimmering of what the coming season is going to be like for it. The Giants, for instance, looked dour and flat in Phoenix last month, in sharp contrast to their demeanor last spring, when they were coming off a strong third-place finish in their division and everyone was talking pennant. But last year the Giants went bad almost from the start—most of all their pitching staff, whose earned-run average skidded from third-best in

the league to eleventh (from 3.30 to 4.16 runs per game)—
and the team finished fourth in the National League West,
nineteen and a half games behind the division-winning Reds.
The various causes of the collapse—the painful proud silence
of Willie McCovey, sadly but inevitably benched at last by
age; the stubbornness of Vida Blue, the club's ace left-handed
fireballer, who persisted in tinkering with off-speed pitches
while his E.R.A. ballooned to five runs per game; the dis-
gruntlement of second baseman Bill Madlock, who complained
so persistently and vehemently about the team's management
and morale that he was traded off to the Pirates, where he
helped win a pennant—were still being murmured about this
year. "Vida got off his pattern, and then we kind of drifted
apart," a member of the team told me. "It was awful. *We* were
awful. We took turns blaming the manager"—Joe Altobelli,
who was replaced in September by Dave Bristol—"and the
pitching coach and the ownership, but when this sort of thing
happens there's never anybody to blame but the players themselves. As you may have heard, we ended up blaming the press.
There were guys on the team last summer who actually believed
that the writers were rooting against us."

Paranoia about sportswriters is on the rise in several major-
league clubhouses, and Phillies pitcher Steve Carlton, the Cubs'
slugger Dave Kingman, and outfielder George Hendrick, of
the Cardinals, are stars who have more or less permanently
broken off diplomatic relations with the press. Various reasons
have been put forward for this breakdown, including the possibility that their very high salaries encourage some players in
the belief that reporters, whose relationship to a ball team and
its athletes has never been easy to define, are now socially
beyond the pale. Clubhouse churlishness, in any case, is not
a new phenomenon, and these recent outbreaks bring to mind
the bad-tempered Jerry Grote, an excellent catcher with the
Mets for many years, who habitually sneered at and foully
reviled members of the New York press who had written less
than rave notices of his work in a given game. Then, early in
a season near the end of his tenure, it was observed that Grote
was trying to be a tad more lovable and sweetly forgiving in
his demeanor toward the same writers, at least to the point of
no longer addressing them with homosexual or incestuous ep-
ithets. One columnist, making note of this unexpected socia-

bility wrote, "Why is Jerry Grote saying hello when it's time to say goodbye?"—a line first coined, about another player in another time, by the late Frank Graham.

The Mariners, on the other hand, looked a trifle better. The Seattle expansion club, which has suffered a drop in attendance every year in its three-year history and has never lost fewer than ninety-five games, is said to be experiencing some financial strain, but better times are perhaps on the way. This summer, the club will play in the outfield a twenty-two-year-old switch-hitting phenom named Rodney Craig, who is the first home-grown product of the Mariners' farm system to make it to the majors. Another, and possibly better, prospect is Dave Henderson, an outfielder said to have formidable power and a wonderful arm, who is still perhaps a year away. And in 1982, according to the present reckoning of the Mariner coaches, fans in the Kingdome should get their first long look at a catcher named Orlando Mercado, who, at eighteen, is already being fervently described as the next Johnny Bench. Young teams are fun to watch, but no one on the Mariners is more entertaining than Willie Horton, the club's designated hitter and senior statesman. Horton is thirty-six now, and his increasingly senatorial embonpoint, when viewed—as I have viewed it—at widely spaced intervals, gives the curious impression that his head is shrinking. Lately, he has adopted a unique, forward-toppling, Leaning Tower of Pisa batting stance, which he checks, just short of demolition, as the pitch is delivered. Last year, Willie whacked twenty-nine homers and drove in a hundred and six runs—pretty good work for a monument. (Horton, by the way, has seven children, and two of his sons have the same name—Darryl I and Darryl II. Trivia fans would love to see them in the same starting lineup someday.)

The most intently watched club in Arizona this year was the worst—Charlie Finley's threadbare Oakland A's, who finished last in the American League West and attracted only 306,763 customers all season. (Six hundred and fifty-three patrons came through the turnstiles to watch them play a game against the Mariners last April.) The 1980 A's don't look much better than the 1979 A's, but their new manager is Billy Martin, the twice-removed Yankee skipper, who was asked to turn in his pinstripes (for good, one may assume) by Yankee owner George Steinbrenner during the off-season, after becoming embroiled in a barroom fistfight with a marshmallow salesman. Billy *redivivus,* in green-and-gold habiliments, attracted swarms of reporters to the A's field at Scottsdale every day, and, as I quickly discovered during some conversations with his players, he had instantly infused the tatterdemalion A's with an almost unrecognizable emotion: hope. "He's not projecting a winner two or three years from now," infielder Wayne Gross said, in awe-struck tones. "He wants it now." A couple of young out-fielders told me that they had learned more about baseball from Billy in the past four weeks than they had previously picked up in their entire professional careers. Matt Keough, a hand-some, thoughtful young pitcher who somehow lost fourteen games in a row for the A's last summer, explained why he believed the new manager would make such a difference. "We're going to be a reflection of Billy Martin, a little" he said. "We're going to have more class and a little more fighter to us. He's created an intensity here we've never had. That can change everything, if you think about it. If you can get rid of the first mistake that leads to the second mistake, then you've broken the whole chain of bad baseball. A pitcher walks a guy, let's say, because he's being too fine—he's had some errors behind him, and he isn't confident about what will happen if somebody hits the ball. There's the first mistake. Now you have a situation where the infielders are tucked around second base, and then there's a hit-and-run and somebody doesn't hold his position, so the ball goes through, and then you've got first and third, instead of what should have been the second out of the inning. Then there's a base hit, and it's a rally. You can't give big-league teams many runs that way and hope to win. We've been last in fielding ever since I've been here, and other teams play against us figuring that we're going to make some kind of mistake in the seventh or eighth inning, letting them back into the ballgame. But now it's going to be the other way around. If we're ahead, or even close, late in the game, the other teams are going to feel the pressure, because of Billy and his strategy. If we can hold them until the eighth, Billy will think of some-thing. Wait and see."

Billy, in his office, looked unchanged—the same cold eyes, hollow cheeks, and thin, apache-dancer's mustache. He is fifty-one years old, but he still has an infielder's body; his hands are large, with long fingers. He often bites the corners of his fingernails as he talks. He speaks in a quiet, low voice, almost a monotone.

"Managing takes a lot out of you," he said during one of his morning levees. "You can be so high one day, and so down the next that you don't want to eat. There's so much to explain, and it's hard to get things across. I go over something in my mind before I talk to a player—I'll go over it twenty or thirty times, rehearsing it, so I'll do it the right way when I talk to that player. You don't want to hurt his feelings or his pride. You don't want to show him up, so you wait until later and then tell him what went wrong. Players are different now from when I came up. Back then, nobody challenged authority or asked questions. Now they all want to know why, and I like that. Every young player wants to learn. 'Show me.' 'Teach me.'

"We've been working a lot on our defense, in order to help our young pitchers. We've made a lot of mistakes—you wouldn't *believe* the things we've done wrong: missing signals, everything. But we're working on things—relays and pickoffs, bunts, hit-and-runs, the suicide squeeze. Hitting the cutoff man, backing up throws in different situations—all the fundamentals. It's all got to be automatic by the time the season starts."

Somebody asked Martin the obligatory question: How did it feel to be managing the A's instead of the Yankees?

"With each club, you have to figure your personnel, and you manage at that level," he said. "Each club you go to, you change your style. Here I'm molding. When I managed at Detroit, there was a lot of ability and some good older players, and I had to break up cliques. In Minnesota, they had great talent, so it was more a question of working on finesse. Texas was like this club, with a lot of young arms and inexperience. When I went to the Yankees, I had to throw the freeloaders out of the clubhouse and stop the country-club atmosphere."

But what about the fame and attention that come to anyone managing the Yankees, another writer asked. What about his pride in that job? Didn't he miss it all?

"I don't care about the credit," Martin said. "I never cared about that." His voice was lower and flatter, and there was a whispery tone to it. "I don't care about being fired. I've been fired when I was winning, so I got nothing to lose here. I don't worry about that. There's something called petty jealousy. If you start to win, there can be people above you sometimes who want to take credit for what you've done, so they begin to step in and interfere."

Did he mean George Steinbrenner?

"No, not him," Martin said. "George and I get along fine. We're friends. Not George—other people. Figure it out for yourself. I don't want to talk about it."

Figuring out Billy Martin is a little beyond me. I think he is a great manager at times, but managing doesn't always seem to satisfy him. Perhaps nothing satisfies him. This spring in Scottsdale, he looked gaunt with hunger, or something like hunger. He looked like a man with a fever. I hope he lasts out the season—Charlie Finley is a notoriously impatient employer. I hope it's for Billy's sake, but even more for his young ballplayers'. If they lose Billy Martin, or lose faith in him, it will be a very long summer out there by the bay.

Every newly appointed manager of a struggling ball team announces, "We're going back to fundamentals," while players on fallen championship teams or disappointed contenders often confess, "We forgot our fundamentals." Brushing up on the basic techniques and tactics of the game is part of what spring training is all about, of course, but anyone who has watched practice at most spring parks becomes aware of an inordinate number of players who appear to be lounging around the batting cage while they await their turn to hit, or standing in cheerful, neighborly clusters in the outfield while they shag flies. In truth, the "training" at many spring-training camps is largely confined to batting practice and getting the pitchers' arms ready, and any further instruction that is offered is conducted in casual, almost slovenly fashion. "I've always been amazed by this," a ten-year veteran pitcher, with service in both leagues, said to me. "I've never seen any signs of a unified system of baseball in any club I've been with. On most teams, there's sort of a religious hierarchy that keeps a big-league manager or a big-league player from ever saying anything to a minor-league player. Whatever a rookie is meant to learn is taught like tribal wisdom, which can only be handed along by word of mouth.

What happens is that the manager talks to the coaches, and then they pass the word along, like disciples. It's discouraging."

This player, I should add, never saw service with the Baltimore Orioles, an organization that for more than a decade has seen to it that every technique and tactic of the game is taught and pursued in exactly the same fashion at every level of its structure. The Orioles' emphasis on correct baseball— never missing a cutoff man, never throwing the ball more than twice on a run-down, never giving the other team an undeserved base or an extra out, and so forth—is taught at the infamously repetitious and wearisome (to players) early-spring drills at the Baltimore camp. ("So dull, so dull!" cried Jim Palmer, quoted in an excellent story by Thomas Boswell in the Washington *Post*. "I hate the cursed Oriole fundamentals. . . . I've been doing them since 1964. I do them in my sleep. I *hate* spring training.") The Oriole system accounts for the team's visibly sparkling, heads-up style of daily play and, to a large degree, for its great success since the mid-sixties, during which span the Orioles have won more games than any other team in the majors, usually while fielding players who are less celebrated and perhaps less talented than those of most of their prime rivals. The Orioles' consistency and zeal are also attributable to the longevity of their coaching personnel—their manager, Earl Weaver, has held the post for a dozen seasons, longer than any other contemporary skipper—and to a famous instruction manual that is distributed to and presumably memorized by every coach and player in the Baltimore organization.

A club now pursuing a similar tradition of precise baseball pedagogy is the Milwaukee Brewers, whose techniques and philosophy are contained in a thickly packed hundred-and-ten-page manual. This volume—I have a copy—begins with a brief hortatory preface by Ray Poitevint, the Brewers' director of scouting and player development, who was once a scout with the Orioles, and its publisher, in effect, is Harry Dalton, the Brewers' executive vice-president and general manager, who was vice-president in charge of player personnel with the Orioles in the late nineteen-sixties and early nineteen-seventies. A third imprimatur on the volume is probably that of the Brewers' manager, George Bamberger, who was formerly the Orioles' pitching coach. The Brewers' manual is a legitimate variant edition or adaptation of the Orioles' textbook, which means only that common sense and good baseball are on the rise in some corners of the game.*

The manual makes vivid and absorbing reading, for it breaks down and explicates almost all the broad physical movements, the minute technical adjustments, the offensive and defensive patterns, and the easy or convoluted strategies of the sport. It contains lists of players' responsibilities categorized by position; reminders about the basics of the game; corrective drills; dos and don'ts of running and throwing and hitting; and mottoes, essays, photographs, and tactical diagrams. I think that a major-league player looking through the book for the first time might be startled at the variety and number of difficult and subtle maneuvers that he has somehow mastered in his lifetime in the game, while a fan—*this* fan, at least—is alternately flattered to find how much baseball he knows already and embarrassed about how much he has overlooked or never understood. The book includes some of Lary Sorensen's tips to the West Side Little Leaguers ("Keep your tail low at all times" is Instruction No. 13 of "Starting Points for Proper Fielding"), but it goes on a bit from there. On page 14, we learn (and somehow understand at once) that pressure on the middle finger will help a pitcher's curveball, and that "pitchers having curveball trouble should throw to hitters having hitting curveballs" in batting practice. Among thirty-six basic hitting fundamentals, on page 33, we might note No. 17: "Don't stand in someone else's footmarks"—in the batter's box, that is. And also No. 28: "When hitting the ball to the opposite field, hit down on the ball," and No. 34: "Hit with top hand and roll wrist." With the aid of such tips, we should get on base in no time, where we will make use of the eighteen numbered items governing our lead off first base (page 39), and later—with a little help from the next batters—of the seven pointers on leading off second base and the five pointers on

---

*Surprising numbers of high-school and college and Little League players and coaches, as well as fans, dads, moms, and (I suppose) Baseball Annies have written me to request a dispatch of this manual by return mail, and I am happy to tell them that the work is now available in bookstores: *Major League Baseball Manual—Prepared and Used by the Milwaukee Brewers*. Dolphin Books; $8.95.

tagging up after a fly ball. We should stay on our toes out there on the base paths, however, because page 36 lists, in three long, extremely detailed paragraphs, the three basic pickoff plays, including the play called by the catcher which is signalled first by an infielder to the catcher (telling him that a man is taking an excessive lead out there) and then by the catcher to the pitcher (using fingers to indicate which base the play is to go to and which infielder is going to cover second), and is begun at the instant that the pitcher and the infielders see the catcher unclench his right fist, which is resting on his right knee.

Knowledgeable fans groan when somebody misses the cut-off man in the infield with a peg from the outfield, but perhaps not every one of them has wondered how many different cutoff situations can occur in a game; the book diagrams twenty-three of them, and adds three further alignments of infielders, covering pop fouls to the catcher, short flies hit behind first base, and passed balls and wild pitches. Cutoff assignments are listed for each position. For the first baseman, for instance, we find:

On all base hits and fly-ball scoring situations to right and center field, you are the cutoff man, except for three situations:
a. Situation #17—Single to right field between 1st and 2nd basemen with runner on 2nd base.
b. Situation #19—Single to right field between 1st and 2nd basemen with runners on 1st and 2nd.
c. Situation #23—Double, possible triple, down right-field line with runner on 1st base.
When 1st base is occupied, you are the cutoff man on *all extra-base hits* except Situation #23, when you are a trailer. When the 3rd baseman dives for the ball and cannot recover to be the cutoff man, you become the cutoff man—Situation #4.

The "situations" are delineated in field diagrams, showing the flight of the ball and the responsive movements of the runners and fielders. Situation #18—a single to right, with men on first or second, or on first, second, and third—offers strategic as well as tactical advice: "ALWAYS keep tying or winning run from going to 3rd with less than two out. Give the opposing team two runs to keep the tying run at 2nd base in this situation."

Like most worthwhile advice, all this looks simple and self-explanatory once it has been laid out. This is also the case with the manual's remarkable extended essay on catching, written by a coach named Jerry Weinstein:

> The ball must be met in the strike zone, not recieved and taken away from the plate. The pitch is more of a strike the closer it is caught to the plate; it is less of a strike the farther away it is caught. In catching the ball, the glove frames the perimeter of the strike zone on close pitches. The ball on the inside corner to a right-handed hitter should be caught with the glove facing into the plate, as opposed to . . . facing the pitcher. If the inside pitch is caught with the glove facing the pitcher, the umpire views the majority of the glove outside the strike zone, whereas if on the inside-corner pitch the glove is facing into the plate, the umpire can see the ball and see that the ball is on the corner.

> There is much more of this—how to position the glove for low pitches, outside-corner pitches, high pitches, and so on— but the purpose of these techniques (somewhat to my surprise) is not to deceive the home-plate umpire but to assist him in calling a strike that really *is* a strike. "Any time a ball is dropped," the text murmurs as an aside, "the umpire's tendency is to call it a ball."

As Dave Garcia pointed out, one of the wonders of baseball is that every aspect of the game is visible, but another wonder, I know now, is how much of it we can watch, summer after summer, and never see at all.

The umpires, who were on strike for higher wages last spring, worked the spring games as usual this year, but some of them appeared to be feeling a mite irritable for the preseason, when games are customarily conducted in a lighthearted, almost off-hand fashion. In the contest between the Cubs and the Angels, a National League ump named Jim Quick tossed Rod Carew out of the game for an infinitesimal glance or murmur over a called strike—a rare happening for a famous hitter like Carew.

When the teams changed sides a minute or two later, Quick suddenly ejected Carew's celebrated teammate Don Baylor for a comment offered on the previous penalty. Then the Angels' manager, Jim Fregosi, who took further exception to *Quick v. Carew et al.*, got the heave-ho as well. The next day, some players with the Brewers asked Baylor about the incident, and Baylor, laughing, said, "I don't know what-all happened. I asked the man why he was running me, and he said, 'You said I was unprintable.' I said, 'I never called you unprintable, but now that you bring it up, you *are* unprintable, and you are also a deleting dash and an adjectival omission, too!'"

In Florida, during a Reds-Tigers game at the Tigers' home park in Lakeland, the Detroit manager, Sparky Anderson, got into a shouting match with the home-plate ump, Greg Kosc, who suddenly ordered him from the premises. "But you can't do that!" Sparky cried indignantly. "This is *my* house." Kosc, unnerved by this heartrending plea, reversed himself and allowed Sparky to sit out the rest of the game in the dugout. A few days later, during a Braves-Orioles game at the Braves' home field in West Palm Beach, Earl Weaver, a Torquemada-like persecutor of the arbiters, got on National League ump Joe West after West had called a balk on a Baltimore pitcher. "We don't call that a balk in the major league!" Weaver yelled. "He understood me right away," Weaver said a couple of days later, "and I was *gone.* I told him I wasn't going to leave for any goddam ump during a goddam spring-training game—I'd heard what Sparky had done, and I didn't see why I couldn't stay there, the way he had. West said the game couldn't go on until I'd left the bench, and I said, fine, that was O.K. with me. It was a real standoff for a few minutes, but then I saw a lot of my players were looking at me and hoping we could get along with it, no matter what I said or the goddam ump said, and get the goddam game played and over with, and get back on our bus and go home, so I changed my mind and went." He laughed and shook his head. "That goddam traffic in West Palm is a killer if you don't get out of there by four o'clock."

FLA. FLASHES

On a blowy, sunny afternoon in Dunedin, a record crowd of more than three thousand old gents and old ladies turns up at

Grant Field—a bijou ballpark set about with feathery pine trees—to watch the home-team Toronto Blue Jays take on the Pirates. The Blue Jays lost a hundred and nine games in the regular season last summer, and the only thing like a star in their lineup is a shortstop named Alfredo Griffin, who was the American League Rookie of the Year in 1979. Everybody in Dunedin loves the Jays, but today the folks are here to see the World Champions, and there is some stirring and mumbling in the crowd when it is realized that Phil Garner and Dave Parker and, worst of all, Willie Stargell did not make the trip from the Pirates' camp, down in Bradenton. Everybody cheers up, however, when Bill Madlock, the Pirates' third baseman, makes three glaring errors in the game—two terrible throws to first on successive plays in the third, and a muffed easy bouncer in the fifth. When Madlock fields a routine ground ball in the eighth and throws out the Toronto base runner, fans applaud, and Madlock gallantly tips his cap. Something better has already happened in the game, though. In Pittsburgh's fifth inning, with nobody out and Matt Alexander, a good runner, on first base, the Pirates signal for a sacrifice; Alexander takes off with the pitch, and Tim Foli squares around to bunt. Foli is a right-handed batter, but, unaccountably, it is Griffin, the Toronto shortstop, who leaves his position to cover second; Foli, suddenly straightening up, swings away and whacks the pitch precisely through the vacated left side of the infield, sending Alexander to third. A few minutes later, Foli himself gets to third, and then he tags up and tries to score on a medium-short fly ball to left by Manny Sanguillen; the throw in has Foli cleanly beaten, but he kicks the ball out of the catcher's glove and is safe. Only a few people yell, but these are the lucky few who know that what we have seen is just as good as watching Dave Parker hit a home run, any day. Better.

The Tigers are loaded with strong, exciting-looking hitters—Steve Kemp, Lance Parrish, Jason Thompson, and young Kirk Gibson. The most riveting Detroit player to watch in the batter's box, however, is the backup catcher John Wockenfuss, who waits up there in a righty stance, with bat held high, and with his lead, or left, foot placed on the ground a bare inch or so in front of his right foot, heel to toe. He opens up with the pitch, of course, but until then he looks exactly like a man trying to play ball while balancing on top of a back-yard fence. Somehow, it works: Fuss batted .264 and hit fifteen homers last year. Whatever feels comfortable to you . . .

I catch up with the Yankees in Lakeland (because it is easy for me to see the Yankees at home once the season starts, I don't often spend much time scouting them in spring training), and talk to young Ruppert Jones, who came over from the Mariners in a trade and will play center field for the Yankees' new manager, Dick Howser, this year. Jones was a .267 hitter last year, but he has good speed (thirty-three stolen bases) and a reputation as a superior defensive fielder. Only his arm is suspect. He is a good deal smaller than Reggie Jackson, but there is something of Reggie's eagerness and garrulous charm about him. "I was getting respect from my peers out at the Kingdome, but my career wasn't going that fast," Jones says. "Plenty of people didn't know who I was. Now I'm here, and the whole country knows the Yankees. Denver, Colorado, knows the Yankees! Pocatello, Idaho, knows the Yankees! I see myself as a great center fielder, so the challenge is just right for me."

I exchange glances with another baseball writer; both of us, perhaps, are thinking of the immense green reaches of the Yankee outfield, and of how small and alone outfielders have sometimes looked out there when things were going wrong for their team. The other man says, "Yankee Stadium is a little different, you know. Everything that happens there is—well, it's sort of magnified."

"Good!" says Ruppert. "If I do great, then I'll be magnified, too."*

Earl Weaver again, in mid-disquisition at Winter Haven (fifteen or twenty reporters are listening, for Earl is the Samuel Johnson of baseball): "I don't go in so much for that *strategy*. You have a man on second base and one out, and the batter hits a ground

---

*Ruppert Jones soon won the admiration of Yankee Stadium fans for the eagerness and dash of his outfield play—the same qualities that were so evident in his springtime remarks to me—but his luck with the Yankees ran out very quickly. In May, he underwent emergency surgery to correct an intestinal blockage and did not return to the lineup until early August. Two weeks later, he crashed into the center-field wall in Oakland while attempting a spectacular catch and suffered a concussion and a separated shoulder, ending his season. Just before the beginning of the 1981 campaign, he was dealt to the Padres (along with Joe Lefebvre) in a trade for their fine switch-hitting center fielder, Jerry Mumphrey. No more magnification.

ball to the right side and he's out at first, and everybody says 'How pretty! How nice!' But that makes two out, and then the next man comes up and swings from his ass to score the run from third and he strikes out, and everybody says 'Look at *that* stupid son of a bitch!' If you're always givin' yourself up, the way the book says, they'll say nice things about you, but what you're really doing is passing the blame along to the next man."

Ted Williams, enormous in a navy-blue warmup jacket, is standing to one side of a batting cage on a minor-league diamond of the Red Sox complex at Winter Haven; the fingers of his left hand are looped in the cage netting, and he is holding a bat, with a strip of white tape wrapped around the fat of it, in his right hand, dangling it by the knob. He is wearing white uniform pants, worn long on his extremely long legs, which seem to be no heavier than they were when he was still a player, twenty years ago. His chest and midsection look massive now, but it's hard to be sure about their real dimensions, for he appears to be wearing two or three layers of shirts under the jacket. His tan face is heavy but still youthful in appearance, perhaps because it is dominated by his piercing brown eyes. When he was playing, I recall, it was said of him that he could see at a hundred feet what the rest of us were meant to see at twenty: 100/20 vision. Williams is watching a very young right-handed batter taking his cuts at the plate, and when I introduce myself Williams shakes hands with me almost without taking his gaze from the man at the plate. Williams lives in the Florida Keys most of the year, and he is a fishing consultant for Sears, Roebuck (he is almost as famous a fisherman and flycaster now as he was a batter in the nineteen-forties and fifties), but every spring he comes up to Winter Haven to help the Red Sox players—the minor-leaguers in particular—with their batting. Here on the field he looks larger and more handsome than anyone else in sight—just the way a legend ought to look.

"You've got to like this kid," Williams says to me at once. "He swings pretty good, and he thinks he can run, too. His name is Keenan, or Kennan—something like that." Keenan or Kennan swings at the next pitch, and Williams, talking louder, says, "Quicker. *Quicker!* Get yourself relaxed up there. If your bat is quicker, then you can wait a little, see?"

The batter swings again, and Williams steps by me and goes out in front of the cage. "Look at me," he says. "Look over here." He takes up his left-handed batting stance, with his right knee cocked a little, and a thousand baseball memories sweep over me. It is ridiculously exciting. Williams slaps his right hip—the lead hip for him—with his right hand. "Hold this," he says to the batter. "Hold it back, see?... That's it—you understand me. Then do this—" He leans forward, flexing the knee even more, then shifts his weight onto that leg and swings slowly through an imaginary pitch, snapping his wrists at the last instant. An imaginary ball flies off his bat—a line drive, of course.

The batter swings again, imitating him a little, in reverse, and Ted, behind the cage again, cries, *"That's* it! That's a better swing, for sure! You were in front of the pitch for the first time today." He drops his voice again. "Sometimes I don't even know their names, but after a few times you begin to recognize them and tell them apart, and then you think, Hey, *that* kid's got a little something. He might do something for us. There was one here today—" He calls over to another coach. "Who was that switch-hitter we liked, a little while ago today—Ramos? Yes, Ramos—I'll remember him now. He looks just like Jim Rivera. And that other one we were talking about yesterday, he's just like Billy Consolo."

There are three diamonds, separated by low chain-link fences, that face out from the large central field here, like spokes of a wheel, and players assigned to different levels of the Boston minor-league system—the Class AAA Pawtucket Red Sox, the Class AA Bristol Red Sox, and the Class A Winston-Salem Red Sox—are in action on different fields, most of them wearing what look to be old Boston road uniforms, which are gray with red numbers on the back. Ted Williams keeps moving from one field to another, and although I'm never quite sure which squad we are with, it is clear after watching the next couple of batters take their cuts that we are at a higher level than the last. The young man up at the plate now is a muscular catcher who bats left-handed, and Ted talks to him in a louder, more cheerful way, as if he were talking to a teammate. "This is our Mr. Gedman," he says to me loudly. "Mr. Gedman can hit. If Mr. Gedman doesn't make it to the Hall of Fame, it's going to be his own damned fault. He can play ball a little, but the jury is still out on him from the neck up." He watches in silence as Gedman hits a few more pitches, and then steps around the cage again with his bat and says, "It seems to me you've got all your attention up here [he gestures, drawing a line at shoulder level], but if you can just do this [a very slight crouching movement makes Williams into a relaxed, perfectly balanced batter], then you've got the center of your swing just where you want it."

Ted scoots back behind the cage, and Gedman takes another cut at a pitch. "Better," Williams says. "You're cocking your hips real good, the way I said yesterday. I can see you thought about that last night, the way I told you to." Gedman pops the next pitch foul, and Ted shouts, "Oh, get your damned fists up on top of that damned fastball!" Another swing, and there is a loud report. *"There!"* Williams cries. "I told you! Remember what you said to me yesterday—that I could be your agent? You're learning real fast, aren't you?" He is laughing.*

The morning goes by quickly as Williams watches twenty batters or more and says something to each of them. He seems to take the most pains with the least talented hitters, and when a thin left-handed player who looks not much bigger than a junior-high-school player is at bat, he murmurs, "Just a little quicker. Then you can wait. . . . No, you waited too long that time. . . . No, that's a sweep. Try not to sweep the bat. You're too big. Make it more compact." The boy swings and hits a modest grounder, and Williams, delighted, cries, "That's it! You did it! Hey, don't you feel better now?"

A few fans have wandered down to the runways between the fields, and now and then two or three of them make a little mouse-like dart out onto the field, behind the batting cage, and ask Williams for an autograph. One man wearing a mesh, fan's-model Red Sox cap introduces his daughter, a girl of about eight, and when Ted leans over and shakes her hand, her father says to her, "Mr. Williams hit .406 in 1941."

"You don't look old enough to remember that," Williams says to the man cheerfully. "I bet you read it in a book."

It is time for me to get back to the main Boston field, to talk to the players there before the upcoming Red Sox–Orioles game—to ask about Yaz's leg and Fisk's arm and a new young Boston pitching whiz named Bruce Hurst—but I linger a little longer at the practice field, for it has come to me that I am watching the other kind of baseball instruction here. This is tribal wisdom—the Word, handed down. For me, this has been a teaching sort of spring.

Williams is standing beside Eddie Popowski, a small, pot-

---

*Gedman matriculated to the Red Sox in 1981, where his .288 batting average helped ease the pain caused by the departure of Carlton Fisk.

bellied, mahogany-tan man who used to coach at third base for the Sox and now works with the youngest players in the Boston system during the summer. Popowski is off to one side of the batting cage, and after each pitch to the batter there he hits a grounder with his fungo bat to a lithe, slick-looking shortstop named Juan Bustabad.

"He's sure got that Aparicio look to him," Ted Williams says.

Popowski hits another grounder, and Bustabad, gliding to the ball, drops his glove hand nearly into the dirt and opens it at the last instant, and the ball almost seems to dive into the glove pocket.

"He ain't got much range, but he sure gets that glove down," Pop says. "I don't know why more of them don't get the idea of that."

Williams steps back closer to the cage to watch a strong-looking right-handed batter named John Morgan. "This one's a little raw," he says to me, "but he comes from up New England way, so he hasn't had time to play a lot of ball. You have to be patient. You see these players here every year, and after about two or three years, or sometimes more, you begin to make up your mind about them. I like that part of it—coming back and seeing what a kid has made of himself. That's why I come back here every year like this." He raises his voice so Morgan can hear him. "Carlton Fisk was a whole lot like this fellow. He didn't show us much at first, and then everybody knows what happened. But Mr. Morgan hits much better than Fisk did at the same age. He's way ahead of Carlton Fisk. . . . Not too high, not so high! Don't swing at that one!" He turns to me again and says, "Everybody thinks where they hit the ball is a little lower than it was."

As I walk back to the upper field, I suddenly remember that I have forgotten to ask Ted Williams about a doubleheader I saw him play in during the summer of 1946 in which he went seven for eight at the plate for the day. I can't recall which team that was against, and he surely would have been able to remind me. Then I think about John Morgan perhaps sitting down tonight and writing home to his family in New England to tell them that Ted Williams said he was ahead of Carlton Fisk, for his age. But now a terrible thought comes to me. I wonder if young John Morgan knows who Ted Williams is— who he *really* is: the best hitter I ever saw swing at a pitch.

* * *

On a warm, sunny morning shortly before the end of my spring trip, I sat on a little green bench behind the home-plate screen and watched a B-squad game between the Mets and the Cardinals at Huggins-Stengel Field, which is the Mets' practice ground at St. Petersburg. The Mets and the Cards both play their regular spring games at Al Lang Stadium, in downtown St. Pete, each taking a turn there while the other is on the road, but the two clubs also fit in a lot of informal morning games like the one I was attending, so that their pitchers can get the work they need. On this particular day, there was a handful of Mets' and Cardinals' coaches and executives watching the game from other benches and chairs behind the screen, and I counted seventeen fans, two babies, and one dog in the miniature bleachers behind the Mets' shedlike dugout on the first-base side of the diamond. Birds were chirping, and from my vantage point there was a nice view of some low palms and other trees set about the perimeter of the field. Beyond the trees was a little lake. Beside the Mets' clubhouse, over by right field, a bus was parked with its engine running, and every now and then three or four Mets players, in full uniform except for their spikes, ambled out of the building and climbed aboard it for the ride down to Bradenton, where an A-squad game against the Pirates would be played that afternoon. I was sharing my bench with Red Schoendienst and Claude Osteen, a pair of Cardinals coaches, who came over from the Cards' dugout and sat there whenever their team was in the field, in order to get a better line on their pitcher's stuff. The man on the mound just now was Donnie Hood, a left-hander, who had been signed on as a free agent during the winter to give the Cards some needed depth in their bullpen. Now Hood wound and threw, and the Mets batter, Joel Youngblood, swung and missed, striking out.

"Forkball," Schoendienst and Osteen murmured in unison, standing up again, and Schoendienst added, "Seems like he's got real good control over it now."

"Yes, but up to this batter he didn't throw good," said Osteen.

The teams changed sides, with a right-hander, John Pacella, taking the mound for the Mets, and a moment or two later there was a startlingly loud report as a big lefty-swinging Cardinal hitter named Leon Durham (he is called Bull, of course) came around on one of Pacella's deliveries and whaled the ball down the line and all the way out to the fence in deep right.

He galloped into third base, yards ahead of the throw. There were exclamations and grins in the seats around me and Joe Torre, the Met's manager, came out of his dugout shaking his head. "Why don't you keep him with the big guys?" he shouted over to the coaches on the Cardinals' side of the field. "Doesn't he know these B-game stats don't count on the spring averages? He can keep track of these hits on a matchbook cover, because they don't mean a damn thing."

Torre was a star catcher and first and third baseman with the Cards in the early nineteen-seventies, when Schoendienst was managing the St. Louis club, so all this had a friendly, first-tee sound to it.

"What are you doing here, anyway?" one of the Cards coaches called back. "Why aren't you going off down there with your first string?"

"I'm going, I'm going," Torre said. "If I get down there too early, I'll probably have to pitch batting practice again."

Everyone was laughing, but Torre's smile looked a bit wan, because Bull Durham is a prime property—perhaps the most admired young player to surface with any club during spring training this year. He is a twenty-two-year-old first baseman, who batted .310 with the Cards' Class AAA Springfield Red-birds in the American Association last year, and so far this spring in St, Petersburg—in the games with the big guys, where stats *are* kept—he was batting .455 in twelve games, with three homers and thirteen runs batted in. The Cardinals have another first baseman, however—Keith Hernandez, who led the National League with an average of .344 last summer and was then voted the league's Most Valuable Player, sharing that honor with Willie Stargell. Hernandez is only twenty-six, so the Cardinals were hastily converting Durham into an outfielder this spring, although there wasn't much chance that he would crack their starting outfield of Bobby Bonds, George Hendrick, and Tony Scott. Joe Torre should have such problems. The Mets have no one like Bull Durham at any level of their organization.

Another observer of this pageant was Frank Cashen, who had been named general manager of the Mets on February 21st and will have absolute control over the club's baseball decisions from now on. He is a roundish, Cagney-size man, with sandy gray hair, a pleasant, Galway-touched face, and a businesslike manner. Here, out in the hot morning sunshine, he was wearing gray pants, a blue oxford button-down Brooks Brothers shirt with the sleeves rolled up, a green golf visor, and a tan knitted tie—the only necktie I observed anywhere during spring training. I had caught up with Cashen early that morning in his office at Huggins-Stengel Field—something of a feat, for he had been working on the run ever since taking on his new post; in the previous two days, I knew, he had flown to Phoenix and back, and today, he had told me, he would see both Mets games—the morning B-game here and the afternoon game against the Pirates—and when he got back from Bradenton he would probably put in a couple of hours more at his office. Then, at home after dinner, he expected to be on the phone for two or three hours talking to his scouts in Florida and Arizona and to front-office men from other clubs as well. All in all, he looked pretty cheerful for a man who had just taken on the toughest job in baseball, which is to breathe life into the New York Mets, a club that lost more than ninety-five games in each of its past three seasons and suffered the disaffection of almost two million fans in the past decade.

"We're trying to make changes at the top and at the very bottom, too, and I just hope we'll meet somewhere in the middle," he told me in his office. "Fans think that because of free-agency you can turn a ballclub around very quickly, but that isn't a useful way to go about what we have in mind here. Sure, I'd like us to get some new faces, because the fans deserve to see signs of change in a losing team, but I'm fighting the idea of a trade just for its own sake. We have four out of the first-twenty-seven picks in the draft of high-school and college players this June, because we finished so low and then lost two free agents in the off-season. That's a start—maybe our first chance to make a difference."

I said that as a onetime Mets fan I had been encouraged by the news that the new club owners—Nelson Doubleday, Jr., and Fred Wilpon, a young real-estate executive who, although he owns a lesser share in the new Mets, is the new club president—had expressed a willingness to invest considerably more than their initial purchase price of twenty-one million dollars in order to bring the club back into contention.

Cashen nodded, and said, "The only question I asked before I agreed to come to work here was whether the new people just wanted to spend and spend to get a winner or whether they really wanted to be in the business of baseball. They sort of smiled, and said that they looked forward to making a little money out of this in the end, which was the right answer for me. I had no interest in working for anyone who was after a winner at any price, because people like that go sour very quickly. We've had some examples in baseball of how *that* works."

Cashen, who is fifty-three but still has a rumpled, boyish air, is one of the most admired front-office men in baseball. He spent ten years—from the mid-sixties to the mid-seventies—with the Orioles, serving as executive vice-president of the club during its swift and entirely unexpected rise to eminence. Prior to that, he had been a sportswriter for seventeen years with the old Baltimore *News-Post*, where he started as a copy boy at the age of fifteen, and along the line had also managed to graduate from Loyola in Baltimore (doing four years there in twenty-five months), to pick up a law degree at the University of Maryland, and to serve as general manager of two Baltimore race tracks. His father, who came to this country from Ireland, was a trainer of jumping horses, and at one point Frank Cashen had dreams of becoming a breeder of thoroughbreds. "The mare I bought kept coming up barren and my wife kept coming up pregnant," he told me, "so I finally decided that was the wrong line of work for me." He said that for years he had played softball—the fast-pitch game—three evenings every week in Baltimore, and his team, the Esquires, had once won simultaneous titles in the Monday Night and Thursday Night Leagues. "We played until our wives were ready to divorce us," he said. "In one way or another, baseball has always been a passion with me."

I asked him how he planned to breed passion into the new Mets.

"Doing the little things right is what's important in baseball," he said. "Hitting the cutoff man"—I almost whispered the words along with him—"making the double play, knowing when to bring in the man from the bullpen. There's no great charismatic secret to winning—it's just executing. The same thing carries over to the business side. A winning team is built out of successful scouting and a sound farm system, which is the production line of the business. You can help yourself with a good trade sometimes. Players don't really learn how to win when they're at the major-league level, which means that you change your team only by working systematically with young players when they're still in the minors. We want to be a respectable ball team. After that—well, who knows if you're going to win and how soon? A lot of that is up to the other teams anyway, but that's the pleasure of the game."

I said that I had begun to learn a few things this spring about the systematic instruction of baseball—most of all about the old Orioles' way of doing things.

Cashen moved a stack of letters and papers on his desk and found a thickish bound notebook, which he held up, with a brief smile. He riffled the pages for a moment, and I had a swift, unmistakable glimpse of two or three of the "situation" diagrams that I had been studying in my Brewers instruction manual.

"Now there's going to be a *Mets* way of doing things," he said.

A little later on in the Mets-Cardinals B-squad game, I was joined on my green bench by Fred Wilpon, the Mets' president, who was wearing white cotton pants, white loafers, and a pink gingham shirt. He is forty-three, but he looks about thirty. I had heard that Wilpon and Sandy Koufax had been classmates at Lafayette High, in Brooklyn, years ago, and I asked him now if they had both played on the ball team there.

"Yes, but it was *my* ball team—I was the captain and the first-string pitcher, and Sandy played first base," Wilpon said. "We were friends, and he came out for the team only because of that. He couldn't hit at *all*. Basketball was his main sport then, and I played basketball at Lafayette because of Sandy. Later on, I went to Michigan on a baseball scholarship, but I gave up the game after my sophomore year. Now I'm back."

I asked him if he and Koufax were still friends, and he said, "As a matter of fact, he and I and our wives had dinner together in Vero Beach a couple of days ago. Sandy Koufax has a wonderful, high-level, inquiring mind. We can't conceal the affection we still hold for each other."

The Cardinal pitcher now was another left-hander, Buddy Schultz. He threw an off-speed pitch to a Mets batter, Mike Jorgensen, who swung at it tentatively and fouled it off.

"Good pitch," said Claude Osteen. "Good speed." He was perched on a chair just to our left.

"What's the optimum differential in speed between a fastball and a change-up?" Wilpon asked him.

"Well, your change-up should be about sixty-eight or seventy miles an hour," Osteen said. "The fastball might be about eighty-four or eighty-five."

"What if it's *seventy*-five?" Wilpon asked.

"Not enough," Osteen said. "That's a base hit."

Jorgensen fanned, and another Mets batter stood in.

"Why is your pitcher throwing so many change-ups?" Wilpon asked Osteen. He sounded like an honors student in a baseball seminar.

"He's working on that pitch," Osteen said. "I'm looking for a fastball from him myself."

"There!" Wilpon said. "Wasn't that a fastball?"

"Pretty near," said Osteen. "About eighty."

Schultz threw again, and the batter took the pitch. "Streeuh!" the home-plate ump said, throwing up his fist.

"Better," said Osteen. "About eighty-four."

As the teams changed sides, I got ready to leave, saying goodbye to Wilpon and to Frank Cashen, and wishing them good luck in the coming season. I turned my back to the field for a moment, so I missed what happened next, but by the noise of it I had a pretty good idea what it was. I turned around in time to see two Mets outfielders chasing the ball out by the fence once again and, a moment later, the batter pulling into third base. Bull Durham had hit another triple. Joe Torre, leaning back on the bench with his arms folded, had tipped his cap down so that it covered his face, hiding his sight of the field. School was out.

11

Distance

On the afternoon of October 2nd, 1968—a warm, sunshiny day in St. Louis—Mickey Stanley, the Detroit Tiger shortstop, singled to center field to lead off the top of the ninth inning of the opening game of the 1968 World Series. It was only the fifth hit of the game for the Tigers, who by this time were trailing the National League Champion St. Louis Cardinals by a score of 4–0, so there were only minimal sounds of anxiety among the 54,692 spectators—home-town rooters, for the most part—in the stands at Busch Stadium. The next batter, the dangerous Al Kaline, worked the count to two and two and then fanned, swinging away at a fastball, to an accompanying roar from the crowd. A moment later, there was a second enormous cheer, louder and more sustained than the first. The Cardinal catcher, Tim McCarver, who had straightened up to throw the ball back to his pitcher, now hesitated. The pitcher, Bob Gibson, a notoriously swift worker on the mound, motioned to his battery mate to return the ball. Instead, McCarver pointed with his gloved hand at something behind Gibson's head. Gibson, staring uncomprehendingly at his catcher, yelled, "Throw the goddam ball back, will you! C'mon, c'mon, let's *go!*" Still holding the ball, McCarver pointed again, and Gibson, turning around, read the illuminated message on the center-field scoreboard, which perhaps only he in the ballpark had not seen until that moment: "Gibson's fifteenth strikeout in one game ties the all-time World Series record held by Sandy Koufax." Gibson, at the center of a great tureen of noise, dug at the dirt of the mound with his spikes and then uneasily doffed his cap. ("I *hate* that sort of thing," he said later.) With the ball retrieved at last, he went to work on the next Tiger, Norm Cash, a left-handed batter, who ran the count to two and two, fouled off several pitches, and then struck out, swinging at a slider. Gibson, a long-legged, powerfully built right-hander, whose habitual aura of glowering intensity on the mound seemed to deepen toward rancor whenever his club was ahead in the late stages of a game, now swiftly attacked the next Detroit hitter, Willie Horton. Again the count went to two and two and stuck there while Horton fouled off two or three pitches. Gibson stretched and threw again, and Horton, a righty batter, flinched away from the pitch, which seemed headed for his rib cage, but the ball, another slider, broke abruptly away under his fists and caught the inside corner of the plate. Tom Gorman, the home-plate umpire, threw up his right hand, and the game was over. McCarver, talking about this moment not long ago (he is now a radio and television broadcaster with the Phillies), said, "I can still see that last pitch, and I'll bet Willie Horton thinks to this day that the ball hit him—that's how much it broke. Talk about a batter *shuddering!*"

Bob Gibson's one-game World Series record of seventeen strikeouts stands intact, and so do my memories of that famous afternoon. In recent weeks, I have firmed up my recollections by consulting the box score and the inning-by-inning recapitulations of the game, by watching filmed highlights of the play, and by talking to a number of participants, including Gibson himself. (He had had no idea, he told me, that he was close to a record that afternoon. "You're concentrating so hard out there that you don't think of those things," he said.) Gibson seemed to take absolute charge of that game in the second inning, when he struck out the side on eleven pitches. By the end of four innings, he had run off eight strikeouts. Not until I reëxamined the box score, however, did I realize that there had been only two ground-ball outs by the Tigers in the course of nine innings. This, too, must be a record (baseball statistics, for once, don't tell us), but the phenomenally low figure, when taken along with the seventeen strikeouts, suggests what kind of pitching the Tiger batters were up against that afternoon. Most National League batters in the nineteen-sixties believed that Gibson's fastball compared only with the blazers thrown by the Dodgers' Sandy Koufax (who retired in 1966 with an arthritic elbow) and by the Reds' Jim Maloney. Gibson's pitch flashed through the strike zone with a unique, upward-moving, right-to-left sail that snatched it away from a right-handed batter or caused it to jump up and in at a left-handed swinger—a natural break of six to eight inches—and hitters who didn't miss the ball altogether usually fouled it off or nudged it harmlessly into the air. The pitch, which was delivered with a driving, downward flick of Gibson's long forefinger and middle finger (what pitchers call "cutting the ball"), very much resembled an inhumanly fast slider, and was often taken for such by batters who were unfamiliar with his stuff. Joe Pepitone, of the Yankees, concluded the All-Star Game of 1965 by fanning on three successive Gibson fastballs and then shook his head and called out to the pitcher, "Throw me that slider one more time!" Gibson, to be sure, did have a slider—a superior breaking pitch that arrived, disconcertingly, at about three-quarters of the speed of the fastball and, most of the time, with exquisite control. Tim McCarver, who caught Gibson longer than anyone else, says that Gibson became a great pitcher during the summer of 1966 (his sixth full season in the majors), when he achieved absolute mastery of the outside corner of the plate while pitching to right-handed batters and—it was the same pitch, of course—the inside corner to left-handed batters. He could hit this sliver of air with his fastball or his slider with equal consistency, and he worked the opposite edge of the plate as well. "He *lived* on the corners," McCarver said. A third Gibson delivery was a fastball that broke downward instead of up and away; for this pitch, he held the ball with his fingers parallel to the seams (instead of across the seams, as was the case with the sailer), and he twisted his wrist counterclockwise as he threw—"turning it over," in mound parlance. He also had a curveball, adequate by unextraordinary, that he threw mostly to left-handers and mostly for balls, to set up an ensuing fastball. But it was the combination of the devastating slider and the famous fastball (plus some other, less tangible assets that we shall get to in time) that made Gibson almost untouchable at his best, just as Sandy Koufax's down-diving curveball worked in such terrible (to hitters) concert with his illustrious upriding fastball.

"Hitting is rhythm," McCarver said to me, "and if you allow major-league hitters to see only one pitch—to swing repeatedly through a certain area of the plate—eventually they'll get to you and begin to hit it, even if it's a great fastball. But anybody who can control and switch off between two first-class pitches will make the hitters start reaching, either in or out, and then the game belongs to the pitcher. Besides all that, Bob had such great stuff and was so intimidating out there that he'd make the batter open up his front shoulder just a fraction too fast, no matter what the count was. The other key to good hitting, of course, is keeping that shoulder—the left shoulder for a right-handed batter, I mean, and vice versa—in place, and the most common flaw is pulling it back. Gibson had guys pulling back that shoulder who normally wouldn't be caught dead doing it. Their ass was in the dugout, as we say."

Mike Shannon, who played third base behind Gibson in the 1968 Series opening game (he didn't handle the ball once), remembers feeling pity for the Detroit batters that afternoon. "Most of them had never seen Gibby before," he said, "and they had no *idea* what they were up against." Shannon, who is now a television game announcer with the Cards, told me that he encounters some of the 1968 Tigers from time to time in the course of his baseball travels, and that they almost compulsively want to talk about the game. "It's as if they can't believe it to this day," he said. "But neither can I. I've never seen major-league hitters overmatched that way. It was like watching a big-league pitcher against Little League batters. It was frightening."

Gibson, of course, was already a celebrated winning pitcher by 1968. Like many other fans, I had first become aware of his fastball and his unique pitching mannerisms and his burning intensity on the mound when he won two out of the three games he pitched against the Yankees in the 1964 World Series, including a tense, exhausting victory in the clinching seventh game. Then, in 1967, I had watched him capture three of the Cardinals' four October victories over the Red Sox, again including the seventh game—a feat that won him the Most Valuable Player award for that Series. I had also seen him work eight or ten regular-season games over the previous five years or more. Although he was of only moderate size for a pitcher—six feet one and about a hundred and eighty-five pounds—Gibson always appeared to take up a lot of space on the mound, and the sense of intimidation that McCarver mentioned had something to do with his sombre, almost funereal demeanor as he stared in at his catcher, with his cap pulled low over his black face and strong jaw, and with the ball held behind his right hip (he always wore a sweatshirt under his uniform, with the long, Cardinals-red sleeves extending all the way down to his wrists), and with his glove cocked on his left hip, parallel to the ground. Everything about him looked mean and loose—arms, elbows, shoulders, even his legs—as, with a quick little shrug, he launched into his delivery. When there was no one on base, he had an old-fashioned full crank-up, with the right foot turning in mid-motion to slip into its slot in front of the mound and his long arms coming together over his head before his backward lean, which was deep enough to require him to peer over his left shoulder at his catcher while his upraised left leg crooked and kicked. The ensuing sustained forward drive was made up of a medium-sized stride of that leg and a blurrily fast, slinglike motion of the right arm, which came over at about three-quarters height and then snapped down and (with the fastball and the slider) across his left knee. It was not a long drop-down delivery like Tom Seaver's (for contrast), or a tight, brisk, body-opening motion like Whitey Ford's.

The pitch, as I have said, shot across the plate with a notable amount of right-to-left (from Gibson's vantage point) action, and his catchers sometimes gave the curious impression that they were cutting off a ball that was headed on a much longer journey—a one-hundred-foot fastball. But with Gibson pitching you were always a little distracted from the plate and the batter, because his delivery continued so extravagantly after the ball was released that you almost felt that the pitch was incidental to the whole affair. The follow-through sometimes suggested a far-out basketball move—a fast downcourt feint. His right leg, which was up and twisted to the right in the air as the ball was let go (all normal enough for a right-handed pitcher), now continued forward in a sudden sidewise rush, crossing his planted left leg, actually stepping over it, and he finished with a full running step toward the right-field foul line, which wrenched his body in the same direction, so that he now had to follow the flight of the ball by peering over his *right* shoulder. Both his arms whirled in the air to help him keep his balance during this acrobatic maneuver, but the key to his overpowering speed and stuff was not the strength of his pitching arm—it was the powerful, driving thrust of his legs, culminating in that final extra step, which brought his right foot clomping down on the sloping left-hand side of the mound, with the full weight of his body slamming and twisting behind it. (Gibson's arm never gave him undue trouble, but he had serious difficulties with his knees in the latter stages of his career, and eventually had to have a torn cartilage removed from the right knee, which had pushed off to start all the tens of thousands of his pitches over the years and had then had to withstand the punishing force of the last stage of his unique delivery.) All in all, the pitch and its extended amplifications made it look as if Gibson were leaping at the batter, with hostile intent. He always looked much closer to the plate at the end than any other pitcher; he made pitching seem unfair.

The players in the Detroit clubhouse after Gibson's seventeen-strikeout game had none of the aggrieved, blustery manner of batters on a losing team who wish to suggest that only bad luck or their own bad play kept them from putting away a pitcher who has just beaten them. Denny McLain, the starting Tiger pitcher, who had won thirty-one games that summer but had lasted only five innings in the Series opener, said, "I was awed. I was *awed,*" and Dick McAuliffe, the Detroit second baseman, said that he could think of no one he had ever faced with whom Gibson could be compared. "He doesn't remind me of anybody," he said. "He's all by himself."

I was awed, too, of course, but nothing I had seen on the field at Busch Stadium that afternoon startled me as much as Gibson's postgame comportment in the clubhouse. In October of 1964 and again in 1967, I had noticed that Bob Gibson often appeared to be less elated than his teammates in the noisy, jam-packed, overexuberant World Series locker rooms—a man at a little distance from the crowd. But somehow I must have expected that his astounding performance here in the 1968 opener would change him—that his record-breaking turn on the mound would make him more lighthearted and accommodating; he would be smiling and modest and self-depreciating, but also joyful about his feat, and this would diminish that almost immeasurable distance he had just established, out on the field, between himself and the rest of us. He would seem boyish, in short, and we, the grown-up watchers of the game, would then be able to call him by his first name (even if we didn't know him), and forgive him for what he had done, and thus to love him, as is the ancient custom in these high sporting dramas. But Gibson was unchanged. Talking to the sportswriters gathered in a thick, uncomfortable crowd around his locker, he looked at each reporter who asked him a question (Gibson is an exceptionally handsome man, with small ears, very dark skin, and a strikingly direct gaze) and then answered it gravely and briefly. When one writer asked him if he had always been as competitive as he had seemed on this day, he said yes, and he added that he had played several hundred games of ticktacktoe against one of his young daughters and that she had yet to win a game from him. He said this with a little smile, but it seemed to me that he meant it: he couldn't let himself lose to anyone. Then someone asked him if he had been surprised by what he had just done on the field, and Gibson said, "I'm never surprised by anything I do."

The shock of this went out across the ten-deep bank of writer faces like a seismic wave, and the returning, murmurous counterwaves of reaction were made up of uneasy laughter and whispers of *"What* did he say?" and some ripples of disbelieving silence and (it seemed to me) a considerable, almost visible wave of dislike, or perhaps hatred. This occasion, it should be remembered, was before the time when players' enormous salaries and their accompanying television-bred notoriety had given birth to a kind of athlete who could choose to become famous for his sullenness and foul temper, just as another might be identified by his gentle smile and unvarying sweetness of disposition. In 1968, ballplayers, particularly black ballplayers in near-Southern cities like St. Louis, did not talk outrageously to the press. Bob Gibson, however, was not projecting an image but telling us a fact about himself. He was beyond us, it seemed, but the truth of the matter is that no one at Busch Stadium should have been much surprised by his achievement that afternoon, for it was only a continuation of the kind of pitching he had sustained all through that summer of 1968—a season in which he won twenty-two games for the Cardinals while losing nine, and also compiled an earned-run average of 1.12 runs per game: the best pitching performance, by that measurement, in the history of modern baseball.

When Bob Gibson retired, at the age of thirty-nine, at the end of the 1975 season, after seventeen summers with the Cardinals, he had won two hundred and fifty-one games, and his record of 3,117 strikeouts was second only to Walter Johnson's 3,508. Last year, however, Gaylord Perry, who is still going strong at the age of forty-two, passed Gibson on the lifetime-strikeout list (Perry is now with the Yankees and has 3,267 whiffs to his credit at this writing), while three other active pitchers— Nolan Ryan, Tom Seaver, and Steve Carlton—may surpass Gibson's mark next summer.* This kind of erosion of the game's most famous fixed numbers—the landmarks of the pastime—by swirling tides of newcomers is always happening, of course; it is the process that makes baseball statistics seem alive and urgent to the true fan. But Gibson's displacement unsettled me, and when I read in the sports pages last spring that he was among the players who would become eligible for election to baseball's Hall of Fame at the end of this season, after the obligatory five-year post-retirement waiting period (the qualifications for official immortality are established by the Baseball Writers Association of America, whose three hundred-odd members conduct a Hall of Fame balloting in the off-season each year), I sensed that Gibson might be about to slip away into the quiet corridors of baseball history. It is always a discomfiting moment for a long-term follower of the game when a favorite player, whose every feat and gesture on the field still retain clarity and color, is declared safe for embronzement, but the possibility of Bob Gibson's imminent apotheosis at Cooperstown came as a shock to me. He seemed too impatient, too large, and too restless a figure to be stilled and put away in this particular fashion; somehow, he would shrug off the

*By the end of the 1981 season, Gaylord Perry had accounted for 3,336 lifetime strikeouts, while Ryan stood at 3,249, Carlton at 3,148, and Seaver at 3,075. Steve Carlton's total is a new National League record, eclipsing Gibson's old mark, because unlike Perry and Ryan, he has pitched only in that league.

speeches and honorifics when they came, just as he had busied himself unhappily on the mound when the crowd stopped the rush of the game to cheer him at Busch Stadium that afternoon in 1968. For me, at least, Bob Gibson was still burning to pitch to the next batter. But in another, oddly opposite sense it seemed wrong to think of Gibson as a participant in the soft, sweet rituals with which newly elected baseball immortals are inducted into the Hall of Fame at the ceremonial in Cooperstown each August—the reading of the players' records and their official citations; their speeches of acceptance and gratitude; the obligatory picture-taking, with the still-young heroes, in civilian clothes, holding up their plaques and standing among the smaller, white-haired, earlier great figures who have come back for the occasion: old gents at a reunion, blinking in the hot upstate sunlight—because baseball up to now has never quite known what to make of Bob Gibson, and has slightly but persistently failed to pay him his full due as a player and as a man. With this conviction in mind, I determined early this summer to look up Gibson and try to get to know him a little better. I wanted to see how he was faring now that he could no longer stare down at the batters of the world from the height of the pitcher's mound. I knew that he was still living in Omaha, his home town, and when I reached him there by telephone he told me to come on out if I wanted to. Not a warm invitation, but not a wary one, either. In the next week or two, I mentioned my forthcoming trip to some friends of mine—good baseball fans, all of them—and noticed that many of them seemed to have forgotten Bob Gibson's eminence and élan, if, indeed, they had ever been aware of them. In the history of the game, it seemed, as in his playing days, he already stood at a little distance from the crowd, a little beyond us all. But then I talked about Gibson with some players—old teammates or opponents of his—and they responded more warmly.

Pete Rose, who talks in the same runaway-taxi style in which he runs bases, said, "I'm always afraid I'll forget some pitcher when I start rating them, because I've faced so many of them. I started out against people like Warren Spahn, you know. But the best pitcher I ever batted against was Juan Marichal, because he threw so many goddam different kinds of good pitches against you. The hardest thrower of them all was Sandy Koufax, and the greatest competitor was Bob Gibson. He worked so fast out there, and he always had the hood up. He always wanted to close his own deal. He wasn't no badman, but he never talked to you, because he was battling you so hard. I sure as hell don't miss batting against him, but I miss him in the game."

Billy Williams, now a coach for the Cubs, who hit four hundred and twenty-six home runs during his sixteen years with that team and two years with the Oakland A's, told me, "Bob Gibson always got *on* with it. He didn't stand around out there and look around the park, you know. You always got the same message from him: 'Look, I'm goin' to throw this pitch and either you hit it or I get your ass out.' You like a guy like that. The infielders were never on their heels out there behind him. Everyone's on their toes, and it's a better game for everybody. I used to love the afternoon games at Wrigley Field when Gibby pitched against our Fergie Jenkins, because you could always plan something early for that evening. They *hurried*. Gibby was as serious as anybody you ever saw, and you had to be ready at all times. There was hitters that tried to step out on him, to break his pace, but if you did that too often he'd knock you down. He let you know who was out there on the mound. Made himself felt. He never let up, even on the hottest days there in St. Louis, which is the hottest place in the world. Just walked out there in the heat and threw the ball past people."

Tim McCarver said, "He was an intimidating, arrogant-looking athlete. The arrogance he projected toward batters was fearsome. There was no guile to his pitching, just him glaring down at that batter. He wanted the game played on his own terms. He worked very fast, and that pace was part of his personality on the mound, part of the way he dominated the game. One of the things he couldn't stand was a catcher coming out there to talk to him. In my first full year with the Cardinals, when I was only twenty-one years old, our manager was Johnny Keane, who was a fanatic about having a catcher establish communications with his pitcher. So I'd get a signal from Keane that meant 'Go on out there and settle him down,' but then I'd look out and see Hoot glaring in at me." McCarver laughed, and shook his head. "Well, sometimes I'd walk out halfway, to try to appease both parties!"

McCarver is an intimate friend of Bob Gibson's, and he told me that Gibson was much the same off the field as on the mound. "Bob is relatively shy," he said. "He's a nice man, but he's quiet. He doesn't enjoy small talk. He doesn't like to waste his time with anything that's weak or offhand. He wants to deal from strength all the time. That's why he projects this uppity-black-man figure that so many people in baseball seem to hate. He's very proud, you know, and he had a ghetto upbringing, so you could understand why he was so sensitive to bigotry—up to a point. But we have a great relationship—me, a kid from Memphis, Tennessee, and him, an elegant black man from Omaha. Any relationship you get into with Bob is going to be intense. He's a strong man, with strong feelings."

Joe Torre, the manager of the New York Mets, who played with Gibson from 1969 to 1974, is also a close friend. When I called on him late in June, in the clubhouse at Shea Stadium, and told him I was about to go west to visit Gibson, he beckoned me over to a framed photograph on one wall of his office. The picture shows the three friends posing beside a batting cage in their Cardinals uniforms. Torre, a heavy-faced man with dark eyebrows and a falsely menacing appearance, and McCarver, who has a cheerful, snub-nosed Irish look to him, are both grinning at the photographer, with their arms around the shoulders of Bob Gibson, who is between them; it's impossible to tell if Gibson is smiling, though, because his back is turned to the camera. "That says it all," Torre said. "He alienated a lot of people—most of all the press, who didn't always know what to make of him. He has this great confidence in himself: 'Hey, I'm me. Take me or leave me.' There was never any selling of Bob Gibson. He's an admirable man. On the mound, he had very tangible intangibles. He had that hunger, that killer instinct. He threw at a lot of batters but not nearly as many as you've heard. But he'd never deny it if you asked him. I think this is great. There's no other sport except boxing that has such a hard one-on-one confrontation as you get when a pitcher and a hitter go up against each other. Any edge you can get on the hitter, any doubt you can put in his mind, you use. And Bob Gibson would never give up that edge. He was your enemy out there. I try to teach this to our pitchers. The more coldness, the more mystery about you, the more chance you have of getting them out.

"I played against him before I played with him, and either way he never talked to you. Never. I was on some All-Star teams with him, and even then he didn't talk to you. There was the one in Minnesota, when I was catching him and we were ahead 6–5, I think, in the ninth. I'm catching, and Tony Oliva, a great hitter, is leading off, and Gibby goes strike one, strike two. Now I want a fastball up and in, I think to myself, and maybe I should go out there and tell him this—tell him, whatever he does, not to throw it down and in to Oliva. So I go out and tell him, and Gibby just gives me that look of his. Doesn't say a word. I go back and squat down and give him the signal—fastball up and in—and he throws it *down* and in, and Oliva hits it for a double to left center. To this day, I think Gibby did it on purpose. He didn't want to be told *anything*. So then there's an infield out, and then he strikes out the last two batters, of course, and we win. In the shower, I say, 'Nice pitching,' and he still doesn't say anything to me. Ask him about it."

Torre lit a long cigar, and said, "Quite a man. He can seem distant and uncaring to some people, but he's not the cold person he's been described as. There are no areas between us where he's withdrawn. Things go deep with him. I miss talking to him during the season, and it's my fault, because I'm always so damn busy. He doesn't call me, because he never wants to make himself a pain in the ass to a friend. But he is my friend. The other day, I got a photograph of himself he'd sent me, and he'd signed it 'Love, Bob.' How many other ballplayers are going to do that? How many other friends?"

Most ballplayers who are discussing a past rival or a teammate go directly to the man's craft—what pitches he could hit, his arm, his range afield, or (with pitchers) his stuff and what he threw when the count was against him. But I had begun to notice that the baseball people talking about Bob Gibson all seemed anxious to get at something deeper; Gibson the man was even more vivid and interesting to them than Gibson the great pitcher. Bill White, the well-known TV and radio announcer with the Yankees, played first base behind Gibson with the Cards for seven years, and was then traded to the Phillies and had to play against him. "He was tough and uncompromising," White told me. "Koufax and Don Drysdale were just the same, with variations for their personalities—they had that same hard state of mind. But I think a great black athlete is sometimes tougher in a game, because every black has had it tough on the way up. Any black player who has a sense of himself, who wants to make something of himself, has something of Bob Gibson's attitude. Gibson had a chip on his shoulder out there—which was good. He was mean enough. He had no remorse. I remember when he hit Jim Ray Hart on the shoulder—he was bending away from a pitch—and broke his collarbone. Bob didn't say anything to him. I'd been his roomie for a while on the Cards, but the first time I batted against him, when I went over to the Phillies, he hit me in the arm. It didn't surprise me at all."

And, once again, Mike Shannon: "I think every superior athlete has some special motivation. With Bob Gibson, it wasn't that he wanted to win so much as that he didn't want to lose. He *hated* to lose. He just wouldn't accept it."

It was ninety-seven degrees at the Omaha airport when I landed there early one evening in July, and when I called Bob Gibson from my motel he invited me to come on out and cool off with a dip in his pool. He picked me up in his car—a black 1972 Mercedes SEL, lovingly kept up, with CB equipment (his call signal is Redbird) and terse "BG" license plates. Gibson looked well kept up himself, in tailored jeans, a white polo shirt, thin gold spectacles, a gold bracelet on his left wrist, a World Series ring, and a necklace with a pendant "45" in gold—his old uniform number. He is forty-four years old, but only his glasses spoiled the impression that he was perfectly capable of working nine tough innings the next afternoon. I asked him what he did for exercise these days, and he said, "Nothing." I expressed surprise, and he said, "I played sports hard for thirty years, which is enough. Now I'm tired of all that." No apology, no accompanying smile or joke: no small talk. He spoke pleasantly enough, though, in a light, almost boyish voice, and when he did laugh—a little later, after we were more used to each other—the sound of it made me realize that only in the world of sports would he be considered anything but a young man. There were some quiet spells in the car during our longish drive out to his house, in Bellevue, a comfortable suburban district on the south side of town, but by the time we got there I had lost any sense of foreboding that I might have had about imposing myself on such a famously private man.

Bob Gibson has done well for himself in Omaha. He was

born and grew up there in the black North Side ghetto; his mother was a laundress, and his father died before he was born. He was the youngest of seven children—his three sisters and three brothers are all still living—and at the time of his birth the family lived in a four-room shack. When he was an infant there, he was bitten on the ear by a rat. By the end of his playing days, Gibson was earning more than a hundred and fifty thousand dollars a year, which made him one of the two or three best-paid players of his time, and he invested his money with care. Today, he is the chairman of the board—an interracial board—of the Community Bank of Nebraska, which he helped get started seven years ago, and which does most of its business in the black community of Omaha. He is also the co-owner and the active, day-to-day manager of a new and successful medium-sized bar-restaurant called Gibby's, a couple of blocks away from Creighton University, which Gibson entered as a freshman on a basketball scholarship in 1954. Much of Gibson's life these days seems new. Gibby's opened in late 1978, and last November he was married to Wendy Nelson, whom I met at their home, to the accompaniment of frenzied barking from their four-month-old miniature schnauzer, Mia. ("Kill, Mia!" Gibson said delightedly. "Kill, girl!") Wendy Gibson, a composed, striking-looking blond woman in her late twenties, is in the financial division of the local telephone company, where she works, by preference, on the very early shift, driving to work each day shortly after dawn in the family's *other* Mercedes. (Gibson's previous marriage, to Charline Johnson, ended in divorce some years ago; their children, Renee and Annette, are grown up and have moved away from Omaha. A captivating oil portrait of the two girls and their father—all of them much younger then—hangs in Gibson's study in his new house; the artist is an old friend and teammate, Curt Flood.) Wendy and Bob Gibson moved into their house last May. It is a spacious, comfortably furnished and carpeted three-story contemporary wooden structure, with a sundeck that looks over a steep hillside and a thick green growth of oaks and cottonwoods. A flight of steps leads down from the deck to a big swimming pool, which had had its inaugural only a week before my arrival. Bob Gibson is handy. He helped design the new house, and he put in the deck stairs and built a raised wooden patio beside the pool, and also did most of the landscape work on the grounds, laying in some old railroad ties to form a rose garden and planting shrubs and young trees everywhere. The pool was built to Gibson's design; its sides and bottom are painted black—a da Vinci-like idea of his, meant to help the water hold the heat of the sun in the spring and fall. Somehow, though, he had not remembered the warmish midsummer Nebraska sunshine, and when he and I slipped into the inky waves, the water temperature stood at ninety-two degrees—only a fraction cooler than the steamy, locust-loud night air. "Another mistake," Gibson said mildly. Swimming was a bit like sloshing through black-bean soup, but after a couple of turns up and down the pool he and I settled ourselves comfortably enough on the top steps at the shallow end, with our legs dangling in the water, and while Mia sniffed and circled me warily we talked a little baseball.

I asked Gibson if he recalled the low-and-inside pitch he had thrown to Tony Oliva in that All-Star game, against Joe Torre's signals.

"Well, I never really liked being on the All-Star team," he said. "I liked the honor of it, being voted one of the best, but I couldn't get used to the idea of playing with people from other teams in the league—guys who I'd have to go out and try to beat just a couple of days later. I didn't even like having Joe catch me—he was with the Braves then—because I figured he'd learn how to hit me. In that same game, he came out and told me not to throw the high fastball to Harmon Killebrew, because the word was that he ate up that pitch." Gibson's voice was almost incredulous as he said this. "Well, hell. I struck him out with three high fastballs. But in any of the All-Star games where I got to pitch early"—Gibson was voted onto the National League All-Star squad eight times—"I'd always dress right away and get out of there in a hurry, before the other players got done and came into the clubhouse. I didn't want to hang around and make friends. I don't think there's any place in the game for a pitcher smiling and joking with the hitters. I was all business on the mound—it *is* a business, isn't it?—and I think some of the writers used to call me cold or arrogant because of that. I didn't want to be friends with anybody on the other side, except perhaps with Willie Stargell— how could you not talk to that guy? None of this was meant to scare guys, or anything. It was just the way I felt. When

Orlando Cepeda was with us, I used to watch him and Marichal laughing and fooling around before a game. They'd been on the Giants together, you know. But then Cepeda would go out and *kill* Marichal at the plate—one of the best pitchers I ever saw—and when it was over they'd go to dinner together and laugh some more. It just made me shake my head. I didn't understand it."

I had been wondering how to bring up the business of his knocking down his old roommate Bill White, but now Gibson offered the story of his own accord. "Even before Bill was traded, I used to tell him that if he ever dived across the plate to swing at an outside pitch, the way he liked to, I'd have to hit him," he said. "And then, the very first time, he went for a pitch that was *this* far outside and swung at it, and so I hit him on the elbow with the next pitch. [Some years earlier, Gibson hit Duke Snider after similar provocation, and broke his elbow.] Bill saw it coming, and he yelled 'Yaah!' even before it got him. And I yelled over to him, "You son of a bitch, you went for that outside ball! That pitch, that part of the plate, belongs to *me!* If I make a mistake inside, all right, but the outside is mine and don't you forget it.' He said, 'You're crazy,' but he understood me."

I mentioned a famous moment when Gibson had hit Tommie Agee, of the Mets, on the batting helmet with the very first pitch of the first inning of the first Cardinals spring-training game in 1968. Agee had come over from the Chicago White Sox and the American League in the previous winter, and when Gibson's first swallow of the spring conked him, several Gibson students among the Mets and Cardinals baseball writers in the press box at Al Lang Field called out, "Welcome to the National League, Tommie!" (Agee went to the hospital for observation, but was found not to have suffered serious injury.)

Gibson was silent for a moment, and then he said, "It's very easy to hit a batter in the body with a pitch. There's nothing to it. It's a lot harder to hit him in the head. Any time you hit him in the head, it's really his own fault. Anyway, that was just spring training."

Joe Torre had told me that the Agee-plunking was an accident, but I noted now that Gibson had not quite denied intention in the affair. He had put doubt in my mind, just as Torre had told me he would. He still wanted that edge.

"I did throw at John Milner in spring training once," Gibson went on, paddling his legs in the water. "Because of that swing of his—that dive at the ball." Milner, an outfielder then with the Mets and now with the Pirates, invariably takes a full-scale, left-handed downtown swing at the ball, as if he meant to pull every pitch into the right-field stands. "I don't like batters taking that big cut, with their hats falling off and their buttons popping and every goddam thing like that. It doesn't show any respect for the pitcher. That batter's not doing any thinking up there, so I'm going to *make* him think. The next time, he won't look so fancy out there. He'll be a better-looking hitter. So I got Milner that once, and then, months later, at Shea Stadium, Tom Seaver began to pitch me up and inside, knocking me down, and it took me a minute to realize that it must have been to pay me back for something *in spring training*. I couldn't believe that."

There was a little silence at poolside while I digested this. Gibson sounded almost like a veteran samurai warrior recalling an ancient code of pain and honor. I suggested that there must be days when he still badly missed being out there on the mound, back in the thick of things.

"No, I have no desire to get out and throw the fastball again," he said quietly. "Even if I wanted to, I couldn't."

I had noticed that Gibson limped slightly as he walked around the pool, and the accounts of some of his baseball injuries and how he had reacted to them at the time came back to me. In July of 1967, while pitching against the Pirates in St. Louis, he was struck just above his right ankle by a line drive off the bat of Roberto Clemente. He went down in a heap, but after the Cardinals trainer had treated the injury with a pain-deadening spray, Gibson insisted on staying in the game. He walked Willie Stargell, retired Bill Mazeroski on a pop-up, and then, firing a three-two pitch to Donn Clendenon, came down hard on the right leg with his characteristic spinning follow-through and snapped the already cracked bone. Dal Maxvill, then a Cardinals shortstop and now a Cardinals coach, said to me recently, "That was the most extraordinary thing I ever saw in baseball—Gibby pitching to those batters with a broken leg. Everyone who was there that day remembered it afterward, for always, and every young pitcher who came onto our club while Gibson was still with us was told about it. We didn't have too many pitchers turning up with upset stomachs or hangnails on our team after that."

Gibson came back to win three games against the Red Sox in the World Series that fall, but his next serious injury, in midseason of 1973, took a heavier toll. Leading off first base in a game against the Mets at Shea Stadium, he made a sudden dive back toward the base after an infield line drive was caught, but collapsed when his right knee buckled. The trainer and the team doctor came out to succor him, but Gibson cried "Don't touch it! Don't touch it!" and again refused to be taken out of the game. When the inning ended, he walked to the mound and began his warmup tosses and fell heavily to the ground. The surgeon—Dr. Stan London—who performed the cartilage operation the next day said afterward that Gibson had the knees of an eighty-year-old man. Gibson recovered in time to pitch and win a game that September, and he continued for two more full seasons on the mound, although, as he told me now, he sometimes had to sit in the clubhouse for two hours after a game before he felt able to head for the showers. "I'd had the left knee drained about seventeen times, too," he said. "I'd sit like this"—he hung his head and arms like a broken puppet—"and I'd think, *Why do I put up with this? Why, why?*" He laughed now, mocking himself. "I just couldn't give it up," he said. "Couldn't let go."

I asked if he'd become a different kind of pitcher then, using change-ups and slip pitches, the way many older hurlers do in their final seasons.

"No, I always threw hard," he said. "They didn't use me much in my final season, after I'd announced I was going to retire—I never did understand that. But once, when I hadn't pitched in three weeks, they brought me into a game against Houston in extra innings—I was the last pitcher we had—and I struck out the side on nine pitches that were nothing but fastballs. So I still had something left, even at the end. I always had pretty good control, you know, so it wasn't like I didn't know what I was doing out there. But later that season I gave up a grand-slam home run to Pete LaCock, of the Cubs, and that told me it was about time for me to get off the mound for good." Gibson spoke lightly enough, but at the time this home run was an almost insupportable blow to his pride. A pitcher who was with the Cubs that year told me that as LaCock (who is not exactly famous as a slugger) circled the bases, Gibson stalked after him around the base paths, reviling him for what he had done.

"Pitching is about ninety per cent thinking," Gibson went on. "I threw hard when I was younger, but I didn't know how to get people out. I don't care how hard you throw, somebody's going to hit it if you don't think out there. It's not all that detailed—you don't think of three or four pitches ahead. But one pitch might set up the next two you throw—it depends what the guy does with it. You know. If he misses a fastball by a foot, then he'll see another one. If he fouls it off or *just* misses it, he'll probably get a breaking ball next. It isn't exactly scientific, or anything."

Gibson suddenly laughed in the darkness beside me. "But not everybody understands what a pitcher *does*," he said. "About his control, I mean. I remember when Mike Shannon was moved in from the outfield and began playing third base for us—back in the middle sixties, it was. He was really nervous over there. He kept asking me where I wanted him to play— up or back, near the line or away. He wanted instructions. I always told him I didn't give a damn where he played unless there was a right-handed batter coming up with a man on first and less than two out, but then he should be ready, because he'd be getting a ground ball, right to him or around his area. And I'd throw a sinker down and in, and the batter would hit it on the ground to Mike, to start the double play, and when we came in off the field Mike would look at me with his mouth open, and he'd say, 'But how did you *know?*' He didn't have the faintest idea that when I threw that pitch to the batter he *had* to hit it to him there! He didn't know what pitching was all about."

To go back a little, Gibson also won his second start in the 1968 Cardinals-Tigers World Series—a 10–1 decision in the fourth game, during which he fanned ten batters and whacked a home run. It was Gibson's seventh straight World Series victory—an all-time record. The Tigers, however, captured the Series, rallying in stimulating fashion after trailing by three games to one, and beating Gibson in the memorable finale, when Detroit outfielder Jim Northrup, batting with two out and two on in the seventh inning of the scoreless game, smashed a long drive that was misjudged by Curt Flood in center field, who then slipped on the turf and allowed the ball to go over his head for a triple. The Tigers won the game by 4–1, and the Most Valuable Player award for the Series went to Mickey Lolich, a portly left-handed sinkerball specialist, who won the second, fifth, and seventh games. Gibson, however, had established a Series record of thirty-five strikeouts (still standing), and a few weeks later he was named the Most Valuable Player of the National League for 1968 and became the unanimous winner of the Cy Young Award as the league's best pitcher. The following year, 1969, Gibson compiled a 20–13 record, with an earned-run average of 2.18, and in 1970 his 23–7 won-lost mark and 3.12 E.R.A. won him the Cy Young again. Injuries began to gnaw him after that, but he declined only stubbornly, throwing a no-hitter against the Pirates in 1971 and running off eleven straight victories in the course of a 19–11 season in 1972. His lifetime earned-run average of 2.91 runs per game is the ninth-best in baseball history. (Walter Johnson's 2.37 leads all comers, while Tom Seaver, at 2.62, and Jim Palmer, at 2.73, stand third and fourth on the all-time list at this writing.)

Many observers (including this one) believe that Gibson's 1.12 earned-run average in 1968 is one of the Everests of the game, ranking with Joe DiMaggio's fifty-six-consecutive-game hitting streak in 1941 and Hack Wilson's hundred and ninety runs batted in in 1930. Gibson's record, however, was not much noted or celebrated in its time, partly because it was achieved in a summer during which the pitchers in both leagues established a mesmerizing dominance over the batters. The leagues' combined batting average fell to an all-time low of .237, and twenty-one per cent of all games played were shut-outs. Many pitchers came up with startling performances that summer. Gaylord Perry, of the Giants, and Ray Washburn, of the Cardinals, threw no-hit games on successive days at Candlestick Park; Jerry Koosman, a rookie, won nineteen games for the Mets; Denny McLain, as I have noted, won thirty-one games for the Tigers; and Don Drysdale, of the Dodgers, ran off fifty-eight and two-thirds consecutive shutout innings—a record that still stands. At the end of the year, the baseball fathers studied these figures and determined to rebalance the game by shaving five inches off the height of the mound (reducing it to ten inches), and by closing up the upper and lower limits of the strike zone. Gibson's golden season may always appear a mite tarnished by these circumstances, but even a brief rundown of his 1968 summer outings suggests that in that single season he came as close to some ideal of pitching as most of us are ever likely to witness or wish for. Younger fans may argue for Ron Guidry's marvellous 25–3 season for the Yankees in 1978, when he threw nine shutouts and wound up with a 1.74 earned-run average. Others will cite Steve Carlton's one-man-band performance in 1972, when he finished with an earned-run average of 1.97 and a record of 27–10—all this for a frightful last-place Phillies team that won only fifty-nine games in all—while geezers may bring up Carl Hubbell's 23–12 and 1.66 earned-run mark for the Giants in 1933. But no matter: these great case studies of the game are forever moot.

On May 28, 1968, Bob Gibson lost to the Giants, 3–1, and saw his record for the year decline to three victories and five defeats. Surprisingly, however, his earned run average of 1.52 for the young season was fifth in the National League at this point—an oddity explicable by the fact that his teammates had supplied him with a total of four runs in the five games he lost: starvation fare. On June 2nd, Gibson pitched the Cardinals into first place (this was before the leagues had been subdivided into East and West sectors) with a 6–3 victory over the Mets; the final Mets run—a homer by Ed Charles—came in the seventh inning. It was also the final run that Gibson surrendered in the month of June, for he threw shutout games in his next five outings. Only the last of these brought him much attention from the national press, and that came because reporters had noticed that his next appearance, on July 1st, would be against the Dodgers in Los Angeles, and that his mound opponent there would be Don Drysdale, whose record shutout skein of fifty-eight and two-thirds innings had been set over a span of six games in late May and early June. A matchup between the two seemed exciting indeed, for Drysdale, who was six feet five and threw almost sidearm, had a hostile scowl, a devastating fastball, and a reputation for knocking down batters he didn't care for: another intimidator. Gibson by now had forty-eight scoreless innings to his credit, but the tension of the famous confrontation vanished in the very first inning, when two Dodgers singled and Gibson, while pitching to Ron Fairly, let go a wild pitch that allowed Len Gabrielson to score from third base. Gibson had lost the duel with Drysdale and a shot at his record, but he won the game, by 5–1. He then pitched a shutout against the Giants, beat Houston by 8–1, and afterward shut out the Mets and the Phillies in succession. On July 30th, once again facing the Mets, Gibson surrendered a run with two out in the fourth inning, when Ed Charles scored on a double by Eddie Kranepool—the same Ed Charles who had homered against him on June 2nd. In that span—from June 2nd to July 30th—Gibson had given up two earned runs (and two runs in toto) in ninety-six and two-thirds innings.

Gibson won that Mets game, and he did not lose a game, in fact, until August 24th, when he fanned fifteen Pirates but lost, 6–4, after giving up a three-run homer to Willie Stargell. Between May 28th and August 24th, Gibson had won fifteen straight games, ten of them shutouts. He threw two more shutouts in his next two outings, and somebody figured out that in the course of three straight games in August, Gibson's infielders had to make only eight assists. (His shortstop, Dal Maxvill, told a reporter, "It's like having a night off out there when he's pitching.") Possibly tired by now—or perhaps a bit understimulated, since his club had run away with the league by this point, having established a fourteen-and-a-half-game lead over the second-place Reds by August 1st—Gibson lost three games in September, one of them to the no-hitter by Gaylord Perry. His final victory, on September 27th, was a 1–0 decision over the Astros—his thirteenth shutout. His season was over; the World Series and the Tigers were just ahead.

A further thin cement of statistics will finish the monument. Gibson completed twenty-eight of the thirty-four games he started in 1968, and was never removed in the middle of an inning—never knocked out of the box. His 1.12 earned-run average is second only to the all-time low of 1.01, established by the Red Sox' Hub Leonard in 1914, and it eclipsed the old National League mark of 1.22, set by Grover Cleveland Alexander in 1915. Gibson's thirteen shutouts are second only to the sixteen that Alexander achieved the following summer. But those very low early figures, it should be understood, must be slightly discounted, for they were established in the sludgy, Pleistocene era of the game, when aces like Leonard and Alexander and Walter Johnson and the White Sox' Red Faber regularly ran off season-long earned-run averages of two runs or less per game, thanks to the dead ball then in use. The lively ball, which came into the game in 1921, when the owners began to notice how much the fans seemed to enjoy watching a young outfielder (and former pitcher) named George Herman Ruth hit towering drives into the bleachers, put an end to the pitchers' hold over the game, and none of the four worthies I have cited ever pitched consistently in the less-than-three-runs-per-game level after 1922. Bob Gibson, we may conclude, was the man most responsible for the *next* major change in the dimensions of the sport—the lowering of the mound and the shrinkage of the strike zone that came along in 1969. Gibson, like all pitchers, complained bitterly when these new rules were announced, but Bob Broeg, the sports editor of the St. Louis *Post-Dispatch* and the dean of Cardinals sportswriters, told him he had only himself to blame. "I said, 'Goddam it, Gib, you're changing the game!'" Broeg told me not long ago. "'It isn't fun anymore. You're making it like hockey.'"

On another day, Omaha slowly came to a broil under a glazy white sun while Gibson and I ran some early-morning errands in his car—a visit to his bank, a stop at the drive-in window of another bank, where he picked up the payroll checks for Gibby's—and wound up at the restaurant, where the daytime help greeted the boss cheerfully. Gibson seemed in an easy frame of mind, and he looked younger than ever. I recalled that many of his teammates had told me what good company he was in the dugout and on road trips—on days when he wasn't pitching. He was a comical, shrill-voiced bench jockey, and a grouchy but lighthearted clubhouse agitator, who was sometimes known to bang a bat repeatedly and horribly on the metal locker of a teammate who was seen to be suffering the aftereffects of too many ice-cream sodas the previous evening. While he drove, Gibson, with a little urging, recalled how he had pitched to some of the prime hitters of his day—inside fastballs to Willie Mays (who feasted on breaking pitches), belt-high inside deliveries to Eddie Mathews, low and away to Roberto Clemente, and so on. He said that Frank Robinson used to deceive pitchers with his plate-crowding (Robinson was a right-handed slugger of fearsome power, whose customary stance at the plate was that of an impatient subway traveller leaning over the edge of the platform and peering down the tracks for the D train), because they took it to mean that he was eager for an inside pitch. "Besides," he said, "they'd be afraid of hitting him and putting him on base. So they'd work him outside, and he'd hit the shit out of the ball. I always tried him inside, and I got him out there—sometimes. He was like Willie Mays—if you got the ball outside to Willie at all, he'd just *kill* you. The same with Clemente. I could throw him a fastball knee-high on the outside corner seventeen times in a row, but if I ever got it two inches up, he'd hit it out of sight. That's the mark of a good hitter—the tiniest mistake and he'll punish you. Other batters—well, somebody like Joe Adcock was just a guess hitter. You'd pitch him up and in, and he'd swing and miss every time. He just didn't give a damn. I don't know what's the matter with so many hitters—it's like their brains small up." He shook his head and laughed softly. "Me, too. I got beat by Tommy Davis twice the same way. In one game, I'd struck him out three times on sliders away. But I saw that he'd been inching up and inching up toward that part of the plate, so I decided to fool him and come inside, and he hit a homer and beat me, one-oh. And then, in another game, I did exactly the same thing. I tried to outthink him, and hit the inside pitch for a homer, and it was one–oh all over again. So I could get dumb, too."

I said that he didn't seem to have made too many mistakes in the summer of '68. Gibson thought for a moment or two and said, "You can't say it was a fluke, although some people *have* said that. Just say it was totally unusual. Everything I threw that year seemed to go where I wanted it. Everything was down, all year. I was never that good again, because they went and changed the rules on me. The next year was a terrific struggle. I had a good season, but I never worked so hard in my life, because so many of my breaking pitches were up. I'll never know, but I doubt very seriously I'd have had another one-point-one-two E.R.A., even if they'd left the mound where it was. I'd like to think I'd really perfected my pitching to that point, but I'll never know."

The talk shifted to pitchers, and Gibson (echoing Pete Rose) said he thought that Juan Marichal had been the best hurler of their time, because of his absolute control. "I had a better fastball and a better slider, but he was a better pitcher than me or Koufax," he said. Among contemporary pitchers, he had warm things to say about the Phillies' Steve Carlton, once a young teammate of his on the Cards. "He's always had a great arm," he said. "And if you have a good arm and you're in the game long enough, you're going to learn how to pitch. He sure knows how now. What makes a player great to me is longevity."

I named some other mound stars of the sixties and seventies, and Gibson shrugged and shook his head. "I guess I was never much in awe of anybody," he said. "I think you have to have that attitude if you're going to go far in this game. People have always said that I was too confident, but I think you'll find that most guys who can play are pretty cocky." The locution "He can play"—as in "Carl Yastrzemski can play a little"—is a throwaway line, the professionals' designation for star-quality athletes. "They're not sitting around worrying about who they're going to pitch against or bat against the next day. You hear a lot of talk about the pressure of the game, but I think most of that comes from the media. Most guys don't let things worry them. Pressure comes when you're not doing well. I've always thought that you only really enjoy baseball when you're good at it. For someone who isn't at the top of the game—who's just hanging on somewhere on down the totem pole—it's a real tough job, every day. But when I was playing I never wished I was doing anything else. I think being a professional athlete is the finest thing a man can do."

I asked about the source of his great confidence in himself, and he said, "I've always been that way. After all, I was playing basketball with grown men when I was thirteen years old. I always thought I was good enough to play with anyone. I don't know where that came from."

When Gibson was playing baseball, he was considered one of the two or three very best athletes in the game. His early basketball experience had come when he was a water boy with an itinerant black basketball team, the Y Travellers (named for Omaha's North Branch Y.M.C.A.), which was coached by his grown-up oldest brother, Josh; whenever the Travellers ran up a comfortable lead over some local Nebraska or Iowa all-star club, Josh would send his kid brother into the game, just to rub things in a little. Bob Gibson won city and statewide basketball honors at Technical High School, in Omaha, and a few in baseball, too (he was a catcher in the beginning), and he broke every basketball record at Creighton, where he was the first black student to be given a basketball scholarship—and, for that matter, to play on the team. After leaving Creighton, he played for the Harlem Globetrotters during the 1957–58 season, after he had signed on as a pitcher with the Cardinals organization. "It was all right being with the Trotters," Gibson told me, "but I hated that clowning around. I wanted to play all the time—I mean, I wanted to play to win."

In spite of Gibson's spinning, staggering pitching motion, which certainly did not leave him in the squared-away, weight-on-both-feet attitude that coaches recommend as the proper post-delivery fielding stance for the position, he was agile enough out there to win the Gold Glove award as the best defensive pitcher in his league every season from 1965 through 1973. Fans and writers and players still talk about some of his fielding plays in the same awestruck tones they use for the seventeen-strikeout Series game. In one play (I can still see it) in the 1964 World Series, he scampered over and plucked up a hard-hit ball struck by Joe Pepitone that had nailed him on the hip and caromed halfway to third base; Gibson leaped and turned one hundred and eighty degrees in midair and made an overhead throw to first—a basketball one-handed fall-away jumper— that nipped Pepitone at the bag. There was also a nationally televised game in which he ran down a ball that a Giants batter had bounced over his head out on the mound; Gibson caught up with it while running full tilt away from the plate and toward second base, and he flipped it, underhand and right-handed and away from his body (try it), to first for the out. Tim McCarver, who weighs a solid hundred and ninety pounds, told me that one day when he and Gibson were horsing around on the field, Bob had suddenly seized him and lifted him above his head at arm's length, holding him aloft like some Olympic weight lifter at the end of a clean and jerk. "The man is some-what startling," McCarver said.

Gibby's is a welcoming sort of place—a squared-off, three-sided bar downstairs, with strips of stained-glass decoration on the far wall and a short flight of steps up to the sun-filled upper level, where there are some comfortable wooden-backed dining booths and hanging plants everywhere. On a busy night—on

Saturdays, for instance, when a jazz group comes in to play—Gibby's has room for about a hundred and thirty diners and twenty more customers at the bar. I was not surprised to learn that Gibson had had a hand in the restaurant's design and construction. He is there every day, starting at eight in the morning, when he turns up to check the books for the previous night's business, to inspect the incoming meat and produce (the menu is modest, and is built around steaks and shrimp and delicious hamburgers), and generally to keep an eye on things. "I want to make sure nobody is throwing out the forks with the garbage," he said lightly. He went to bartenders' school for three months before Gibby's opened—not so much to learn how to mix cocktails, although he can now whip up eighty different drinks, as to learn how veteran waiters and bartenders can fleece a rookie owner. "What I *should* have done was to become an accountant," he said. "About ninety per cent of the job is damned paperwork." Gibby's clientele is an interesting mixture of races and ages and sexes—a "neat crowd," according to the owner ("neat" is a favorite word), and perhaps the only such cosmopolitan mixture in Omaha. The waiters are mostly young black men, and the bartenders mostly young black women. Gibson is a calm and approachable boss; the staff seems to care about him, and vice versa. When a small, very young waitress began putting coins into a cigarette machine near us, Bob said reprovingly, "Those aren't for *you*, are they?" (The weren't.) Later on, he let slip that the previous week he had taken the four-year-old daughter of one of his female bartenders out to his new pool for the afternoon when her mother couldn't find a babysitter. At the last moment, he also asked the daughter of one of his regular customers to come along, too. "I used to have little girls myself," he said to me. A lot of the arriving diners and drinkers at Gibby's say hello to him in an easy, friendly way, but there isn't much hearty bar chatter with the host. Not many people would feel impelled to buddy up to Bob Gibson. I suggested that he must be exposed to a good deal of barside baseball expertise at his place of work, and he said, "Who wants to talk to fans? They always know so much, to hear them tell it, and they always think baseball is so easy. You hear them say, 'Oh, I was a pretty good ballplayer myself back when I was in school, but then I got this injury. . . .' Some cabdriver gave me that one day, and

I said, 'Oh, really? That's funny, because when *I* was young I really wanted to be a cabdriver, only I had this little problem with my eyes, so I never made it.' He thought I was serious. It went right over his head."

Gibson's impatience with trifling or intrusive strangers accounted for considerable coolness between him and the media during his playing days—a mistrust that may even keep him out of the Hall of Fame for a year or two, since some members of the Baseball Writers Association have been known to allow personal pique to influence their judgment. (Each writer selects up to ten names of eligible former players he thinks worthy of the Hall of Fame, and a player must be named on seventy-five per cent of the ballots in order to be immortalized.) A couple of years ago, when Willie Mays first came up for election, twenty-three members of the B.W.A. resolutely omitted him from their ballots. A good many St. Louis reporters still recall the time in 1967 when Gibson had the cast removed from his broken leg and then, annoyed by their clubhouse importunings and questions, taped a sheet of paper to his shirtfront on which he had written "1. Yes, it's off; 2. No, it doesn't hurt; 3. I don't know how much longer"; and so on. The club was in a pennant race, of course, and Gibson's condition was a matter of daily concern to Cardinals fans everywhere, so his broadside was not taken in good part.

"I don't like all this personal contact with the press," Gibson told me. "The press expects everyone to be congenial. Everyone's *not* congenial! They want to put every athlete in the same category as every other athlete. It's as if they thought they owned you." I had been told of a St. Louis television reporter who had once done something to offend one of Gibson's teammates and had then tried to reassure Gibson about their relationship. "You know I'll never do anything to hurt *you*, Bob," he said. Gibson looked at him incredulously and said, "Why, hell, the only way you could ever hurt me is if you happened to be a pretty good fastball hitter!" One longtime Cardinals writer said to me, "Bob was a thorny, obdurate personality, and there weren't too many people who were crazy about him. If he'd had a little more give to him, he could have owned this city. If he'd had Lou Brock's personality, he'd still be working for the Cardinals somewhere."

There is a standoff here. The price of Bob Gibson's owning

St. Louis seems to be his agreeing—in his mind, at least—to let the press own him. I have considerable sympathy for any writer who had to ask Bob Gibson some sharp, news-producing questions two or three times a week over the span of a decade or more, but wanting Gibson with a sunny, less obdurate temperament would be to want him a less difficult, less dangerous man on the mound—not quite a Bob Gibson, not quite a great pitcher. The man is indivisible, and it is the wonder of him. It is my own suspicion that both sportswriters and fans are increasingly resentful of the fame and adulation and immense wealth that are now bestowed so swiftly upon so many young professional athletes, and are envious of their privileged and apparently carefree style of living. The resentment is a half-conscious appreciation of the fact that they themselves—the fans and the media people, that is—have to a great degree created these golden youths, and because of that there is indeed a wish to own them; to demand ceaseless, inhumanly repeated dazzling performances from them on the field, and to require absolute access to their private lives as well. Most athletes, who are very young when they first come to prominence and, for the most part, have a very limited experience of the world, respond to these demands either with a convulsive, wholly artificial public "image" of affability, or (more often, of late) with surliness or angry silence. Bob Gibson did neither. Somehow, he has always kept his distance and his strangeness, and there is something upright and old-fashioned about such stubborn propriety. He is there if anyone really wants to close that space—the whole man, and not a piece of him or an image of him—but many of us may prefer not to do so, because at a distance (from sixty feet six inches away, perhaps) he stands whole and undiminished, and beyond our envy: the athlete incarnate, the player.

Gibson had allowed me to close this space a little by his willingness to talk about himself, and I had begun to sense the intensity of relationships with him that Tim McCarver had told me about, and the absence of any withdrawn places in him that Joe Torre had mentioned. There is reason to believe that he has allowed himself to become more approachable since he left the game. Bob Broeg, who covered Gibson from his first day in spring training as a rookie, in 1958, to his retirement at the end of the 1975 season, said to me, "Bob didn't know how his personality worked against him. I don't think I wrote many things about him over the years that weren't appreciative of his great skills—he and Dizzy Dean were the two best pitchers I ever saw here—but he was always indifferent to me. One day, late in his career, I was in the clubhouse with him, and he was as closed off as ever, and I finally said, 'You've never said a kind or personal word to me in the years I've known you.' I walked away, and he chased me all the way across the room to ask what I meant. I'd pinked him, and he was extremely upset. He just didn't realize how cold he could be in everyday relationships."

But other intimates of Gibson's from his Cardinals days have a very different view of him. Gene Gieselmann, the team's trainer—he is thirty-three years old but looks much younger—counts Gibson among his closest and warmest friends. "My memories of baseball are all shiny where he's concerned," he said. "I cherish him. I think his problems with people go back to his never having had a father. He never knew him, you know. He dearly loved his mother, but I don't think he was very close to anyone else in his family. So when somebody, especially a white person"—Gieselmann is white—"showed him over a long period of time that he could be more than just a trainer or more than just another ballplayer, and that there could be something deeper in their relationship—well, that meant a lot to him, and then he showed how sensitive and generous he really was."

Gibson is a compulsive truthteller, and he appears to have a wry understanding of the burdens of that self-imposed role. At one point, he was talking with me about the difference between himself and Joe Torre when it came to dealing with writers and other strangers, and he said, "Joe knows everybody, and he recognizes them right away. I don't. I always had a hard time remembering people's names and recognizing their faces." There was a moment of silence, and then he added, "That's only half of it. I didn't *care*. And if I think somebody's wrong I'm going to say it."

I suddenly recalled an incident some years ago involving Gibson and another player, a well-known American League infielder, who were members of a small troupe of ballplayers making a postseason tour of military bases in the Pacific. Gibson's roommate on the trip was a public-relations man with one of the major-league teams, who was acting as an escort and travel agent for the group. Early in the trip, the infielder let drop some plainly anti-Semitic remarks about the P.R. man, who was Jewish, and Gibson stopped him in mid-sentence and advised him to keep his distance and not to talk to him for the remainder of the trip. "And if I ever pitch against you," Gibson said levelly, "I'm going to hit you on the coconut with my first pitch." Fortunately (or perhaps *un*fortunately), the two never did play against each other.

Gibson told me that racism had been easy to find when he came into baseball. When he first reported to the Cards' spring-training camp, in St. Petersburg, in 1958, he presented himself at the Bainbridge Hotel, where the club was quartered, and asked for his room, but he was guided out a side door, where a taxi picked him up and drove him to the house of a black family on the other side of town; the same arrangement had been made for all the team's black players. (Three years later, the entire club moved to a different, unsegregated hotel in St. Pete.) Earlier, when he was an eighteen-year-old sophomore at Creighton, Gibson and the rest of the college's basketball team had gone to Oklahoma by train for a game against the University of Tulsa, and on the way Gibson was told that he wouldn't be able to eat or sleep with his teammates there. "I cried when I was told that," Gibson said to me. "I wouldn't have gone if I'd known. I wasn't ready for that."

At one point, I said to Gibson that when I had seen him play I had always been very much aware of the fact that he was a black athlete; somehow, his race had always appeared to be a considerable part of what he brought to the mound when he went to work out there.

He didn't respond—he simply said nothing at all—and I understood that my remark was not a question that anyone could easily respond to; it was not a question at all. But a little later he mentioned the many times he had been harassed by semi-official white people—hotel clerks and traffic cops and the like—who later began fawning on him when they learned that he was *the* Bob Gibson, the famous pitcher. "It's nice to get attention and favors," he said, "but I can never forget the fact that if I were an ordinary black person I'd be in the shit-house, like millions of others." He paused a moment, and then added, "I'm happy I'm *not* ordinary, though."

All this was said without surface bitterness or cynicism but with an intensity that went beyond his words. Some days later, Bill White, who is also black, commented on this tone of Gibson's. "He was always so proud," he said to me. "You could see it in his face and in the way he met people and talked to them. He never dropped it. I used to tell him, 'You can't be as tough on people as you are—it hurts you.' And he would say, 'You can do that, take all that, but I can't.' We didn't agree. But, of course, you never know what it's been like for another person. Some people have the ability to forget these things, but Bob Gibson always had the ability to make everybody remember what he had been through."

Gibson and I spent the afternoon at the restaurant, and he and Wendy had me to dinner at their house that night: steaks and mustard greens, prepared by the Gibsons together, and a Cabernet Sauvignon. (He is a demanding, accomplished cook; when he was playing, he invariably got his own meals at home when he returned from road trips and road cooking.) It was our last evening. Bob showed me some of the nineteenth-century American antiques he collects—a delicate bevelled-glass-front walnut secretary, an immense Barbary Coast-style sideboard, and so on—and took me into a basement room where he keeps his HO-gauge model-railroad set: an entire railhead in miniature, with yards and sidings and a downtown terminal, complete with surrounding streets and buildings. He said he didn't use the trains much anymore. The three of us took another swim in the pool, and Bob and I played a little noisy one-o'-cat with Mia in the living room with an old tennis ball. Gibson was relaxed and playful, but, as always, there was a silence about him: an air not of something held back but of a space within him that is not quite filled. At one point, I asked him if he liked Omaha, and he said, "Not all that much. It's all right. It's what I know." Then I asked if he liked the restaurant business, and in the same brusque way he said, "It isn't much, but it sure is better than doing nothing."

I knew that Gibson had had a brief career in sports television with the American Broadcasting Company, shortly after his retirement as a player. He was a "color man" with ABC's "Monday Night Baseball," and on one occasion he conducted an impromptu, nationally televised interview with the Pitts-

burgh Pirates' John Candelaria, just after Candelaria had pitched
a no-hit game. Gibson's questions centered on the future financial rewards of Candelaria's gem, but this insidey banter
between co-professionals was evidently not a line of sports talk
that the network brass approved of, and Gibson's media career
declined after that, although he has since done some baseball
broadcasts with the HBO cable network. It was a disappointment to him.

When Gibson was out of the room for a moment, I said to
Wendy that I sensed something missing or incomplete in Bob,
and she said, "Yes, he's still looking for something, and I don't
know if the right thing for him will ever come along. It's sad."

Last winter, Gibson made inquiries with the Cardinals and
the Royals and the Mets and the Giants in the hope of landing
a job as a pitching coach; interest was expressed, but nothing
quite worked out. One difficulty may be the very modest salaries of big-league coaches, but when I talked to Bob about
his joining some team in this capacity I got the feeling that he
might be willing to make a considerable financial sacrifice in
order to get back into the game. Several of Gibson's old friends
and teammates told me later that they had heard of his wish to
get back into baseball, and without exception they hoped he
would. They said that the game would be better off with a man
of Gibson's character back in uniform. But some of them went
on to express their doubt that he would be satisfied with a job
of such limited rewards as that of a pitching coach. "It won't
be enough for him," one man said. "Nothing will ever be
enough for him now."

"I don't miss pitching," Gibson said to me on that last
evening, "but I can't say that I don't miss the game. I miss it
a *little*. There's a lot I don't want to get back to. I don't want
the fame or the money or all that attention. I always hated all
the waiting around a pitcher has to do. I used to wish I could
press a button the minute I'd finished a game and make the
next four days just disappear. I sure as hell don't miss the
travelling. I think it's the life I miss—all the activity that's
around baseball. I don't miss playing baseball but I
miss . . . baseball. *Baseball*. Does that sound like a crazy man?"

For the first time in our long talks, he seemed a bit uncertain.
He did not sound crazy but only like a man who could no longer
find work or a challenge that was nearly difficult enough to

nurture his extraordinarily demanding inner requirements. Maybe there was no such work, outside of pitching. Baseball is the most individual and the most difficult of all team sports, and the handful of young men who can play it superbly must sense, however glimmeringly, that there will be some long-lasting future payment exacted for the privileges and satisfactions they have won for themselves. Like other team sports, baseball cannot be played in middle age; there is no cheerful, companionable afternoon to the game, as there is for old golfers and tennis players and the like. A lot of ex-ballplayers become sentimental, self-pitying, garrulous bores when they are cut off from the game. Some of them, including some great stars, go to pieces.

Thinking of what Wendy had said, I told Bob Gibson that I was sometimes aware of a sadness in him.

"Sad?" he said uncomprehendingly. "No, I'm not sad. I just think I've been spoiled. When you've been an athlete, there's no place for you to go. You're much harder to please. But where I am right now is where the average person has been all along. I'm like millions of others now, and I'm finding out what that's like. I don't think the ordinary person ever gets to do anything they enjoy nearly as much as I enjoyed playing ball. I haven't found my niche now that that's over—or maybe I have found it and I don't know it. Maybe I'll still find something I like as much as I liked pitching, but I don't know if I will. I sure hope so."

Maybe he will. Athletes illuminate our imagination and raise our hopes for ourselves to such an extent that we often want the best of them to become models for us in every area of life—an unfair and childish expectation. But Bob Gibson is a tough and resolute man, and the unique blend of independence and pride and self-imposed isolation in his character—the distance again—will continue to serve him in the new and even more difficult contest he is engaged in. Those who know him best will look to him for something brilliant and special now, just as they have always done. Even those of us who have not been spoiled by any athletic triumphs of our own and the fulfillment of the wild expectations of our early youth are aware of a humdrum, twilight quality to all of our doings of middle life, however successful they may prove to be. There is a loss of light and ease and early joy, and we look to other exemplars—mentors and philosophers: grown men—to sustain us in that loss. A few athletes, a rare handful, have gone on, once their day out on the field was done, to join that number, and it is possible—the expectation will not quite go away—that Bob Gibson may be among them someday. Nothing he ever does will surprise me.

12

Pluck and Luck

OCTOBER 1980

Begin with the ending. The turbulent, continuously absorbing World Series just past, in which the Phillies overcame the Royals in six games—six *hard* games—still fills the mind with its noises and movements and pleasures, and the rest of this long baseball year should perhaps be put aside for the moment while we give ourselves at once to that finale. Or, in the indelible words of a Peter De Vries hero, foreplay later. Phillies fans, who had slogged through eighty consecutive years of summer warfare without an ultimate victory—fifty-one losing seasons, three humiliating successive defeats in the league-championship eliminations of 1976, 1977, and 1978, and bad beatings in each of their two previous, generations-apart World Series appearances, in 1915 and 1950—will have an understandable impatience with any news but their own just now, and why should we not indulge such hard-won solipsism? The Phillies have won more games in the past five years than any other club in their league, but the combination of their habitual postseason ineptitude and the high salaries and lofty self-regard of many of their star players and talented veterans has sometimes made their clubhouse resemble a private sanatorium for privileged depressives—a place of moneyed calm and secret self-doubt. Over the years, the glumness and abysmal unfellowship of the clinic have been sustained by the patients' openly expressed skepticism about their senior therapists, past and present, and their suspicious stares and silences when visitors are on the floor—which is to say that this Phillies squad has always distrusted its manager and hated the press. The new manager this year, Dallas Green, may have dissipated some of the festering malaise early in August, when he blew up between the games of a doubleheader and blistered the Phillies for their detachment and languid play, and the team's brand-new championship may finish the cure. The Phillies' clubhouse, by the way, has often reminded me of the Red Sox' unhappy home up at Fenway Park, which exudes a similar aura of misanthropy; veteran reporters on both beats have sometimes wondered whether such bad clubhouse vibes were the result of so many annual disappointments or part of their cause.

Phillies fans are typified for me by a friend of mine, a Philadelphia-born editor now in his fifties—a lifelong Phillies invalid, whose sombre, withdrawn visage bears the unmistakable psychic scars of 1964, when his team threw away a sure pennant by dropping ten straight games in late September, and the fainter, pathetic signs of a wasting illness in his boyhood, when his team easily lost more than a hundred games a year for five successive seasons. This man was on his feet at Veterans Stadium, along with a friend and 65,836 other disbelieving partisans, as the sixth game ran down to its last out, and was startled to discover that he felt exactly like the victorious but expiring Lord Nelson at the Battle of Trafalgar. Tug McGraw wound and threw, Willie Wilson swung and missed, and as the last great roar of pleasure split the night sky and the green Astro Turf below was suddenly emptied of baseball and filled, weirdly, with police horses and police attack dogs, my friend, tottering, leaned toward his companion and croaked, "Kiss me, Hardy." I cannot claim such an ancient, passionate, and triumphantly rewarded affiliation (nor will I ever, unless some other famous battle—a Lepanto or a Jutland—should be fought and won some autumn in the Strait of Fenway), but, like a great many other fans, far and near, I was so stirred and pleased by this World Series that a hundred visions and flashes of the games are still in my memory and crowd forward at times, almost unbidden:

Pete Rose, coming up to bat again, pauses for a moment to assess the situation and its possibilities, cocking his head in a succession of alert, robinlike stares and twitches, as he looks out at the pitcher, then at his third-base coach, then at the infielders, then at a teammate leading off first. He steps up and goes into his crouch, peering over the barrel of his bat, while the encircling tiers of Phillies fans pelt him with their cheers: "LetsgoPete! LetsgoPete! LETSGOPETE!" A moment later, he is bucketing down the line, his thick legs churning, and he slaps one hand onto the top of his red batting helmet, holding down his hat like some comedian rounding a street corner in a silent-movie chase, as he leans in and turns the bag. . . . Tug McGraw, again bugled forth to put down some vile disorder, standing at attention on the mound, facing first base and squaring his shoulders like a cadet, and then snapping his head to the "dress right" position to pick up the sign from his catcher; his left arm is at a perfect perpendicular, with the gripped ball in line with the red pants stripe of his uniform—the Steadfast Tin Soldier. ("TUG SAVES" proclaims a fan's banner behind third base in the top deck of the Vet.) . . . Willie Aikens, the young K.C. slugger, collapsing his left leg and dropping his left shoulder down a foot or more as he comes around on a pitch with his big, uppercutting lefty swing—a terrible stroke, really—but making violent contact once again, nailing the ball so hard that it jumps out of view for an instant before your eyes can find its distant new path. . . . Steve Carlton, a tall tower, impassive save for some twitchings around the nose and eyes of his small face, leaning back a bit, tilting his head a fraction, cranking and striding—a seven-league step toward the batter—and delivering a burrowing slider to the lower outer-most rim of the strike zone. . . . Manny Trillo, in short right, receiving and continuing a peg from the outfield to the plate, wheeling in mid-relay with the motion of the arriving ball and then plucking it out of his glove so quickly that you wonder if it touched there at all. . . . The home fans at Royals Stadium, standing up between innings in the lovely autumn-angled sunlight and clapping their hands and waving their blue-and-white paper pompons in time to some thumping, cornball polka from the park organ, in an orgy of wholesomeness and self-congratulation and good cheer. . . . Amos Otis hovering with his back foot just inside the batter's box and his front foot just outside it while he fiddles with his bat, fiddles with his shirt, fiddles with his helmet, fiddles with his batting glove; what he is really fiddling with is the pitcher, of course, who is going bananas out there waiting for him to move up that other foot and get *on* with it, man. The Kansas City locals, eating this up, start their old, quick chant: "A.O.! A.O.! A.-OH!" There has never been a noisier World Series. . . . And, best of all, George Brett batting—a brilliant repeated exhibit of precision and style and success. At the outset, he is far back in the box, with his weight way back as well, so that the spikes of the front (right) foot barely touch the dirt, but he is still in balance, still comfortable up there. The stride begins with the oncoming pitch and moves him swiftly forward and much closer to the plate. His weight is now entirely on the solidly planted front leg, with the foot almost toed inward, and his hands, well extended, lead the bat through its level swing as the hips open smoothly. Now, in mid-swing, his torso is facing center field while his shoulders are still back, parallel to the lines of the batter's box, almost until the moment of contact, which is made with a final, body-opening thrust that brings the back foot completely off the ground as the ball is struck. The follow-through of the bat is extended, pulling Brett's left, top hand off the bat and imparting a casual, almost lackadaisical look to the swing, as if this batter were some father rapping out weekend grounders to his son in the park. The whole swing is so fluid, so easy and elegant, that you must watch Brett bat a few dozen times before you begin to pick up the instant of power and violence in its midst, when the full force of Brett's legs, trunk, shoulders, arms, and fists is wheeling through the fulcrum, and his head, pulled sharply downward, focusses on bat and ball with such concentration that he does not lift his gaze until the bat is behind him and the classic swing completed. Most of the time, I am convinced, George Brett is the last man in the ballpark to see where he has just hit the ball to, and how hard.

The first World Series game is often a sombre, low-scoring sermon on pitching and defense. Not this one, in which the visiting Royals, it will be recalled, quickly ran up a four-run lead at Veterans Stadium and then as quickly fell behind, all in the space of three innings. The Phillies' five-run response was initiated by a modest leadoff single and a wholly unexpected steal of second by shortstop Larry Bowa, and included a pitch taken on the calf by Pete Rose and then a three-run homer by right-fielder Bake McBride. Willie Aikens whacked two homers for Kansas City, the second of which, in the eighth, brought on Tug McGraw, to nail down the 7–6 win. It was the Phillies' fourth straight come-from-behind victory in post-season play this year, and McGraw appeared in all of them. The long, painful marriage between Phillies fans and Phillies players has been a neurotic tangle, which often shows itself in a months-long opprobrious chill and reflexive booing directed at some highly paid resident star or estimable long-term journeyman (Bob Boone and Mike Schmidt were in the doghouse most of last year, and Larry Bowa moved in late this summer), but the line between Tug McGraw and the upper-deck regulars at the Vet is healthy and direct, perhaps because his joy in the game is so evident: the upraised fist after an inning-ending strikeout, the broad-jump off the mound when the last screwball of the day has been fired and the game is put away. "I love the crowd," he said at one point last month. "Whenever I need something extra, I look up and there it is. I keep saying to them, 'Give it to me, give it to me.'" It was the same at Shea Stadium in 1973, when Tug was a Met and his "You Gotta Believe!" (along with his twenty-five saves) helped take that modestly ferocious club all the way to the seventh game of the World Series. Tug, who is thirty-six now, seemed to be throwing with exceptional heart and heat this fall (his regular-season earned-run average of 1.47 was the best of his career), and his appreciation of the dour, self-doubting Phillie-bitten citizenry goes a good deal beyond mere public relations. "I think it takes kind of a second effort to get to know the fans and identify with them, but that's easy for me, because I'm such a fan myself," he told me. "I don't understand the game of baseball as well as a Pete Rose or a Larry Bowa does. The positioning of the players, the strategy, when to put on the hit-and-run—those things have always sort of baffled me, which is why I've never thought about staying in the game once I retire as a player. It's the entertainment and the emotional aspect of baseball that I understand—the whole fun of it."

Phillies fans, who had waited ever since October 8, 1915, for their second victory in a World Series, got their third one in just twenty-four hours, when their club, rallying still again, scored four times in the eighth inning of Game Two and won by 6–4. The Phillies looked resolute and, above all, patient—which is the mark of a tested, senior club—and their ace left-hander, Steve Carlton, gave us a textbook lesson in how to win on an off night. He struggled from the outset, running up high counts on most batters and walking several of them, and sometimes bouncing his best pitch, the slider, in the dirt—the fifty-nine-foot delivery that catchers so detest—but he hung in there, making minute adjustments in his delivery and just skinning out of trouble until the seventh, when three walks led to three runs and put the Royals ahead by 4–2. Carlton's prime weapon on this night was his pickoff motion to first base and its baffling, near-balk variation when he goes to the plate—a tantalizing tilt and sway that he probably learned from Jerry Koosman. Running is a big part of the Royals' attack—they led their league with a hundred and eighty-six stolen bases this year—but their rabbits were so bemused by Carlton's snaky moves that on several occasions Kansas City base runners could be seen ducking back toward first base at the instant that a Carlton pitch was crossing the plate. This time, the Phillies' uprising came against Dan Quisenberry, the Royals' side-wheeling relief specialist, who gave up a ringing pinch-hit double to left by Del Unser and, a moment later, a louder, longer double—the gamer, it turned out—by Mike Schmidt, the Phillies' muscular slugging champion (forty-eight homers this year, forty-five homers last year). Most of this got into the newspapers the next day, amid some amazingly extended medical bulletins, for this was the game when George Brett, sorely afflicted, had to leave the lineup in the sixth inning, and several hundred sportswriters learned, once and for all, how to spell "hemorrhoid."

In Game Three, played on Tartan Turf at Royals Stadium (this was the first All-Carpet Championship of the World), the Phillies rallied not once but thrice, scoring solo runs in the second, fifth, and eighth innings, each time countervailing a K.C. tally and sustaining a tie, which brought the teams into the tenth inning all even at 3–3. Brett, just out of the hospital, had started things off with a sharply pulled homer in the very first inning—an unarguable announcement—and one immediately sensed that the first Series game ever to be played in this enclosure would come out all right for the home folks.

Luck had a hand in it, to be sure, for the visitors stranded fifteen base runners (a record), and in the top of the tenth Schmidt's low line-drive smash flew into the glove of the Royals' second baseman, Frank White, who turned it into a double play. In the bottom half—to a vast, imploring din—the Royals' remarkable switch-hitter and base runner Willie Wilson (he had two hundred and thirty hits this year and seventy-nine stolen bases) got to first on a walk, stole second (beating a pitchout), and flew home when Willie Aikens hit a good, low outside Tug McGraw fastball to left center, where the ball seemed to lift and bend and sail, all on its own, so as to elude the pursuing Garry Maddox, and at last bounced free for an end to the delightful game.

Suspense was given the day off in Game Four, in which the Royals, effulgent in the Saturday sunshine, batted around, and also batted for the cycle, in the very first inning: two singles, two doubles, a screeching triple by Brett, and a homer by Aikens, all good for a paltry (under the circs) four runs. They added another run in the next inning, on another Aikens down-towner (a standing ovation summoned him to the dugout steps each time, where he waggled his upraised cap delightedly), and the margin held up for a 5–3 win that tied the Series. The important event of the day may have been the fourth-inning fastball thrown by a muscular right-handed Phillies reliever named Dickie Noles, which very nearly struck Geroge Brett in the face. Brett flung himself backward at the last instant and then stared out at Noles in disbelief while lying in the dirt in the batter's box. His manager, Jim Frey, put up a fearful ruckus, sprinting onto the field to roar in protest to the umpires and then almost charging Noles on the mound. There was no acting here. The pitch was a knockdown, plain and simple. The score and the count and the batter all made that clear (Brett was batting .500 for the Series at that juncture, and Willie Aikens, who was waiting in the on-deck circle at the time, said later that *he* had been expecting a knockdown, in retaliation for his two homers), but conclusions about the scary business are harder to agree upon. After the game, Frey said that while brushback deliveries were part of the game, blatant intimidation—and possible serious injury to a player—was not. Brett himself, who sees a good deal of such incoming fire in the course of a season, thanks to his batting average and his forward surge

toward the plate when he swings, was unruffled, and the testimony of other bystanders and expert witnesses seemed to
depend on their own professional prejudices: batters, past or
present, expressed a preference for having such a message
arrive in the vicinity of the knees instead of the chin, while
mound people (including Tom Seaver, who was part of the
NBC television team covering the Series) admired it as "a
pitcher's pitch." It should be pointed out that the Royals scored
no runs in the game after Noles's pitch, and that they won no
games after that one, and that Brett hit only three insignificant
singles for the rest of the Series. I don't think that he or his
teammates were intimidated by the knockdown, but I believe
its meaning was sensed and absorbed, perhaps unconsciously,
by both teams. Baseball is a war sometimes.

I don't much admire the much admired Royals Stadium, a
contemporary sports palace so denuded of leaf and lawn that
the gentle sobriquets "field" and "park" are no longer heard
there; it is a "facility," and when it is taken with its adjoining
football facility, Arrowhead Stadium, and their shared parking
prairies it becomes the Harry S Truman Sports Complex—a
peculiar posthumous honor for a President whose sole athletic
interest, to the best of my recollection, consisted of those brisk
morning walks and an occasional dip in the White House pool,
during which latter diversion he always wore his glasses. The
stadium, which is kept so clean that one almost looks for the
"Sanitized" paper wrapper across one's grandstand seat upon
arrival, is famous for its illuminated fountains, which plash
and pulse between innings in a lakelet beyond the right-center-
field fence, but these are far less noticeable than a towering
and epochally ugly gold-crowned scoreboard in dead center,
which rises to a height of twelve stories, dwarfing the playing
surface and its occupants, and is given over to blinding commercials between innings. Like any Holiday Inn, the stadium
appears forever new (it was opened in 1973), and thus without
history—the wrong overtones for a sport so devoutly attached
to its ancestors and its family records. Kansas City is in fact
an old and honorable baseball town, with tribal memories and
histories that run deep in the local fan consciousness. The
present club arrived as a newborn expansion team in 1969,
when the franchise was purchased by Ewing M. Kauffman, a

local pharmaceuticals executive, who is still the Royals' president and All-father; during the seventh-inning stretch at most home games, Mr. and Mrs. Kauffman—or Ewing and Muriel, as everyone thinks of them—come forward in their upper-level enclosed box behind home and wave cheerfully to the multitudes below, who wave back. Kansas City baseball has prospered under the Kauffmans. The Royals have won their divisional pennant in four of the past five years, but they fell before the Yankees in their first three league-championship series (1976, 1977, and 1978) in painful and heartbreaking fashion, twice losing hard-fought playoffs in the ninth inning of the fifth and final game. This year's club, under the management of Jim Frey, who succeeded the long-term incumbent, Whitey Herzog, last fall, dominated its division all year, leading the pack by twenty games at the end of August, and its restorative, almost effortless three-game sweep of the Yankees in the playoffs this fall probably meant more to the players and the fans than any old World Championship. The club, incidentally, drew 2,288,714 fans this year, which was the best attendance-to-local-population ratio achieved by any club in the league. It was not always thus. The previous K.C. team, Charlie Finley's Athletics, arrived from Philadelphia as a shifted franchise in 1955 and never once came close to a respectable season in its thirteen-year incumbency. The renamed A's became a fond, wry local joke (they finished forty-seven and a half games out in 1961, for instance), but there were grim feelings in town when Mr. Finley abruptly folded his tent and took the club to Oakland after the 1967 season—a bitterness that hardened when that team (whose roster included youngsters named Reggie Jackson and Catfish Hunter) grew up into the fearsome three-time World Champion Oakland A's in the early nineteen-seventies.

Much of this midlands cultural history was given to me during a memorable supper of ribs and baseball (and frosty pitchers of draft beer) in the side room of Arthur Bryant's Restaurant, a Tour d'Argent of barbecue, just after Game Four. My friendly companions were Jim and Dana, both faculty members of the University of Kansas; a free-lance writer named Bill; and Jim's seventeen-year-old son, Mike. All these humanists had watched and thought about Kansas City ball throughout their lives, and as they talked and laughed and argued their voices seemed to flow and part and intermingle into a single river, a murmurous Missouri of baseball memories.*

—No, no, the resignation about baseball here started long before those Yankee games. For me, it always began with the fact that St. Louis had the Cardinals and at this end of the state we just had the Blues. Until the A's came, we were always minor-league.

—I think we were more minor-league *after* the A's came. I mean, the Blues were better, weren't they?

—But you have to admit this doomed feeling had a lot to do with losing those playoffs to the Yankees, even though it started before that. It always showed itself in the way the fans began to get down on some player. They'd blame him for everything. There was that anti-Freddie Patek faction here for years. There was an anti-Amos Otis faction. . . .

—Still is!

—Still is. If you go back a little, there was an anti-John Mayberry faction. And then Clint Hurdle came along to take Mayberry's place, and in his first game as a starter he hit that shot that landed in the fountains and bounced right out of the stadium. . . .

—I saw that! I was there that day!

—Of course you were there—we were there together. But then it turned out that Hurdle was still a year away—a year away at least—and so then, of course, you had an anti-Hurdle faction.

—And before that—way back—there was even an anti-Lou Piniella faction, when he was here.

—The *reason* for it—the reason for all the factions, for everybody getting down on so many players—was that the fans just had to protect themselves against losing. Everybody

*These good companions deserve further identification, but only Bill will be asked to step forward here. He is Bill James, a lanky, bearded, thirty-two-year old baseball scholar who writes the invaluable *Baseball Abstract* (Ballantine: $7.95), an annual most notable for its dazzling use of statistics and its original analytical theorems. These include such Jamesean elucidations as Runs Created, the Defensive Efficiency Record, V-IRBI (Victory-Important Runs Batted In), the VAM (Value Approximation Record), and even the HOFPS (Hall of Fame Prediction System).

had to learn not to have such high hopes, see, because that way you don't get your heart broken.

—You don't get your heart broken *so much*.

—Right now, Hal McRae is sort of senior man on the club. He's the most respected by the fans and the most respected by the players. There isn't any anti-McRae faction.

—Well, I don't care. The one I like most is Amos Otis. I *love* Amos Otis.

—So do I.

—Me, too.

—All that great stepping out of the box. But it's on the field where he's so special. That elegance and, uh, *restraint* that make so many people think he really isn't trying out there. He'll get booed for not making some catch or play that he had no chance at all on, but then later in the game, like as not, he'll make a much more difficult catch—an impossible play, you know—and the fans will change their minds and cheer him, and then he'll tip his hat in that *ironic way*.

—Right! Right!

—Oh, I love Amos.

—I think there are three ghosts watching this Series—Mayberry, Whitey Herzog, and Steve Busby.

—And Cookie Rojas.

—Well, O.K., four ghosts. I mean, Busby back when he was going good—the best pitcher we ever saw here. Before he got the fashionable rotator-cuff injury. Busby the dominator, with those two no-hit games.

—Old Steve. The Buzz . . .

—Whitey? Well, he was pretty good at using all his players, but a lot of people faulted him for the way he handled pitchers. And I always thought he played the left-hand, right-hand game kind of mindlessly.

—Well, I'll always remember where I was when he brought in Doug Bird to pitch to Thurman Munson in the eighth inning in '78, when he had Hrabosky all warmed and ready.

—Everybody remembers where they were that afternoon.

—Where I was was in the car, because we were driving to Colorado on a trip. I had the radio on, of course, and when I got the news that it was going to be Bird we were on I-70, just this side of Wa Keeney, and I let out this *groan*, because of course I knew what was coming. [*What was coming was Thur-*

*man Munson's four-hundred-and-twenty-foot home run into the
center-field monuments at Yankee Stadium, which helped win
the 1978 American League championship for the Yankees.*]

—I think the feeling about players here was a lot better back
when we had the Blues. They were always pretty well stocked,
even though we kept losing all those guys when they'd get
called up to the Yankees. The first game I ever saw here,
Rizzuto was playing short for the Blues, and they had Jerry
Priddy and I think Johnny Lindell.

—Do you remember Walt Lochman doing the Blues' road
games over the radio—those re-creations, with the funny fake
game sounds and the telegraph ticker going in the background?
And do you remember going to see the Monarchs play at Municipal Stadium when the Blues were on the road—the Monarchs, of the old Negro League?

—Well, I hate to say it, but you're a little older than I am.
The guys I remember best were the first Athletics team here,
in '55—the first Kansas City A's. Gus Zernial. Elmer Valo.
Jim Finigan—Jim played third base. . . .

—No, no. Jim played second that year, didn't he? And we
forgot Art Ditmar.

—And Arnold Portocarrero.

—[*In chorus*] Arnold Portocarrero! [*The three older men
laugh uproariously.*]

—But listen, when you said Walt Lochman it made me
think of Buddy Blattner. He taught a lot of people around here
about baseball. I mean, he was always on the tube telling
everybody about how you're supposed to hit to the right side
of the infield in order to move up a base runner, and then . . .

—And then Cookie would come up to bat and *do* it!

—Old Cookie . . .

I thought about these friends again and again during the next
afternoon (Jim and Mike were at the game, I knew, sitting out
in short left field), when the Royals and the Phillies played the
best game of this stirring Series, and the Phillies—coming
from behind of course—won in the ninth, 4–3, under excruciating circumstances, and took command of things for good.
A different outcome had seemed very likely in the middle
innings, after Amos Otis made a dazzling running catch of
Larry Bowa's drive to deep left center, and the Royals began

to rock the Phillies' young starter, Marty Bystrom, with solid base hits. A salvo of blows in the sixth, including a low, hurrying leadoff homer by A.O., only added up to a bare 3–2 lead for the home side, however, because the Phillies executed a picture-play relay—right fielder McBride to second baseman Trillo to catcher Boone—to nail the middle runner, Darrell Porter, at the plate and break the back of the rally. By the ninth, it was Quisenberry vs. McGraw again—or, rather, Quisenberry vs. Mike Schmidt, who led off with a single off Brett's glove, a bullet that George knocked down but could not quite retrieve. (Schmidt had homered in the fourth, for the Phillies' first two runs.) Del Unser, pinch-hitting again, doubled just inside first base—an inch or two beyond Aikens' backhand stab at the ball—and the game was tied. Trillo then won it with a sinking, deadly little darter that caromed off the tip of Quisenberry's gloved left hand and the tips of the fingers of his bare right hand and rolled behind him, just too slowly and too far for Brett to make the play at first. Inches each time—to be recalled and remeasured in years to come, I'm sure, by my grieving river chorus of friends. Tug McGraw, in the K.C. half, walked the bases full but also, along the way, fanned Brett on three terrific pitches, survived a shot into the left-field seats by Hal McRae that hooked foul at the last possible instant, and, with everyone in the place screaming and roaring, fanned Jose Cardenal for the last out.

The Phillies, back at home before their own convalescent sufferers, won their World Championship in a 4–1 game that was never quite close, because Steve Carlton, throwing mostly fastballs this time, seemed absolutely in charge of things during his seven-inning tenure. The Royals lost it with two trifling misplays in the third inning—a throw by Frank White that pulled shortstop U. L. Washington a foot or so off the bag in what should have been a force play, and a bunt by Pete Rose that pitcher Rich Gale should have fielded but didn't. Mike Schmidt then delivered the necessary two runs with a brusque single to right. Schmidt has a compact, business-like, microscopically tuned swing—most unusual for a man of such awesome strength—and he meets the ball so solidly and so far in front of the plate that he appears to have ruled out the lucky hit, the nubber or little blooper, as part of his repertoire. He batted .381 in the Series, hitting safely in all six games, and won the Most Valuable Player award. Tug McGraw came in one more time, and again made things interesting by loading the bases in the eighth and ninth, before the tears and the air horns and the riot police (what were they protecting? *Astro Turf?*) and the champagne and the flapdoodle took over. A few conclusions can be ventured. Dallas Green seemed to have handled his pitchers better than Jim Frey handled his, and the Royals, perhaps made overcautious by the weight of the event, never quite showed us the dashing, opportunistic, boyish brand of baseball that had taken them so far this season. For contrasts, there was young Willie Wilson, who somehow lost his good stroke as the games progressed, and ended up fanning twelve times, and thirty-five-year-old Del Unser, who somehow found his at just the right moment, and who has been around long enough to know how big a part chance plays in such matters. Unser, a contemplative man, said of the Series and its ending, "Probably the younger guys don't appreciate how rare this is." Then he smiled and added, "Now I don't know what I want to do when I grow up." There was a lot of talk in the clubhouse and in the newspapers the next day about the Phillies' newfound "character"—a dubious business. Just before the Series began, Pete Rose (he was speaking of the Phillies' terribly close five-game victory over the Astros in the National League playoffs) had said, "I don't know if the fans understand how much luck is involved in these things. You always have to have luck to win, and sometimes the best team is just the luckiest." And Mike Schmidt, in the champagne-soaked clubhouse when the games were over, said, "The only difference between this club and those other Phillies teams that everyone was complaining about for so long is a few key hits. Four or five hits gave us all that character."

The season just past (if we may now reset our clocks to summer time) sometimes seemed overstuffed with melodrama, as if the standings and averages had been taken over by the scriptwriters for "Dallas." George Brett launched a three-month-long assault on the snowcapped pinnacle of a full-season batting average of .400 (last attained by Ted Williams in 1941), sustaining an astounding .500 over twenty-one games in July and batting .460 for the first three weeks of August. He fell just short in the end, possibly because the Royals were out of the pennant race by then (they had won it), or perhaps because from August 17th, when he first broke through the .400 level, until the last days of the season his every move and word and gesture, on the field and off the field, were under scrutiny by hordes of newspaper and magazine reporters, television and radio crews, and assorted promotion people and hangers-on of our celebrity machine—the unwinking, irony-proof, gigantic eye of the Brett Watch. He wound up at .390. . . . Meanwhile, at midseason James Rodney Richard, the six-foot-eight strikeout artist of the Houston Astros, began to complain of a vague weariness and of an odd dead feeling in his pitching arm; when he missed some turns on the mound, he was subjected to extended innuendos and a few open accusations of malingering by the pennant-hungry Houston press, and even by some of his teammates, although he was leading his league at the time, with a 10–4 record and an earned-run average of 1.89. On July 30th, Richard collapsed during a workout at the Astrodome and was taken to the hospital, where it was discovered that he had suffered a stroke. He underwent two operations to remove blood clots, and is expected to recover fully, although it is not known if he will ever pitch again. Whether he should *want* to pitch again is another question. . . . Earlier in the year, the players and the owners had come within hours, or perhaps minutes, of a full-scale players' strike over the issue of compensation for teams losing players to the annual free-agent draft. The strike was averted only after the news came that two or three teams had refused to board the planes that would take them to the cities where they were scheduled to play the following day—the day of the strike deadline previously announced by the Players Association. All spring, most of the owners and front-office people I had talked to assured me that the stars of the game were far too well paid nowadays ever to go out on strike over such a trifling issue; they said this with such assurance (and usually with an accompanying amused half-smile, as if they and I understood reality in such matters) that I almost suppressed my own conviction that the players were entirely serious about their announced refusal to play, because they believed that the owners' team-compensation plan posed such a direct threat to the future of free-agency. The airport unembarkations put a sudden halt to the smiles, it turned out, and the side issues between the two sides were then quickly resolved, while the compensation issue, by mutual consent, was put over for another year—all in time to permit an announcement, at five in the morning, that the season would continue after all. The compensation problem will be studied in the coming twelvemonth by a committee made up of two players (Sal Bando, of the Brewers, and Bob Boone, of the Phillies), two front-office executives (Frank Cashen, of the Mets, and Harry Dalton, of the Brewers), and Marvin Miller and Ray Grebey, who are, of course, the labor negotiators for the players and the owners, respectively. Offhand, I can't think of four baseball men whom I admire more than the new appointees, but since it has yet to be proved that the owners are willing to compromise their position in the team compensation issue in any significant manner, there is still not much that I can see to smile about.

The strike threat, which hovered over the sport for weeks on end, probably cost the leagues another record-breaking season at the gate (the total of 43,014,756 was off by half a million from last year), but there were healthy signs as well: the Yankees played to an all-time-high American League audience of 2,627,417 at the Stadium, and every club in the National League was over a million at the gate, for the first time ever.... Nothing in recent baseball history has been healthier, or more melodramatic, than the late pennant races staged in both divisions of the National League, in which two famous old contenders—the defending World Champion Pirates and the Cincinnati Reds—grudgingly gave way as September waned, leaving the Dodgers and the Astros (in the West) and the Expos and the Phillies (in the East) to have at each other in violent fashion in the final moments of the season. Montreal died at home on the very last weekend, just as it did last year—this time going down before the Phillies, 6–4, in the eleventh inning of the rain-soaked, miserably played, miserably close Saturday game. Out in Los Angeles, the Dodgers, trailing Houston by three games, with three games to play, swept the set, beating the fine Astro pitchers with a thrilling home run each day—by Joe Ferguson on Friday, Steve Garvey on Saturday, and Ron Cey on Sunday—to the accompaniment of the most uproarious and fervent fan noises of this fervent year. By Monday, the Dodger fans seemed yelled out, and no wonder, and their injury-worn, self-exhilarated heroes lost the one-game divisional playoff to the Astro knuckleballer Joe Niekro by 7–1.

It didn't seem likely that the league-championship series between the Astros and the Phillies could be better than that, but it was. Yet our recollections of that extraordinary semifinal, which the Phillies won in five games—the last four of them going to extra innings—should not let us forget the brilliant, combative kind of baseball that the National League had given us all through September. On one evening, for instance, the Expos beat the Cardinals with a three-run pinch-hit homer in the bottom of the ninth, while the Phillies beat the Cubs, 6–5, with a three-run rally in the bottom of the fifteenth. On another, a twenty-one-year-old Montreal rookie named Bill Gullickson struck out eighteen Cubs batters in the course of a 4–2 win, while the Astros, playing at home, beat the Dodgers, 6–5, with a home run in the twelfth inning; the two previous Houston innings had ended with a Dodger outfielder throwing out an Astro base runner (and the winning run) at home plate. Too *much*.

The American League, obdurately persisting with a schedule that does not permit all its divisional teams to play against each other in September, will probably pretend to ignore the Merlin-like foresight of the N.L. chartmaker and its wonderful results. The Royals' runaway in the West would not have been altered in any case, but the league's senior executives ought to be dismayed and embarrassed by the clear evidence that the only riveting series of the entire summer—a wonderful eight-game, home-and-home battle between the first-place Yankees and the onrushing Orioles—was over and done with by August 18th, and the rest of that pennant struggle took place in the reading-room atmosphere of the daily standings, since the clubs did not meet again for the rest of the year. The Yankees, as we know, did not quite give up their foothold (or toehold: it was down to a half-game for a full week in August) on first place, and won by a three-game margin before falling to the Royals in the startlingly short playoff. The Orioles, the defending A.L. champs, cannot quite be dismissed as losers, since their hundred wins were the second-highest record in either league. Their rising star, Eddie Murray, had his best year ever, batting .300, with thirty-two homers and a hundred and sixteen runs batted in, and Steve Stone won more games than any other pitcher this year: twenty-five. The young Oakland A's, under the tutelage of Billy Martin, soared to a second-place finish in the A.L. West, with an 83–79 season, picking up an astounding twenty-nine games in the win column and a half-million new fans at the gate. They had the league's best pitching, perhaps the league's best pitcher in Mike Norris (twenty-two wins and a 2.54 earned-run average), and the league's most electrifying base runner in outfielder Rickey Henderson, whose hundred stolen bases broke Ty Cobb's ancient league mark of ninety-six. The long-rumored sale of the Oakland team came to pass late this summer, when the franchise was acquired by Walter A. Haas, Jr., the chairman of the board of Levi Strauss & Company (the bluejeans people), who seems likely to give the club a larger investment of time and money and energy than it has received from Charlie Finley in recent times. The A's may be even better next year.

The list of losers is far more crowded. Never, it seemed, was there a season of longer falls or more frightfully shattered hopes. The Angels, divisional champions a year ago, played without the services of the injured Don Baylor, Brian Downing, and Dan Ford for most of the going, and without any pitching to speak of (they had allowed Nolan Ryan to depart as a free agent), and finished thirty-one games behind the Royals. The Red Sox, suffering, as always, from shortages of pitching, speed, and imagination, got indifferent (for them) years from Jim Rice and Fred Lynn, and slid gloomily to a fourth-place finish. They now face the necessity of trading some of their expensive long-ball hitters in order to lighten their heavy payroll and their sludgy style of play. Red Sox fans, perhaps worn down by so many years of summer hopes and autumn mopes, turned out in smaller numbers this year. In September, a Bosox addict named Stephen Burke wrote to the Boston *Globe* to announce the formation of Ball-Anon, a local organization of Red Sox "fans or former fans who, thinking that they are experiencing pennant fever, feel a sudden impulse to turn on the game, read about it, talk about it, or to buy or use tickets to actually go see a game. Ball-Anon members will talk on the phone to those afflicted at any hour of the day or night, and will make home visits, if necessary." Other branches, it seems to me, could be opened in Milwaukee, where the muscular, forever-promising Brewers finished seventeen games back, in spite of Ben Oglivie's forty-one homers and Cecil Cooper's .352 batting average and league-leading hundred and twenty-two R.B.I.s; or, for that matter, in Seattle, where the apparently budding Mariners organization fell apart, in the front office and on the field, and the team finished dead last.

In the N.L., the Mets escaped the cellar, but only barely—a terrible disappointment after an amazing midseason burst of energy and good pitching that had brought them to .500 (and to within four games of first place) in late July. The Cardinals, picked by many to take over their division this year, wound up with the best hitting (five of their regulars hit over .300) and the worst pitching in the league, and never came close to contention. The club also fired its general manager and its manager (and let go two replacements); both posts will be filled next year by Whitey Herzog. Six other managers went under during the season or at its close—about average for this occupation, whose survival rate is something like that of an R.F.C. wing commander in the First World War. Among the fallen was the estimable and resilient Don Zimmer, of the Red Sox, who left an office desk on which he had carved over a hundred notches—one for each time he had read or heard about his imminent firing over the past three years. The Serpent's Tooth Watch Fob, awarded each year (starting right now) to the most ungenerous executive in the game, was won hands down by John McMullen, the principal owner of the Houston Astros, who recently fired the Astros' president and general manager, Tal Smith—the man most responsible for building Houston's new divisional champions. Mr. McMullen cited "philosophical differences" as the reason for the deed—possibly a heated Heideggerian debate over Inexplicable Difficulty, which may govern more baseball events than anyone suspects.

Saddest of all—to me and perhaps to a great many other baseball-watchers who recall their rare team fellowship and the splendid quality of their play in the World Series last fall—was the third-place finish of the Pittsburgh Pirates, who lost their field leader, Willie Stargell, to a knee injury (and to age, it must be said: he is thirty-nine) and yearned for the vanished magic touch of reliever Kent Tekulve, who was 8–12 this summer. What hurt them most, surely, was the ingratitude of their bleacher fans, who turned savagely on right fielder and former M.V.P. Dave Parker, pelting him with abuse and hate mail and at times—horrifyingly—with deadly missiles, including a nine-volt electric battery. Parker, as it happened, was playing all summer with a painfully damaged knee, for which he underwent surgery at the end of the season, but the combination of his very high salary and the team's sagging fortunes was apparently unpardonable to some of the Pirate fans—if that is the word for them. The violence and drunkenness of the crowds in many ballparks have lately reached such a point that many of us now hesitate to take children or unwary friends to the games. Few owners and executives have seriously addressed themselves to the problem of assuring the safety and comfort of their more restrained customers, since the appropriate measures of control—including the control of beer sales—might have an adverse effect on attendance. Commissioner Bowie Kuhn habitually talks about the wholesome image of baseball, and recently pointed out that the game is "a family sport appealing to young children, women, mothers, and family groups" (this was in defense of his suspension of pitcher Ferguson Jenkins after his arrest on drug charges in Canada, although Jenkins's case had not, and has not yet, come to court), but I wish Mr. Kuhn would leave his box seat once in a while and take a stroll through the outer grandstands and upper decks of his bailiwick, in the interest of preserving his game instead of its image. The problem is not really beyond solution. Last June, Detroit president and general manager Jim Campbell closed the center-field bleachers at Tiger Stadium for a Tigers-Brewers game, because the fans out there had been so foul-mouthed and had thrown so many things at Brewer outfielders the previous night. He also apologized to the Milwaukee team.

A few peeps of sunlight broke through. One day in Detroit, Baltimore manager Earl Weaver, the Kwazy Pwofessor of the game, wrote in pitcher Steve Stone as his designated hitter, in the No. 6 slot of his batting order, although Stone happened to be in another city observing a Jewish holiday at the time. The next night, Weaver selected Tippy Martinez, who was attending a funeral in Colorado, for the same position. There was method, as always, in Earl's tinkering. In both cases, his d.h. was a straw man, for whom he would pinch-hit, when the time came, with either a right-handed or a left-handed hitter, who would thus not be wasted if the enemy pitcher should have been knocked out instantaneously and a pitcher who threw from the opposite wing brought in in his place. (Think about it.)...Seattle pitcher Rick Honeycutt was suspended for ten days when umps discovered a thumbtack taped to the inside of his glove, on the presumption that it was there not to help him spear line drives but to rough up the surface of the ball and thus add a pretty variety to the flight path of his pitches. This form of cheating is more traditionally accomplished by means of a sharpened point or projection on a pitcher's belt buckle, but Honeycutt was forced to improvise because the Mariners wear those beltless doubleknit jammies when on the field. Bring back the old uniforms!...Oakland shortstop Rob Picciolo, who has evidently decided that getting to first by means of a base on balls gives him an unfair advantage at the plate—he walked three times in 1979, with three hundred and forty-eight at-bats—had no walks at all this year when he came up to bat against White Sox pitcher Richard Dotson on October 2nd. When the count on Picciolo went to 2–0, writers in the press box leaned forward in their seats, in wild surmise, like watchers of the final outs of a potential no-hitter. The count went to 3–0, then to 3–1, and Picciolo, having been flashed the "take" sign, looked unhappily at an eye-high pitch and trotted down to first, where umpire Steve Palermo stopped the game and presented him with the ball....And a first-things-first, early-autumn headline from a newspaper in Philadelphia, just when it was beginning to be noticed that this might be a different kind of year down there after all: "PHILLIES FAN WINS NOBEL PRIZE."

O my Mets! I came back to Shea—came back home, really, after a sensible defection of several summers—when they began to win, or almost win, a lot of games in June, mostly on nerve and pitching and some plain luck. I have a private score-card symbol for an eye hit—two tiny circles under the pencil stroke that indicates a single—and a good many of my Mets scorecards saved from midsummer, I notice, have those beads peeping out from the thickets of some Mets rally. No matter. As I have noted before, runs made out of wormy singles and topped rollers and sacrifices and stolen bases are sometimes more beautiful than a cathedral-high homer, especially if they are happening to the right people, and I recall with particular relish a winning three-run rally against the champion Pirates that was built around an eighty-foot bingle by Lee Mazzilli (and the game then held by some stout pitching by young Ed Glynn, who was once a hotdog vender at Shea); and a 6–5 comeback win over the Dodgers (who had led by 5–0) which was patched together mostly out of four singles—one of them zapped between the legs of the L.A. pitcher—and two providential Dodger errors, and which held up because Neil Allen pitched so beautifully in relief and because Ron Cey, frazzled by the screaming of the Mets sans-culottes, "walked" on a ball-three count, causing the similarly deluded Steve Garvey, on first base, to amble over toward second, where he was tagged out for an embarrassing (hee-haw!) end to an inning. The Mets didn't always win flukily. Mike Jorgensen, brought in as a defensive replacement during the late innings of another game, hit a grand-slam homer in the tenth to beat the Dodgers in a different way. "I haven't seen the fans as excited as this since I played here," manager Joe Torre said one night. "Players used to dread coming here. The wind is blowing, the planes are roaring, and the fans are screaming. I *love* the crowd here."

Me, too. I sat, by choice, out in the farthest left-field grandstand for one Sunday doubleheader against the Pirates, where the fans in my section became a neighborhood of sorts during the six or seven hours we spent together: the beefy, noisy renegade Pirates fan who kept yelling "You're a piece uh *gahbage!*" at each Mets batter, and then yelled "Let's go, Bucs!" when the wrong guys were up there (until a woman across the aisle from him—she was wearing taped-together glasses—told him to make up his own damned cheer); and the white gent in white shoes and plaid pants who suddenly stood up and handed some bills to a Hispanic gent in the row behind him (a bet of some kind), who gave him his Pirates cap in return; and the two black kids just behind me (brothers, I figured) who kept the venders busy all afternoon ("I don't know why you're not spending much," said one. "Hey, man, I'm spending," said the other. "I spent two-fifty. What you spend—something like a dollar thirty-five?"); and the Mets unexpectedly coming from way back to win the first game (yahoo!); and then the long, long between-games parade of fans' banners down the left-field line and up the right-field line (it was Banner Day), with kite banners and balloon banners and bedsheet banners tromping along, with about ten "THE BUCS STOP HERE" messages, and about twenty variations on "STRAWBERRY'S FIELD FOREVER" (the Mets had just signed their No. 1 choice in the rookie draft, a phenom named Darryl Strawberry—*Darryl Strawberry!*), and so on and on, with the banners flapping and wrinkling and tacking in the windy sunshine, and then, at last, the banners going away, thank God, and the players and umps reappearing way off down there around home plate, and the baseball resuming, and all the fans in our section—well, almost all—craning their necks and staring in and yelling "Sweep! Sweep!" and clapping and whistling and carrying on for the Mets, who *didn't* sweep, as it happened, but it was a great day and you can't have everything, can you?

That was in June, and there was more of the same (including one very late night at Shea when the Mets, held hitless until the sixth, when they were down six runs to the Giants, came back to win it, 7–6, in the ninth, with a three-run, two-out homer by Steve Henderson, who had been knocked down by the Giants pitcher with the previous pitch). But all this Mets joy had to be paid for later on, it turned out. Catcher John Stearns broke a finger and was lost for the season, and Doug Flynn, the dandy second baseman, went out with a broken wrist, and Pat Zachry, the skinny, bearded, introverted super-starter, went out with assorted ailments, and the thinly defended, once lucky, once mettlesome Mets began to lose. They lost and lost, at one point dropping twelve straight games and then going two for seventeen, and five for thirty-two—awful, really; almost too hard to bear—and even lost their fans again, there at the end. But now, with the season over, I notice that the memory of that payment, the down side of the sport, has just about disappeared, and that what I remember are the good days and the winning, which is foolish, I suppose, but a good thing, too, for why would we ever go back, any of us, if we remembered only the hard times and felt we had to protect ourselves against them? Let's go, Mets!

A loss of a different kind for me was the famous double series between the Orioles and the Yankees in mid-August, during which the O's swept three games from the Yanks at Yankee Stadium and then, after a three-day interval, won three of five at Memorial Stadium, before huge, jam-packed crowds, to close to within two and a half games of the leaders. I was out of town—out of both towns—and missed the whole wonderful business, but so many friends told me about the games later on and insisted on my listening to each riveting moment that I have almost begun to think I actually *did* see Steve Stone's two-hitter; and Willie Randolph's first-inning, first-pitch homer against Mike Flanagan, which was matched by Al Bumbry's leadoff homer against Tommy John in the bottom of the same inning; and Bumbry's catch against Reggie at the fence in New York; and Ruppert Jones's heartstopping leap and grab at the fence in Baltimore to pull back Eddie Murray's shot; and Reggie's catch against Doug DeCinces and his frightening full-tilt crash into the bullpen gate; and much more, I suppose. Until their sudden October expungement, the Yankees had a vivid and rewarding summer. Reggie Jackson, who is thirty-four now, seemed to make peace with himself this year (and worked out a truce of sorts with the demanding Bronx bleacher fans), winding up with a .300 average, forty-one homers (tying him with Ben Oglivie at the top of the league), and a hundred and eleven runs batted in—his best season, all in all, since his M.V.P. summer of 1973. I admired him most during the second half of the year, when he kept his poise despite the very few decent pitches he was given to swing at (Graig Nettles was ill, and the loss of his bat in the lineup allowed enemy pitchers to work around Jackson), and then suffered through a debilitating slump in mid-September. Reggie has slightly altered his batting stroke and now stands a bit farther away from the plate than he used to; when the count goes to two strikes against him, he abandons that awesome, flailing hack at the ball and goes the other way or up the middle, sensibly settling for singles or sliced doubles. (All this, by the way, owes a good deal to the tutelage of Yankee batting coach Charley Lau, who was also the main architect of George Brett's lovely stroke.) It was this shortened, flatter swing that allowed Reggie to fight his way out of his slump and finish the season with a shower of hits and homers. I also felt great admiration for Dick Howser, the Yankees' astute, low-key freshman manager,*who kept calm when his squad seemed on the point of collapse in mid-August,

---

Too low-key for Mr. Steinbrenner, who removed Howser from the helm in the off-season, after the expungement of the Yankees in the A.L. play-offs.

and got it winning again in spite of some chronic pitching problems, outfield defensive problems (after center fielder Ruppert Jones went out for good), and owner problems. Not everyone seemed to notice that the Yankees won eighteen of twenty games between August 26th and September 18th, which is why they were able to stave off another typical late-season cavalry charge by the Orioles. Howser's use of his great bullpen star, Rich Gossage, seems a model of managerial restraint. He brought him in mostly for bite-size, one-inning or two-inning chunks, which is why the Goose—fearsomely rearing and thrashing out there, with his face sometimes seeming to disappear altogether between those hulking shoulders and the pulled-down cap—stayed so strong and was able to run off such formidable numbers this year: thirty-three saves, one run surrendered in nineteen games, twenty-eight consecutive batters retired, and so on. Some of the Yankee and Red Sox players may still be talking about the night up at Fenway Park when, with the bases loaded, the Goose struck out Tony Perez on three straight meteorlike fastballs, each of which seemed to flame past the veteran righty slugger just before he could touch off the synapses of his swing: "Yes! Now!...*Damn!*"

I suspect that George Steinbrenner is widely disliked by Yankee fans for his meddling in the day-to-day operations of his club—most of all when he subjects lesser members of the Yankee cast to his bullying public tongue-lashings for their deficiencies at the plate or on the field. This execrable habit probably should not distract us from a proper appreciation of Mr. Steinbrenner's baseball acumen—most of all, his eager and astute player trades and purchases. This year's winners would never have come close had it not been for Steinbrenner's off-season moves last year, when he picked up outfielder Ruppert Jones, pitchers Tom Underwood and Rudy May (who would have guessed that the Yankees would need more *pitching* this year?), first baseman-d.h. Bob Watson, and catcher Rick Cerone, who all played considerable roles in the Yankees' divisional championship.* Watson batted .307, and May, a much traded veteran southpaw, led the league with an earned-run average of 2.46, but Cerone was probably the most useful

---

*Steinbrenner did just as well or better in 1981, when he traded for Jerry Mumphrey, Larry Milbourne, and Rick Reuschel.

pickup of them all. A mobile, durable receiver, he batted close to .300 for the last two-thirds of the season and delighted Stadium fans with his combustible ways at the plate. On three occasions in one game against Detroit back in May, Tiger skipper Sparky Anderson ordered a Yankee batter walked in order to bring the supposedly weaker Cerone up to the plate, and Cerone responded with two singles and a grand-slam homer. To return to George Steinbrenner for a moment, it seems curious to me that his eagerness to win should often reach such proportions that he apparently expects to control the outcome of every Yankee game through the imposition of his will on his employees, because this, of course, is precisely what one can't do, in baseball or in any other sport, once the play begins. What makes any hard-fought, well-played game so attractive and interesting is the perfect unpredictability of the outcome when a player is up at the plate or out on the pitcher's mound, alone before the crowd and entirely in charge of his own fortunes—exactly the opposite situation and view of things that we have about our own jobs and most of the rest of our lives. But Mr. Steinbrenner doesn't appear to find any pleasure in that moment; in fact, he can hardly bear it when his carefully selected, highly paid athletes actually have to go out there and play, and he and they and all the rest of us must wait to find out what will happen. I think he's in the wrong line of work.

No one took charge of his team's fortunes more suddenly or more decisively in this baseball year than George Brett, with his enormous, first-pitch, three-run homer into the top right-field tier at Yankee Stadium in the third game of the American League playoffs. The blow was so swift, so loud (the explosion of his bat as it collided with a Rich Gossage fastball could be heard in every corner of the great yard), and so terminal in its results and meanings that even before the ball had disappeared among the high-perched rows of fans out there I could hear people all around me in the lower grandstand uttering the same strange cry that I, rising and craning, halfway out of my seat, was uttering myself: "That's *it!*" The Royals, to be sure, were already two games up in this championship series, having beaten Ron Guidry and Rudy May on successive days in Kansas City, but the Yankees were ahead in this game, 2–1, with two gone in the top of the seventh, and when Gossage took the mound in relief of Tommy John (Willie Wilson had just doubled) there was good reason to believe that the Yankees might struggle out of their difficulties and once again break the hearts of the upstart Westerners. The next batter, U. L. Washington, the Kansas City shortstop, was the out that Gossage and Dick Howser badly wanted at this juncture, and when he beat out a short infield bouncer over the mound—barely beat it out— one suddenly became aware of all the possibilities and overtones of Gossage vs. Brett, who was now stepping up to bat. *Started* to become aware of them, I should say, because the whole thing was over in a twinkling: the pitch, the swing, the noise, the cries and groans, the playoffs, and the Yankees (who did, to be sure, load the bases in the eighth before Cerone lined into a sudden double play). Going down the Stadium ramps, and later in the subway, I heard no one among the murmurous, disappointed, now baseball-deprived Yankee rooters—that tough, insatiable critical mass—say anything angry or bitter about the outcome; a lot of them, in fact, were saying, "Well, it was their turn," or something like that. I think all of us felt a thrilling satisfaction, even in the midst of our gloom, over the way it happened—how one man, with one swing, had changed so many things. None of us had ever done such a thing in our own lives—not even George Steinbrenner.

No such vivid termination and release was given to anyone during the five-game Astros-Phillies playoffs, which, from first to last, were so close and tense and tiring, so filled with adventure and accident and emotion, that one longed at times for something like Brett's clarifying bang. Any one of the four concluding, extra-inning games was almost good enough to be placed alongside such Louvre pieces as Game Six of the 1975 Reds—Red Sox World Series or the 1978 Red Sox–Yankees one-game divisional playoff, and yet there were such varieties of style and structure among them—the accruing tension and austerity of ten classic innings of double-shutout ball in Game Three; the mistakes and disputations and slapstick amazements of Game Four (baseball of the High Baroque, surely); and the grim attrition and sadness (because one of the two teams now had to give way in the end) of the finale, in which the score was retied or reversed five times before the Phillies won it in the tenth—that none of them can properly stand for the whole.

Recapitulation is beyond me, but there were some secondary shifts and discoveries that come to mind. Even though the Astros lost, after suffering a succession of disabling injuries to some of their regulars, these playoffs were a means of introducing most of us to a whole squad of interesting and capable players who have been mostly unknown to fans outside their own region. I had paid a brief visit to the Astrodome for an Astros-Reds series a couple of weeks before the end of the season, and I was struck by the modest, approachable character of the Astro players and the old-fashioned virtues of their light-hitting, stout-pitching brand of ball—a team character that is summed up in the person of Bill Virdon, a skipper in steel-rimmed spectacles, who reminds one of a small-town high-school math teacher who doubles as coach of the volleyball team. Astro stars like Joe Morgan and Nolan Ryan and Cesar Cedeno are not exactly strangers to the national baseball scene, but outfielder Jose Cruz (an exceptional athlete, who has sustained a .300 batting average for the past five years), and young Terry Puhl, and the gawky-looking, bald thirty-three-year-old first baseman Art Howe (who came into baseball late and almost by accident after starting a career as a computer programmer with Westinghouse) are newer friends, whose fortunes we will now follow and care about in the seasons just ahead. I was most pleased and startled by the work of Vern Ruhle, a pitcher who had been discarded some years ago by the Tigers because of a sore arm, and who came on valiantly for the Astros this summer after the club suffered the loss of James Rodney Richard. I saw Ruhle throw a masterly four-hit shutout against the Reds, not only beating Tom Seaver in a game of real significance to both sides but swiftly dismissing each of those dangerous Cincinnati batters with a handful of pitches—sinkers and sliders—throughout the evening. "My philosophy is that the hitter is either on or out in three pitches," he said afterward. Many of the Astros seemed to have a fondness for a self-depreciating line of talk ("I like to think we've shown a little perseverance," said Art Howe. "We can move through airports kind of quietly," said reliever Joe Sambito) that reflected a cheerful awareness of their own low profile. Everything about the Astros is a little odd, a little different, starting with their home park and certainly including their audience. The Astrodome no longer strikes me as quite such an outlandish envelope for baseball as it first did, and for some reason the lofty, windless chamber seemed smaller than on my previous visits. It still conveys an odd sense of containing its own weather— the aqueous, twilight silence of a summer lakeside cottage just before a thunderstorm. That eerie light and air confer a perpetual advantage on the home team's pitchers and fielders (two of the games I saw turned on uncharacteristic mistakes by the Reds' outfielders), and since no one can hit the ball very far through the stilly, contained sky of the Dome, the place also rewards the Astro lineup of punch hitters and their one-base-at-a-time attack.

The Astros drew good crowds this summer, but almost until the end their fans were a mannerly, gently involved bunch, who seemed to have trouble understanding that their team was now being followed and watched and talked about by baseball people everywhere. The Astros and their fans have always thought of themselves as a little band of baseball warriors encamped deep in football country, for the team that Houston really cares about is the Oilers, of the National Football League; even in midsummer the Houston Airport souvenir shops carry vast stocks of pale-blue Oiler mugs and Oiler T-shirts and Oiler light bulbs and "LUV YA BLUE!" Oiler banners, and almost no tangerine-colored Astrojunk. The sizable late-season crowds at the games I saw kept up a hopeful cheering and cajoling, but on my last day in Houston I was puzzled by sudden little bursts of noise and spatters of applause that had no connection with the action on the field. Then I remembered that it was Sunday, and I understood: everyone was following the Oilers, too— they were playing the Bengals on the road—by means of radios and portable TV sets they had brought to the baseball game. But all that may be over now. At some point in the midst of the last three wonderful Astros-Phillies games at the Astrodome (I saw these at home, on television, since I had opted for the Yankees-Royals series at the Stadium), I was suddenly convinced that the older, quieter game had at last taken root in South Texas for good. Maybe it happened in Game Four, whose four hours of horrors and heroics and never-saw-it-before vicissitudes—runners tagging up to leave a base before the catch or forgetting to tag up at all; two or three abysmal calls by the umpires; a squirting, comically misthrown peg from the outfield that was still converted into a key out; a triple play that was debated for twenty minutes by the six umps and league president Chub Feeney and then declared a double play; and also some splendidly aggressive play and courageous pitching and a lot of timely big hits—seemed designed to provide the wildly excited and roaring Astro rooters ("HOUS-TON...AS-TROS!" they cried again and again, in thunderous chorus) with an entire lifetime of baseball varieties and possibilities, all in a single evening. If such a shift of attachments and passions did come to pass, then those same fans may have concluded on the next evening—as I did during that last, long test of courage and luck and will—that sometimes the game can hold us too closely, when its unique events and their attendant hopes and anxieties so seize us and wear us down that we almost wish ourselves free of such exorbitant pleasures.

Let's end with something lighter, then—perhaps a weekend swatch of games I saw in Baltimore early in September, when Billy Martin's rising, nothing-to-lose Oakland A's took the measure of the older, deeper, better Orioles in three out of four games, beating them in almost every department of the game, and (it turned out later) just about ruining the Orioles' pennant hopes for the year. I had come down to root for the Orioles, who are longtime favorites of mine, but the dash and zest and impetuous optimism of the young Green-and-Yellows turned me around in no time. Oakland's leadoff man, Rickey Henderson, stole six bases over the four games, while its second batter, Dwayne Murphy, went eight for fourteen at the plate—a partnership that helped the A's score in the first inning of each game—and their teammates chipped in with a passel of bunts and stolen bases and sacrifices that flustered the Baltimore Old Guardsmen no end. Henderson leading off first base is a sketch—a perfect image of skulking thievishness. With his head hunched between his shoulders, his body bent almost double, his legs oddly splayed and knock-kneed, and his fingertips just touching the tops of his knees, he looks like Sylvester Pussycat about to pluck Tweety out of his birdbath. I was similarly entertained by pitcher Mike Norris's hot-dog mannerisms on the field—his stiff-backed, duck-footed saunterings around the mound while he rubbed up the ball and coolly eyed the crowd, and then the pitch delivered, right-handed, with an unorthodox upright, three-part, over-the-top (mostly) motion that finishes with his right leg kicking up behind him, and the ball, much of the time, flicking the wrong way as it crosses the plate: screwball. Norris has a great variety of outstanding pitches: two speeds on his fastball (a "two-seamer" and a "four-seamer" in mound parlance), two speeds on his curve, a change-up, possibly a spitball (or so say a great many indignant American League batters, who claim that Oakland coach Art Fowler has taught most of the A's young staff how to throw the slinking, illegal, wonderfully useful pitch), and the excellent screwball—a pitch he learned years ago from Juan Marichal when the Giants' ace, looking for a place to work out during a spring baseball strike, turned up at San Francisco's Balboa High School diamond, where Norris was a fifteen-year-old star pitcher on the team. In the Friday game, Norris had given up one hit to the Orioles over seven innings when Billy Martin determined to rest his young ace, and entrusted the 5–2 Oakland lead to his bullpen—a mistake, it turned out, because the A's *have* no bullpen to speak of (and not much of an infield, either, if truth be told). The Orioles scored three runs in the eighth inning and three more in the ninth, to win it, 8–7, and Martin, who *hates* to lose—cannot bear it—stormed into his clubhouse and threw over the food table. The appalling welter of scattered cold cuts, far-flung beans, strewn fruit salad, and broken ketchup bottles, and the grieving, hungry faces of the young Oakland players presented a Cruikshank tableau out of *Oliver Twist*. Poor form, I concluded, and bad leadership, too—but I was wrong, it seems, because the next night the team whipped Jim Palmer, 3–2, in a terrific duel, won by the bald, bearded, resolute right-hander Rick Langford, who pitched his twenty-fourth complete game of the year (No bullpen, see?) All three of the Oakland outfielders—Henderson, Murphy, and Tony Armas—have superior arms, and the game ended with a sensational peg from the deep-left-field corner by Henderson that cut down Benny Ayala (who had just hit a single and was impetuously trying to stretch it into a double) at second—got him by yards. When Martin came back to the clubhouse, he found six or seven of his players standing guard in front of the restocked food table with their arms folded and mock-serious glares on their faces: Not tonight, Billy!

On the next afternoon—a dazzling, cool late-summer Sunday—Mike Norris, resplendent in a three-piece tan suit, narrow tie, and pink boutonnière, sat in the press box eating ice cream and watching his teammates while they took on the league's leading pitcher, Steve Stone, and rapped him for three first-inning runs, in a game that they won by 5–2. Norris had been given the day off by Billy Martin, perhaps as balm for his disappointment over his cruelly lost Friday victory. Norris is a thin, striking-looking young man, with long fingers and a small mustache and a gentle, lighthearted way of talking. He had taken that sudden hard turn of events with great composure, I had noticed, and he told me now that he had endured some other difficult times this year, including a pair of back-to-back 1–0 losses in May and an exhausting game against these same Orioles that he had won only after pitching fourteen full innings. Hardly anyone knows more about the vagaries of baseball fortune than Norris, who threw a shutout in his very first major-league start, at the age of twenty, but later underwent arm surgery and returned to the minors three times while struggling to regain his strength and form. Just two years ago, he suffered a 2–6 season with a Class AA team in Jersey City, and his tatterdemalion major-league record at the beginning of this season was 12–25. Now, taking his ease in the Memorial Stadium press box in September, he stood at 18–8 and 2.31 for the season, with a very good chance at the Cy Young Award as the best pitcher in the American League. (As it turned out, he finished just behind Steve Stone in that post-season balloting.) Luck and character and Billy Martin (and pitching coach Art Fowler) had all had a hand in Norris's sunstruck summer, but I found the whole thing a little hard to believe just the same.

Down on the field, Tony Armas walked to start off the A's fourth, and Wayne Gross stroked a hit past first base and tried to turn it into a double; the throw from right field had him dead to rights, but Gross flew into shortstop Kiko Garcia with a fiery slide and body block and kicked the ball a good thirty feet away, while Armas scored. Jeff Newman beat out a nifty speed bunt to the third-base side of the mound, moving Gross to third, and Dave McKay instantly scored him with a bunt— the team's fourteenth successful suicide squeeze of the year. Then Rob Picciolo bunted safely, too. By this time, Mike Norris and I and everyone else in the press box—even the Baltimore writers—were laughing and exclaiming and shaking our heads over this wonderful outburst of Billy-Ball and the discomfiture of Steve Stone and the helplessness of the Orioles and the frustration of Earl Weaver and the joy of the Oakland players, who, of course, were jumping around in their dugout and slapping palms in the air and having the time of their lives. Baseball is hard, as I have been saying here, but there are days when it yields a little to good luck and good play, and suddenly seems almost easy. It becomes a game again, instead of a business or a war or a test of character, and for once we can smile and simply enjoy it.

One Hard Way to Make a Living

APRIL 1981

THE FLAGS ARE RUN UP, THE PLAYERS ARE ON THE FIELD. THE early standings shift ridiculously from morning to morning in the papers, April weather is already messing up some pitching rotations, the first feats and shocks of the season appear in the late-night news and the next day's box scores—the four authoritative victories (three of them shutouts)* thrown by the Dodgers' portly twenty-year-old rookie southpaw, Fernando Valenzuela; the Oakland A's' record-breaking bolt from the starting gate with eleven straight wins—and hope and attention stir again like seedlings in the south-facing beds of the mind. Baseball has begun, and surely we should all feel better because of that. I feel terrible. Maybe it's all those new names in the lineups—or, rather, the appearance of so many old names with the wrong teams, after a winter of expensive and frantic buying and trading in the player market. Maybe it's the distraction of the price tags and business squabbles and owners' statements and press releases that are now attached—in this fan's mind, at least—to so many stars and teams, and even to the simplest and most cheerful scraps of early baseball news. It's not quite

---

* Valenzuela won eight in a row, with five shutouts, before his first defeat.

right, for instance, to say that baseball has begun again. It has begun for the present, but it may stop again on May 29th, when the Major League Players' Association has voted to halt play unless the issue of compensation for teams losing players to free-agency is resolved between the players and the owners. This is the same disagreement that brought the sport within hours of a full-scale strike last May, and a year of subsequent study and discussion by groups representing the two sides has carried the matter no closer to resolution. The details and sub-strategies of the difference, which centers on the idea (and definition) of a "prime player," whose loss to free-agency would require the team that signed him to dispatch one of its own players to the roster of his old club, will not be reëxplicated here, but the deeper causes of the conflict are easy to perceive. The owners wish the players to agree to some plan that would curb the owners' own unbridled extravagance in bidding for free-agent players. The players, for their part, claim that the owners' compensation proposal would effectively put an end to free-agency (by punishing each owner who acquires a player through free-agency with the instant loss of another player already on his team), which has been responsible for increasing the average major-league salary from forty-six thousand dollars in 1975 to one hundred and forty-three thousand dollars last year. "But that's too much money!" cry the owners. "Some of the new salaries are insane! Some owners will do *anything* to buy a pennant. Only the rich clubs can play this game now, and the rest of us are going broke. Help!" To this the players reply, "How much is 'too much,' anyway? Who started these big salaries? You did. Wouldn't *you* take all that loot if it was offered to you? Why should we punish our teammates who are going to be the next free agents by agreeing to solve your problem? Go talk to George Steinbrenner—or throw a net over him."

The players may be right in all this, but neither side, I realize, now has my sympathy, or even much of my interest. The compensation dispute does not appear to be beyond compromise, but the inflation and devaluation of the game may be beyond control. I have no idea whether there will be a strike, but if one comes I don't think the fans will easily forgive either party, or perhaps ever feel the same about the old game, which is *their* game, after all, and not just a lucrative occupation for a few hundred athletes or an investment and tax dodge and plaything for a couple of dozen millionaires. I think baseball is in bad trouble.

Most of all, I guess, it's the money that's got me down. For several summers now, I have carefully reminded myself that the irony of our laying out hundreds of thousands of dollars in salary for a fireballing young relief pitcher or an indomitable veteran switchhitter but only a small fraction of such sums for a first-class teacher or a promising poet or pathologist says a good deal about our society but can't quite be blamed on baseball itself. In much the same fashion, I have argued, reasonably or heatedly, with friends of mine who claimed that today's players just aren't good enough, at the plate or on the mound, to deserve such gargantuan rewards. ("That's not the point!" I have said. "It's the *market* that sets those prices.") But now I have been silenced. That market keeps going up, and the top salary figures, whatever their explanation, are beyond ignoring and beyond rational defense, for they deform and shame the sport.

Last winter, George Steinbrenner, the owner of the Yankees, signed Dave Winfield, a free-agent outfielder lately of the San Diego Padres, to a ten-year contract that will bring him a million and a half dollars per year, and may total more than twenty million dollars by the end of that period, thanks to various deferrals and subclauses. Winfield thus steps into the cleanup slot on the 1981 All-Star Money Team that I drew up one evening during spring training, with expert advice from Peter Gammons, of the Boston *Globe*. The players we chose were picked by the value of their current contracts, position by position; the figures are careful estimates of their annual salaries, subject to some uncertainties of information about the details of the contracts:

1B:	Eddie Murray (Orioles)	$1,000,000
2B:	Rennie Stennett (Giants)	600,000
3B:	George Brett (Royals)	1,300,000
SS:	Rick Burleson (Angels)	767,000
C:	Ted Simmons (Brewers)	820,000
OF:	Dave Winfield (Yankees)	1,500,000
OF:	Fred Lynn (Angels)	1,300,000

OF:	Dave Parker (Pirates)	1,000,000
	or	
	Andre Dawson (Expos)	1,000,000
DH or Utility:		
	Rod Carew (Angels)	900,000
	Pete Rose (Phillies)	800,000
	Garry Maddox (Phillies)	800,000
	Gary Matthews (Phillies)	800,000
	George Foster (Reds)	700,000
P:	Nolan Ryan (Astros)	1,170,000
	J. R. Richard (Astros)	1,000,000
	Phil Niekro (Braves)	1,000,000
	Joe Niekro (Astros)	900,000
	Don Sutton (Astros)	900,000
	Bruce Sutter (Cardinals)	800,000

This lineup is less stable than any in baseball, for the owners and the players' agents now engage in year-round bargaining and renegotiation which will continue to produce fresh rookies and restore old stars for the Mammons. Sometime this summer, Reggie Jackson and George Steinbrenner will, in all likelihood, come to terms over a new contract that will put Reggie out ahead of his teammate Dave Winfield as the best-paid player in the game (unless Mike Schmidt gets there first), and the autumn free-agent class of 1981 may include Ken Griffey, Bill Madlock, and Mike Norris. Conversely, some of the best-paid players of the past half decade have become benchwarmers on this squad; just three years ago, Pete Rose's $800,000 topped every other salary in the game, but he gave way, in turn, to Parker, who was then pushed aside by Ryan, and so on. A similar lineup of player plutocrats set forth in these pages only four years ago* was topped by Reggie Jackson and his five-hundred-and-eighty-thousand-dollar salary, and it included five players who were manfully struggling along at about three hundred thousand dollars per year. It averaged $346,562 per man, as against this year's All-Star Money average of $952,850.

Two more salary figures for this season seem significant: the six hundred thousand dollars awarded to Tiger outfielder

* See pages 11 and 12.

Steve Kemp by the process of salary arbitration, and the seven hundred thousand dollars offered by the Braves' flamboyant owner, Ted Turner, to Claudell Washington, a free-agent outfielder who batted .278 while playing for the White Sox and the Mets last summer. Salary arbitration was once considered a routine apparatus for adjudicating wage differences between a club and a player who had no wish to jump ship but felt himself undervalued; its unique feature is a clause that requires the arbitrator to award either the club's offer or the player's demand but nothing in between. Last year, however, an arbitrator (the arbitrators are professional labor consultants, often with no baseball background or expertise) astounded the Chicago Cubs by awarding seven hundred thousand dollars to their ace relief pitcher, Bruce Sutter. This, when taken with Kemp's arbitrated six hundred thousand dollars this year, suggested that the arbitrators are now counting free agents' salaries as a fair basis for comparison when making their decisions—a development that no owner and no player had ever foreseen, and one that may inflate the basic pay scale of the game far more than free-agency itself. Ninety-eight players put in for preliminary salary arbitration last winter.

Claudell Washington's new salary of seven hundred thousand dollars tells us once again that the skills of a free-agent player have very little to do with what a fast-spending and ambitious owner may be willing to pay him. Washington had played for four previous teams during his seven-year stint in the majors, compiling a lifetime average of .280 and a total of fifty-seven home runs. Similarly modest credentials have not hampered other free agents, who have occasionally seemed to embody a shimmering, holy vision vouchsafed to some prayerful and ambitious owner—a vision of the one true star player needed to fill out a fragile pitching staff or plug a leaky infield. Stennett, the second baseman on my 1981 Gold Sox, is no longer a full-timer with the Giants, whom he joined as a free agent after the 1979 season; he has batted .275 and has struck forty homers during his nine-year career, and has yet to show much fondness for executing the pivot at his bag in the midst of a close double play. Claudell Washington's new contract with the Braves was cited by R. R. M. (Ruly) Carpenter III, the president of the World Champion Phillies, as a prime factor in the Carpenter family's decision, announced a few weeks ago, to put their club on the market. The Carpenters are dedicated baseball people who worked for thirty-seven years to bring home their present championship, but they are getting out of the game because of "deeply ingrained philosophical differences" between them and "some of the other owners as to how the baseball business should be conducted." Ruly Carpenter also said, "I don't blame the players. It's just that a few of my peers don't think the same way I do." Mr. Carpenter's peers include nine owners who have acquired major-league clubs within the past five years—more than one-third of all the teams, that is—and while some of the new executives (Edward Bennett Williams, of the Orioles, for instance, and Roy Eisenhardt, of the A's) seem to represent a rare infusion of intelligence and business acumen into the game, the departure from the field of old baseball gentry like the Carpenters is an ominous sign indeed.

The fans, I think, have their own reasons for depression. Many lifelong loyalists have begun to understand that imbalances of financing and demographics make it more and more unlikely that their particular club will be able to compete on even terms with gold-platers like the Yankees, the Dodgers, the Angels, the Phillies, and the Astros. This spring, someone noticed that the sum of the salaries paid by the 1981 Astros to only five of their pitchers (Nolan Ryan, J. R. Richard, Don Sutton, Joe Niekro, and Joe Sambito) exceeded the entire team salaries paid by eighteen major-league clubs last year. It is true that careful free-agent purchases, patient player development, canny trades, and enlightened salary negotiations can still produce winners in limited-market areas, as the Orioles and the Kansas City Royals have demonstrated in the past five years (the Baltimore team re-signed virtually all its young stars to multi-year contracts last winter), but front-office brilliance is rarer in baseball than the triple play. More often, it happens that long-term contenders suddenly take on the appearance of dying brontosaurs, drooping with the weight of their bloated payrolls. Last winter, the Red Sox appalled their pain-gnarled rooters when they traded away Rick Burleson and Freddie Lynn, the best shortstop and the best center fielder in the American League, and then distractedly lost their splendid catcher Carlton

Fisk to free-agency through a front-office blunder. The losses were explained or defended in various ways, but they were in fact the result of the club's unwillingness or inability to pay the sums that all three stars could have been awarded this spring by salary arbitration. The Red Sox have entered the Ice Age.

Fans in the park, at a game, may feel a deeper malaise. Dave Winfield is six feet six inches tall and weighs two hundred and twenty pounds, but each time he steps up to bat this year he will be virtually invisible. Watching him, many of us will be unable to keep from thinking, There's a million and a half bucks up at the plate! As the count progresses, we may even do a little figuring ("A million five divided by a hundred and sixty-two—well, make that a hundred and fifty, because it's easier and probably he won't play every day . . ."), and then we'll suddenly think, My God, this man is pulling down ten thousand dollars per game. Winfield hits with power (twenty homers last year, thirty-four the year before that), and he has a strong arm and runs the bases exceptionally well, but none of this will matter much now. The team and the pitcher that Winfield is facing will have lost their interest and excitement, for what the man is batting against this season is a million and a half dollars. He can't succeed out there—who could bat or field or run well enough, or hit enough homers, to earn that much money? Babe Ruth? Ty Cobb?—but that no longer matters, either, because Dave Winfield is no longer a ballplayer but a celebrity.* We have lost him, and we will lose more and more like him, as the subtle, ancient bonds of imagination and appreciation and expert knowledge that have connected each true fan to each player of this beautiful and difficult sport

---

* Winfield played with such dash and spirit in his first season with the Yankees—batting .294 and running the bases elegantly and making those off-the-wall-and-into-the-stands leaping catches in left field—that, contrary to these premonitions of mine, he often did make us forget about his salary. He fell into a severe batting slump at the end of the year, however, batting .154 in the League Championship Series and .045 (one hit in twenty-two at-bats) in the World Series, and one heard disparaging and cynical remarks on all sides about his enormous wages. Contemporary stars can run away from the spectre of their money, it seems, but if they pause or falter even for an instant it will catch up with them again.

become frayed or severed by distraction and greed. It is no wonder that ballpark crowds are so angry these days, and so often drunk and violent. The ballplayers we come to see are no longer close to us, no longer part of our team or, by that psychic extension that gives all sport its meaning, part of us. They are entertainers, and the game is just another hyped, grossly expensive show, guaranteed to gain our initial attention and our ultimate boredom and self-loathing. About half of all the ballgames played are not especially close or interesting; about a quarter of them—half of that half—are truly tedious. Fans know these ratios and accept them without much distress, for bad games prepare us for better ones and our appetites for the unequalled pleasures of a great game. But if we are lured to the park by money and celebrity, we expect something big in return—a guaranteed million-and-a-half-dollar, thrill-a-minute special. We know it won't happen, of course, and when that sullen inner conviction is confirmed by a foolish, 10–2 laugher or by a dim, error-filled performance by our home team, we are consumed with rage, for we have been gulled again, just as we knew we would be. So baseball, the quiet show, slips away from us, season by season, and, as with so many of our other lost amenities and gifts—our cities, our countryside—we don't seem to know how to reverse what is happening and win back something we had prized and counted on always.

Most of the owners have no such feelings about the game. George Steinbrenner knows baseball—an attribute that cannot be ascribed to all of his fellow-owners—but his true business—and he is a genius at it—is publicity. He has won the crowd and the media, and he himself is the central player, Numero Uno, on his team. He and Reggie Jackson play the fame game with skill and passion, and their moves and fakes grab us, even against our will, right through the year. Reggie turned up two days late at the Yankees' spring-training camp, in Fort Lauderdale, this March, and was fined five thousand dollars. George Steinbrenner let it be known that Reggie's tardiness had so displeased him that he was postponing the negotiations over Jackson's new contract, which could again make him the highest-paid player in the game. Reggie had already said that he didn't know if he was "secure enough not to have the largest numbers next to my name," so the delay upset him. All this was reported at great length in the sports pages, of course. A few days later, Jackson announced that the postponement of the confrontation with his boss had turned him into "a walking keg of dynamite," and that he wanted to "tear this building down." Then he added, "I'm tired of the whole situation."

Me, too, Reggie baby. Me, too.

Spring training is always optimistic, but no club I visited this March looked younger or more lighthearted than Billy Martin's Oakland A's, at Scottsdale. By the time I arrived, at mid-Ides, the Camp Billy nine had won five of its first six games, stealing fourteen bases in that brief span, while the club pitching stats showed an earned-run average of 2.00, with no saves at all. The team, in short, had taken up exactly where it left off last year, when it finished a dashing second in the American League West, improving its 1979 record by twenty-nine games, and delighting classicists everywhere with its combination of brilliant pitching, great outfield play, and fiery speed on the bases. Winter trading did not turn up much help for the club's considerable remaining deficiencies, in power, the infield, and the bullpen, but these young A's feed on hope and suggestibility. "Nobody has better arms than we do," said pitcher Matt Keough. "We had ninety-four complete games last year"—an astounding total in this day of bullpen specialists—"and once you begin to expect to finish what you start out there, you pitch a whole lot smarter and better." Rickey Henderson, the twenty-two-year-old left fielder, who set a league record last year with a hundred stolen bases, was working hard at his bunting every day, in the expectation, he told me, of adding thirty or forty points to his 1980 average of .303. ("Three-forty is a lot," I said when he mentioned the figure. "Why not?" he said at once. "Why not three *fifty?*") Manager Billy Martin, still lacking much team muscle at the plate, had hired Eddie Mathews and Harmon Killebrew as joint spring batting coaches, thus suggesting that fame and the long ball may be contagious, like the measles, and at morning practice in Scottsdale the sense of exuberant hope around the batting cage could be sniffed and savored, along with the aroma of the reporters' coffee and the smell of fresh-cut grass, on the bright desert air.

"Oh, this man is sweet-swinging today," said Eddie Mathews as first baseman Dave Revering hit a low liner to center field. Mathews and Killebrew were side by side behind the netting, each wearing sunglasses and each with one foot up on the metal frame of the cage. Revering pulled a shot to right and gave way to Wayne Gross, who was wielding an aluminum bat—a "cheater," in player parlance, since metal bats are not permitted at the major-league level. Gross whaled a pitch (a musical *ping!* from the bat), and the ball flew away toward the 430-foot marker on the green outfield fence.

"You're going to put a hitch in your swing with that thing," Killebrew said mildly.

"It's only a hitch when you're in a slump," Mathews murmured. "When you're hittin' the ball, it's called rhythm. Hitches are just a superstition."

"I once asked Hank Greenberg if he had any superstitions," Killebrew said after the next pitch. "He said yes, he had one—he liked to touch all four bases after he hit a home run."

During his team's spring games, Billy Martin always sits on a folding chair set out on the grass beyond the Oakland dugout, with his coaching staff—Clete Boyer, Art Fowler, George Mitterwald, Jackie Moore, Lee Walls, Camilo Pascual, Harmon Killebrew, and Eddie Mathews—ranged alongside. The tableau suggests Napoleon on a knoll at Austerlitz or Jena, with Ney and Bernadotte and the other marshals in close attendance. Mathews and Killebrew always seemed to sit together—one thousand and eighty-five lifetime homers leaning back in two little chairs, catching the sun.

Leathery baseball visages were even more numerous (and more elderly) at the Cubs' training ground, in Mesa. Lunchtime in the little pressroom at Ho-Ho-Kam Park offers the finest spring flowering of scouts' hats in the land—identical circular canvas buckets, in a tasteful range of colors and band stripes, each surmounting a large, heavily tanned outdoor face, a deep voice, and a dome stuffed with baseball anecdotes and diamond strategies left over from the nineteen-thirties and forties. The Cubs have been owned by the Wrigley family for more than sixty-five years, and belonging is the name of their game. When the team played its first exhibition of the spring season this year, against the Taiyo Whales, of Japan, *nine* living Cub managers (including the incumbent, Joey Amalfitano) turned up for the occasion.*

I looked up another famous Cub before a game at Mesa—Billy Williams, the Chicago batting coach, who batted .290 and hit four hundred and twenty-six homers during his sixteen years with the Cubs (and two with the Oakland A's), and at one time ran off a skein of one thousand one hundred and seventeen consecutive games played, which is a record for the National League—and we talked hitting. Billy talked, that is; I listened.

"There are some little things you learn to do after a while," he said. "Against some pitchers who threw real hard—a Koufax, a Bob Veale—I'd sometimes turn my back foot in a little, just an inch would do it, in order to open up my body that much faster. If a pitcher went the other way, with a lot of slow stuff, maybe I'd do it the opposite way—twist that foot back a mite. I never did like to move my hands, adjust them, although some batters do that, you know. The Cubs' uniforms always had this insignia in the same place here on the shirt, and when I'd go take batting practice for the first time each day, I always checked to make sure my hands were at the level of this 'C,' which was just right for me. My weakness was overstriding. When that'd begin to happen, I'd try to stay with the pitch just a little longer and drive it up the middle, because most of the time if you're going bad, you're coming off the ball too quick, and pulling too much. But each time I was in a slump it seemed like I'd have to go out and face a Drysdale, a Koufax, or a Marichal that particular afternoon. It never failed.

"You have to stay aggressive, though. 'Go out and *get that pitch!*' is what Henry Aaron always said. And Rogers Hornsby, who helped me when I was coming up, always emphasized the strike zone. 'Hit the strikes!' he said. You know, when you're up there you're most always going to get one good pitch to swing at. The good hitters hit the hanging curve, the bad hitters

---

* The Old Cubbies gents' club was soon to be altered in shocking fashion, when the team was sold to the parent corporation of the Chicago *Tribune* on June 17th, 1981, for twenty and a half million dollars. The Cubs will go on, of course, and they may do much better on the field under their new directors, but the end of the Wrigley era is another hard loss to the game.

miss it. Henry Aaron would sometimes hit the pitcher's *best* pitch, but he never let the bad one get by him. There's only about twenty or thirty hits a year difference between a bad hitter and a good one, you know. You hit those thirty hangers and you'll see your name up there in the papers."

Bill Buckner, the Cubs' first baseman, stands in the batter's box in a squared-up, easy stance, with his left foot (he bats lefty) on the back line of the batter's box. His stride is short, and his rip at the ball is brusque and economical. He hits lots of line drives—enough of them last year to rack up a batting average of .324, which was the best in his league. He has a thick mustache and heavy eyebrows, and he runs with a slight limp—the result of a severe injury to his left ankle and subsequent surgery, which almost terminated his career in 1975. When I talked to him in Mesa, he struck me as being simultaneously intense and relaxed, if that is possible. At the time, I thought that this might be caused by his boredom at having to answer a lot of dumb questions from reporters during a week when he was anxiously hoping for word that he had been traded back to his old club, the Dodgers (the trade never came off), but later on it occurred to me that this air of intense calm, of burning imperturbability, is the ideal condition for any man who must go up there all summer and swing against major-league pitchers. A lot of the hitters I watched and listened to this spring gave off exactly the same vibrations; the machine was at rest, but you could almost feel the engine ticking over just under the hood.

"Hitting is confidence," Buckner told me. "It's the feeling that you can hit certain pitchers in certain situations. The hard thing for young hitters is knowing that—just knowing they can do the job. You've got to keep it simple. There are a lot of guys who can hit the ball nine miles in batting practice, but when they get up there they begin thinking about this pitch or looking for that pitch, guessing and wondering, and they tie themselves up. You make a few adjustments—as few as possible. Against a fastball pitcher like Nolan Ryan, I try to stay on top—hit the ball on a line drive down, so I don't just pop up every time. But it's the difference of speeds that makes major-league pitching so hard—the fastball and then the slider, which gets you leaning. You've got to go out there and decide to do well every day. Don't let an at-bat slip away here and another there. You might lose ten, twelve hits that way, and there goes a good year gone."

Nothing to it, I decided that evening. Well, almost nothing. Hit the hangers, don't let the at-bats get away. Keep it simple. Both Billy Williams and Bill Buckner had pointed out that a handful of hits could make quite a difference, but when I got out a pencil and paper I was startled to see what a big difference that was. A man racking up a hundred and fifty hits in five hundred and fifty official at-bats (close to a full season) is hitting .272. Ten more hits raises his average to .290. Another five hits—a hundred and sixty-five hits in the same five hundred and fifty at-bats—and he's a .300 hitter. If he's bumping along around .250, fifteen extra hits means .276 and respectability. Fifteen extra hits spread over a summer is a bit more than three extra hits per month—less than one extra base hit every week.

Nothing to it, perhaps, but when I gave a little more thought to the real nature of the hitter's job—the business of making contact with a blurry white missile that is flying at you at a speed that ranges between seventy-five and ninety-five miles per hour, of hitting a ball delivered with guile and spin (or no spin), and sometimes with extreme ill will, which will sail or sink or bend through a narrow panel of the strike zone (or just miss it: don't swing!) in something less than a quarter of a second after its launching, and must be intercepted with your bat, which is (most unfairly) a cylinder, of course, and then redirected with enough force and plan and muscle and confidence and plain luck to land it untouched somewhere out there on that ruled, overdefended pasture, so that—Well, let's forget it, folks, because it clearly can't be done. A fairer and more realistic appraisal of the hitter's prospects will always take away that extra hit—the crisp, low line drive that zaps into the shortstop's glove; the mighty shot (I got it all *this* time, man!) that hooks foul at the last second; the terrible call by a rookie ump on a pitch that was two inches off the black; or, worse, the strike-three fastball, up and in, that really ate you up, made you look like a real jerk up there, because you were looking for the slider away, of course. So forget that extra hit; let's take away a hit instead. Or take away two hits every week. Let's face it: .250 is much more like it—no, better make that .238.

I talked to hitters all spring—dozens of them, in the end:

young hitters and older ones, retired hitters and free-swinging kids, Hall of Famers and hangers-on, and a lot of coaches and managers, too. I hadn't exactly planned this crash course, but once I started I could hardly wait to go on with it. Learning something new is said to be the quickest way to combat a depression, and I badly wanted to shake my miseries over the money side of the game. Hitting is certainly the hardest part of baseball, and possibly the hardest thing to do in any sport, so the curriculum would keep me busy. As it happened, I ended up talking to a lot more National League than American League hitters along the way, but that was pure accident and didn't much influence my education. I did steer clear of some of the very best hitters of our time—Rod Carew and George Brett, for instance—because I had already read so much about them or listened to them so often, and because anyone *that* good always seems to make hitting sound easy. I also skipped most of the great contemporary philosophers of bat-and-ball and their theorems (Ted Williams: Cock the hips. Study the zones of the plate. Hips open first, *then* shoulders. Swing slightly upward. Harry Walker: Be late. Wait, wait, wait, then wait some more. Do it *my* way! Waitwaitwaitwaitwait. Talktalktalktalktalk. Wally Moses: Throw the head of the bat at the ball. Charley Lau: Stance *and* rhythm. Be back. Swing back to front. Swing through the ball. Head down at point of contact. Don't turn the top hand over before contact. Keep a tension-free swing), because I didn't want to entangle myself in doctrine and heresy, and also because most of them seem to be saying the same, sensible sort of thing. Some of the batters I did corner sounded surprised at being asked about their demanding line of work. Pitchers are usually more cheerful than batters, I have noticed, probably because their success ratio looks so much rosier; there are twenty-seven outs per team in a game, and less than a third that many hits most of the time. Pitchers are full of ideas; at least they and their catchers know what the ball is meant to do each time it is pitched, while the batters are forever in the dark. "It's always two against one out there," a .257-hitting outfielder said to me sombrely. "Or *three* against one, if you count the umpire. No wonder it's so damned tough."

Tommy Davis poured me a glass of orange juice in his motel room in Phoenix, and told me to watch the inside of his knees.

Batting righty, he was standing up at an imaginary plate, just at the foot of his bed, and his knees were bent slightly inward. "Knee-knockers!" David said. "Balance!" Then he told me to watch his left hip and his left knee; he dipped the knee, and the hip rotated slightly inward with the motion. "See what happened!" Davis cried. "Now watch me swing. Excuse me—" He stepped past me and picked up a bat from a group of three bats standing in a corner, and resumed his position. "Here comes the pitch," he announced. He held the bat high, dipped the knee, and then swung the bat in slow motion, stopping it just short of mid-swing. "Can you see what's happened to that hip now, because I began with that bend?" he said. "It's still there, before the ball gets to the plate! It hasn't gone away yet. Now look at the end of the bat. I've added four or five inches to the outer end of the bat. I've added four or five inches to the outer end of my swing, and I'm covering the whole plate, all because of this hip! It's easy! Everything I tell my batters is easy."

Davis, a large forty-two-year-old man with a large, wide smile, is the batting coach for the Seattle Mariners. This is his first year at the job, and he told me that he had to keep things simple, because in the spring-training period he had arranged for each member of the Mariners squad to visit him in his motel room in the evening, so they could talk about hitting at their ease and come to understand each other's ideas. I was a late rookie—an ancient Mariner—but Davis was still eager about everything he had to tell me. He urged me to turn my head and really look at the pitcher—not peek at him around a corner. He told me to be selfish at the plate during my first two or three times up in a game—to hit for myself then, since later on I might have to hit for the team, because we might be behind in the game. He told me to close my stance a fraction against a left handed pitcher, so that the second baseman became the center of the diamond for me, because a southpaw's fastball tends to tail away from a righty batter. Then he told me to imagine that I was deformed and had been born with no bone or muscle between my left shoulder and my left elbow.

"What?" I said.

"How would you swing at a pitch then?" Davis said. "Show me how you'd swing with just your wrist and elbow there."

I stood up and executed an awkward, twisting little flip of

my wrists and hands. "You see it!" Tommy cried. "You see that! See how fast that was!"

He made the same kind of swing, and the end of his bat whipped across the foot of the bed. "You couldn't extend your arms, so you got quicker," he announced. "You're *much* quicker, and you've covered the inside of the plate with your swing. Now you've got to step up closer to the plate to cover that outside corner, don't you? But you don't mind that! You don't mind that one little bit, because now you've got bat speed, and the man out there can't jam you. You don't care how close you are to that pitch, or how big you are or how small, because you can get that bat around so fast. And if the bat goes first, the body will follow, and then you're a *hitter!* See how easy it all is? Now, when you're up there in a game and you hear old Tommy yell out 'Midget!'—or maybe 'Hip!' or 'Knee-knockers!'—you'll know ex*actly* what to do. You'll remember this talk we had and think, Hey, maybe old Tommy had an idea!"

He put away the bat and sat down on the edge of his bed, smiling. "If you can relax, that is," he said in a quieter voice. "Relaxed is the key, but I don't know if that can be taught. I just don't know. They used to call me lazy or lackadaisical, but the lazier I felt the better I'd hit."

I nodded my head, remembering. I could still see Tommy Davis coming up to the plate again for the Dodgers back in 1962 or '63, with the bat almost falling out of his hands, and then hitting another line drive. He batted .346 in 1962, with two hundred and thirty hits. A lazy, terrifying hitter.

"Anything that works," Frank Robinson said. "Anything that feels comfortable to you."

Robinson, the only man to win a Most Valuable Player award in both leagues, is now the manager of the Giants, and he was talking to Larry Herndon, a lanky Giant outfielder, who was taking extra batting practice at Phoenix Stadium, which is the Giants' springtime park. It was late in the afternoon, with shadows falling across the field. Robinson and Herndon and Jim Lefebvre, the San Francisco batting coach, were the only Giants left on the field. Lefebvre was pitching to Herndon, throwing from behind a low screen on the mound; a batboy loped around in the outfield shagging Herndon's flies and grounders. Herndon, a right-handed swinger, would hit two or three hard drives and then he'd pop up or half-top a pitch. Now and then, Robinson would stop him and walk slowly to the front of the cage. "Do me a favor," he said once, in his quiet, slow voice. "Bend just a little more from your waist here. Flex your knees. Loosen yourself." He walked away slowly, and Herndon whacked the next pitch on a line. "That's it," Robinson said softly. "Super!" Jim Lefebvre called in from the mound. "You got it, Lar!"

This has been going on for some time. Lefebvre has a quick, excitable manner. He talks rapidly and with great intensity—especially if the subject is hitting. Earlier, when Robinson had been the man on the mound, Lefebvre had stood beside Herndon, with a bat in his hands, showing him things. "Get your weight more centered," he said. "Don't spread out so much. Don't get ahead. Get your stride shortened up and block down along here"—he pointed to his front hip and thigh—"and then your weight is behind the swing. *Voom!* You see that? *Voom!*"

When Robinson became the tutor, he murmured to Herndon, "Slow it down, slow it down. The quickness comes with your hands, not the body," and I had a sudden impression of two veteran detectives working over a suspect in the classic pre-cinct-house fashion. One was shrill and excitable, and then the fatherly, gentler partner took over. The two partners were after the same thing, of course, and it took me only a minute or two now to see that Lefebvre and Robinson had been giving Herndon exactly the same advice.

Later, Lefebvre and I sat in the Giants' dugout for a few minutes in the gathering dusk. He told me that he considered it a great luxury to have Frank Robinson on hand as an example to the Giant hitters. "You need a source," he said. "It's so hard to reach batters at the major-league phase, because they've already come so far and they don't like to change. They don't want to be *told* things, and hitting is so hard that it can get through only if you can find the batter's own terminology or steer him to a source."

Lefebvre's terminology, I discovered, was technical. He explained for me the Axis of the Swing, and how it was de-stroyed if the batter moved forward in the box too quickly. He demonstrated the Setup Position and the Power Position. He touched on the Focussing Phase and the Decision Phase.

He explicated the Lever Actions of a swing—Lever No. 1, which was the leading forearm, and Lever No. 2, which was the bat—and showed me how the two, taken together, became Lever No. 3 when the bat met the ball, unless the batter had turned his wrists over before the impact, in which case the lever was broken. I was awed.

"Oh, I love to talk about all this," he said, sitting down again at last. "I played ball in Japan after my major-league career was over"—Lefebvre was an infielder with the Dodgers from 1955 to 1972—"and I discovered that the Japanese care a lot about the style of the swing: how it's done. I can remember reading their newspapers and seeing something like 'The American hit a very long home run in the third inning, but it was done without proper form.' So I began to think about form and dynamics. I wish I had some of my pictures and charts here to show you. It's all there, once you start taking it apart. The difficulty about hitting is the emotional side. That's much, much harder to master. You know something?" His voice dropped and took on a wondering tone. "Great hitters have it *here*." He pointed to his belly, below his belt. "It's all inside here with the great ones. The tougher it is out there, the more they love it. They thrive on it. A Reggie Jackson in the World Series. A Pete Rose with men on base. Did you ever look at Pete Rose's face when he makes out in a spot like that? He can't *believe* it! He wants it every time. He feeds on it. He lives on it! I tell you, if we could bottle that somehow, the job of teaching hitting would be a whole lot easier."

"We didn't have any batting coaches in my time. I was always curious about the game and how it was played, so I asked questions, and they were mostly questions about how to hit the ball. In my first couple of years up with the Giants, my roomie was John Mize. He's just been taken into the Hall of Fame, you know. He had that beautiful swing—the prettiest thing you ever saw—but he couldn't exactly communicate what he was doing up there, so I just watched him. This was around 1947 and '48 we're talking about. In 1947, the Big Cat and I hit sixty-eight homers, which was good going for a couple of roomies. Maybe it's a record. He had fifty-one and I had seventeen. If we were on the road, he'd wake up early in the morning in our hotel room, and the very first thing he'd do was light up a big cigar. The very first thing in the day. Then he'd go over to the window and put up the shade and look out to see which way the flags on top of the buildings were blowing—I can still see him looking out like that, in his underwear. If the wind was going the right way—blowing out at the ballpark, I mean—the Cat would come back and lie down on the bed and blow out some smoke, and he'd say, 'Roomie, I think I'll hit two out today.' But if the wind was wrong, he'd yank down the shade and come back and stump out the cigar in the ashtray, and I'd think, Oh-oh, we'd better pitch a *shutout* today."

The speaker and former Giant is my friend Bill Rigney, later a manager of that club (and manager of the California Angels and the Minnesota Twins: seventeen years at the helm, in all), who is now a super-scout for the Angels. On this afternoon, he is wearing his super planter's broad-brimmed straw hat, for we are sitting in the stands behind home plate at Sun City, watching the Angels and the home-team Milwaukee Brewers play, and the day is a desert blazer, with the temperature well up in the eighties and the humidity (I heard it on my car radio, driving over) at eight per cent. There is a pleasant smell of coconut oil wafting over the grandstand, and if you didn't care about the baseball you could draw up an interesting clothes-for-age chart here today: from near-nudity for the college kids on up to gloves and parasols for the blue-haired older female fans, or Geezerettes, who live in this retirement community. But nearly everybody cares about the baseball today. The Angels and the Brewers are dynamite at the plate this year (although a bit more like Play-Doh on the mound). Both clubs improved themselves with major purchases and trades in the winter market, and when the lineups are announced today one can count fourteen All-Stars among the starters. The game begins, and the visiting Angels take things in hand at once. They rack up nine runs and thirteen hits in their first four innings. But the Brewers are larruping the ball, too, so there is a lot of time in which to study batting styles and batting approaches: Rod Carew's tipped-back torso and droopy, flattened bat; Freddie Lynn's classical, elegant left-handed stroke; Disco Dan Ford's closed-up, almost cross-legged stance; Brian Downing's utterly opposite, open posture—his front foot so far in the bucket before the pitch that he looks as if he had given up on the idea of batting today and had started back for the dugout. Cecil Cooper, who batted .352 for the Brewers last year, has clearly modelled his batting stance on Carew's bent knees and lightly touching front toe, but Cooper is six feet two, so the impression is of a blown-up poster of Rodney. Ben Oglivie, who weighs just a hundred and seventy pounds, whacked forty-one homers for the Brewers last summer, and when you watch his short, sneaky-fast cut at the ball you can pretty well guess how he did it: Aaron wrists.

"Everyone starts differently, but most hitters meet the ball pretty much the same," Rigney says. "There's no *right* way to hit. I think there's much more hitting to the opposite field now than there was when I was coming up. That's because of the slider, of course. We didn't see that pitch so much back then, and batters could just lay back and pull the ball. I'll tell you, though, if I was starting out coaching today, down at the Class A level or in the rookie leagues, I'd sure try to get all my players to stand up closer to the plate. You just can't let a big pitcher throw two kinds of good pitches at you, and if you're up on top of the plate you've almost taken the best part of the sinker-slider thing away from him. You've made his plate seventeen inches wide again, instead of the twenty or twenty-two inches he's working with. You have to do something up there, you know. You have to think. And a pitcher hates it when he sees you right up on top of the plate. He thinks, Why is he standing *there?* Does he have a weakness he's hiding? Does he want the ball outside? It messes up their thinking. And all you have to do is be a little quick up there, so he won't jam you."

On the field, the Angels are doing frightful things to Brewer pitcher Jim Slaton, and when Bobby Grich lines a bulletlike double to right-center field, off a low, outside fastball, Rigney winces with admiration. "That's murder," he says. "It isn't manslaughter, it's *murder.*" He shakes his head. "I'll tell you what I like to see, though, and that's a batter who can go from the inside out—a right-hand batter who can slap the inside pitch to right field. A Clemente. If you're doing that, you can use your bottom hand and slide the whole length of the bat against the ball, and really hit to all fields. If the pitch is down and in, O.K., fine—you can pull it. But if it is up and in, you should try to go to right. I lasted two whole extra years with the Giants because Leo"—Leo Durocher was Rig's manager at the time—"knew that with a man on first or second I'd never hit it at *him* or *him*." He points to the third baseman and the shortstop. "No! I'd slap it at *him* and *him*"—the second base-man and the first baseman—"and, a lot of the time, past them. So they'd never get two."

Rig smiles and tips his hat a little lower over his eyes. "Well, *hardly* ever," he says.

"Bottom hand is one approach," Ted Simmons told me later that day. "Top hand is another, and it's more common. Almost every player has to make some kind of an adjustment when he gets to the major-league level, and for me it was because of the trouble I had with a pitch inside, where I was looping the bat. Even if I got a good cut, I'd just foul the pitch off. So I had to learn to tomahawk the ball, which was top-handing. It took me less time to get from back up here to *here,* over the plate, and I could keep the ball fair then, because I'd changed the angle of the bat on the ball. So top hand was right for me."

Simmons, a switch-hitting catcher, moved from the Car-dinals to the Brewers during the off-season as part of a com-plicated multiplayer trade; he batted .298 during his eleven years with the Cards, and he hits with enough power to have twice batted in over a hundred runs in a season. A lot of baseball people think that his acquisition by the Brewers will take them all the way to a pennant this year. Simmons has a square-jawed, alert face (he looks very much like an Ivy League football player from the eighteen-nineties), and he talks base-ball as articulately as anyone I know. By this time, however, I had begun to sense an overload in my hitting comprehension. The more I heard about it, the more difficult and impossible it had begun to seem to me. I said something to this effect to Simmons.

"Well, hitting is a physical art, and that's never easy to explain," he said. "And it's hard. It's one hard way to make a living if you're not good at it. Hitting is mostly a matter of feel, and it's abstract as hell. If I'm in a slump, it's because I've lost the feel of making solid contact with the ball on the thick part of the bat, and I get a pitcher and go out and take extra batting practice until that feeling comes back—maybe ten minutes, maybe half an hour: for as long as it takes. I've made some kind of physical adjustment in order to attain a better mental state, a better psychic condition. You have to feel good if you're going to hit aggressively and with confidence. But I *know* I can hit—I've been doing it all my life— and that breeds confidence, too."

I asked Simmons about batters' picking up the spin on the pitch—the part of hitting that most startled me when I first heard batters mention it. Simmons said that Carl Yastrzemski had once told him that the players who hit the ball hardest and most often are simply the ones who are quickest to see the spin and identify it. Some pitches can be read before they leave the pitcher's hand, Simmons said—the curveball, much of the time, because it is delivered from a wider angle (I recalled Billy Williams saying that a ball delivered from the upper, outer limits of a pitcher's reach which was headed for his chin was almost surely a curve, "because big-league pitchers just ain't that wild")—but most pitches are identified by the precise appearance of the ball in mid-flight. The fastball has a blurry, near-vertical spin. The curveball spins on a slight axis. The slider—well, there is more than one kind of slider.

"If a pitcher holds the ball with his forefinger and middle finger between the wide part of the seams, out at that horseshoe-shaped part of the ball, you see a big, wide white spot when it's pitched—sort of a flickering," Simmons said. "The better slider comes when he grabs the ball where the seams are close together. Then the red laces on the ball make a little red spot out there. That's because the ball is spiralling so hard that it's like the tip of a football that's just been passed. The seams make a little circle—that red dot—and you think, *Slider!* The red-dot sliders are the hard ones to hit—like J. R. Richard's. The white ones tend to hang. You can read the white one when it's about three feet out of the pitcher's hand. The red dot I can pick up about five feet from his hand."

"I still can't believe it," I said.

"It's just data," Simmons said. "You learn it and you use it. What's much harder—what makes the biggest disadvantage for any hitter—is not knowing the pitchers. If you see a batter facing a pitcher for the first time ever, the odds are way, way in the pitcher's favor. It's not just knowing what the pitcher has—sinker, slider, a riding fastball; whether he has a change; whether he'll throw you a breaking ball when he's behind in the count—but what kind of speeds he throws them with. That identifies him in your mind. That's his pitcher's character. Without that, you're at a gross disadvantage. I'll be up against that for the first few weeks this year, because this is a new league for me. It's more of a breaking-ball league than the National League. But it doesn't take *that* long to learn it, because you compare every pitcher with someone you've faced before. Just a couple of at-bats against him, and you begin to say to yourself, 'O.K., you pitch like Sutton.' Or 'Your fastball is a little like Seaver's.' Or 'You come at a batter like Jerry Reuss.' And then it's all a lot easier. Your data grows. That's why a young pitcher will do so well sometimes in his first year in the majors. He might win ten or fifteen games out there—because the batters don't know him yet—and then he's never heard of again. The hitters have caught up."

Baseball is not just hitting, and spring training had other rewards for me this year. In Florida, before a Tigers–Red Sox game at Winter Haven, the new Boston manager, Ralph Houk, looked across the field at Mark Fidrych, who was warming up for the Tigers, and recalled the kind of pitcher Fidrych had been in that one great summer of 1976, when he ran off a 19–9 record, with an earned-run average of 2.34, and became the most attractive, most talked-about rookie of our time: the Bird. Fidrych hurt his knee the next spring, and then damaged his arm, and he has spent most of the ensuing four years on the bench or in the minors. Now he was making another comeback try. Houk, who was Fidrych's manager in Detroit that first year, said, "He knew one thing, which was to go right at the hitters and to keep the ball low. Everything he threw that summer was down, and it was all strikes. He never had to learn to pitch to a hitter's weakness, because he made them hit his pitch. That low fastball moved around so much nobody could touch it. He was so strong that if he was ahead in the seventh or eighth inning you could already put up that 'W' beside his name. The things he did for our club that summer! The games he won and the crowds he got! I remember us going in to play the Twins, who hadn't been drawing *anybody*, and he filled the ballpark for them. I never saw anything like that before in baseball."

The Red Sox fans applauded happily when Fidrych's name

was announced in the starting lineup, and they laughed and clapped some more when he took the mound and we could watch and remember his odd, deep crouch on the mound, with the ball and glove held close to his belly as he got the catcher's sign. Fidrych is only twenty-six, and he still has an eager, boyish, stalking way about him out there. But most of his pitches to the Bosox batters were up, and there was no pop to his fastball. He gave up three walks and a double and a two-run homer (to Jim Rice) in the first inning, and was soon gone. Gone for good, almost surely.

In the same game, the Red Sox moved a base runner (Tony Perez) from first base to third base with a hit-and-run single poked to the right side, just behind the Tiger second baseman, by the next batter, Carney Lansford; Perez then scored on a sacrifice fly, while I swooned with surprise. To the best of my recollection, my Bosox had not scored a run in such austere, classical fashion since the mid-nineteen-thirties. The Major (Houk, that is) also seemed to have persuaded some of the Boston pull-hitters to take a pitch now and then. The new incumbent at short, Glenn Hoffman, is clearly no Burleson—who is?—but there was some stout Boston pitching by a young rookie right-hander named Steve Crawford and some sound arms at last in the bullpen, and if the Boston fans can get used to the idea of their heroes winning (or losing) some games in which the total of runs scored does not always climb into football-game figures, there may be a few happy hours up at the Fens this summer after all.

Over at St. Petersburg, I found Bob Gibson behind a batting cage at the Mets' practice ground, Huggins-Stengel Field—Gibson in uniform again. The retired Cardinal ace and brand-new Hall of Fame designee had been appointed to the Mets' coaching staff last winter; because the Mets already had a pitching coach, Rube Walker, manager Joe Torre was calling Gibson his "attitude coach," which meant he was there to help the team win. Gibson said he had been pitching a lot of batting practice, his first work on a mound in six years, and told me he almost wished he were a rookie mound candidate again.

"You'd be Rookie of the Year," I said.

Gibson smiled but did not laugh; he was considering his chances.

A little later, Gibson and Torre and Walker stood together behind the cage and watched Pat Zachry, the Mets' sepulchral, bearded right-hander, working to a batter from the mound. Torre asked Zachry to throw off a stretch. The pitch came in— a pretty good slider—and Torre said, "There—he did it again."

"I missed it," Gibson said. "I don't have my glasses on."

Torre asked Zachry to throw another slider, and this time we all saw it. At the top of his stretch, Zachry wiggled his glove minutely as the fingers of his pitching hand gripped the ball for the slider. A smart batter, I knew by now, would pick this up in an instant.

"It'll be fixed," Torre said. This, among other things, is what spring training is *for*.

A couple of days later, a sellout crowd turned up at Al Lang Stadium, in St. Pete, to watch the visiting Yankees take on the Cardinals. During batting practice, the foul-ground territory around home was jam-packed with local cityside reporters, fence-hopping autograph hunters, children in baseball caps, young women with Instamatics trying to look like A.P. photogs, old codgers with baseballs to be autographed for their grandchildren, and middle-aged gents who eagerly accosted one Yankee or another with recollections of some years-past lobby encounter or with the insistent request to be remembered relayed from the player's fourth-grade teacher in Terre Haute. This is the World Series atmosphere that the Yankee entourage never escapes, even in spring training, and during the game the same overheated love-hate response showed itself in savage little eruptions of jeering from the stands when Dave Winfield leaped for a long drive at the left-field wall and missed it, and when Reggie Jackson struck out in the second inning and again in the sixth. But I didn't care; it was too nice a day to care about anything. I sat in the stands and watched the breeze fluttering the fronds of the palm trees out beyond the fences. A lot of teen-age kids were perched on top of the green outfield wall, with their bare legs dangling; the park loudspeaker ordered them down from there, but nobody moved, of course. The second-stringers began to filter into the game, and I gave up keeping score. The Cardinals' batting helmets were brilliant scarlet in the sunshine. A pterodactyl flapped slowly across the field, headed for Tampa Bay. Out beyond the 388-foot marker in right center, a man in a scarlet shirt was sitting in a tree. The Cardinals won, 3–1, and the whole thing was over in less than two hours. I yawned and stretched. Could that have been a pelican?... It was time to head for the pool.

I went back to the hitters. On a frigid, wind-torn gray morning in Clearwater, I asked Pete Rose what he did about slumps.

"Well, I don't think there's anybody's going to get me out for long," he said. "Nobody's got a book on me. I switch-hit and I hit the ball everywhere. I can hit the fastball and the breaking ball, and I might hit you down the right-field line one time and up the other way the next time. If some pitcher's been getting me out, I'll do one of six things. I might move up in the box or move back. I might move away from the plate or come closer. I might choke up more or choke up less. I can usually tell what I'm doing wrong by the flight of the ball. I've seen guys play major-league ball for ten, twelve years, and if they go oh-for-fifteen they want to change their stance, like it's the end of the world. That's ridiculous. The only thing that's rough about this game is that you can't turn it on and off like a faucet. If I'm swinging good, I'll come to the park even on an off day, just to keep it going. This game is mental. There's a lot of thinking in it. You watch the pitcher from the batter's box and see what's going good for him. You watch the ball and it's sending you messages—the knuckleball don't spin, screwball's got backspin, slider's got that dot. It's easy. I like to watch the ball leave the pitcher's hand, and I like to watch the catcher catch it and throw it back to him. It's a habit I got into. I like the umpire to tell me where the ball is. He says, 'Strike one,' and I say, 'O.K., you missed one. Now give me one.'" Rose had a bat in his hands and had taken up his exaggerated, crouching at-bat posture (he was batting lefty, perhaps because I was taking notes right-handed), and was staring back in disbelief at some imaginary umpire behind him. A little crowd of writers and Phillies laughed at the pantomime. Pete Rose could draw a crowd in a cemetery.

"It never changes," he went on. "The pitchers don't change. Tom Seaver don't change. If you're a good hitter, hitting in the majors is easier, 'cause you're facing the same pitchers all the time. I'm particular about that. I have to know the way a guy throws. If you don't believe me, look at my Championship

Series record, where I got more hits than anybody in the game, and then look at my World Series average. I don't know the pitchers in the World Series, unless they were in my league once, but look at what happens in the fifth and sixth and seventh games, when I begin to see the same guys out there pitching. Look that up."

I looked it up. In the five World Series in which Rose has played (in 1970, 1972, 1975, 1976, and 1980), he has gone hitless at the plate—0 for 16—in the opening games. His second-game average is .157. His third-game average is .285. His fourth-game average is .285. His fifth-game average—he has been in four of them—is .375. His sixth-game average, for three games, is .416. He is 4 for 9 in his two seventh World Series games—.444. Nothing about Pete Rose surprises me anymore, but still . . .

Steve Garvey always seems to be standing at attention in the batter's box. As he waits for the pitch, his back is straight and his bat shows not a tremor of anxiety or anticipation. His feet are apart, of course, but perfectly parallel with the back line of the box. When he swings, his head snaps down, as if he were checking the shine on his tunic buttons. What he is doing, of course, is watching the ball—*really* watching the ball. He swings exactly the same way at every pitch: perfect swings. Last year, he batted .304, which is exactly his lifetime average in eleven seasons with the Dodgers. Last year, he had exactly two hundred hits; the year before, he had two hundred and four hits; the year before that, it was two hundred and two. Garvey is a soldier of hitting.

"No mannerisms—right?" Garvey said after he had seen me studying him in the batting cage one evening at St. Petersburg. He is entirely aware that his play and his personality give the appearance of bland, mechanical perfection. "I'll have to try to do something about that," he said, shaking his head in mock distress. "Actually, I make a conscious effort to limit all that extra activity at the plate so I can just take the bat back and step into the pitch. It's hard enough to do that, without having to compensate for a lot of little movements and habits you can get into up there. I did change my stance back in 1972 and '73, when our batting coach, Dixie Walker, worked with me on going right toward the pitcher, so that I could hit the outside pitch on a line to the opposite field—to right, for me. Hitting that pitch on a line drive *down*." (Buckner, an old teammate of Garvey's, had used this same phrase.) "Most of the time when you try to go that way, you have a tendency to drag the head of the bat, and if you don't have great strength"— Garvey's forearms are like ships' cables—"you'll just hit a lot of fly balls to right. Now about a third of my homers are to right or right center. Once I learned how to stay on top of that outside pitch, my average went up about thirty points, because the pitchers couldn't pitch me just one way.

"I always aim to hit the top half of the ball. You try to meet it square, but if I had my druthers I'd always hit *through* the ball, to give it backspin. People don't realize that a lot of home runs are caused by backspin. If the ball is rotating toward you as it goes out, like a tennis ball when you slice it, it will carry a lot further. Sometimes you'll see a line drive that suddenly goes like this"—a diving motion with his hand—"because there's no backspin on it. That isn't to say that there aren't hitters who aren't doing the opposite—trying to hit the ball with topspin, so it'll go through the infield. You'll see players with a lot of speed chop at the ball that way, so they can beat out the hit when it takes that big hop, particularly on Astro-Turf. But that's not my style."

He smiled almost apologetically. Of course it isn't his style. Last year, he hit twenty-six homers; the year before that, he hit twenty-eight homers. In the spring of 1977, Garvey's manager, Tom LaSorda, asked him to hit a few extra homers—to sacrifice some points on his batting average in order to help the Dodgers score runs. Garvey said he'd try. That year, his batting average went down by twenty points and he hit exactly twenty more homers than he had in the previous year.

As I went from one spring ballpark to another, and from clubhouse to batting cage to dugout, listening to the hitters, I began to sense a continuous batters' dialogue going on in my head. I was still a student, still a beginner (I would always be), but I knew enough, at least, to be grateful for the difficulty of the material. Broad shapes of general theory and scraps of lectures from my preceptors and savants stayed with me, so I always seemed to be engaged in some great seminar of swing.

I could summon up Jackson (Prof. Reggie, that is) on Slumps:

"You wake up in the morning with the feeling 'I'm in a slump,' and it stays with you all through the day. Everyone knows it, wherever you go—you can see it in their faces—and *you* know it. You know that no matter how well you've played, no matter what you've done in the past, your numbers for this week and last week are all that matter now. You're in trouble, and it won't go away of its own accord. You get quiet. You lose that intensity, that bounce, that's necessary to do things well in sports. You're fatigued, so you try to compensate mentally, but some of the compensations can make you worse. Then you begin to understand how many little things there are that might be wrong with what you're doing. If you know you're dragging the bat through the hitting zone, say, it might be because you're lowering your hands, which causes them not to get back in the right hitting position, or you might be wrapping the bat back around your neck, which causes the swing to get a little longer, or you could be dropping the head of the bat, which causes you to top the ball, or you could be pulling off the ball, which causes your front shoulder to fly out. Those are just a few of the possibilities. Anything that changes your regular swing is going to mess up your natural feeling at the plate, and if you're not natural you're nothing: you're in a slump. And so it goes on."

There was Frey on Difficulty (Jim Frey, the manager of the Kansas City Royals, who was a batting coach with the Orioles for many years): "The average hitter is a struggling hitter. If you're at .250 or .260, where most players find themselves, it never comes easy. You have to go out and *grind* it out, day after day, just to stay at that level. It's hard to take, because when you get into one of those ten-day or two-week slumps, it's a long road back for you. A .250 hitter hits one ball good every night, and if it happens to go right at somebody out there, he's in trouble. But the .320 hitter always hits two or three balls good, so his chances are better and he won't run into so many discouragements. I don't know if hitters are better than they used to be, but the pitching sure is. It's not just the slider, it's the development of the bullpen—the star pitcher who comes in in the eighth or ninth to shut the door. Twenty years ago, all the great pitchers were starters, but now the staffs are complete. And today all the clubs chart hitters—they know where to pitch to them, how to get them out. A lot of the parks are bigger, and the pitchers are bigger, too—and they're *good*. Hitting never seems to get easier."

I recalled inspirational themes, as expounded by two great sluggers. George Foster, the awesome, slit-eyed Cincinnati thumper (he drove in one hundred and forty-nine runs in his M.V.P. year, 1977): "You can still be disciplined at the plate when the count is against you. Sometimes when the count is oh-and-two, the pressure is on the *pitcher*. I'm a better hitter when things are against me. The more the challenge, the more mental and spiritual strength you can come up with, and the stronger you're going to be in some other situation, away from the ballpark. Baseball is part of life, maybe only a small part, but the important thing is what you overcome inside yourself."

Mike Schmidt, who has hit more homers in the past seven years (two hundred and sixty-four of them) than anyone else in the game: "I don't think I can get into my deep inner thoughts about hitting. It's like talking about religion. It's hard to explain what goes through my mind during a game that makes me a better hitter. Let's just say that I know I'm still not getting the best out of my abilities. I've got twenty-ten vision and great strengths and a great knowledge of the game, and there's no reason in the world I shouldn't be better than I am. I work at hitting and improving all the time."

The tone of voice of these various messages, I had begun to notice, mattered almost more than their content. Hitting is confidence, Bill Buckner had said, and Pete Rose's brusque garrulousness, Steve Garvey's verbal printouts, and Mike Schmidt's near-mysticism were perhaps only different evidences of a professional optimism thickly armored against unrelenting and excruciating difficulty. Lesser hitters, I discovered, are in awe of a batter who appears truly unconcerned about the painful odds that afflict their work. Art Shamsky, who batted .253 during an eight-year career in the outfield and at first base with the Reds and the Mets, told me that he had once asked Hank Aaron how it felt to come to the ballpark every day with the assurance that he would get two hits. The question was put while Shamsky, playing first base, was holding Aaron, a base runner, close to the bag. Hank, watching the pitcher, took a few steps down toward second and said over his shoulder,

"Hell, I don't ever know if I'm going to get two hits. What I know is if I don't get 'em today, I'm sure going to get 'em tomorrow."

When older players and those who have retired from baseball talk about the game, they don't sound the way young regulars do. The heedless grace and silvery reflexes of their youth have given way to appreciation and understanding, and even to aesthetics, and a quiescent sadness envelops them. Against their will, they have become fans.

Art Shamsky said, "I still think about baseball all the time. I'm disappointed that I didn't become a better hitter. I had a better bat than ninety per cent of the other guys, but I didn't apply myself until I was older, and then it was too late. I think I cheated myself."

Sal Bando, now in his fifteenth year in the majors, batted .197 for the Brewers last season and came to spring training this year half expecting to be cut from the active-player roster. Instead, he slightly altered his batting style, adopting a more rhythmic beginning to his stroke, and enjoyed the best spring of his career. He made the club. "Isn't that *strange?*" he said to me. "Fifteen years, and I'm still learning. You know, there are so many young guys with ability who don't listen, don't learn. But why should they, when they're doing great?" He shook his head.

Richie Ashburn, a veteran broadcaster with the Phillies, compiled a lifetime .308 average during his fifteen years in the majors (he led all National League batters in 1958, batting .350), but he has now decided that he didn't understand much about his work until the very end. "I wish I'd known early what I had to learn late," he said to me. "When I was young, I could run so fast that I never had to learn how to hit. The last year of my career was with the Mets—it was their *first* year—and playing in the Polo Grounds there, with its short lines and that endless center field, taught me that you should probably never hit the ball in the air down the middle. I'd try to hit the breaking ball on the ground down the middle and the up pitch in the air down the line to right or left. I think that's how you should hit in all parks."

The insouciance of young hitters, by contrast, startles even their managers and veteran teammates. "You see some guys up there who don't think about *anything*," one batting coach said to me. "They see a pitch and they swing and hit it. It's kind of beautiful." And Del Unser, a thirteen-year veteran now with the Phillies, mentioned the difficulty his club had in pitching to the young Kansas City first baseman, Willie Mays Aikens, during the World Series last fall. "We'd set him up just right and pitch him right—good, tough fastballs—and he *still* kept hitting those dingers," Unser said. Some of this same kind of dazzled, carping praise has been directed at Garry Templeton, the Cardinals' twenty-five-year-old shortstop, who has the best glove and the strongest arm at his position in the National League, and who may be the best artificial-turf hitter in baseball. He switch-hits, starting from a closed stance, and his eager, swiftly opening slash at the ball results in clusters of line drives up the outfield alleys, or hard, high-bouncing infield singles that he can beat out with his great speed afoot. Templeton can *hit*. Two years ago, when he batted .314, he banged out one hundred hits batting right-handed and one hundred and eleven batting lefty—a new record in the game. Templeton, a pleasant, mild-spoken young man, chatted with me briefly after morning practice one day at Al Lang Stadium while he fielded some very short grounders being tossed to him by his two-year-old son, Garry II. Templeton I was wearing a bright-red Cardinals jacket with "JUMP" emblazoned across the back—short for "Jump Steady," which is his nickname. He told me that he was still learning how to bat left-handed. "Swinging right-handed is natural for me," he said, "and they only started me switching five years ago. The ball still looks kind of strange to me from that side, especially in the spring." Strange but not unrecognizable, perhaps: last year, Templeton batted .321 left-handed, as against .317 from his natural side.

I asked Garry if certain pitchers or situations ever put him at a disadvantage, and he said, "I'm not up on counts and taking pitches. I swing the bat. If you can concentrate, hitting is easy. If a person could gear his concentration in, he should be able to hit the ball every time he comes up to the plate."

He picked up the baseball that young Garry, throwing righty, had just launched unsteadily across the grass, and this time he put it in the boy's left hand. "Throw it left-handed," Garry said gently. "C'mon, now." Frowning with effort, the boy made a little left-handed heave, and Templeton said, *"That's* it." He handed the ball back to his son. "You see that?" he said, smiling. "Switch-pitcher."

Templeton's teammate Keith Hernandez is a tall, extremely handsome first baseman who throws and bats left-handed and hits with power to all fields. Two years ago, he batted .344 and was voted co-winner (with Willie Stargell) of the National League's Most Valuable Player award. Hernandez is twenty-seven, and his great abilities, one senses, are somewhere at mid-stage—halfway between the gift and the art. "I like the pitch away, and I look for the ball in a certain zone out there," he said to me. "I can cover the majority of the plate hitting that way, but I can't cover the good inside pitch. Anything on the inside two inches of the black I won't be able to handle, and the pitchers know it. If I get five pitches in an at-bat, I guarantee you three of them will be inside. But the pitcher has to make a hell of a pitch to me to get it in there every time, and sooner or later he'll make a mistake. It'll be out there and I'll get him. It's a matter of being patient. If he starts me out with a nasty pitch, I'm not afraid to let it go by. I've still got two more swings. Even if I'm down oh-and-two or one-and-two, I don't get defensive. Then I'm like a wounded animal that's cornered next to a cliff. I'm a tougher out, because I'm fighting for my life."

Perhaps there *is* no norm for players of such a demanding game. Some great hitters seem to attain full maturity at the plate during their very first season; their reactions are so marvellous that the pitchers never do find a useful way to get them out, and these hitters' subsequent accrual of at-bats and knowledge of the pitchers does not seem to be a significant factor in their continuing success. Such golden creatures—a young Willie Mays, say—are awesome to observe but not especially rewarding as a subject for study: one can take apart a pocket watch but not a sunset. Mike Schmidt has always been a slugger—he has led his league in homers four times in seven years—but last season, as the result of intensive scrutiny of himself and his sport, he became a hitter, at the age of thirty-one. His forty-eight homers and one hundred and twenty-one runs batted in were the best such totals of his career, and his batting average of .286 was more than thirty points above his lifetime level. Schmidt used to lead his league in strikeouts, but in the past three years he has had about forty fewer whiffs per season than he used to. Somewhere in the middle of last August, Schmidt appeared to have finally mastered his long, forward-driving movement at the plate, which he begins from the very back of the box, in a way that brought the full power of his awesomely muscular swing through the outer sector of the strike zone with the smoothness and control of a singles hitter. In September and October, when he was punishing the ball with a severity and consistency that brought him the double reward of Most Valuable Player in both the regular season and the World Series, he looked like some marvellous new young hitter up at bat—a natural. But he was better than that—to me, at least—for he had made it all happen.

During a game, Schmidt brings such formidable attention and intelligence to bear on the enemy pitcher that one senses that the odds have almost been reversed out there: it is the man on the mound, not the one up at the plate, who is in worse trouble from the start. "A lot of times, a pitcher will change his patterns against you if you've happened to hit his best pitch once," Schmidt told me. "Because he remembers the one fast-ball you hit out, he'll forget all the ones you missed or popped up, and he'll feed you something else—something less than his best. This is total nonsense for him, of course, but you try to pick up on it if it's happening. Pitchers' patterns are what you have to keep studying—how they are thinking about you. But the catchers have patterns, too—how they call a game against you—and so do teams. Some teams are fastball-pitching teams, and some are breaking-ball teams. Their philosophy may come from the manager or from a pitching coach. St. Louis has been an away-pitching team for years, probably because of Ted Simmons. Now that he's gone, they may pitch some other way. We'll see. The Dodgers like to pitch you inside. In fact, they've pitched me in so much over the years that I finally had to back away at the plate, and that began to make me a better hitter. Pitchers should be smart enough to find out, when a team comes to town, how a certain batter on that club is going—whether he's been swinging the bat good or not—and if they know that, they should know how to pitch to him. I'd like to think that they do that, but maybe I'm giving them too much credit. I don't know how many pitchers know that I'm sitting here in the dugout all through the game, thinking about what they're doing. But I am. I don't mind if they know it, though. I'm *watching*."

Fear comes into it, Hawk told me. I was relieved at the news. Again and again, I'd asked hitters whether they were afraid up at the plate—afraid of being struck by a ninety-mile-an-hour fastball, the way I would be. Again and again, they'd said no. Some of them had confessed to a fear of failure. Some had said that certain pitchers inspired "respect." But fear—real nervousness out there—would destroy them at the plate, they'd said. It didn't exist.

Ken Harrelson (Hawk to his friends, because of his strong, beaky nose) is a television commentator with the Red Sox; he and his partner, Ned Martin, are just about the best pair in the business, to my way of thinking. He is a large, cheerful, ham-handed man who plays golf well enough to have competed on the professional circuit after his baseball career came to a close. He batted .239 in the majors in the late sixties and the early seventies, but his baseball intelligence and his opinions are of a Hall of Fame level of intensity. I sometimes have the impression that he relishes a heavy thundershower in the middle of a Red Sox game, so that he can get on with some good, serious baseball talk during the delay.

"Of *course* fear comes into it," he said to me one morning at Winter Haven. "The players won't admit it, because it diminishes their macho. They think the pitchers will hear them say it, and take advantage. Anyone who says he's never scared up there is lying. I played nine years in the majors scared to death. I've seen great players who were intimidated at the plate in certain situations, and anybody who's been around this game for long has seen pitchers who made fear part of their repertoire. Look at Jim Lonborg in 1967—there's never been a pitcher who dominated a whole league the way he did that summer, because of fear. Before the World Series that year, all the Cardinals said, 'We aren't going to let him intimidate *us*,' but in the second game Lonnie's first pitch, to Lou Brock, was between his helmet and his head, and that was it. The game was over. He pitched a one-hitter. Or just think back to the way Dickie Noles knocked down George Brett in the World Series last fall. That pitch changed the whole tempo of the Series. There isn't as much throwing at hitters as there used to be, and it isn't as vicious when it's done. It isn't done to *maim*. But it's part of the game, all right. It's just part of the main question out there: Who's going to dominate the situation—the pitcher or the batter? This is the struggle in any close game, and the best line about it came from Sandy Koufax, who said, 'Show me a guy who can't pitch inside and I'll show you a loser.' And Al Kaline was saying the same thing—the same thing *exactly*—when he said, 'Show me a guy who can't be jammed and I'll show you a horseshit hitter.' They're all out there, hitters and pitchers, fighting to dominate the plate."

Harrelson reminded me that the struggle for dominance is not always waged in such melodramatic terms. Some of the best pitchers, to his way of thinking, were those whose pitching knowledge and subtlety utterly mastered the batters in some games. Catfish Hunter, for instance. "He established the inside fastball to righthanded hitters early in the game," Harrelson said, "so by the time the seventh and eighth innings came along they were all looking in *here*, under their hands, and he was working to a plate that was about twenty-two inches wide. He only had a semipro-level fastball, but he broke more bats than anyone else, because of where he put it. He thought about hitters. If you'd ever asked him before a game how he was going to pitch to Frank Robinson, I'd bet he'd say, 'I'm going to go two-and-oh on him,' because he thought that Frank was less of a hitter that way—with the count in his favor. Maybe only Tommy John pitches like that nowadays. T.J. threw a two-hit shutout against the Red Sox in Fenway Park two years ago, and he never threw a right-handed hitter an inside strike all day. He was up against a lineup of big right-handed sluggers that had been pumping home runs, and he turned that knowledge to his advantage. He just walked the ladder, down and away. It was like T'ai Chi—he used the batters' strength to destroy them. It was one of the most beautiful things I've ever seen in my twenty-one years in the game. Sometimes you can see one pitcher do that to one batter—even to a real good, first-class hitter—and do it so bad that it almost destroys his mind. They can do it with one pitch. Two years ago, Mike Flanagan threw Jim Rice a hundred-mile-an-hour slider that put Jimmy into a two-week slump. I swear it. A pitch like that can turn a batter's head around. He won't look outside again for a long, long time.

"The better the pitcher, the more of the plate you have to concede. This is what's going on out there so much of the time between a good pitcher and a good hitter. Sometimes you just have to pick a third of the plate and try to make that yours. You've got to decide where you want the pitch—inside or away, up or away and down—and wait for it. It's the heart of the game."

I had heard something like this before, and when I remembered it there was a strange stir, a small knock of pleasure, inside me. I was beginning to understand—a little. Hitting seemed as difficult and complicated as ever, but I suddenly felt as if a door had opened and I could see a little farther into the game. What I had remembered was Ted Simmons sitting in the Brewers' clubhouse after that Brewers-Angels game in the desert heat at Sun City and talking about his struggle to master a special responsibility in baseball, which was batting in the cleanup position in the lineup. Seven years earlier, he told me, the Cardinals had asked him to take over the No. 4 spot in their batting order, and he had had to refashion his way of swinging at the ball and his way of thinking about the game. He had been a line-drive hitter, but now he taught himself to pull the ball more and to try to hit it out of the park down the foul lines, which was the only way it could be done in Busch Memorial Stadium, where the Cards play. It took him three years to become a competent cleanup hitter, he said, and along the way he talked to some other cleanup sluggers around the league, to get their counselling. Most of all, he talked to Willie Stargell.

"It would be stupid not to talk to someone like that," Simmons said to me. "Here's a man who's hit forty-four homers and batted .300 in the same year, so he can *hit,* and he understands situations. He told me that he admired what I'd been doing—how I'd gone about changing myself. What we talked about a lot was the win-the-game situation. You've been up three times, say, and now you've got a chance to win the game. Before you go up there, Stargell said, you've got to decide what kind of a pitch you're going to get to swing at. Is this guy going to give me the fastball or isn't he? And if he isn't— if he isn't going to throw it to you when the count is up and the pitch really matters—then you'd probably better decide *I'm going to get the slider.* Willie said that you might have seen nothing but the fastball all day, three times in a row, but that the man isn't going to throw it to you now, with two strikes on you and with men on base in the ninth inning, because if he does and you hit it he ain't going to *sleep* that night! It's as simple as that. But if he gives you the slider there, and you hit it just right and beat him the ballgame, he'll say to himself, 'Well, I did my best and I guess he's quite a hitter,' and that way he won't mind so much."

Simmons was very anxious for me to understand that this waiting for a certain pitch was not the same as guessing. "It takes discipline to wait for the slider in that situation," he said. "It takes discipline to take the oh-and-oh fastball on the outside corner, and then the slider or sinker down and away, and whatever, all the rest of it, because you still *know* that that slider is coming—because you know and he knows that if he gasses you up and you take him deep for the salami, he'll never forget it! If you're batting No. 4 and you do get the slider then, that isn't guessing—it's *design*."

Ted paused, recalling some past ninth inning of some game, no doubt, and then he said, "Guys like that, who can combine power and performance, are what I admire. I'm talking about a Ted Williams, a Stan Musial. And some other hitters—a Reggie Jackson, a Willie Stargell—can fan three times in a game and walk up to the plate in the tenth inning, and still the pitcher is scared out there, and the fans are scared and excited, too, because that man is *feared*. Everyone lives vicariously through a Reggie Jackson or a Willie Stargell coming up to bat in that situation, and if he comes through, they come through. That's what this game is all about. I've been in that position a few times. Some people have that kind of ability given to them, but I've had to learn it. I have it now—I have that respect. As far as I'm concerned, there is no greater pleasure in the world than walking up to the plate with men on base and knowing that you are feared."

14

The Web of the Game

JUNE 1981

AN AFTERNOON IN MID-MAY, AND WE ARE WAITING FOR THE game to begin. We are in shadow, and the sunlit field before us is a thick, springy green—an old diamond, beautifully kept up. The grass continues beyond the low chain-link fence that encloses the outfield, extending itself on the right-field side into a rougher, featureless sward that terminates in a low line of distant trees, still showing a pale, early-summer green. We are almost in the country. Our seats are in the seventh row of the grandstand, on the home side of the diamond, about halfway between third base and home plate. The seats themselves are more comforting to spirit than to body, being a surviving variant example of the pure late-Doric Polo Grounds mode: the backs made of a continuous running row of wood slats, divided off by pairs of narrow cast-iron arms, within which are slatted let-down seats, grown arthritic with rust and countless layers of gray paint. The rows are stacked so closely upon each other (one discovers) that a happening on the field of sufficient interest to warrant a rise or half-rise to one's feet is often made more memorable by a sharp crack to the kneecaps delivered by the backs of the seats just forward; in time, one finds that a dandruff of gray paint flakes from the same source has fallen on one's lap and scorecard. None of this matters, for this view and these stands and this park—it is Yale Field, in New Haven—are renowned for their felicity. The grandstand is a low, penumbrous steel-post shed that holds the infield in a pleasant horseshoe-curved embrace. The back wall of the grandstand, behind the uppermost row of seats, is broken by an arcade of open arches, admitting a soft back light that silhouettes the upper audience and also discloses an overhead bonework of struts and beams supporting the roof—the pigeonland of all the ballparks of our youth. The game we are waiting for— Yale vs. St. John's University—is a considerable event, for it is part of the National Collegiate Athletic Association's northeast regional tournament, the winner of which will qualify for a berth at the national collegiate championships in Omaha in June, the World Series of college baseball. Another pair of teams, Maine and Central Michigan—the Black Bears and the Chippewas—have just finished their game here, the first of a doubleheader. Maine won it, 10–2, but the ultimate winner will not be picked here for three more days, when the four teams will have completed a difficult double-elimination tournament. Good, hard competition, but the stands at Yale Field are half empty today. Call them half full, because everyone on hand— some twenty-five hundred fans—must know something about the quality of the teams here, or at least enough to qualify either as a partisan or as an expert, which would explain the hum of talk and expectation that runs through the grandstand even while the Yale team, in pinstriped home whites, is still taking infield practice.

I am seated in a little sector of senior New Haven men— Townies rather than Old Elis. One of them a couple of rows in front of me says, "They used to fill this place in the old days, before there was all the baseball on TV."

His neighbor, a small man in a tweed cap, says, "The biggest crowd I ever saw in here—the biggest ever, I bet—was for a highschool game. Shelton and Naugatuck, about twenty years ago."

An old gent with a cane, seated just to my left, says, "They filled it up that day the Yankees came here, with Ruth and Gehrig and the rest of them. An exhibition game."

A fan just beyond the old gentleman—a good-looking man in his sixties, with an open, friendly face, a large smile, and a thick stand of gray hair—leans toward my neighbor and says, "When *was* that game, Joe? 1930? 1932?"

"Oh, I can't remember," the old man says. "Somewhere in there. My youngest son was mascot for the Yankees that day, so I could figure it out, I suppose." He is not much interested. His eyes are on the field. "Say, look at these fellows throw!" he says. "Did you see that outfielder peg in the ball?"

"That was the day Babe Ruth said this was about the best-looking ballpark he'd ever ever seen," the man beyond says. "You remember that."

"I can remember long before this park was built," the old man says. "It was already the Yale ballfield when I got here, but they put in these stands later— Who is this shortstop? He's a hefty-looking bird."

"How many Yale games do you think you've seen, Joe?" the smiling man asks.

"Oh, I couldn't begin to count them. But I haven't seen a Yale team play in—I don't know how long. Not for years. These fellows today, they play in the Cape Cod League in the summers. They let the freshmen play here now, too. They recruit them more, I suppose. They're athletes—you can see that."

The Yale team finishes its warmup ritual, and St. John's— light-gray uniforms with scarlet cap bills and scarlet socks— replaces it on the field.

"St. John's has always had a good club," the old man tells me. "Even back when my sons were playing ball, it was a good ball team. But not as good as this one. Oh, my! Did you see this catcher throw down to second? Did you see that! I bet you in all the years I was here I didn't have twenty fellows who could throw."

"Your sons played here?" I ask him. "For Yale?"

"My son Joe was captain in '41," he says. "He was a pitcher. He pitched against my son Steve here one day. Steve was pitching for Colgate, and my other son, Bob—my youngest— was on the same Colgate team. A good little left-handed first baseman."

I am about to ask how that game turned out, but the old man has taken out a small gold pocket watch, with a hunting case, which he snaps open. Three-fourteen. "Can't they get this *started?*" he says impatiently.

I say something admiring about the watch, and he hands it to me carefully. "I've had that watch for sixty-eight years," he says. "I always carried it in my vest pocket, back when we wore vests."

The little watch has a considerable heft to it: a weight of authority. I turn it over and find an inscription on the back. It is in script and a bit worn, but I can still make it out:

PRESENTED TO JOE WOOD
BY HIS FRIEND A. E. SMITH
IN APPRECIATION OF HIS SPLENDID
PITCHING WHICH BROUGHT THE
WORLD'S CHAMPIONSHIP
TO BOSTON IN 1912.

"Who was A. E. Smith, Mr. Wood?" I ask.

"He was a manufacturer."

I know the rest. Joe Wood, the old gentleman on my left, was the baseball coach at Yale for twenty years—from 1923 to 1942. Before that, he was a sometime outfielder for the Cleveland Indians, who batted .366 in 1921. Before *that*, he was a celebrated righthanded pitcher for the Boston Red Sox— Smokey Joe Wood, who won thirty-four games for the Bosox in 1912, when he finished up with a record of 34–5, pitching ten shutouts and sixteen consecutive victories along the way. In the World Series that fall—one of the two or three finest ever played—he won three of the four games he pitched, including the famous finale: the game of Hooper's catch and Snodgrass's muff and Tris Speaker's killing tenth-inning single. Next to Walter Johnson, Smokey Joe Wood was the most famous fastballer of his era. Still is, no doubt, in the minds of the few surviving fans who saw him at his best. He is ninety-one years old.

None of this, I should explain—neither my presence at the game nor my companions in the stands—was an accident. I had been a fervent admirer of Smokey Joe Wood ever since I read his account of his baseball beginnings and his subsequent career in Lawrence Ritter's *The Glory of Their Times*, a cherished, classic volume of oral history of the early days of the pastime. Mr. Wood was in his seventies when that book was published, in 1966, and I was startled and pleased a few weeks ago when I ran across an article by Joan Whaley, in *Baseball Digest*, which informed me that he was still hale and still talking baseball in stimulating fashion. He was living with a married daughter in New Haven, and my first impulse was to jump in my car and drive up to press a call. But something held me back; it did not seem quite right to present myself uninvited at his door, even as a pilgrim. Then Ron Darling and Frank Viola gave me my chance. Darling, who was a junior at Yale this past year, is the best pitcher ever to take the mound for the Blue. He is better than Johnny Broaca, who went on to pitch for the Yankees and the Indians for five seasons in the mid-nineteen-thirties; he is better than Frank Quinn, who compiled a 1.57 career earned-run average at Yale in 1946, '47, and '48. (He is also a better all-around ballplayer than George Bush, who played first base and captained the Elis in 1948, and then somehow drifted off into politics instead of baseball.) Darling, a right-handed fastball thrower, won eleven games and lost two as a sophomore, with an earned-run average of 1.31, and this year he was 9–3 and 2.42, with eighty-nine strikeouts in his ninety-three innings of work—the finest college pitcher in the Northeast, according to major-league scouts, with the possible exception of Frank Viola, a junior left-handed curveball ace at St. John's, who was undefeated this year, 9–0, and had a neat earned-run average of 1.00. St. John's, a Catholic university in Queens, is almost a baseball powerhouse—not quite in the same class, perhaps, as such perennial national champions or challengers as Arizona, Arizona State, Texas, and Southern California, whose teams play Sun Belt schedules of close to sixty games, but good enough to have gone as the Northeast's representative to the national tournament in Omaha in 1980, when Viola defeated the eventual winner, Arizona, in the first round. St. John's, by the way, does not recruit high-school stars from faraway states, as do most of these rival college powers; all but one player on this year's thirty-three-man Red-men squad grew up and went to school in New York City or in nearby suburbs. This 1981 St. John's team ran off an awesome 31–2 record, capturing the Eastern College Metro (Greater New York, that is) elimination, while Yale, winning its last nine games in a row, concluded its regular season with a record of 24–12–1, which was good enough to win its first Eastern Intercollegiate League championship since 1956. (The tie in

Yale's record was a game against the University of Central Florida, played during the Elis' spring-training tour in March, and was called because of darkness after seven innings, with the score tied at 21–21. Darling did not pitch that day.) The two teams, along with Central Michigan (Mid-America Conference) and Maine (New England Conference), qualified for the tournament at New Haven, and the luck of the draw pitted Yale (and Darling) against St. John's (and Viola) in the second game of the opening doubleheader. Perfect. Darling, by the way, had indicated that he might be willing to turn professional this summer if he were to be picked in an early round of the annual amateur draft conducted by the major leagues in mid-June, and Viola had been talked about as a potential big-leaguer ever since his freshman year, so their matchup suddenly became an obligatory reunion for every front-rank baseball scout east of the Ohio River. (About fifty of them turned up, with their speed-guns and clipboards, and their glowing reports of the game, I learned later, altered the draft priorities of several clubs.)

Perfect, but who would get in touch with Mr. Wood and persuade him to come out to Yale Field with me for the game? Why, Dick Lee would—Dick Lee, *of course*. Richard C. Lee (he was the smiling man sitting just beyond Smokey Joe in our row) is a former Democratic mayor of New Haven, an extremely popular (eight consecutive terms, sixteen years in office), innovative officeholder who, among other things, presided over the widely admired urban renewal of his city during the nineteen-sixties and, before that, thought up and pushed through the first Operation Head Start program (for minority-group preschoolers) in the country. Dick Lee knows everybody in New Haven, including Smokey Joe Wood and several friends of mine there, one of whom provided me with his telephone number. I called Lee at his office (he is assistant to the chairman of the Union Trust Company, in New Haven) and proposed our party. "Wonderful!" he cried at once. "You have come to the right man. I'll bring Joe. Count on me!" Even over the telephone, I could see him smiling.

Dick Lee did not play baseball for Yale, but the nature of his partisanship became clear in the very early moments of the Yale-St. John's game. "Yay!" he shouted in a stentorian baritone as Ron Darling set down three St. John's batters in order in the first. "Yay, Ron *baby!*" he boomed out as Darling dismissed three more batters in the second, fanning the last two. "Now *c'mon,* Yale! Let's get something started, gang! Yay!" Lee had told me that he pitched for some lesser-known New Haven teams—the Dixwell Community House sandlot team and the Jewish Home for Children nine (the Utopians), among others—while he was growing up in the ivyless Newhallville neighborhood. Some years later, having passed up college altogether, he went to work for Yale as its public-relations officer. By the time he became mayor, in 1953, the university was his own—another precinct to be worried about and looked after. A born politician, he appears to draw on some inner deep-water reservoir of concern that enables him to preside effortlessly and affectionately over each encounter of his day; he was the host at our game, and at intervals he primed Joe Wood with questions about his baseball past, which he seemed to know almost by heart.

"Yes, that's right, I did play for the Bloomer Girls a few games," Mr. Wood said in response to one such cue. "I was about sixteen, and I was pitching for our town team in Ness City, Kansas. The Bloomer Girls were a barnstorming team, but they used to pick up a few young local fellows on the sly to play along with them if they needed to fill out their lineup. I was one of those. I never wore a wig, though—I wouldn't have done that. I guess I looked young enough to pass for a girl anyway. Bill Stern, the old radio braodcaster, must have used that story about forty times, but he always got it wrong about the wig."

There was a yell around us, and an instantly ensuing groan, as Yale's big freshman catcher, Tony Paterno, leading off the bottom of the second, lined sharply to the St. John's shortstop, who made a fine play on the ball. Joe Wood peered intently out at the field through his thickish horn-rimmed spectacles. He shook his head a little. "You know, I can't hardly follow the damned ball now," he said. "It's better for me if I'm someplace where I can get up high behind the plate. I was up to Fenway Park for two games last year, and they let me sit in the press box there at that beautiful park. I could see it all from there. The grounds keeper has got that field just like a living room."

I asked him if he still rooted for the Red Sox.

"Oh, yes," he said. "All my life. A couple of years ago, when they had that big lead in the middle of the summer, they asked me if I'd come up and throw out the first ball at one of their World Series games or playoff games. But then they dropped out of it, of course. Now it looks like it'll never happen."

He spoke in a quiet, almost measured tone, but there was no tinge of disappointment or self-pity in it. It was the voice of age. He was wearing a blue windbreaker over a buttoned-up plaid shirt, made formal with a small dark-red bow tie. There was a brown straw hat on his bald head. The years had imparted a delicate thinness to the skin on his cheeks and neck, but his face had a determined look to it, with a strong chin and a broad, unsmiling mouth. Watching him, I recalled one of the pictures in *The Glory of Their Times*—a team photograph taken in 1906, in which he is sitting cross-legged down in front of a row of men in baggy baseball pants and lace-up, collared baseball shirts with "NESS CITY" across the front in block letters. The men are standing in attitudes of cheerful assurance, with their arms folded, and their mushy little baseball gloves are hanging from their belts. Joe Wood, the smallest player in the picture, is wearing a dark warmup shirt, with the sleeves rolled halfway up his forearms, and his striped baseball cap is pushed back a little, revealing a part in the middle of his hair. There is an intent, unsmiling look on his boyish face—the same grave demeanor you can spot in a subsequent photograph, taken in 1912, in which he is standing beside his Red Sox manager, Jake Stahl, and wearing a heavy woollen three-button suit, a stiff collar, a narrow necktie with a stickpin, and a stylish black porkpie hat pulled low over his handsome, famous face: Smokey Joe Wood at twenty-two. (The moniker, by the way, was given him by Paul Shannon, a sportswriter for the Boston *Post;* before that, he was sometimes called Ozone Wood— "ozone" for the air cleaved by the hapless batters who faced him.) The young man in the photographs and the old man beside me at the ballpark had the same broad, sloping shoulders, but there was nothing burly or physically imposing about him then or now.

"What kind of a pitcher were you, Mr. Wood?" I asked him.

"I had a curve and a fastball," he said. "That's all. I didn't even have brains enough to slow up on the batters. The fastball had a hop on it. You had to be *fast* to have that happen to the ball."

I said that I vividly recalled Sandy Koufax's fastball, which sometimes seemed to jump so violently as it crossed the plate that his catcher had to shoot up his mitt to intercept it.

"Mine didn't go up that far. Just enough for them to miss it." He half turned to me as he said this, and gave me a little glance and an infinitesimal smile. A twinkle. "I don't know where my speed came from," he went on. "I wasn't any bigger or stronger-looking then than I am now. I always could throw hard, and once I saw I was able to get batters out, I figured I was crazy enough to play ball for a living. My father was a criminal lawyer in Kansas, and before that out in Ouray, Colorado, where I first played ball, and my brother went to law school and got a degree, but I didn't even graduate from high school. I ate and slept baseball all my life."

The flow of recollection from Joe Wood was perhaps not as smooth and rivery as I have suggested here. For one thing, he spoke slowly and with care—not unlike the way he walked to the grandstand at Yale Field from the parking lot beyond left field, making his way along the grass firmly enough but looking where he was going, too, and helping himself a bit with his cane. Nothing infirm about him, but nothing hurrying or sprightly, either. For another, the game was well in progress by now, and its principals and sudden events kept interrupting our colloquy. Ron Darling, a poised, impressive figure on the mound, alternated his popping fastballs with just enough down-breaking sliders and an occasional curveball to keep the St. John's batters unhappy. Everything was thrown with heat—his strikeout pitch is a Seaver-high fastball, but his slider, which slides at the last possible instant, is an even deadlier weapon—but without any signs of strain or anxiety. He threw over the top, smoothly driving his front (left) shoulder at the batter in picturebook style, and by the third or fourth inning he had imposed his will and his pace on the game. He was rolling. He is a dark-haired, olive-skinned young man (he lives in Millbury, Massachusetts, near Worcester, but he was born in Hawaii; his mother is Chinese-Hawaiian by birth) with long, powerful legs, but his pitcherlike proportions tend to conceal, rather than emphasize, his six feet two inches and his hundred and ninety-five pounds. He also swings the bat well enough (.331 this year) to play right field for Yale when he isn't pitching; in our game he was the designated hitter as well as the pitcher for the Elis.

"That's a nice build for a pitcher, isn't it?" Joe Wood murmured during the St. John's fifth. Almost as he spoke, Darling executed a twisting dive to his right to snaffle a hard-hit grounder up the middle by Brian Miller, the St. John's shortstop, and threw him out at first. ("Hey-*hey!*" Dick Lee cried. "Yay, Ronnie!") *"And* he's an athlete out there," Wood added. "The scouts like that, you know. Oh, this fellow's a lot better than Broaca ever was."

Frank Viola, for his part, was as imperturbable as Darling on the mound, if not quite as awesome. A lanky, sharp-shouldered lefty, he threw an assortment of speeds and spins, mostly sinkers and down-darting sliders, that had the Yale batters swinging from their shoe tops and, for the most part, hammering the ball into the dirt. He had the stuff and poise of a veteran relief pitcher, and the St. John's infield—especially Brian Miller and a stubby, ebullient second baseman named Steve Scafa—performed behind him with the swift, almost haughty confidence that imparts an elegance and calm and sense of ease to baseball at its best. It was a scoreless game after five, and a beauty.

"What was the score of that game you beat Walter Johnson in, in your big year?" Dick Lee asked our guest between innings.

We all knew the answer, I think. In September of 1912, Walter Johnson came to Fenway Park (it was brand-new that year) with the Senators and pitched against young Joe Wood, who then had a string of thirteen consecutive victories to his credit. That summer, Johnson had established a league record of sixteen straight wins, so the matchup was not merely an overflow, sellout affair but perhaps the most anticipated, most discussed non-championship game in the American League up to that time.

"We won it, 1–0," Joe Wood said quietly, "but it wasn't his fault I beat him that day. If he'd had the team behind him that I did, he'd have set every kind of record in baseball. You have to remember that Walter Johnson played for a second-division team almost all through his career. All those years, and he had to work from the bottom every time he pitched."

"Were you faster than he was?" I asked.

"Oh, I don't think there was ever anybody faster than Walter," he murmured.

"But Johnson said just the opposite!" Dick Lee cried. "He said no one was faster than *you*."

"He was just that kind of fellow, to say something like that," Wood said. "That was just like the man. Walter Johnson was a great big sort of a pitcher, with hands that came clear down to his knees. Why, the way he threw the ball, the only reason anybody ever got even a foul off him was because everybody in the league knew he'd never come inside to a batter. Walter Johnson was a prince of men—a gentleman first, last, and always."

It came to me that this was the first time I had ever heard anybody use the phrase "a prince of men" in non-satiric fashion. In any case, the Johnson-Wood argument did not really need settling, then or now. Smokey Joe went on to tie Johnson with sixteen straight victories that season—an American League record, subsequently tied by Lefty Grove and Schoolboy Rowe. (Over in the National League that year, Rube Marquard won *nineteen* straight for the Giants—a single-season mark first set by Tim Keefe of the Giants in 1888 and untouched as yet by anyone else.) Johnson and Wood pretty well divided up the A.L. mound honors that summer, when Johnson won thirty-two games and lost twelve, posting the best earned-run average (1.39) and the most strikeouts (three hundred and three), while Wood won the most games and established the best winning percentage with his 34–5 mark (not including his three World Series wins, of course).

These last figures are firmly emplaced in the baseball crannies of my mind, and in the minds of most students of the game, because, it turned out, they represent the autumn of Joe Wood's pitching career as well as its first full flowering. Early in the spring of 1913, he was injured in a fielding play, and he was never near to being the same pitcher again. One of the game's sad speculations over the years has been what Joe Wood's status in the pantheon of great pitchers would be if he had remained sound. I did not need any reminder of his accident, but I had been given one just the same when Dick Lee introduced me to him, shortly before the game. We had stopped to pick up Mr. Wood at his small, red-shuttered white house on Marvel Road, and when he came down the concrete path to join us I got out of Lee's Cadillac to shake the hand that once shook the baseball world.

"Mr. Wood," I said, "this is a great honor."

"Ow—*ow!*" he cried, cringing before me and attempting to extricate his paw.

"Oh, oh . . . I'm *terribly* sorry," I said, appalled. "Is it—is this because of your fall off the roof?" Three years ago, at the age of eighty-eight, he had fallen off a ladder while investigating a leak, and had cracked several ribs.

"Hell, no!" he said indignantly. "This is the arm I threw out in 1913!"

I felt awful. I had touched history—and almost brought it to its knees.

Now, at the game, he told me how it all happened. "I can't remember now if it was on the road or at Fenway Park," he said. "Anyway, it was against Detroit. There was a swinging bunt down the line, and I went to field it and slipped on the wet grass and went down and landed on my hand. I broke it right here." He pointed to a spot just below his wrist, on the back of his freckled, slightly gnarled right hand. "It's what they call a subperiosteal fracture. They put it in a cast, and I had to sit out awhile. Well, this was in 1913, right after we'd won the championship, and every team was out to get us, of course. So as soon as the cast came off, the manager would come up to me every now and then and want to know how soon I was going to get back to pitching. Well, maybe I got back to it too soon and maybe I didn't, but the arm never felt right again. The shoulder went bad. I still went on pitching, but the fastball had lost that hop. I never threw a day after that when I wasn't in pain. Most of the time, I'd pitch and then it would hurt so bad that I wasn't able to raise my hand again for days afterward. So I was about a halftime pitcher after that. You have to understand that in those days if you didn't work you didn't get paid. Now they lay out as long as they need to and get a shot of that cortisone. But we had to play, ready or not. I was a married man, just starting a family, and in order to get my check I had to be in there. So I pitched."

He pitched less, but not much less well. In 1915, he was

15–5 for the Red Sox, with an earned-run average of 1.49, which was the best in the league. But the pain was so persistent that he sat out the entire 1916 season, on his farm, near Shohola, Pennsylvania, hoping that the rest would restore his arm. It did not. He pitched in eight more games after that—all of them for the Cleveland Indians, to whom he was sold in 1917—but he never won again.

"Did you become a different kind of pitcher after you hurt your arm?" I asked. "More off-speed stuff, I mean?"

"No, I still pitched the fastball."

"But all that pain—"

"I tried not to think about that." He gave me the same small smile and bright glance. "I just loved to be out there," he said. "It was as simple as that."

Our afternoon slid by in a distraction of baseball and memory, and I almost felt myself at some dreamlike doubleheader involving the then and the now—the semi-anonymous strong young men waging their close, marvellous game on the sunlit green field before us while bygone players and heroes of baseball history—long gone now, most of them—replayed their vivid, famous innings for me in the words and recollections of my companion. Yale kept putting men aboard against Viola and failing to move them along; Rich Diana, the husky center fielder (he is also an All-Ivy League half-back), whacked a long double to left but then died on second—the sixth stranded Eli base runner in five innings. Darling appeared to be struggling a little, walking two successive batters in the sixth, but he saved himself with a whirling pickoff to second base—a timed play brilliantly completed by his shortstop, Bob Brooke—and then struck out St. John's big first baseman, Karl Komyathy, for the last out. St. John's had yet to manage a hit against him.

In the home half of the sixth, Yale put its leadoff batter aboard with a single but could not bunt him along. Joe Wood was distressed. "I could teach these fellows to bunt in one minute," he said. "Nobody can't hardly bunt anymore. You've got to get your weight more forward than he did, so you're not reaching for the ball. And he should have his right hand higher up on the bat."

The inning ended, and we reversed directions once again. "Ty Cobb was the greatest bat-handler you ever saw," Wood said. "He used to go out to the ballpark early in the morning with a pitcher and work on hitting the ball to all fields, over and over. He batted that strange way, with his fists apart, you know, but he could have hit just as well no matter how he held it. He just knew what to do with a bat in hand. And baserunning—why, I saw him get on base and steal second, steal third, and then steal home. *The* best. A lot of fellows in my time shortened up on the bat when they had to—that's what the St. John's boys should try against this good pitcher. Next to Cobb, Shoeless Joe Jackson was the best left-handed hitter I ever saw, and he was always down at the end of the bat until there were two strikes on him. Then he'd shorten up a little, to give himself a better chance."

Dick Lee said, "That's what you've been telling Charlie Polka, isn't it, Joe?"

"Yes, sir, and it's helped him," Wood said. "He's tried it, and now he knows that all you have to to is make contact and the ball will fly a long way."

Both men saw my look of bewilderment, and they laughed together.

"Charlie Polka is a Little League player," Dick Lee explained. "He's about eleven years old."

"He lives right across the street from me," Wood said. "He plays for the 500 Blake team—that's named for a restaurant here in town. I've got him shortened up on the bat, and now he's a hitter. Charlie Polka is a natural."

"Is that how you batted?" I asked.

"Not at first," he said. "But after I went over to Cleveland in 1917 to join my old roommate, Tris Speaker, I started to play the outfield, and I began to take up on the bat, because I knew I'd have to hit a little better if I was going to make the team. I never was any wonder at the plate, but I was good enough to last six more years, playing with Spoke."

Tris Speaker (Wood had called him by his old nickname, Spoke) was the Joe DiMaggio or Willie Mays of the first two decades of this century—the nonpareil center fielder of his day. "He had a beautiful left-handed arm," Joe Wood said. "He always played very shallow in center—you could do that in those days, because of the dead ball. I saw him make a lot of plays to second base from there—pick up what looked like a clean single and fire the ball to second in time to force the base runner coming down from first. Or he could throw the ball behind a runner and pick him off that way. And just as fine a man as he was a ballplayer. He was a Southern gentleman—well, he was from Hubbard, Texas. Back in the early days, when we were living together on the beach at Winthrop during the season, out beyond Revere, Spoke would sometimes cook up a mess of fried chicken in the evening. He'd cook, and then I'd do the dishes."

Listening to this, I sensed the web of baseball about me. Tris Speaker had driven in the tying run in the tenth inning of the last game of the 1912 World Series, at Fenway Park, after Fred Merkle and Chief Meyers, of the Giants, had let his easy foul pop fall untouched between them. A moment or two later, Joe Wood had won his third game of the Series and the Red Sox were champions. My father saw that game—he was at Harvard Law School at the time, and got a ticket somehow— and he told me about it many times. He was terrifically excited to be there, but I think my mother must have relished the famous victory even more. She grew up in Boston and was a true Red Sox fan, even though young women didn't go to many games then. My father grew up in Cleveland, so he was an Indians rooter, of course. In 1915, my parents got married and went to live in Cleveland, where my father began to practice law. Tris Speaker was traded to the Indians in 1916—a terrible shock to Red Sox fans—and Joe Wood came out of his brief retirement to join him on the club a year later. My parents' first child, my older sister, was born in Cleveland late in 1916, and the next year my father went off to Europe—off to the war. My mother once told me that in the summer afternoons of 1917 she would often push a baby carriage past League Park, the Indians' home field, out on Linwood Avenue, which was a block or two away from my parents' house. Sometimes there was a game going on, and if she heard a roar of pleasure from the fans inside she would tell herself that probably Tris Speaker had just done something special. She was lonely in Cleveland, she told me, and it made her feel good to know that Tris Speaker was there in the same town with her. "Tris

Speaker and I were traded to Cleveland in the same year," she said.

A yell and an explosion of cheering brought me back to Yale Field. We were in the top of the seventh, and the Yale second baseman and captain, Gerry Harrington, had just leaped high to snatch down a burning line drive—the force of it almost knocked him over backward in midair. Then he flipped the ball to second to double off a St. John's base runner and end the inning. "These fellows came to *play!*" Dick Lee said.

Most no-hitters produce at least one such heaven-sent gift somewhere along the line, and I began to believe that Ron Darling, who was still untouched on the mound, might be pitching the game of his young life. I turned to ask Mr. Wood how many no-hitters he recalled—he had seen Mathewson and Marquard and Babe Ruth (Ruth, the pitcher, that is) and Coveleski and the rest of them, after all—but he seemed transfixed by something on the field. "Look at *that!*" he said, in a harsh, disbelieving way. "This Yale coach has his own coaches out there on the lines, by God! They're professionals—not just players, the way I always had it when I was here. The coach has his own coaches . . . I never knew that."

"Did you have special coaches when you were coming up with the Red Sox?" I said, hoping to change his mood. "A pitching coach, I mean, or a batting coach?"

He didn't catch the question, and I repeated it.

"No, no," he said, a little impatiently. "We talked about the other players and the pitchers among ourselves in those days. We players. We didn't need anybody to help us."

He was staring straight ahead at the field. I thought he looked a bit chilly. It was well past five o'clock now, and a skim of clouds had covered the sun.

Dick Lee stole a glance at him, too. "Hey, Joe, doesn't this Darling remind you a little of Carl Hubbell on the mound?" he said in a cheerful, distracting sort of voice. "The way he picks up his front leg, I mean. You remember how Hubbell would go way up on the stretch and then drop his hands down by his ankles before he threw the ball?"

"Hubbell?" Joe Wood said. He shook his head, making an effort. "Well, to me this pitcher's a little like that fellow Eckersley," he said slowly. "The way he moves forward there."

He was right. Don Darling had exactly the same float and glide that the Red Sox' Dennis Eckersley conveys when he is pitching well.

"How do today's players compare with the men you played with, Mr. Wood?" I asked.

"I'd rather not answer that question," he said. He had taken out his watch again. He studied it and then tucked it away carefully, and then he glanced over at me, perhaps wondering if he had been impolite. "That Pete Rose plays hard," he added. "Him and a few more. I don't *like* Pete Rose, exactly, but he looks like he plays the game the way we did. He'd play for the fun of it if he had to."

He resumed his study of the field, and now and then I saw him stare again at the heavyset Yale third-base coach on our side of the diamond. Scoreless games make for a long day at the ballpark, and Joe Wood's day had probably been longer than ours. More than once, I had seen him struggle to his feet to catch some exciting play or moment on the field, only to have it end before he was quite up. Then he would sit down again, leaning on his cane while he lowered himself. I had more questions for Mr. Wood, but now I tried to put them out of my mind. Earlier in the afternoon, he had remarked that several old Yale players had dropped in at his house before the game to say hello and to talk about the old days. "People come by and see me all the time," he had said. "People I don't even know, from as far away as Colorado. Why, I had a fellow come in all the way from Canada the other day, who just wanted to talk about the old days. They all want that, somehow. It's gone on too long."

It had gone on for him, I realized, for as long as most lifetimes. He had played ball for fourteen years, all told, and people had been asking him to talk about it for nearly sixty years. For him, the last juice and sweetness must have been squeezed out of these ancient games years ago, but he was still expected to respond to our amateur expertise, our insatiable vicariousness. Old men are patronized in much the same fashion as athletes; because we take pride in them, we expect their intimacy in return. I had intruded after all.

We were in the eighth now . . . and then in the ninth. Still no score, and each new batter, each pitch was greeted with clappings and deepening cries of encouragement and anxiety from the stands and the players alike. The close-packed rows hummed with ceaseless, nervous sounds of conversation and specula-tion—and impatience for the dénouement, and a fear of it, too. All around me in our section I could see the same look of resignation and boredom and pleasure that now showed on my own face, I knew—the look of longtime fans who under-stand that one can never leave a very long close game, no matter how much inconvenience and exasperation it imposes on us. The difficulty of baseball is imperious.

"Yay! Yay!" Dick Lee cried when Yale left fielder Joe Dufek led off the eighth with a single. "Now come *on,* you guys! I gotta get home for dinner." But the next Yale batter bunted into a force play at second, and the chance was gone. "Well, all right—for *breakfast!*" Lee said, slumping back in his seat.

The two pitchers held us—each as intent and calm and purposeful as the other. Ron Darling, never deviating from the purity of his stylish body-lean and leg-crook and his riding, down-thrusting delivery, poured fastballs through the dimin-ishing daylight. He looked as fast as ever now, or faster, and in both the ninth and the tenth he dismissed the side in order and with four more strikeouts. Viola was dominant in his own fashion, also setting down the Yale hitters one, two, three in the ninth and tenth, with a handful of pitches. His rhythm—the constant variety of speeds and location on his pitches—had the enemy batters leaning and swaying with his motion, and, as antistrophe, was almost as exciting to watch as Darling's flair and flame. With two out in the top of the eleventh, a St. John's batter nudged a soft little roller up the first-base line—such an easy, waiting, schoolboy sort of chance that the Yale first baseman, O'Connor, allowed the ball to carom off his mitt: a miserable little butchery, except that the second base-man, seeing his pitcher sprinting for the bag, now snatched up the ball and flipped it toward him almost despairingly. Darling took the toss while diving full-length at the bag and, rolling in the dirt, beat the runner by a hair.

"Oh, my!" said Joe Wood. "Oh, my, oh, my!"

Then in the bottom of the inning Yale suddenly loaded the bases—a hit, a walk, another walk (Viola was just missing the corners now)—and we all came to our feet, yelling and plead-ing. The tilted stands and the low roof deepened the cheers and sent them rolling across the field. There were two out, and the Yale batter, Dan Costello, swung at the first pitch and bounced it gently to short, for a force that ended the rally. Somehow, I think, we knew that we had seen Yale's last chance.

"I would have taken that pitch," I said, entering the out in my scorecard. "To keep the pressure on him."

"I don't know," Joe Wood said at once. "He's just walked two. You might get the cripple on the first pitch and then see nothing but hooks. Hit away."

He was back in the game.

Steve Scafa, leading off the twelfth, got a little piece of Darling's first pitch on the handle of his bat, and the ball looped softly over the shortstop's head and into left: a hit. The loud-speakers told us that Ron Darling's eleven innings of no-hit pitching had set a new N.C.A.A. tournament record. Everyone at Yale Field stood up—the St. John's players, too, coming off their bench and out onto the field—and applauded Darling's masterpiece. We were scarcely seated again before Scafa stole second as the Yale catcher, Paterno, bobbled the pitch. Scafa, who is blurrily quick, had stolen thirty-five bases during the season. Now he stole third as well. With one out and runners at the corners (the other St. John's man had reached first on an error), Darling ran the count to three and two and fanned the next batter—his fifteenth strikeout of the game. Two out. Darling sighed and stared in, and then stepped off the mound while the St. John's coach put in a pinch-runner at first—who took off for second on the very next pitch. Paterno fired the ball quickly this time, and Darling, staggering off the mound with his follow-through, did not cut it off. Scafa came ten feet down the third-base line and stopped there, while the pinch-runner suddenly jammed on the brakes, standing himself be-tween first and second: a play, clearly—an inserted crisis. The Yale second baseman glanced twice at Scafa, freezing him, and then made a little run at the hungup base runner to his left and threw to first. With that, Scafa instantly broke for the plate. Lured by the vision of the third out just a few feet away from him on the base path, the Yale first baseman hesitated, frac-tionally and fatally, before he spun and threw home, where Scafa slid past the tag and came up, leaping and clapping, into the arms of his teammates. That was the game. Darling struck out his last man, but a new St. John's pitcher, a right-handed fireballer named Eric Stampfl, walked on and blew the Elis away in their half.

"Well, that's a shame," Joe Wood said, getting up for the last time. It was close to six-thirty, but he looked fine now. "If that man scores before the third out, it counts, you know," he said. "That's why it worked. I never saw a better-played game anyplace—college or big-league. That's a swell ball-game."

Several things happened afterward. Neither Yale nor St. John's qualified for the college World Series, it turned out; the University of Maine defeated St. John's in the final game of the playoffs at New Haven (neither Viola nor Darling was sufficiently recovered from his ordeal to pitch again) and made the trip to Omaha, where it, too, was eliminated. Arizona State won the national title. On June 9th, Ron Darling was selected by the Texas Rangers at the major-league amateur-player draft in New York. He was the ninth player in the country to be chosen. Frank Viola, the thirty-seventh pick, went to the Minnesota Twins. (The Seattle Mariners, who had the first pick this year, had been ready to take Darling, which would have made him the coveted No. 1 selection in the draft, but the club backed off at the last moment because of Darling's considerable salary demands. As it was, he signed with the Rangers for a hundred-thousand-dollar bonus.) On June 12th, the major-league players unanimously struck the twenty-six big-league teams. The strike has brought major-league ball to a halt, and no one can predict when play will resume. Because of this sudden silence, the St. John's–Yale struggle has become the best and most vivid game of the year for me, so far. It may stay that way even after the strike ends. "I think that game will always be on my mind," Ron Darling said after it was over. I feel the same way. I think I will remember it all my life. So will Joe Wood. Somebody will probably tell Ron Darling that Smokey Joe Wood was at the game that afternoon and saw him pitch eleven scoreless no-hit innings against St. John's, and someday—perhaps years from now, when he, too, may possibly be a celebrated major-league strikeout artist—it may occur to him that his heartbreaking 0–1 loss in May 1981 and

Walter Johnson's 0–1 loss at Fenway Park in September 1912 are now woven together into the fabric of baseball. Pitch by pitch, inning by inning, Ron Darling had made that happen. He stitched us together.

15

The Silence

I

JULY 1981

LAST WEEK, MY WIFE AND I CAME UPTOWN LATE ONE NIGHT in a cab after having dinner with friends of ours in the Village. We wheeled through the warm and odorous light-strewn summer dark on the same northward route home we have followed hundreds of times over the years, I suppose: bumping and lurching up Sixth non-stop, with the successive gateways of staggered green lights magically opening before us, and the stately tall street lights (if you tipped your head back on the cab seat and watched them upside down through the back window of the cab: I had drunk a bit of wine) forming a narrowing golden archway astern; and then moving more quietly through the swerves and small hills of the Park, where the weight and silence of the black trees wrapped us in a special summer darkness. The cabdriver had his radio on, and the blurry sounds of the news—the midnight news, I suppose—passed over us there in the back seat, mixing with the sounds of the wind coming in through the open cab windows, and the motion of our ride, and the whole sense of city night. All was as always, I mean, except that now it came to me, unsurprisingly at first but then with a terrific jolt of unhappiness and mourning, that this radio news was altered for there was no baseball in it. Without knowing it, I had been waiting for those other particular sounds, for that other part of the summer night, but it was missing, of course—no line scores, no winning and losing pitchers, no homers and highlights, no records approached or streaks cut short, no "Meanwhile, over in the National League," no double-zip early innings from Anaheim or Chavez Ravine, no Valenzuela and no Rose, no Goose and no Tom, no Yaz, no Mazz, no nothing.

The strike by this time was more than a week old, and I had so far sustained the shock of it and the change of it with more fortitude and patience than I had expected of myself. The issues seemed far removed from me—too expensive or too complicated, for some reason, for me to hold them clearly in my mind for long, although I am an attentive and patient fan. I would wait, then, with whatever composure I could find, until it was settled, days or weeks from now, and in some fashion or other I would fill up the empty eveningtimes and morningtimes I had once spent (I did not say "wasted"; I would never say "wasted") before the tube and with the sports pages. It might even be better for me to do without baseball for a while, although I could not imagine why. All this brave nonsense was knocked out of me in an instant, there in the cab, and suddenly the loss of that murmurous little ribbon of baseball-by-radio, the ordinary news of the game, seemed to explain a lot of things about the much larger loss we fans are all experiencing because of the strike. The refrain of late-night baseball scores; the sounds of the televised game from the next room (the room empty, perhaps, for the moment, but the game running along in there just the same and quietly waiting for us to step in and rejoin it when we are of a mind to); the mid-game mid-event from some car or cab that pulls up beside us for a few seconds in traffic before the light changes; the baseball conversation in the elevator that goes away when two men get off together at the eleventh floor, taking the game with them; the flickery white fall of light on our hands and arms and the scary sounds of the crowd that suddenly wake us up, in bed or in the study armchair, where we have fallen asleep, with the set and the game still on—all these streams and continuities, it seems to me, are part of the greater, riverlike flow of baseball. No other sport, I think, conveys anything like this sense of cool depth and fluvial steadiness, and when you stop for a minute and think about the game it is easy to see why this should be so.

The slow, inexorable progression of baseball events—balls and strikes, outs and innings, batters stepping up and batters being retired, pitchers and sides changing on the field, innings turning into games and games into series, and all these merging and continuing, in turn, in the box scores and the averages and the slowly fluctuous standings—are what make the game quietly and uniquely satisfying. Baseball flows past us all through the summer—it is one of the reasons that summer exists—and wherever we happen to stand on its green banks we can sense with only a glance across its shiny expanse that the long, un-hurrying swirl and down-flowing have their own purpose and direction, that the river is headed, in its own sweet time, toward a downsummer broadening and debouchment and to its end in the estuary of October.

River people, it is said, count on the noises and movement of nearby water, even without knowing it, and feel uneasy and unaccountably diminished if they must move away for a while and stay among plains inhabitants. That is almost the way it is for us just now, but it is worse than that, really, because this time it is the river that has gone away—just stopped—and all of us who live along these banks feel a fretful sense of loss and a profound disquiet over the sudden cessation of our reliable old stream. The main issue of the baseball strike, I have read, concerns the matter of compensation for owners who have lost a player to free-agency, but when this difficulty is resolved and the two sides come to an agreement (as they will someday), what compensation can ever be made to us, the fans, who are the true owners and neighbors and keepers of the game, for this dry, soundless summer and for the loss of our joy?

II

OCTOBER 1981

THE STRIKE BEGAN ON JUNE 12TH AND CONTINUED FOR SEVEN weeks and a day, wiping out seven hundred and thirteen games—

a third of the 1981 schedule. The financial losses, it has been estimated, exceeded seventy million dollars in ticket, concession, and broadcast revenues and twenty-eight million in player salaries. The damage inflicted upon the status of baseball in the affections and attention and loyalty of its fans can never be measured—a circumstance that may permit the owners to skip this page in the ledger once again. If the strike proved anything, it was that the owners do not hold themselves accountable in any way to their customers. The crisis left a very sour feeling, not just because of the loss of the dailiness and flow of summer baseball, or because of the bitterness and hostility of the negotiations, but because no one on the owners' side could ever put forward a brief, reasonable explanation of the deadlock or prevent its prolongation until the last moment at which some vestige of the season could be retrieved. From first to last, the crisis was an invention of the owners—the inevitable result of their determination to radically alter or put an end to the basic structure of player free-agency, and thus to win back by force what they had lost in bargaining and in the courts and through mediation. Their plan for achieving this unlikely end (as previously set forth here in Chapter 10) was to demand that any team signing a free-agent player of tested worth be subject to a penalty so costly as to make the signing an unacceptable risk. The penalty was to be the loss of a player from the middle level of the signing team's roster—the sixteenth player, according to one early form of the proposal—and the assigning of that player to the team from which the free agent had just departed. This stratagem had a spuriously reasonable look to it, as if the Player Relations Committee (the eight-man body that represented the owners throughout the negotiations) were saying, "Look, it isn't as if we're asking a club to give up a George Brett or a Nolan Ryan in the deal. We're talking about a benchwarmer—a nobody, just about. So what's the problem?" Casual followers of the game might swallow this, but every player and manager and thoughtful fan knew better. One need only consult the box scores of a team over the span of a week's play to realize once again how many different skills and strengths are needed on a well-balanced contemporary ball team, and to notice that the collective makeup of a contender's bench and bull-pen is far more significant than the performance of any one or two of its stars; this depth, indeed, is a distinguishing mark of a pennant-bound club.

Strangely enough, the owners were never even able to state the true nature of their difficulties, which all had to do with money. They never came right out and said that some of the clubs could no longer compete on even terms with the others because they couldn't afford the astronomical level of present-day free-agent contracts—for this would have obliged them to open their books during the negotiations or else face the charge that they had refused to bargain in good faith. The National Labor Relations Board at one point did attempt to prevent the coming strike on just such a charge, which forced the owners and the Commissioner and Ray Grebey, their labor negotiator, to swear to a federal district judge, in direct and embarrassing contravention of a great many prior statements to the contrary, that money had never played a part in the dispute, and that none of them had ever said, in public or even to each other, that the game was getting too damned expensive. Nothing at all like that, sir, they said, and the judge took their word for it, which left the owners in the peculiar position of looking as if they believed that their free-agent player-compensation plan was a natural right—something they *had* to have, like some freedom guaranteed in the Constitution—and that this justified their bringing the national pastime to a halt until they had obtained it.

These deceptions and ironies were so apparent that a good many newspapers and magazines and television commentators felt obliged to draw attention to them, thus clearly putting the media down on the players' side, almost for the first time. Sports columnists also pointed out that the National Football League has a costly and punitive system of compensations for the loss of a free-agent player, which has resulted in a freeze-out of free-agent signings in that sport. Just last spring, Walter Payton, the great running back of the Chicago Bears, ventured into the free-agent marketplace and received not a single offer for his services. There never was a chance, then, that the Players Association would agree to the proffered scheme, or would misunderstand its intentions. But the fans, it turned out, were not much interested in these complexities. Polls taken during the strike showed that public opinion was almost equally divided between the warring parties, with a small plurality actually favoring the owners' side of the dispute. The fans, it seems to me, could never bring themselves to care much about the players' cause, because they were so offended and alienated by the vast sums of money these athletes were earning—by Dave Winfield's salary of a million and a half dollars, say, but perhaps even more by the players' average current salary of a hundred and seventy-five thousand dollars per year. The notion is very widely held, at all levels of society, that this is too much money for anyone to make at such trifling, pleasant work. The fans seemed to think that these young men should feel ashamed of their own good fortune, or at least become less difficult about it, and not object to a limit to free-agency now, because so many of them were already rich. If the fans' voice could have been heard, it probably was saying, "Let them take home a little less loot and let's see them try a little harder out there, and let's have the games again, for God's sake." This wish was very close to the owners' perception of what would happen once the players' salary checks stopped coming in, and it was dead wrong. The players stood fast, out of principle and self-interest and in defense of their younger members, who had not achieved the right to bargain for themselves as free agents. In response to the great, free-floating question, "Aren't you making too much money?" they simply answered, "How much is too much?" They would not give back any significant employee rights or sources of income they had already won, and they proposed another, less arguable hard question: "Would *you?*"

Miserable over the loss of their sport and angered by the very high financial stakes involved in this family dispute over the division of baseball's revenues, the fans were never able to understand how these matters had been pushed to such an impasse—why some reasonable accommodation could not have been offered and accepted, in a time when the game's popularity and income and attendance were at close to an all-time high. That is, in truth, the hardest question of all. Its answer, for me, lies in the remarkable degree of wishful thinking and self-deception that permeated the front offices of baseball on the eve of the strike, and, even more, in the owners' extraordinary way of conducting their side of this labor dispute. A strike over the player-compensation issue almost took place last year, it will be recalled, and the players' willingness to stop play over the matter came as a true shock to most baseball executives, who, with many a smile over my naïveté, had reassured me again and again that the young, overpaid athletes would never hang together over such a trifling matter. The near-miss apparently did not convince them of the seriousness of the Players Association, for the little smiles were back again, I noticed, in early June this year. "They won't strike," one lifelong baseball executive told me just before the last game that was to be played in his team's ballpark until August 14th. "I know the players." But he didn't. He was telling me a wish.

The same wish, I believe, impelled the twenty-six quite various millionaires or corporate identities who are "the owners" to hand over their case from the beginning to a handful of the most obdurately conservative members of their group—the six men who, along with the two league presidents, make up the Player Relations Committee—and then to engage a labor negotiator, Ray Grebey, who was known as an abrasive hardliner, and also to purchase fifty million dollars' worth of strike insurance: preparations for war. And they went farther, weirdly binding themselves with a semi-secret gag rule that could exact a five-hundred-thousand-dollar fine from any executive or front-office person who publicly commented on any aspect of the issues under negotiation with the players. A fine of fifty thousand dollars was actually levied against Harry Dalton, the executive vice-president of the Milwaukee Brewers, for a supposed aside—a murmured hope for accommodation and common sense on both sides during the crisis—to a Washington *Post* reporter before the strike, but it is not clear if the sum was ever actually paid.

The Commissioner of Baseball, Bowie Kuhn, was excluded from the strike discussions by the owners' Player Relations Committee, and in his absence Ray Grebey—a man almost wholly unknown to the fans or the sports world—became baseball's only spokesman during the seven weeks of the strike. Mr. Grebey, it must be said, conducted his side of the long bargaining in a manner, by turns pugnacious and evasive, that infuriated the player representatives and others on the scene. At one point, he did offer sufficient signs of reasonableness to the federal labor mediator, Kenneth Moffett, to encourage that official to produce a compromise settlement plan to both parties—only to have it shot down by Mr. Grebey himself, with the accompanying insulting suggestion that it had been written by someone on the players' side. Several owners attempted to see the text of this proposal, but were told by Grebey that Mr. Moffett had demanded secrecy, which was not the case. When the strike was over, the Players Association's veteran labor negotiator, Marvin Miller, pointedly refused to pose for the customary treaty-signing photographs with his opposite number.

These tactics and self-strictures of the owners were so damaging to reasonable discourse, so masochistic and puritanical in their intentions, that one must read them as a code. To me, they suggest that many of the owners privately acquiesced in the angry cries for action, for punishment, for any kind of retributive enforced return to an older and simpler time that were voiced by their least restrained and most vocal minority. I have heard the hard line for years now, in front offices and stadium-club bars all around both leagues. "These players are getting too much money for their own damned good," it goes. "These salaries are insane—they're ruining the game. Sure, we know who bid the contracts up to where they are, but now it's got to stop. And these are just kids—don't forget that. Look at the way they all vote one way as soon as Marvin Miller gives them his spiel. They're country boys and he's a fast-talking city slicker who can outsmart them all. Hell, he's outsmarted *us*, so far. Now it's time to teach them a lesson. Let's stick it to them just once and see what happens. Let the season go down the tubes, if that's what it takes. We'll hang tough and show them what life is all about. Look, I like these kids—don't get me wrong—but they shouldn't get paid so damned much money and have all those girls on the road and get on TV all the time, when all they're doing is playing ball in the same old half-assed way, most of the time. And they shouldn't be able to quit working for good when they're thirty-five—can you beat that!—and . . ." And so on.

But this bitter contretemps, the whole issue of the strike and its origins and its miserable, self-destructive passions, is sadder and more serious than any harangue can suggest. What is going on here, I believe, is the same old psychodrama about American fathers and sons, work and play, money and sex and sports, which is always being enacted deep within our national unconscious. It is the Tom Seaver–M. Donald Grant parable that I put forward earlier in this book, but we certainly have not seen its end in baseball. It was restaged again in 1981 by the owner of the Yankees, George M. Steinbrenner, and the various Yankee players and managers whom he must browbeat and humiliate in the pursuit of success or dismiss if they do not apologize for their expressions of resentment at such patronizing and patriarchal gestures. "I feel like a father scorned," Steinbrenner declared when he fired his unhappy but unrepentant manager, Gene Michael, in September—and he spoke, I think, for a great many other owners and front-office executives (and not a few senior baseball writers), who control every part of this game except the one that most matters: the moment when it must be handed over to the lucky, well-paid, and unforgivably young men who can actually play it.

The deadlock at the bargaining table began to loosen late in July, when eight American League clubs—the Orioles, Yankees, White Sox, Rangers, A's, Angels, Indians, and Mariners—broke ranks at an owners' meeting and proposed that the issues between the Player Relations Committee and the Players Association be submitted to binding arbitration. The actual terms of the agreement—a very complex document providing some solace for both sides: for teams losing a prime free agent, compensation in the form of a player selected from a pool of players drawn from all the clubs; varying levels of protected players, from twenty-four to twenty-six per club, who would not be available in such a pool; the exempting of as many as five clubs from having to contribute to the pool if they promised not to enter the free-agent market for a period of three years; and so forth—were then worked out between Marvin Miller and the president of the American League, Lee MacPhail. One of its key clauses provided that no player would be docked for service time lost because of the strike—a bitter and potentially divisive issue that could have deprived many of this year's free agents of their right to bargain on the open market at the end of the season. Another clause extended the term of the existing basic agreement between the owners and the players for an additional year, to 1984—a hiatus designed to provide healing time for the game's great wounds. There were other clauses and tradeoffs—too many for most of us to remember now in dazed retrospect. The common wisdom about the players' strike of 1981 is to say that neither side won, but this is not true. What happened, in fact, is that the central feature of the owners' plan—the direct punishment, through the loss of a player, of a team signing a free agent—was not accepted. The players did not give way on this or on any other issue of major consequence; they were more unified at the end of the fifty-day (or two-year: depends on how you look at it) war than at its outset, and the owners are unlikely to challenge their resolve at any point in the near future. There is even some small hope that the emergence of some quieter and less intransigent owners—among them Edward Bennett Williams, of the Orioles; Eddie Chiles, of the Rangers; Jerry Reinsdorf and Edward Einhorn, of the White Sox; and Roy Eisenhardt, of the A's—during the draggy days and nights of the strike may begin a long-overdue shift of power in baseball away from the entrenched father-figures of the Player Relations Committee and toward a more flexible and rational sort of executive, who does not permit his repressed boyhood dreams to infect his business judgment or to damage his long-term dealings with his players, who are, after all, the product that he must sell to the American public if baseball is to last and to thrive.

The fans were the losers. They were left with a patchwork, freakishly twisted two-part season that not only crammed an extra round of postseason elimination playoffs into the already over-extended league schedules but also managed to disqualify the teams with the best and third-best records of the year (the Reds and the Cardinals) from further competition while admitting the seventeenth-best team (the Kansas City Royals) to those same playoffs. The suddenly-declared first-half winners—the Yankees, A's, Phillies, and Dodgers—played without much motivation or zeal throughout the remainder of the summer, together accounting for a vapid 104–101 record in that span. There were thirty-two post-season games this year— so many that it is difficult even for the most dedicated fans to recall which games among them, such as the Astros-Dodgers pitching wars in the National League West, or the last encounters of the Expos-Dodgers N.L. championships, offered the tension and zest and sustained difficulty that one expects from baseball at its best. The World Series, which the Dodgers won by coming back from a two-game deficit to defeat their old oppressors, the Yankees, in six games, was poorly played at times, but it *felt* bad—trivial and almost drained of meaning—all the time, because it came after so much miserable baseball news this year. The Dodgers' courageous, well-deserved World Championship was damaged in memory by the inflation and distortion of their sport. The fans, furthermore, will not even have the solace of this year's statistics to fit into their baseball musings during the off-season, for these will be pockmarked with asterisks and truncated totals—a reminder of the harm done by this careless and destructive summer to the lifetime marks being compiled by the star players of our time.

The fans did not relish the owners' fiddlings and tinkerings with their season, or the puffing-up of the playoffs, either. A careful extrapolation of the 1981 attendance figures to a full-scale season shows that the clubs lost four and a half million customers at the gate this year, not counting the losses during the strike itself, while poststrike network television audiences for the season were down by more than twenty per cent. And no wonder. The wonder is that the owners may still vote for some form of artificial schedule realignment for the seasons just ahead; in the hope of permanently embedding the extra round of postseason play in the sport. Three leagues are a distinct possibility, with the first- and second-place finishers qualifying for the playoffs, along with two "wild-card" teams—the ultimate devaluation of the fairness and logic of a full season of competition that eliminates every team except the ones to finish on top in their divisions, and thus sustains the difficulty and the day-to-day interest of the long summer campaigns. Many of the owners are tempted, I believe, not just by the additional post-season round of games that can be sold to the networks but because the gimcrack scheme will make for apparently closer competition at the end of the regular season and thus help conceal the deep ineptitude of their own teams.

Fans looking back on the strike—this fan among them—can hardly remember now what it was all about. They were left with the numbing knowledge that they were never consulted about it and that, as usual, they have no place to go with their grievance. They sense that the old fixed shape of the game has shifted somehow, away from its past pleasures and assured summer sounds and rituals, and that the only response available to them now is to give way to their anger—to care less about what they once cared about so much, and perhaps to stay away from games altogether. They have been silenced.

16

In the Country

AUGUST 1981

Baseball is a family for those who follow it, and members of close families like to exchange letters. Three years ago, I received a letter from a woman named Linda Kittell, who was living in Clinton, Montana.

"I was born in 1952," she wrote. "I remember listening to the Yankees—with Mel Allen, it must have been—on a little yellow transistor radio on an island in Lake Champlain, where we spent our summers. Not listening but sort of doing the everyday things of an eight- or ten-year-old—drinking chocolate milk and eating animal crackers—while my sister, two years older, flirted with her boyfriend, who *listened* to the Yankee games on the yellow radio. I only paid attention when I heard Mickey Mantle's name or Roger Maris's name. And I was in love with Whitey Ford. Maris was hitting home runs as often as we went uptown that summer—every day. . . .

"I forgot about baseball later, except in September, when I paid attention if the Yankees were close to getting into the Series. I went to college, and then to graduate school in Montana. One night in a bar in Missoula, I met a man who just about fell flat when I complained about the games on the TV set there because they didn't put on the Yankees enough. He looked at me as if he'd been struck. You're a *Yankee* fan? I told him I had a perfect right, because I was from upstate New York and because I'd been in love with Whitey Ford all my life, practically. Ron was a Mantle fan (his name is Ron Goble; he's a lanky six feet five), and I tended more toward Maris, but we both loved Whitey Ford. We talked and drank beer. He'd played Legion ball for five years in his home town of Boise, Idaho, and he'd won a baseball scholarship to Linfield College, in Oregon. He'd been scouted in school by the Yankees, the Angels, and the Pirates. He's a left-handed pitcher. His fastball was clocked at more than ninety m.p.h., and he told me he'd held back on it, at that, because he was afraid of hurting his arm. He said how he'd recognized the scouts in the stands because they were all tan in May and June in southern Idaho. He talked about how he'd come to think a college education was more important than athletics, and how the student riots in the late nineteen-sixties had turned him against sports, so he'd stopped playing. He talked about Vietnam and drugs and what it was like then, and what a waste it had been for him to forget about ball.

"We started living together about three years ago. Christmases, birthdays, surprises from me—all those special days had to do with baseball. A baseball book, a baseball picture, a pack of new baseball cards—anything. Then last year Seattle got the Mariners. Our vacation from Montana was a twelve-hour train ride and three days' worth of games—*Yankee* games: the Yankees at the Kingdome. I cried when I saw them out there. Ron said I was being silly. But, God, there was Mickey Rivers. I mean, Mickey Rivers! . . .

"The third day, I found a sympathetic usher who let us stand down close to the field with about ten little kids trying to get autographs. I lied through my teeth and said one of them was my little brother. Sparky Lyle and Catfish and Chambliss were playing pepper, and then a player out beyond them called, 'Hey, you girl!' I looked up. 'Yeah, you,' and he threw me a ball. Paul Blair threw me a baseball. All the little boys waist-high around me looked disgusted. "Why'd he throw *her* a ball?' . . . 'Mom, Dad, that one threw that *girl* a ball.' It was an Official American League ball. I read it over and rushed up to my seat, where Ron was waiting for the game to start. 'It's a real ball,' I told him. '*Look* at it.' There I was, a perfectly sensible, sensitive twenty-four-year-old woman getting goose bumps over a baseball. I asked Ron if I should go down for more autographs, but something had changed. He rubbed the ball and kept looking at it. He was years away, and sad about it. . . . I went back down, and the autograph I got in the end was Elston Howard's. Memory and imagination make you think about anything you want. I'd picked Ellie Howard—and not Mickey Rivers or Catfish Hunter or Thurman Munson—because I thought it would make him happy, and because his name reminded me of my little yellow radio back in Vermont on August afternoons. Because I'm sentimental.

"We drove back to Montana with a friend, and Ron and I sat in the back seat. 'Can I see the ball again?' he said. I handed it to him and watched Ron hold it for a fastball, a slider, a curve. He looked far-off still. . . .

"This spring, there was an article in *The Sporting News* about a Class A team being formed in Boise, called the Buckskins. Tryouts were in June, and you needed three thousand dollars from a sponsor if you made the team. Something different, all right, but it was a chance to play ball. They'd signed the Sundown Kid—Danny Thomas—and a twenty-seven-year-old catcher form southern Idaho. I wanted Ron to go down and try out. He said he wasn't in shape. He said he was happy playing on the Clinton Clowns, our town's fast-pitch softball team. It was obvious that he *wasn't* happy playing softball, and especially obvious in the fall, when he'd pitch by himself—pitch baseball by throwing rotten apples from our tree against a telephone pole, and call balls and strikes, hits and outs. . . ."

Linda persuaded Ron to try out for the Buckskins, but he didn't get around to it until a few days before their season was about to begin. A letter from the Buckskin manager, Gerry Craft, said they were looking for a left-handed pitcher, and that did the trick.

"Our truck broke down," Linda's letter went on. "Planes were on strike. Finally, Ron's brother George drove him down. Ron was signed on the first day he threw—a good rotation on his curveball, they said. I didn't even know what Ron meant by that when he told me about it by long-distance. Gerry Craft had said he could go far in baseball, but what Gerry didn't know was that Ron had thrown his arm out—just about ruined it, it turned out—with the second curve he'd thrown. So Ron waited, in ice packs. Three days later, he came home with a swollen arm and a professional baseball player's contract. Five hundred dollars a month. We started packing up his stuff and spent long hours looking for a sponsor. We ended up putting up our own money. Three thousand dollars may not sound like much to some people, but it was everything we had. I served Ron a steak dinner and kissed him goodbye.

"I don't think it really sank in until I made the trip down to Boise to see the Buckskins play in their first home stand. Ron was standing there in his tan-and-black uniform, with a satin warmup jacket and real cleats, and I was just as excited about that as I'd been when I saw Mickey Rivers on the field in Seattle. I was goofy. . . .

"Now, anyone will tell you that this Buckskins team is different. The general manager, Lanny Moss [Lanny Moss is a woman], is very religious, and so is Gerry Craft. In right field at their park there's a huge billboard with 'JESUS' written on it in twelve-foot letters. In left field there's a strange picture of Christ Himself. Craft says he had a vision that told him to look around Spokane for a cabin in the woods, and that's where he found Danny Thomas, the Sundown Kid. Danny left major-league ball [Thomas, an outfielder, had played for two seasons with the Brewers] because his religion required him to read the Bible from sundown Friday to sundown Saturday, which meant he mostly couldn't play on those days. And Craft has game strategy confirmed to him by the Bible, and stuff. Some of his ballplayers have been baptized on their road trips—I picture a clean white sink at the Salem Inn as the font, with the neat sample Ivory soap tablets resting at the side. But these ballplayers are the nicest people I've ever met.

"I'm not the typical wife/girlfriend of a baseball player—those women you see on TV with their hair done up and their Rose Bowl Parade wave to the crowds. I like to watch baseball. I love the game, and I'm one of the loudest fans in the stands. And when Ron's pitching I find myself almost praying for a win. But the Buckskins don't win many games. The newspapers around the league have put too much stress on the religious aspect of the team. The players aren't all Jesus people. Most of them drink beer and swear. Gerry Craft rhubarbs with the umps with his hands in his jacket pockets. Danny Thomas hits a grand-slammer half an hour before sunset and trots around the bases on his way to his Bible. It's all wonderful. The beer, the hot dogs with everything on them, and seeing old Ron Goble out on the mound working on his curveball and about to turn twenty-seven. What a good way to turn twenty-seven— finally doing something you've tried to ignore for eight years. I love it. It's a hit in the bottom of the ninth, with the score tied and the ball sailing over the right-field wall."

I answered this letter, needless to say, and in time Linda wrote back. We became baseball correspondents and baseball friends. She wrote in October that year and told me about the rest of the Buckskins' season. The team had gone bad, at one point losing eleven straight games. Money was short, and the team's religious fervor made for difficulties. After the Buckskins suffered a 25–3 loss to the Salem Senators, Gerry Craft released the losing pitcher, saying that God had made it clear to him that He didn't want that pitcher on the team. In Eugene, Oregon, Craft announced that God had told him they were going to lose a game to the Emeralds, and, sure enough, they did, blowing a 6–4 lead in the ninth. Some of the benchwarmers on the club began to wonder if they were being kept on the roster because of their three-thousand-dollar sponsor deposits—an inevitable development, perhaps. The Buckskins finished last in the Northwest League, fourteen games behind their divisional winner, Eugene, and twenty-five games worse than the eventual champions, the Gray's Harbor (Washington) Loggers. Danny Thomas led the league with a .359 batting average, but the Buckskins had the worst pitching in the league—a club earned-run average of 6.42. Ron Goble wound up with a 2–3 record and an earned-run average of 8.18—his lifetime figures in professional baseball.

There were some good moments, even in a season like that. "I went down to Boise in August," Linda wrote in that next letter. "Ron met me at the airport, and we went straight to the field. There was talk that Charlie Finley had sent for the Sundowner, to help his Oakland A's, and talk that two new pitchers were coming from Milwaukee. It was hot—a hundred degrees, easy. I sat in the only shade in the ballpark and watched batting practice. Danny Thomas was running around with a coonskin cap on, and Bo McConnaughy, one of my favorites on the team, came out in a bright-yellow hard hat. Bo was the Buckskins' shortstop—a ballplayers' ballplayer. He had been in the minor leagues for years, in the Orioles organization—the wrong place at the wrong time, because the Orioles had a shortstop named Mark Belanger. Then Bo had gotten too old to be of any interest to them. Bo loves baseball, and you don't notice his gray hair until he's back in street clothes.

"Raymie Odermott started the game against Bend that night, and went six and two-thirds innings, until Gerry brought in Ron with the score 4–3, Boise. Two outs, men on first and second. Ron went in, and this left-hand batter was waiting for him and got a hit that tied the score. Boise scored two runs in the seventh and one in the eighth, and Ron held Bend scoreless the rest of the game, striking out their last two batters. Just fine.

"He was off in the ozone the rest of the night. He sat over a beer with friends, quietly reviewing the game. His curveball had been right for the first time since the June tryout. We both thought—or hoped, I suppose—that the days of Tenderyl and the threat of cortisone were over. It's hard to explain how happy he was that night. It's as if he believed for a moment that he wasn't eight years too late. . . .

"Still, there were rumblings on the team. Pitchers went to Gerry and complained that they didn't get to pitch. Mark Garland was one, and he got to start. He got blown away. The next night, it was Dennis Love, who'd also complained. He looked real bad, too, and Gerry brought in Ron. Ron let up a home run—to the first batter. It was a bad time. The next day, at batting practice, Dennis Love said he'd been released, along with Mark Garland. Ron went in to talk to Gerry about *his* future, and I drove down to the Circle K to get some pop. Mark Garland was crying beside a bridge over an irrigation canal. And I hoped I wouldn't end up comforting Ron some day, squeezing his hand and talking softly to him, the way Mark's wife stood comforting him.

"The last two weeks of the season, the team played without pay, until Lanny Moss could borrow the money to pay their checks. Danny Thomas left, saying he wasn't going to play ball for free. There was no money for hotels or food. Once, the bus broke down, and the team had to sleep on the floor of a church. They left on a last road trip to Victoria and Bellingham. I went up to visit friends in Seattle and to catch some of the Bellingham games. The Kingdome didn't wow me so much this time. The Yankees were there again, but I knew more about people on the field than I used to. I got Ron Guidry's autograph, and I still loved Mickey Rivers, but it was different. People, not heroes. In Bellingham, I spent a rainy evening watching 'Monday Night Baseball' with Ron and Bo. Then I danced with all the team, at Bellingham's imitation disco.

"Season's over. Ron's been back a month. Two weeks ago, he went grouse hunting with the dogs and a friend, and came home tipsy drunk. He'd remembered his doctor's appointment the next day, and had spent his time trying to forget about it. He made a mock pitch for me, and his elbow *clicked* at the end of the motion. He said, 'At least, Gerry Craft told me I could have been in the bigs. I know that much. It's enough.'

"A shot of cortisone and rest. Ron doesn't lie to the scouts about his age, you know. He and Bo are honest about that. We have tons of fallen apples, if Ron's arm starts to come around. Bo's in Boise, studying to be a mechanic. Gerry's been released. Everybody's waiting through the winter."

There were more letters back and forth. It meant a lot to me to hear from someone—from two people, really—who could tell me what baseball was like far from the crowds and the noise and the fame and the big money that I had been writing about for many summers. And by this time, of course, I cared about Ron and Linda, and worried about what would happen to them. Linda wrote me that Ron and his brother George and a friend named Ray were spending a great deal of their time that winter playing an extremely complicated baseball-by-dice game called Extra Innings. From time to time, Ron would get out his mitt and persuade someone to catch him, but when he threw, in gingerly fashion, he found that his elbow was still horribly painful. He couldn't get over how foolish he had been to throw that hard curve during his Buckskins tryout. He read a book by Jim Bouton, in which Bouton said that his sore arm felt as if it had been bitten by alligators; Ron's felt exactly the same way. The Buckskins, in any case, had folded. The Phillies had expressed some interest in picking them up as a farm team, but the city of Boise would not refurbish its ancient ballpark, so the Phillies went elsewhere. Then the Northwest League adopted a rule favoring younger players and making it harder for older players to find a place on its team rosters—the last blow for Ron. That winter, he sent letters to all the major-league clubs asking for some kind of employment in their organizations, but the answers were a long time coming back. He told Linda he had really been collecting major-league letterheads. Linda described an evening of theirs on the town, and its ending: "We walked through the streets of Missoula in the 4 A.M. drizzle, Ron in his Buckskin jacket and me feeling very maudlin, remembering the walk from the field to the Buckskins' dressing room. What fun it was being a Baseball Annie, arm in arm with some semblance of a professional ballplayer, rain drizzling on my arm and on the satin warmup jacket. How romantic and far away it seems now."

At about this time, I wrote an article about the difficulties that women sports reporters had experienced in gaining access to the clubhouses of major-league ball teams on their beat, and Linda commented on that, too: "Oh, as to women in the clubhouse, I think they're a necessity. Why, this summer when the Buckskins got locked out of their locker room, I was the only one who could fit through the window and over the top row of the lockers, to unlock the door. And for that one quiet moment between lockers and door I imagined myself in uniform, imagined the feel of oiled leather and dust, the long trip from this town to the next."

There was a long trip just ahead for Ron and Linda—from Montana to northwestern Vermont, where they moved into a farmhouse about forty miles from Burlington: "It took us six days to drive across the country in a calico Chevy truck, with the two dogs in back and a U-Haul in back of that. I think the only thing that got Ron across the plains was the radio reception. We kept tuning in game after game, from all the big-league cities along the way, including a French-Canadian station, near the end, with the Expos on it. French baseball cracked me up. We're close to Montreal here, and we went to an Expos-Cardinals doubleheader last weekend. Saw Cash's grand slam and drank Canadian beer. Ron was frustrated by the French and English announcements—a whole bunch of French with 'Ellis Valentine' in the middle of it. Whenever the Expos did anything, the French-Canadians sitting around us would slap each other on the back and pull on their pints of vodka."

Linda had come East to be closer to her family for a while.

(She was born in Troy, New York, and Burlington is on Lake Champlain, where she passed those early summers listening to the Yankees.) She went to work as a feature writer and sports editor for a Vermont newspaper, the *Lamoille County Weekly*. The main object, she wrote me, was to get as many players' names as possible into her stories, so that their mothers would buy the paper. "I have a funny press pass that the publisher made up," she added. "It's an attempt to make me seem very professional, but the publisher, who's an old friend of mine, can't spell very well. 'This card,' it says, 'entitles the barer...' It didn't get me into the press room in Montreal."

Ron was working as a carpenter and a substitute high-school teacher, and he and Linda were excited by the discovery that Burlington had a team (more than one team, it turned out) in a local semipro league. Ron hoped to play there—hoped to pitch, in fact, if he got any help from a local orthopedist who was said to specialize in sports medicine. "We'll see," Linda concluded. "I'd rather see Ron pitching and playing than substituting Great Civilization." She urged me to come and visit them, and watch Ron pitch.

I put it in my mind to keep that date—it would be the coming summer, the summer of 1980—but the next letter changed my plans. Ron had cancer. They had found a lump in his abdomen, which was removed by surgery. Subsequently, he underwent another operation and lost one testicle. It was seminoma—a highly curable form of the disease, the doctors said. Ron was going into the Burlington hospital every day for radiation treatments. "I can't stand to see him hooked up to all those tubes in the hospital, and worried about how he's going to look in the locker room," Linda wrote. "I'm not sure I understand why it is that good people and athletes can be struck this way. It's pretty weird, is all. But Ron is unflappable. He's out pitching snowballs at trees and making plans to play on the Burlington team somehow. But I have a feeling it's going to take a lot to get the boy in shape this spring. Street & Smith's are out [the early-season baseball yearbook]. Ron and his buddies are ranking the teams and giving them their finishing places this year. Winner gets a six-pack from each loser."

Ron Goble had a good summer, though—much better than he or anyone else had expected. In May and June, he coached a team of thirteen-to-fifteen-year-olds in the local Babe Ruth League, and at the same time he tried out for the Burlington A's, in the semipro Northern League, and made the club. For a time, he was so weak from the effects of his illness and the radiation that he could pitch no more than two or three innings at a stretch, but he learned how to conserve his energy by warming up only briefly and by trying to throw ground-ball outs. By the end of the brief season, he was able to pitch a full game, and he wound up with a respectable 4-1 record. He never told anyone on the club, last year or this year, that he had had cancer. Last winter, he worked as a teacher's aide at the Bellows Free Academy, in St. Albans, Vermont, and as a custodian at the local rink, but most of his energy went into an attempt to organize a new Northern League club in St. Albans. It fell through—not enough local money, not enough local commercial enthusiasm—but by springtime Ron had been signed on as a regional commission scout by the Milwaukee Brewers (Gerry Craft, his old manager, was a Brewers district scout, and had recommended Ron), and he was umpiring high-school games. He would pitch again for the A's this summer. Linda was teaching humanities courses at the local community college. Things were looking good; they wanted me to drive up and see them.

The bad news, Linda wrote, had come earlier and from far away: Danny Thomas had hanged himself in a jail cell in Alabama, where he had been facing trial on a rape charge. "It came as a real shock," Linda wrote. "What bothers me is that baseball has been a savior for Ron. Last spring, it brought back his confidence in himself and in his body. And here's someone like Danny Thomas who saw baseball as his pain. Danny had a strange look in his eyes when he talked about religion, and reporters were always after him to talk about his beliefs. Everyone knew he was slightly wacko, but the man had principles. His wife, Judy, was really afraid he'd take Charlie Finley up on that offer to come back to major-league ball. She said she couldn't stand that stuff again. Ron says Danny could hit a baseball farther than anyone he's ever seen. I saw him hit a home run out of every ballpark where I saw the Buckskins play. The last day I saw him play was in Bellingham. It was raining, and Danny's little daughter, Renee, was sitting up in the bleachers with Gerry Craft's daughter, Maizee, and singing

'Take me out to the ballgame, take me out to the ballgame,'
slapping their hands on their thighs. The girls didn't know any
of the other words, so they sang that over and over again."

On a cool, windy-bright Saturday at the end of last June, I
drove straight north through Connecticut, through Massachusetts, and into Vermont, crossing and recrossing the narrowing
Connecticut River along the way, and at last, over the river
one more time, I found the Burlington A's at play against the
Walpole (New Hampshire) Blue Jays on the Walpole home
field—a neat little American Legion diamond just beneath a
steep, thickly wooded hillside, hard by the Hubbard Farms
fertilizer plant. At play and then *not* at play, since the A's had
knocked off the Jays, 4–1, at the moment of my arrival, in
the first game of a doubleheader. I met Linda Kittell at the
field—a dark-haired young woman in faded bluejeans, with
pale eyes, an open, alert expression, and an enormous smile.
Then I shook hands with the A's manager, Paul Farrar; with
Paul's wife, Sue; and, at last, with Ron Goble—a pitcher, all
right: long arms, long hands, long body, very long legs, a sun-
burnished nose, a surprising blondish Fu Manchu mustache, a
shy smile, and one bulging cheek (not tobacco, it turned out,
but sunflower seeds). Ron and Paul said what a shame it was
I'd missed the opener, and then quickly ducked back out onto
the field and into their little concrete dugout to get ready for
the next one—Ron to chart pitches and keep score (he would
pitch the next day, down in Brattleboro), and his skipper, of
course, to worry. Linda and I sat down in an upper row of a
tiny rack of bleachers in short right field. We had no trouble
finding seats. My quick count of the house, after the nightcap
had begun, came to thirty-three, including babies in strollers.
Several young women—players' wives or players' girlfriends,
probably—were lying on blankets spread out behind the backstop, where they took turns slathering each other's backs with
suntan goop. Near the Walpole dugout, a ten- or twelve-year-
old girl on an aluminum camp chair watched the game in
company with a big chocolate-brown Labrador, holding him
out of the action (and breaking his heart) with a yellow leash.
Whenever a foul ball few past us, someone in the audience
would get up and amble after it, while we in the bleachers
called out directions ("More right, more right—*now* another

step!") until it had been tracked down in the thick meadow weeds around the field. There was a lot of clapping and cries of encouragement ("Good eye, batter! Good eye!") from the little crowd, and between batters and innings you could hear the cool, gusty northwest wind working through the green treetop canopies of ash and oak and maple on the hillside out beyond right field.

In the first inning, the Walpole batters whacked some long drives against the visitors' starting pitcher, and some short ones, too, and pretty soon Burlington's designated hitter, Darcy Spear, came out of the dugout and began warming up with a catcher—not a good turn of events, Linda told me, because the team had been able to scrape up only four pitchers for its two-day, four-game weekend road trip here to the southern end of the league. The players had driven down in their own cars and pickups, but the team, she said, would pay for their motel accommodations in Brattleboro that night. There were no programs, and I was lucky to have Linda there to identify some of the A's, whose style afield or at the plate I was beginning to pick up—a diminutive second baseman, Greg Wells, who had a nice way of looking the ball into his glove on grounders; a strong-armed shortstop named Rob DelBianco; and Tinker Jarvis, at third, who had driven in a pair of runs in the top of the first inning with a line-drive double and then singled sharply in the third. The A's wore the same combination of garish buttercup-yellow shirts, white pants, and white shoes first made famous by the Oakland A's, while the Walpole nine sported a variation of Toronto Blue Jays home whites, but there was no connection between these local teams and their big-league namesakes, Linda explained; rather, the manufacturer supplying the Northern League had offered bargain rates on these prestyled uniforms—sort of like a Seventh Avenue dress house knocking off mass copies of Diors and Balmains. A distinguishing feature of this particular summer line was the names of various home-town commercial sponsors that the players wore on their backs, and before long I realized that I had begun to identify the different A's players by these billboards rather than by the names that Linda had murmured to me. Thus Darcy Spear became Uncle Sam's Dairy Bar, and it was Coca-Cola, the left-handed first baseman, who kept up a patter of encouraging talk to Red Barn on the mound (Red Barn had settled down after that first inning), while Slayton's Roofing (Manager Farrar) paced up and down in front of his dugout and waited for a chance to send the large and menacing-looking Cake World up to pinch-hit and get something started out there. Linda said it was all right for me to think of the players this way, because they often called each other by the sponsors' names anyway, for fun—except for Ron (Community Bingo), who was called Pigeon, because of his sunflower seeds. The A's players had been expected to hunt up their own sponsors at the beginning of the season, but not all of them, I noticed had been successful. Each sponsor had put up a hundred dollars for his walking (or running and throwing, and sometimes popping-up-in-the-clutch) advertisement, and each sponsored player had sewn on his own commercial or had prevailed upon someone else—his mother, perhaps—to sew it on for him.

The Northern League, which encompasses six teams—the Burlington A's, the Burlington Expos, the South Burlington Queen City Royals, the Walpole Blue Jays, the Brattleboro Maples, and the Saxtons River Pirates—and also plays against the Glens Falls (New York) Glensox, is a semiprofessional circuit, with the stronger emphasis, I had begun to understand, falling on the "semi." In the distant past, semipro ball teams were often composed of skilled local amateurs plus a handful of ringers—a couple of hard-hitting rookie outfielders just starting on their professional careers, perhaps, or a wily, shopworn pro pitcher at the very end of his—who played for modest salaries, or even for a flat per-game fee. This system fell into difficulties when increasing numbers of young athletes began to go off to college, where they found that they were not permitted to play varsity ball, because their semipro experience had compromised their status as amateurs. An earlier, extremely popular Northern League, with teams at Burlington, Montpelier, Rutland, St. Johnsbury, and other northwestern New England towns, came apart in 1952, partly because its Big Ten college stars were withdrawn by their schools to prevent the loss of their amateur status, and thus no longer appeared in games with professionals of the likes of Johnny Antonelli, Robin Roberts, Ray Scarborough, Snuffy Stirnweiss, Johnny Podres, and Boo Ferriss, who had all played on its diamonds at one time or another before moving on up through the minors and then to fame and success as major-leaguers.

Nowadays, many semipro teams simply find summer jobs for their players—a lumber company, let's say, putting a college fastball pitcher to work in the drying sheds by day so that he may advertise the concern out on the mound at the town field by night or on weekend afternoons—but only the Burlington Expos, who are looked upon as the Yankees of the Northern League, had managed to arrange this kind of tie-in this summer, and then only for a few of their players.

The Northern League is an independent body, with its own commissioner, its own set of rules (the d.h., aluminum bats for those who want to use them), and its own ways (including a ritual handshake between the players on rival clubs at the conclusion of every game—a pleasing custom probably lifted from the National Hockey League, whose teams line up and shake hands at the conclusion of each Stanley Cup elimination series). The six clubs play an official two-month schedule, from late May to late July, with playoffs and a Championship Series thereafter—about twenty-five or twenty-seven games each, with a good number of additional, informal, outside-the-standings games thrown in whenever they can be arranged. A minimum team budget, I learned, runs about three thousand dollars, and, beyond the obvious expenditures for equipment, goes for umpires (two umps, at twenty-five dollars each, for every game), a league fee of two hundred dollars (to keep statistics, handle publicity, and stage the league's All-Star Game), a modest insurance policy covering minor player injuries, and so forth. Income, beyond sponsorships, comes from ticket sales—a dollar for adults, fifty cents for children, babies and dogs free. The Burlington A's' entire season's operation probably costs less than a major-league team's bill for adhesive tape and foul balls during a week's play, but the Northern League, now in its third year, is doing well and expects to add at least two more clubs next summer.

All semipro leagues, it should be understood, are self-sustaining, and have no farm affiliation or other connection with the twenty-six major-league clubs, or with the seventeen leagues and hundred and fifty-two teams (ranging from Rookie League at the lowest level, to Class A and Summer Class A, up to the AAA designation at the highest) that make up the National Association—the minors, that is. There is no central body of semipro teams, and semipro players are not included among the six hundred and fifty major-leaguers, the twenty-five hundred-odd minor-leaguers, plus all the managers, coaches, presidents, commissioners, front-office people, and scouts, who, taken together, constitute the great tent called organized ball. (A much diminished tent, at that; back in 1949, the minors included fifty-nine leagues, about four hundred and forty-eight teams, and perhaps ten thousand players.) Also outside the tent, but perhaps within its shade, are five college leagues, ranging across the country from Cape Cod to Alaska, where the most promising college freshman, sophomore, and junior-year ballplayers may compete against each other in the summertime without losing their amateur status; the leagues are administered by the National Collegiate Athletic Association and receive indirect support—bats, balls, uniforms, and the like—from the major leagues, whose scouts keep a careful eye on their young stars. If the college leagues are semipro, the accent there probably should fall on the second word, for a considerable number of their best batters and pitchers are snapped up in the major-league amateur draft toward the end of their college careers. Scouts cover the Northern League as well— two pitchers with the Burlington Expos were signed to professional contracts this June, and they moved along at once to join their assigned minor-league clubs—but the level of play is not up to that of the college leagues. Most of the A's players, I learned in time, are undergraduates or recent graduates of local or eastern colleges (five of them from the University of Vermont, one from the University of New Hampshire, one from Amherst, one from the University of New Haven, and so on) who play for the fun of the game and the heat of the competition, and perhaps with half an eye turned toward the stands between pitches, in search of a major-league scout sitting there one afternoon who might just possibly be writing notes about this one good-looking outfielder or batter out there, whom he had somehow passed over the first time around. Ron Goble, at twenty-nine, was the oldest regular with the Burlington A's, and one of the few players in the league with any experience in professional ball.

How well did the A's play baseball? I found the question a difficult one at first, for the over-all quality of play in any one game tends to blur one's baseball judgment, but it did seem plain that most of the young players here on the Walpole ball field were far too slow afoot to merit comparison with professionals. Some threw well, as I have said, and others attacked the ball at the plate with consistency and power, but these two gifts did not seem to coexist in any one player. Most of all, the A's seemed young. They were all extremely cheerful, and, as I now found out, they loved to win. Down a run in their last at-bats (the seventh inning, in this doubleheader), the A's put their leadoff man aboard on a walk and instantly moved him up with a dazzling bunt by second baseman Greg Wells, who also knocked the catcher's peg out of the first baseman's mitt as he crossed the bag, and was safe. A moment later, with the bases loaded, Uncle Sam's Dairy Bar (Darcy Spear) whacked a single, good for two runs, and then the commercially anonymous catcher (Bob Boucher) tripled to deep center. Walpole, whose handful of wives and parents had gone speechless with dismay, changed pitchers, but Churchill's (Tinker Jarvis) singled, too, and before it was over the visiting A's had scored six runs and won the game, 9–4, sweeping the doubleheader. Ron Goble, ambling over to join us, hugged Linda and grinned at me and asked if I couldn't take the rest of the summer off to watch the A's and thus bring them through the rest of their season undefeated.

Steve Gallacher pitched the opener against the Brattleboro Maples the next afternoon—a strong twenty-two-year-old right-hander with a good, live fastball. The A's took up their hitting where they had left off the previous evening and moved smartly to a three-run lead in the top of the first. Linda and I sat in the last row of the grandstand, behind the decaying foul screen; it was a high-school field, a bit seedy but with a nice view to the south of some distant farms and silos and long fields of young corn sloping down toward the Connecticut River.

Linda told me that Steve Gallacher was said to have been the last man cut at a Pirates' tryout camp a year or two ago, and later had a Dodger scout on his trail, although nothing had come of it. I asked her how many people in the league still hoped to make a career in professional ball someday.

"If you have a chance, you have to see it through," she said at once. "It doesn't mean anything if you don't do something about it—really find out. So many of these players are unrealistic to think they could ever play minor-league ball. They go out and buy these expensive A's warmup jackets, which they can't really afford. I can see them all seventy-five years from now, saying, 'Well, I used to play semipro ball.' And Ron will probably be saying, 'I pitched this one great game for the Boise Buckskins.' I'd like to see something better than that for him in the end. Ron is always looking backward, and I think I like to look ahead. When he goes out scouting for the Brewers, he watches pitchers a lot, and maybe left-handed pitchers most of all. I think he still thinks he's better than most of the young pitchers he scouts."

She had been talking in an edged, hard tone I had not heard before, but now she stopped and shook her head and then laughed at herself a little—a habit of hers, I had begun to notice. "I guess Ron is even more of a hero to me than Whitey Ford was," she said more softly. "I like heroes. I have a lot of trouble with reality, too. I hate it when he plays softball, because all the other players on his team take it so seriously. Softball is—well, it's like badminton, or something. It's nothing, compared to baseball. I've told Ron he'll have to give up baseball when he looks better in his street clothes than he does in his uniform." She laughed again—almost a giggle. "He's still a long way from *that!*" she said.

We watched the game for a while, but Linda seemed tense and distracted, and it came to me at last that she was worrying about how well Ron would pitch in the second game. Suddenly she said, "With all the people I've known in baseball, I can't think of one happy ending. Danny Thomas, Gerry Craft, Ron— none of it came out happily. You know, it isn't like Chris Chambliss coming up in the ninth inning of that playoff game and unbuttoning the top button of his shirt and then hitting that home run. You just don't see that happen. Ron hurt his arm before he got started. Gerry Craft got up as far as Lodi, in the Orioles system, and he was on his way—a good outfielder. Then he got hurt and it was all finished, overnight. Danny Thomas is dead. What's the reality? I ask myself that all the time."

The Brattleboro hitters kept after Steve Gallacher, and then caught up with him and went ahead by 5–4 in the bottom of the fifth, with three solid blows. They were looking for his fastball by this time, and I wondered what would happen if he could show them a breaking pitch now and then in a tough spot. Young pitchers love the heater, but so do good young hitters. The A's put their leadoff man aboard in the top of the seventh, but the Maples' pitcher, a young redhead named Parmenter, threw some impressive-looking sliders and shut off the rally. It was a quick, well-played game, and the local fans—a much better turnout today—gave their boys a good hand at the end.

Ron Goble started the second game, and I found that I was a bit nervous, too. I needn't have worried. He set down the side in order in the first, and even though the Maples touched him up for a pair of runs in the second, on a walk and a couple of singles, he looked unstressed and in control out there, never attempting to force a delivery or to work beyond his capacities. He ended up the inning by fanning the side—a good sign. He is a graceful-looking pitcher. My game notes about him read:

> Tall, v. long legs. Minimal rock & motion. Drops glove behind leg-crook (southpaw). Long upper-bod. and uses good upper-bod. with fastball. Fastball just fair. Good curve. Goes sidearm at times for strikeout. About ¾ otherwise. Good pitcher's build. Control fair. Long stride but doesn't drop down. Curve/slider break down. Changes speed w/o effort. Sense of flow. Pitches patterned. Intell. Knows how to pitch.

On this particular day, Ron also had the A's hitters going for him, for they came up with six runs in the third and six more in the sixth, the latter outburst including two singles, a nifty squeeze bunt, a double, a pinch-hit triple by Cake World, and a home run by Coca-Cola. The last batter of the inning was Manager Paul Farrar, who sent himself up as a pinch-hitter now that matters were in hand. He is a friendly, medium-sized man with curly hair and metal-rimmed glasses—he is also a backup catcher for the club—and his players razzed him happily when he stepped up to the plate, calling him Satch and asking if he didn't want the Maples' pitcher to throw from farther back out there. He fanned, to raucous cheers. The A's won it by 16–4—a laugher, but Ron had pitched well, surrendering only four hits. Near the end, Linda began to relax a little in her seat. At one point, she saw me watching her, and she laughed and shrugged. "Ron's mother used to tell me what to do when he was pitching," she said. "She always said, 'Watch the ball, not the pitcher. Never look at the pitcher.' I wish I could remember that."

Ron and Linda live in a worn brown farmhouse next to a collapsing gray shingle barn, at the very end of a twisting, climbing two-mile-long dirt road. On a map, they are in the upper northwest corner of the state. St. Albans, the nearest real town, is fifteen miles to the west, on the shore of Lake Champlain, and the Canadian border is about the same distance due north. The house, which they rent, is on the side of a hill *(everything* in Vermont is on the side of a hill) and is set about with maples, an elderly lilac bush, and a high stand of burdock. Ron's vegetable garden is up the hill, behind the house. There is a small unpainted front porch with missing steps, which makes it look a little like the front stoop of a sharecropper's place. No matter: the view from here is across many miles of hazy-green rolling farmland toward some distant blue mountains. There isn't much furniture inside—a few castoff schoolroom chairs, with iron pedestal bases, that stand around the dining table, and one overflowing easy chair. The most prominent object is a modern cast-iron heating stove, right in the middle of the room, with a long outlet pipe snaking up through the ceiling. Upstairs, the bathroom has been recently panelled and fitted out with a shower. The best room in the house is a sun-filled upstairs bedroom, five windows wide. A cluster of sports pennants is pinned to one wall there, with their points all streaming to starboard, as if in a stiff breeze: the Mariners, the Yankees, Idaho U., the Clinton Clowns (Ron's old softball team), and one banner with a misshapen felt baseball and the words "I'm a Backer" (a Buckskin backer, that is) on it. On the opposite wall, there is a framed Idaho potato bag depicting (as best one can depict on burlap) a full-rigged ship and inscribed "Tradewind Brand." Linda's desk and Selectric are under one window, next to an overflowing bookshelf: contemporary poets (she writes poetry), classics, English Lit. textbooks—everything. On one windowsill, a philodendron is growing in a small white pot in the shape of a baseball shoe; on another rests a narrow cardboard box containing the complete 1981 Topps bubble-gum base-ball card collection. At the other end of the room, another bookcase offers a considerable paperback collection of contemporary Latin-American fiction, in translation: Borges, García Márquez, Jorge Amado, Machado de Assis, and others. These, I learned, are Ron's. "When I finished my season with the Buckskins, I was told my arm might heal if I could rest it long enough," he told me, "and I began to fantasize that it *would* heal. It was an excuse not to work, so I just sat and read. I was reading García Márquez's 'Leaf Storm' just then, and when I finished that I read 'One Hundred Years of Solitude' and then 'The Autumn of the Patriarch'. I drank a lot of Colombian coffee while I read, and it was like I'd gone off to another country."

When Ron Goble graduated from Capital High School in Boise in the spring of 1969, he accepted a fifteen-hundred-dollar baseball scholarship at Linfield, a small (one thousand students) college in McMinnville, Oregon. He had been an outstanding player in his local American Legion baseball program for several summers (young ballplayers who start in the Little Leagues at the age of eight may graduate to the Babe Ruth League at the age of thirteen and then move along to American Legion teams at sixteen), and he had been named to the all-state team in his senior year at school, as a first baseman. His pitching arm began to mature at about the same time, and when his fastball was clocked at better than ninety miles an hour the scouts began to take notice of him. When he went to Linfield, his real hope was not just to pitch for the varsity team there but to find a more relaxed and varied social and political atmosphere. At Capital High, sports and unquestioning patriotism had seemed to go hand in hand. Capital's teams were known as the Eagles, and varsity athletes were told to keep their hair cut in the "Eagle-pride" style—so short that it couldn't be parted—and there was constant pressure on the larger and quicker boys to make their major school commitment to the football team. Ron played tight end and safety and sometimes quarterback for the Eagles, but he didn't much like football; he was also made uncomfortable by the fact that his own sport, baseball, was considered effete—"sort of a pansy game," as he put it. But things weren't much different at Linfield, he discovered. The jocks there were expected to keep their hair cut short, too, and to think more about winning seasons than about Vietnam and Cambodia and the other political and social crises that were convulsing the nation at the time. Ron was not an activist, but his parents—his father is a state fire-insurance inspector—had always encouraged their three sons to think for themselves. Ron's older brother, Dale, had been an undergraduate at Columbia during the student riots there in 1968, and had brought home tapes he had recorded of the impassioned speeches and the crowd roars during those tumultuous days, and Ron had played these over many times. He was an athlete but he was also a reader and a student, and he felt isolated at Linfield. Early in May of his freshman year, he heard the news of the appalling events at Kent State University, and he and five or six friends went to the Linfield student-union building and lowered the flags there, in honor of the demonstrating students who had been shot by National Guardsmen in Ohio. Only two or three people of the hundreds who walked by stopped to ask what the lowered flags meant, and the next day one of Ron's coaches told him that he had "the wrong orientation" about politics. The next fall, Ron transferred to the University of Idaho and gave up varsity sports.

Ron told me all this in a quiet, almost apologetic manner. His voice is modulated and unforced, and somehow suggests his pitching motion. Like some other young men and women of his generation, or quarter-generation, he takes pains never to sound assured, never to strike an attitude. "I wasn't a real political dissident, you understand," he said. "I cared—I still care—but I didn't know what I was doing. At Idaho, I went down to the R.O.T.C. Building one night and stole Richard Nixon's picture out of his frame there. Big piddly-assed deal."

He laughed, and Linda joined in the laughter. We were sitting out on their porch, drinking beer, and their two English setters, Boone and Hannah, were running and sniffing through an overgrown meadow before us, with their feathery white tails marking their progress through the long grass. Once, Boone got on the trail of something and took off downhill, but Ron turned him with a piercing, two-fingered whistle.

"Tell about the time you decided to go back and play ball," Linda said.

"Oh, geezum," Ron said, smiling. "Well, after a while there at Moscow"—Moscow, Idaho, is the university seat—"I began to reconcile sports and politics a little, and I saw that I wasn't quite the great political radical I'd thought I was. For a while, I'd even stopped collecting baseball cards, but I sure missed playing ball, especially in the spring, and so one day I went down to see the baseball coach. I was going to offer to come out, if he wanted me, but when I got there his office was closed, and I took that as a sign. I decided it wasn't my karma to play ball yet."

"It wasn't your *karma!*" Linda said, doubled over with laughter. "Can you *believe* that now!" They cracked up, thinking about it.

In his last two years at Idaho, Ron lived with two friends on a farm twenty-six miles away from the campus, where they raised chickens and helped the farmer with his planting and other chores. Ron was a pre-law student, majoring in political science, and he had looked forward to going to law school, but now something had changed for him, and he found himself more interested in the farm and in outdoor life. "I just got tired of school," he said. He had let his hair grow long, and he realized that most of his classmates probably thought of him as a hippie. After he graduated, he moved to Missoula because he loved its setting—the high country and the cold streams of the Bitterroot Range and the Garnet Mountains—and found work as a janitor at the University of Montana.

"I just wanted something to do so I could keep on fishing and backpacking," he said. "There were a lot of people with the same idea there at that time. It was what was happening. That's great country, out along the Clark Fork and the Big Blackfoot, if you like fishing. You could walk across the Milwaukee Road railroad tracks behind our house and cross the floodplain and you'd be fishing in just five minutes."

Our house: He had met Linda, and they had moved into a log cabin in Clinton, which is twenty miles southeast of Missoula. She was in graduate school at Montana, majoring in creative writing. She also tutored undergraduates in English and Greek, and after she had picked up her master's degree she worked in a Poetry in the Schools program in the state school system and then became poet-in-residence and a teacher at a private school in Missoula. She and Ron talked baseball and followed the Yankees from a distance, as she wrote me in her first letter, but softball was the only game in town.

Ron said, "Every spring, I'd think, Geezum, I've made it through the winter again—and they were long, long winters there, you know—and I'd get that little urge. I'd go off fishing, and when I got my arm working back and forth with the fishing pole [he said "pole," not "rod"] it was sort of like throwing a curveball. I was spring-strong, and I'd get to wondering what I could have done if I'd gone on in baseball. Each spring was like that. Then when I read that notice in *The Sporting News* about the Buckskins' tryout camp, I realized that it had been eight years since I'd pitched in a ballgame. I couldn't believe it."

This must have sounded self-pitying to Ron when he said it to me, there on the porch, and he corrected himself at once. "It was my own fault," he said. "There was fear, I guess, and then I began to rationalize it all and remind myself that I'd have to go to a tryout camp if I wanted to come back, and maybe I'd fail. What I'd had was a marginal talent—a pretty good high-school fastball—and if I was ever going to do something with it, I would have had to pay the price. I didn't want to have to work at it, I think, or else I just didn't want to work that hard. So I let it go by."

Late one afternoon that week, I watched another team of country ballplayers wearing sponsors' names on the backs of their uniform shirts—Waterville Garage, Tobin Construction, Gerald W. Tatro—in a game played on still another hillside diamond. The field was unfenced, and the woods and brush along the right-field foul line crowded in so close that there wouldn't have been room for bleachers or any other kind of seats there. It was a *field:* the shaggy grass around second base was white with clover blossoms. We were in Belvidere, Vermont—a Green Mountain village a bit to the north and east of Mt. Mansfield—and the game pitted the home team of Belvidere-Waterville against the visiting Morrisville nine. These were Babe Ruth League teams, whose players range in age from thirteen to fifteen years, but the Belvidere-Wavervilles seemed to be outweighed by a couple of dozen pounds and outsized by a couple of inches at almost every position. Outmanned, too: only eight home-team players had turned up for the game, and their coach, Curt Koonz, was filling in at shortstop. The disparity was most noticeable on the mound, for the Belvidere-Waterville pitcher, Earl Domina, was so short that the white pants of his uniform were within an inch or two of swallowing his shoes. He worked hard out there, toeing the rubber in good style and hiding the ball behind his hip while he stared in at his catcher for the sign, but he wasn't big enough to get much stuff on his pitches, and it sometimes looked as if he were throwing uphill against the tall, half-grinning Morrisville boys. Earl was being hit hard—the bases were repeatedly loaded and then unloaded against him in the two or three innings I saw him play—and he also had to put up with a few throwing-uphill jokes from his own teammates, but he kept his concentration and his seriousness, jutting his jaw on the mound and staring the base runners into place before each pitch, and in time the smiles and the jokes died away. He was a battler.

I had heard a good deal about the problems and triumphs of the Belvidere-Waterville Babe Ruth League team from its previous coach, Ron Goble, who had been greeted with hand slaps and jokes and cheerful body blocks by his former troops when we turned up at the game that afternoon. (He and Linda lived in Waterville when they first came to Vermont, but their present house is some thirty miles to the northwest—too far for him to keep up with his Babe Ruth League coaching while he also continues to pitch for the A's.) Now he pointed out some of his stalwarts from the previous year's squad—Peanut Coburn, the team's best shortstop, best outfielder, best first baseman, best everything, who had graduated to assistant coach; the Eldred brothers, Keith and Mike; some others. He said that a few of his players last year had come up through a Little League program, but others had never played an inning of baseball before their season got under way. There weren't many players in either category, to tell the truth, so everybody got a chance to play, including Kim Wescom and Angie Tourangeau, who are girls. Kim, a second baseperson, always wore blue eyeshadow with her game uniform—a complicated announcement, Linda thought. All the teams that Belvidere-Waterville faced were larger and more experienced than they were, and the enemy players razzed them unmercifully for playing girls and for looking like hicks.

"Well, we *were* hicks," Ron said to me. "We were a country team, and most of our players came from poor families, so after a while we took that as our team name. We became the Hicks." The razzing never got entirely out of hand, in any case, because after a couple of innings of it, Frank Machia, the Belvidere-Waterville first baseman, would take a few steps over toward the other team bench and invite the critics there to step forward. Frank was fifteen, but he has a Boog Powell-style chest and belly, topped off by a full beard, and so things usually quieted down in a hurry. The continuing trouble—the real trouble—was that the team wasn't good enough to win. One very bad day came at Stowe, a wealthy ski-resort town at the foot of Mt. Mansfield (its Babe Ruth League team even had different uniforms for home and away games), where the game was called, by mutual consent, when Belvidere-Waterville had fallen behind by 35–3, or 36–5, or something like that.

Ron told me that one of the team's handicaps had been the lack of a decent home field to practice and play on, and after the Stowe disaster he and Linda and a few other devout team backers—Larry and Shirley Brown, Olive McClain, and Emmett Eldred—went over to the abandoned Smithville diamond, in Belvidere, which had long ago turned into a meadow, and attacked it with hand mowers. After three long, hot days' work—a horrendous job, everyone agreed—the hay was cut and raked, and a new backstop had been erected, just in time for the return game against Stowe, which turned up with a considerable entourage to watch the continuation of the slaughter.

"Well, we didn't beat them," Ron said. "It was 9–6, Stowe, in the end, but we *almost* beat them, and they sure knew they'd been in a game. We showed them we could play, and that made the whole season worthwhile."

I asked how the team had fared after that.

"The truth is, we all lost all fourteen games on our schedule," he said. "No, that's not right—we took one on a forfeit, when the other team didn't turn up. But it meant a lot to these kids, learning how to play ball, learning to enjoy it. By the end of the season, they were backing up plays and sometimes hitting the cutoff man on their throws, even though that was mostly because they couldn't throw the ball all the way home anyway. They're all good kids. There isn't much else to do around here in the summers, you know, and that kept them at it."

The game we had been watching ended at 11–4, Morrisville, and the young players began to drift away, some in their parents' cars and pickups, some on bikes, and some on foot. The Belvidere-Waterville bats and batting helmets were stuffed into a gunnysack and toted away. It was evening, or almost evening, by now, but the field was at once repopulated by softball players—a pickup, slow-pitch game, arranged by telephone earlier that day. Ron played and so did Earl Domina—a long pitcher and a very short one, both playing in the same outfield now—and more cars pulled up by the field as the news of the game got around, and soon there were twelve or thirteen players on a side out there in the warm, mosquitoey half-light. Linda didn't play, and I sat it out, too, keeping her company. We were at a worn, teetery old picnic table, where we gnawed on some cold roast chicken she had brought along, and in time we were joined there by Larry Brown, a shy, slightly built, soft-spoken man, who often looks at the ground when he speaks. Larry Brown is the Branch Rickey of Belvidere baseball. He is an asbestos miner—a laborer—with a modest seasonal sideline in maple syrup made from his own hillside sugar bush. Still in his forties, he has six children and two grandchildren.

He told me that he had been a catcher for the Belvidere town team when he was a younger man. "It was all town teams around here then," he said. "I'd like to see those days come back again. Maybe they will. Back when I was a boy, all I had was a bat and one old taped-up ball. It wasn't all organized, the way it is now. I don't think there's a single town team in Lamoille County, but there are eight hundred boys playing Little League and Babe Ruth ball."

His doing—in part, at least. Larry Brown got the Belvidere Little League started, about five years ago. (In fact, a Little League game had been in progress off at the other end of the same field that the Babe Ruth teams were using that afternoon, and I had been struck by the fact that all the players on both teams had full uniforms. Seeing so many players in action at the same time almost reminded me of spring training.) Larry Brown found sponsors, got the parents involved, raised the money for uniforms and bats and balls. Last year, when Ron and Linda turned up in Waterville, he sought out Ron and persuaded him to take on the town's very first Babe Ruth team. Larry didn't know that Ron was still recovering from his cancer surgery and from the debilitating radiation treatments that had ensued, but Larry had been wonderfully persuasive, and the job, Ron must have realized almost at once, was a perfect one for him at that moment: cheerful and funny and full of hope. When the season ended, with most of those hopes still unrewarded, Larry Brown and his wife threw a big potluck dinner for the team. Ron gave a speech, summarizing the summer's high points—the time Mike Eldred lost both sneakers while trying to steal second base (and turned back at once to get them), Angie Tourangeau's single that didn't count because the ump said he wasn't ready, the two games against Stowe.... Everyone had such a good time at the dinner that they all decided to chip in and arrange a team trip up to Montreal for an Expos game. Later in the summer, they did it again. Baseball has caught on in Belvidere.

I asked Larry Brown if anyone from Lamoille County had ever made it to the big leagues.

"No, I don't think so," he said, still smiling and still looking at the ground. "Though there was so many that played ball and watched ball around here in the old days you'd think it'd happen, wouldn't you? Why, I can remember going over to St. Albans when they had a team in the old Northern League here— the Giants, they were—and they'd have a thousand people there at Coote Field. A thousand, easy. But we had some mighty good players around here. Don McCuin played for our team—the Belvidere team, I mean—right after the war. He was a left-handed pitcher. He was signed by the Cardinals organization, but when he got down there he found he couldn't play ball in the heat, there in the South. And there was another good left-hander, named Sonny Davis, just about that time. Funny you'd have two so good, who was both the same kind. He played for Stowe. He signed up with the Braves, back in the nineteen-forties. Sonny told me once that he'd played in a game with young Henry Aaron, who was just a beginner, too, at the time, and when Sonny saw Aaron hit some drives in batting practice he suddenly understood that he was never going to make it in major-league baseball."

All three of us laughed. It was almost dark now, and whenever somebody on the ball field made contact (with that heavy, smacking sound that a softball makes against the bat), the arching ball looked like some strange gray night bird suddenly rising out of the treetops.

"Leonard McCuin was as good as Don was, from all I hear," Larry went on. "He was Don's father. Leonard once played on a team over to Saranac Lake, where Christy Mathewson was his coach. Mathewson was there because he had tuberculosis, you know. I guess he was about dead of it by then. Funny, I always thought Don McCuin had the head for major-league baseball. It was his arm that was at fault. But I liked the way he pitched. I always compared Don to Warren Spahn—a classic left-hander with that high kick. I don't think there was ever a smarter pitcher than Spahn. But I'm not one of those who goes around always saying that the old players were the best. I've been up to Montreal for some games, now that the teams are so close—I almost went *broke* the first summer the Expos was playing!—and I think there's been no better players than some we've seen in our time. You only have to go back a few years to when Aaron and Mays and Clemente were still playing, you know, and you just couldn't come up with a better outfield than that. They say Roberto Clemente was the least appreciated ballplayer of his time. Well, *I* appreciated him."

It was dark now, and the softball game had ended at last. Ron joined us at the picnic table, and some of his friends sat down with us, too, drinking beer and swatting mosquitoes. Little Earl Domina had gone home, waving shyly to us as he walked away into the shadows, and I told Larry how much I'd admired him in the Babe Ruth League game we'd seen.

"He's about half-size for his age, but he always puts out," Larry said. "There are others I wished cared as much about it as he does. Size don't have much to do with it in this game."

Roberto Clemente and Leonard McCuin, Don McCuin and Warren Spahn, Sonny Davis and Hank Aaron, Christy Mathewson and Earl Domina—they were all together in baseball for Larry Brown. For him, the game had no fences.

I was pleased but in fact not much surprised to find someone like Larry Brown here in a corner of Vermont, for I had already met other friends of Ron's and Linda's who seemed sustained and nourished by a similar passion for baseball. One of them was Paul Farrar, the A's manager, who normally gives six or seven hours of his day to the team during the season, beginning at four in the afternoon on weekdays, when he gets off work at the I.B.M. plant in Burlington. If there is a home game (there are also practices on some offdays) at the University of Vermont's Centennial Field, where the A's play, Farrar is usually the first man to arrive. He carries in the field rakes from his car and then unlocks the concession stand and carries out the dusty bases that have been stored there since the last game. The players begin to drift onto the field while he is raking the base paths or carefully laying down the foul lines and the batter's boxes with a lime cart, and he kids them cheerfully and asks about their bruises. Long before this, while he paused at home to put on his uniform, he has picked up the day's team telephone messages from his wife, Sue. Tinker Jarvis will have to work until past seven tonight, she told him, which means not only that he won't be there in time to play but that his girlfriend, Helen Rigby, probably won't be around to work in the hot-dog stand. Southpaw Joe Gay's arm is coming along, his father called to say, but the doctor still thinks it'll be another week before he'll be ready to pitch. One of the troubles is that Joe has this summer job as a housepainter, which makes it hard for him to give his arm the kind of rest it should have. (Why can't Joe paint *right*-handed for a while, Paul wonders for an instant.) The other team tonight will be perfectly willing to play nine innings, instead of seven, if the A's want to, but which of them will pay the seventy-five bucks that U.V.M. wants as a fee for using the lights? Then, there are the automobile arrangements to be made for the weekend doubleheader over at Saxtons River. . . . Paul thinks about some of this while he pitches batting practice, but then he tries to put it all out of his head when he makes out his lineup in the dugout and begins to concentrate on the game at hand. Who's got to play if we're going to win? Who ought to play because he hasn't got into enough games lately? . . .

Paul grew up in the Bronx and, of course, dreamed of playing in Yankee Stadium someday, as a big-leaguer. Then his family moved to South Burlington, and in time Paul went off to Rensselaer Polytechnic, in Troy, New York, where he played catcher for four years on the varsity team. Then he coached at R.P.I. for two years, as an assistant with the varsity, while he got his graduate degree. He is a senior associate engineer with I.B.M. He is twenty-six years old.

"Ron and I and Tinker Jarvis are the old men on the team," he said to me, "but I think it may be more fun for us than for the others. And managing is—well, it's *involving*. These games don't mean anything, but I play them again in my mind when they're over. The bunt signal we missed. The pitcher I maybe took out one batter too late. I lie in bed and play baseball in my head in the middle of the night."

Herbie Pearo lives in East Alburg, Vermont, on a peninsula jutting into Lake Champlain. He is the manager of the East Alburg Beavers, an amateur slow-pitch softball team that Ron plays for whenever the A's schedule permits it. Upstairs in his house there, one walks into a narrow room and a narrow loft above it—a baseball museum—stuffed to bursting with baseball uniforms, autographed baseball bats, autographed baseballs, caps, pairs of spikes, old baseball photographs, albums of baseball tickets, baseball programs, bubble-gum baseball cards, everything. Some of the uniform shirts are framed, showing names and numbers on their backs, and these include the shirts of many present and recently past Expos—Andre Dawson, Ellis Valentine, Steve Rogers, Rusty Staub, Warren Cromartie—for Herbie is a terrific Expos fan. He is also a former terrific Mets fan. The centerpiece of his present collection is Tom Seaver's 1967 Mets uniform (1967 was Seaver's first year in the majors), which Herbie values at one thousand dollars. "Not that I'd automatically sell it," he adds. Selling items like these is Herbie Pearo's business—a baseball-souvenir-and-tradables line known as Centerfield Eight Sales. The business is advertised in most standard baseball publications, and the turnover is brisk. Brisk but often painful, because Herbie, one senses quickly, would much rather hold on to his best stuff. He is still writhing over the recent loss of a genuine Rogers Hornsby St. Louis Browns uniform. "I *had* to do it," he says apologetically. "The man made me an offer I couldn't refuse— seven guaranteed All-Stars' uniforms, plus a lot of other things, but still . . ." His voice trails off, and in his face you can almost see the Hornsby uniform still hanging in its old place on the long wall.

Centerfield Eight is one of the hardest stores to walk out of I have ever walked into. I was there for an hour or more, and each time I edged closer to the staircase my eye would fasten on some new wonder or Herbie would draw me back to look at something else. He wasn't trying to sell me anything; he simply wanted to share it all. He was a great curator, and we were at the Louvre. . . . Here is a ball signed by Sadaharu Oh, and a bat signed by the Babe. Here is Pete Rose's very first

Reds' shirt—with a rookie's number, 33, on the back. Here is a Reggie Jackson Oakland A's shirt; here is a Roberto Clemente shirt (in the old, sleeveless Pirates' style); and over here is an orange Charlie Finley baseball (Finley once lobbied to have the major leagues shift to orange baseballs); and—oh, yes—upstairs, there in the corner, is a player's battered old locker from Connie Mack Stadium, now long gone, alas. And look *here* (here in a desk drawer): a pair of genuine Phillies World Series tickets from 1964—the year the Phillies folded so horribly and didn't make the Series after all. Here is a genuine scout's contract, signed by Connie Mack himself. This is a photograph of the 1908 Portland Mohawks ("Maine's Premier Amateur Baseball Team"), and here are some 1975 White Sox World Series ducats (another blasted hope), and that's an usher's cap from Anaheim Stadium—a bargain at twenty-five bucks. But oh, *wait!* And he holds up a pair of snowy, still pressed Washington Senator home-uniform shirts on wire hangers, with a "1" on one of them and a "2" on the other—commemorative shirts made for presentation to President Nixon and Vice-President Agnew at the Senators' opening game in 1970. I stare at these particular relics in slow surprise, astounded by the possibility that I have at last come upon an object—*two* objects—in this world that may truly be said to have no meaning whatsoever.

Stunned with memorabilia, I descend the stairs at last (the balusters are bats, each with its own history), and Herbie Pearo's voice follows me down. "I wish you'd seen my Carl Furillo shirt, from the 1957 season," he says. "The real thing. I wish I hadn't sold that. I've been *kicking* myself ever since..."

As I have explained, my trip to visit Linda Kittell and Ron Goble was something I had looked forward to for years. It came while the midsummer major-league baseball strike was about two weeks along, but there was no connection between the two events. I was not visiting a semipro player because I would have preferred to call on a big-leaguer. I was not out to prove some connection or lack of connection between the expensive upper flowerings of the game and its humble underbrush. Everyone in Vermont talked about the strike, but not for long; we wanted it over, because we missed the games and the standings and the news of the sport, but I heard no bitter talk about money and free agency, "spoiled" ballplayers or

selfish owners. At the same time, it occurred to me again and
again while I was there (it would have been impossible to ignore
the comparison or not to think about its ironies) to wonder how
many big-league owners and famous players and baseball businessmen (the league presidents, and so forth, and perhaps even
some of the writers) had an involvement in the game—a connection that was simply part of life itself—like Ron Goble's
and Larry Brown's and Linda Kittell's. Not many, I would
think, and yet at the same time it seemed quite likely to me—
almost a certainty, in fact—that if I had stopped and visited
friends in almost any other county or state corner in the United
States I would have found their counterparts there, their friends
in baseball.

Late one afternoon, Linda and Ron and I drove into Burlington
for an A's game against the Queen City Royals. We were in
their wheezy, ancient red Vega, and Ron kept cocking his head
and listening to the engine in a nervous sort of way; a couple
of weeks earlier, the car had conked out altogether on the same
trip, and he had missed the game and his turn on the mound.
He was in uniform tonight, but he wasn't going to play; his
next start would be the following night, against the hated Burlington Expos. We were all eating ice-cream cones.

I asked Ron if he could tell me a little more about his summer
with the Boise Buckskins, when he had pitched in organized
ball for the first time, and everything had gone so badly for
him and his teammates.

"In some ways, it wasn't exactly what you'd call a rewarding
experience," he said after a moment or two. "Our pitching was
downright terrible. We won on opening day, and that was sort
of the highlight. Gerry Craft said opening day was God's greatest blessing but the rest of it was our trial. We had those ugly
uniforms, and the fans got on us because of the religion thing,
and we were always jumping off buses and going right into
some park to play. It was good we had a few things going for
us, like Danny Thomas. The real battle for me was not to let
any of that bother me too much. I was there to prove myself.
That summer answered a lot of questions for me that I would
have gone on asking myself all my life. I got that albatross off
my neck at last. What I discovered was that I'd had a talent
at one time for throwing the ball—maybe not a major-league

talent, at that. But I found out that although I couldn't throw by then—not really—I was at least a pitcher." He paused and then added his little disclaimer: "Although that may be too much of a complimentary term."

What was it about Danny Thomas, I asked. What had made him so special to them and to the whole team?

"Well, he was tall and he had those good long muscles," Ron said. "You know—he looked like a ballplayer."

"And that fantastic smile," Linda said from the back seat.

"Yes, there was never a better-looking ballplayer, anywhere," Ron said. "And his hitting! I remember once when we were playing against the Emeralds on a road trip, and the whole park was down on us for some reason—everyone yelling and booing and laughing. Because we'd been looking so bad, I guess. And then he hit one. I mean, he *hit* it—it went out over the lights and out of the ballpark, and even before he got to first base there was this absolute hush in the place. It was beautiful. He'd shut them up."

"Plus he wore No. 7," Linda said.

"That's right," Ron said at once. "The same number."

It was a minute before I understood. Mickey Mantle's old number had been 7.

At this moment, the Vega gave a couple of despairing wheezes and slowly glided to halt. We came to rest at meadowside on a singularly unpopulated and unpromising stretch of macadam.

"Damn *carburetor*," Ron said. He popped the hood. "Hammer," he said, swinging his long legs out, and Linda, reaching down between her feet, found a hammer and wordlessly handed it to him, exactly like a good instrument nurse working with a surgeon. This operation entailed some thunderous banging noises from up forward—not a promising prognosis at all, I thought—but when Ron reappeared, redfaced, and restarted the engine, it spluttered and groaned but then caught. A miracle. "Remind me to park facing downhill when we get there," he muttered as we resumed our course.

And so I asked him about his pitching now—pitching for the Burlington A's.

"Well, it's still enjoyable," he said. "The thing about pitching is—it's that it requires your concentration. It requires your entire thought. There aren't many things in life that can bring that to you. And every situation, every day and every inning, is different. You have to work on so many little details. Finding the fluidity of your body. Adjusting for different mounds. Bringing the leg up higher, bringing it over more. You kind of expect standards of yourself, and when they're not there you have to find out what's going wrong, and why. Maybe you're not opening up quickly enough. Maybe you're not following through enough, or maybe you're throwing too much across your body. Some days, you're not snapping your wrist so much. Some days, the seams on the ball aren't so nice. It's always different."

He shook his head, and laughed at himself again. "Actually," he went on, "at some level I'm always pitching in the hope that the curveball—the real old curveball—might come back someday. Geezum, wouldn't that be nice, I think to myself. It doesn't happen, though. It's gone. Now it's different, being a pitcher, and sometimes I think it's almost more fun, because you can't just throw it by them now. You've got to trick 'em, because you've got nothing much to get them out with. So you try to get them up—get them looking away and then throw them inside. Get them backing off, and go down and away. I don't play often enough to have that happen that much—just to be able to think about location like that—but that's what it's all about."

He was right: this is what pitching is all about. I have heard a good many big-league pitchers talk about their craft—hundreds of them, I suppose, including a few of the best of our time— and when they got into it, really got talking pitching, they all sounded almost exactly like Ron Goble. He probably would have denied it if I'd said it, but he was one of them, too—a pitcher.

"I know baseball is important to me," he said after another moment or two. "Playing now is like getting a present, and you don't expect presents."

In Burlington, Ron swung into a gravelly downhill road leading to Centennial Field, and then stopped the Vega unexpectedly and walked over to a small shed on the left-hand side of the road and took from it a large, triangular wooden sign, hinged at the top like a kitchen stepladder. He and Linda carried it up to East Avenue, which we had just left, and set it up on the sidewalk there. "BASEBALL TODAY," it read. "6:00." We parked facing downhill and went down to the park—an ancient dark-green beauty, with the outfield terminating in a grove of handsome old trees. The roofed stands were steeply tilted, and the cast-iron arm at the end of each row of seats bore a "UVM" stamped into the metal. Swallows dipped in and out of the shadows under the grandstand roof. Linda and Ron pointed out the football stadium that rose beyond the left-field fence, and then drew my attention to the back of the football press box perched on its topmost rim—a good hundred feet up there, I suppose. This was history: history made about two weeks earlier, when Darcy Spear had whacked a home run against the Expos that cleared the top of the press box—a Kingman shot, an all-timer.

Ron went off to batting practice, and Linda told me she would be selling tickets up at the main automobile gate. It was still a good hour before the game with the Queen City Royals would begin, and I went along. Linda was carrying a big roll of blue tickets and a small envelope of loose change. "Shall we abscond?" I said. She looked into the envelope. "Better wait until a few customers turn up," she said. We leaned on the chain-link fence beside the open gate, listening to the distant crack of bats from the field below, and passed a bottle of warmish beer back and forth. It was a heavy, quiet summer evening.

Linda said she had hardly ever heard Ron talk about his pitching the way he had talked in the car that night. "Basically, I realize I know absolutely nothing about baseball compared to Ron," she said. "But I get tired of the other women around players, who say 'Don't you get tired of him talking about nothing but baseball?' I *hate* that. I think I like the part of Ron that I don't understand. I feel I could get all the knowledge of baseball that he has, and still not understand, because I never played baseball. It's a mystery between us, and I like that. If you know everything about a person, it's sort of a letdown. I just have no idea what he goes through out there on the mound. I get glimpses sometimes, but that's all.

"Ron is truly modest about his talent—you've seen that. I believe all the things about him that he doesn't think or say himself. I believe he could have been a major-league pitcher. I wanted everyone to know about it when he was pitching and was still sick, but he wouldn't let me tell anyone. He didn't want to bother them with it. I think that's sort of heroic. He still doesn't have his fastball back, you know."

The first two or three cars rolled up and stopped for their tickets. "Looks like a nice evening," one man said.

"Yes, it does," Linda said. "Have a nice time, now."

She came back and leaned against the fence again. "I get scared about the day when he can't play ball anymore," she said. "I get teary thinking about it sometimes. He couldn't have planned his life any differently, but sometimes I wish he wouldn't give up on himself so much. There are a lot of other things he could have done. But if he'd planned his life differently I wouldn't be around. There's no one here he can ask, but I get the idea that he knows as much about the technical side of pitching as anyone else. He just learned it himself, I think."

I said I had exactly the same impression.

"Sometimes he asks me to watch a particular thing when he's pitching—whether he's opening his hips, say. But if he asks me about something else afterward—where his foot is coming down, or something like that—then I've totally missed it. I keep wishing his brother George was here, so he could talk baseball with him. There's so much *to* it. To me, baseball is like learning a foreign language. You never learn all the vocabulary, all the endings and idioms. It's what I love about languages."

It came back to me—it was stupid of me not to have re-membered it, all this time—that Linda had gone to college right here. The main college buildings were just behind us, over the top of the hill. This was her campus. I asked her what languages she had taken, here at U.V.M.

"The Classics Department got upset with me, because I always wanted to take up more languages, all at the same time," she said, smiling. "I was studying classical Greek, modern Greek, Latin, Russian, and Japanese. I switched majors over and over. I'd do more than anyone expected of me in one thing—like creative writing—and let everything else slide. If I had to do a Milton paper, or something, I'd do it in twenty minutes and hand it in—I didn't care. But if I was studying something like rondo alliteration or chiastic alliteration, I'd get so excited I'd forget everything else." She shook her head. "Not *organized*."

I asked about her own poetry. She had declined to show me her poems.

"I'll never catch up in baseball, but I have my own world," she said. "Ron can read something I've written and he'll say 'That has a nice sound,' or something, but he doesn't see that for once I've got a good slant rhyme in there. And he'll never see things I suddenly notice when I'm reading—that 'chrysanthemum' is such a perfect iambic word, for instance—that so excite me. When we went out to some friends who were having Hayden Carruth for dinner—Ron had read maybe one poem of Carruth's, I'd say—I said to him, 'Remember, you're having dinner with Mickey Mantle.' But maybe I should have said Catfish Hunter, because Ron respects Catfish Hunter in such a special way." She giggled.

More cars were coming in now. A man in one car said, "I'm one of the umpires," and Linda waved him in. He waved back and drove in. His license plate said "UMP."

"I feel a little disappointed in my own career," Linda went on during the next pause. "But it isn't as if you're ever too old to write a good poem. But I don't know many ninety-year-old pitchers—do you? Maybe Ron and I are both wrong to make baseball so important to us. But what the hell, writing a poem isn't so important, either."

I asked what would happen to Ron in the next couple of years.

"If he isn't going to go on playing ball—and he can't for much longer—and if he can't find something that will take up as much of his attention as baseball, I don't know what's going to happen to him," she said. "Maybe he'll get into teaching, or some kind of coaching. He's supposed to teach in a kids' baseball camp later this summer, and than maybe . . ." She shrugged. "He lets things happen. He's that kind of a person. At least he found out he's a professional-level pitcher, but I think he'd feel better if it had got him to the major leagues. And he'll never feel he knows everything about baseball. Sometimes I'll watch him in the store when we're shopping together, and he'll have a cantaloupe in his hands and he'll be practicing his motion, right there in the store. It's true! And sometimes I'll see him sitting at home in the evening and shaking his head, and I'll ask him why, and he'll say, 'I can't *believe* I threw that pitch.'"

Some cars were rolling up to the gate, and Linda started over to meet them. "I know one thing," she said. "You can't rewrite a pitch."

The A's had another easy time of it that night. Charlie Corbally pitched and went the distance, and Darcy Spear had three hits and four runs batted in, and the team rolled to a 12–3 win over the Royals. I'd had a hard time finding out the A's place in the standings, because Ron said he couldn't always remember which games counted in the league and which were the informal ones, but he asked Paul, who said the club was now four and four in the league, and something like eight and five for the season over all. None of it mattered much. The next night was what mattered—the game against the Expos.

A lot of people turned out for that one—more than three hundred fans, including Larry Brown, who had brought his wife, Shirley, and one of his daughters, Laureen, and one of his sons, Stephen, and Earl Domina. We all sat togther, behind first base. Even before the game began, I could see that the Expos—they wore the same parti-colored red-and-blue-and-white caps that the Montreal players do—were quicker and much more confident than most of the other Northern League players I had seen. They all looked like ballplayers. It was a wonderful game, it turned out, stuffed with close plays and heads-up, opportunistic baseball, and the A's won it, 3–2. Darcy Spear got the big hit once again—a two-run, two-out single in the third. Ron Goble started, but Paul Farrar had said beforehand he wouldn't let him pitch more than four innings; then he would bring in Steve Gallacher to mop up. Both pitchers were tired, and the staff was a little thin just now. Ron retired the first two Expos batters in the first and then gave up a bunt single. He walked the next man. He was falling behind on the count, and I noticed that he didn't seem to have his full, free motion out there. The next batter hit a sure third-out grounder to Greg Wells, but the ball took a bad hop at the last instant and jumped over Wells' glove for a single and an Expos run. Ron walked the next batter, and Paul came out to the mound to settle him down. Ron fell behind on the following batter, too, and eventually walked him, forcing in another run. Linda stared out at the field without expression. The next Expo rammed a hard shot toward third, but Tinker Jarvis made a good play on the ball and threw to second for the force, ending the inning.

In the next inning, Ron gave up two trifling singles through the middle. With two out, the Expos tried a fancy delayed double steal, with the base runner heading toward second intentionally getting himself hung up in the hope that his man from third could score before the out, but Greg Wells made the play perfectly, stopping and wheeling and firing to the plate in time to nail the runner there. Ron also got through the third unscathed, although he surrendered a single and hit a batter with one of his pitches. From time to time, Ron came off the mound between pitches and stared at the ground, his hands on his hips. In the top of the fourth, now defending a 3–2 lead, he walked the leadoff Expos hitter. The next Expos batter, a right-handed hitter, stood in and Ron hit him on the knee with his first pitch, and Paul Farrar came onto the field slowly and took him out of the game. It hadn't been a disastrous outing—with a couple of small breaks, Ron probably could have gone his four innings without giving up a run—but his struggles on the mound in search of his control had been painful to watch, especially for those of us who remembered his easy, elegant dominance over the batters in his previous game, down in Brattleboro. This kind of turnabout is a frightful commonplace for pitchers, as Ron had said himself, the day before in the car: It's always different.

Steve Gallacher came in and got the next Expos man to rap into an instant double play, and then retired the next man on a fly ball, ending the threat. Then Gallacher set down the remaining nine men in succession, fanning four of them—an outsanding pitching performance that nailed down the win. He got a terrific hand when he came off the field, and he deserved it.

After the game, Ron spotted Larry Brown's car just as it was about to leave the parking lot and ran over to say hello. He squatted down beside the driver's side of the car for a good five minutes, talking to Larry about the game. All around the parking lot, you could see the young Expo and A's players standing in their uniforms beside their cars, tossing their spikes and gloves into the back seats, lifting a beer here and there, and laughing with little groups of friends and with their young wives or girlfriends. I was sorry to be leaving. I was staying in Burlington that night, at a motel, so that I could make an early start back to New York the next morning.

Ron and Linda and I went to a bar-restaurant she knew, up a flight of stairs in Burlington. Linda and I ordered drinks and sandwiches. Ron asked for three large glasses of water, and drank them off, one after the other. Then he had a gin rickey and a sandwich, too. He was still in uniform.

"I learned how to drink in here, I think," Linda said, looking around. "A long time ago."

Ron said, "The last time I pitched, I started from the middle of the plate and began to work it out toward the corners. Tonight, it was the other way around. I started on the outside and I never did get it together." He shook his head. "I can't think how long it's been since I hit two batters."

"Well, at least we won," Linda said.

"Yes, at least we won," I said. "You guys ought to keep me around some more."

Ron had stopped listening. He was staring across the room, with a quiet, faraway look on his face. Linda put her hand on his crossed left leg, just above the white part of his cutouts, and watched him with an expression of immense care and affection. He was still in the game.

About the Author

Roger Angell is a writer and senior fiction editor with *The New Yorker*. He lives in New York with his wife and twelve-year-old son.